GW01005414

Strategies for

Strategies for Theory

From Marx to Madonna

Edited by
R. L. Rutsky and
Bradley J. Macdonald

State University of New York Press

Published by
State University of New York Press, Albany

For information, address State University of New York Press,
90 State Street, Suite 700, Albany, NY 12207

Production by Dana Foote
Marketing by Anne M. Valentine

Library of Congress Cataloging-in-Publication Data

Strategies for theory : from Marx to Madonna / edited by R.L. Rutsky and
Bradley J. Macdonald.
     p. cm.
  Includes bibliographical references and index.
  ISBN 0-7914-5729-X (alk. paper) — ISBN 0-7914-5730-3 (pbk. : alk. paper)
   1. Theory (Philosophy) 2. Popular culture. 3. Poststructuralism. 4. Marxist
criticism. 5. Postmodernism. I. Rutsky, R.L. II. Macdonald, Bradley J.
  B842.S77   2003
  306—dc21
                                      2003045633

10 9 8 7 6 5 4 3 2 1

CONTENTS

Introduction
From Marx to Madonna: Theory, Culture, Politics

R. L. Rutsky and Bradley J. Macdonald

Within contemporary theoretical and critical writing, there are few terms that have been more widely used and debated than "theory," "culture," and "politics." The frequency with which these terms have been invoked indicates their importance within the humanities and social sciences, but it also attests to the fact that, as with any commonly used word, we increasingly take these terms for granted, assuming that we already know what they designate, what they mean. To point out this taken-for-granted status is not to say that we can simply escape the history through which these words have come to be known. Nor is it to suggest there should, or could, ever be a priori definitions of theory, culture, or politics, much less of the relations among them. Rather, it is to argue for, as Samuel Weber suggests in chapter 1, "an incessant vigilance about how and why and what we tend to take for granted." The essays presented as the chapters in this volume, drawn from the fifteen-year publishing history of *Strategies: Journal of Theory, Culture and Politics,* are at once part of the history in which "theory, culture, and politics" are inevitably implicated and of this continuing effort to reconsider the meaning and relationship of these terms.

Strategies began as an independently published journal with a limited circulation. For this reason, many of the essays included in this collection never received the attention that they deserved at the time of their original publication. Yet these essays were, in many ways, ahead of their time; even today, they provide thought-provoking perspectives on the intersection of theory, culture, and politics. Theory is highlighted in these essays, particularly the interactions among Marxist, poststructuralist, and "postmodern" theories. Of course, as Weber suggests, such designations have themselves become an increasingly easy means of categorizing theory, delimiting it so that we know in advance what it is and where we stand in relation to it. Thus, for example, one finds attacks on "poststructuralist theory" bent on fitting such diverse figures as Barthes, Baudrillard, and Derrida into a notion of "poststructuralism" that is defined in advance, most often as a matter of apolitical or nihilistic theoretical play. Indeed, such "knowledge" is even applied to new combinations of theoretical approaches, as in critiques that attempt to dismiss "post-Marxist" approaches by showing them to be merely a subset of "poststructuralism," *QED*.

As these examples imply, critiques of "post" theories have often cast not only particular theorists, but theory in general as elitist and aestheticist, removed from everyday political practice and cultural realities. On the other hand, approaches that present themselves as explicitly political have at times been accused of being so rigidly "political" as to border on essentialism, fundamentalism, or even fascism—which is also to say that such approaches lack theoretical acumen or self-awareness. Cultural studies, for its part, has received criticism from several angles. To the extent that cultural studies is presented as providing political evaluations of popular culture, it is sometimes criticized for being "overly political" or "politically correct." Yet, cultural studies has also, quite commonly, been presented as too celebratory in its reading of popular culture (this complaint is generally associated with "postmodern" theorizations of cultural phenomena) and therefore complicit with cultural and political domination. At the same time, however, cultural studies has also been viewed, perhaps by virtue of its association with popular commodity culture, as not only apolitical, but as shallow and undertheorized. These sorts of characterizations are obviously caricatures, but like all caricatures, they merely emphasize already existing tendencies within contemporary debates. In particular, they point to the all-too-common tendency to treat theory, politics, and culture as distinct, a priori categories, which can then be used to evaluate or label various critical approaches in terms of how "theoretical" or "political" or "commodified" they supposedly are.

The essays presented as chapters in this volume, on the other hand, do not treat theory, politics, and culture as static, already-defined entities, but as complex, interconnected, and constantly evolving areas of inquiry. Interdisciplinary in their scope, and often provocative in their choice of materials, these essays challenge the traditional boundaries that have separated the theoretical, the political, and the cultural. They *move* from politics to theory and from theory to culture, connecting Marx and Derrida, Rodney King and "postmodern" politics, Irigaray and Madonna. Indeed, one useful way to think about the issues explored in this volume, and in the essays that constitute it, is to consider them in terms of movement and direction.

If the name of Marx has often served to represent the very idea of politics and political theory, it has also been linked to a politics defined in terms of directed movement—a movement with definite theoretical and historical aims. Conversely, the name of Madonna has frequently been invoked as emblematic of popular mass culture, often with the assumption that popular culture is in some way inimical to authenticity, including theoretical and political authenticity. Like Madonna herself, popular culture has often been accused of being shallow, simulated, inconstant, of continually shifting its position and direction over time. If politics ostensibly has been about "getting somewhere," about moving *from* where we are now *to* a different, and presumably better, place at which we will arrive in the future, culture has often been presumed to move without direction, caught in the *to-and-fro* of cultural shifts and fads.

From this point of view, of course, leftist political theory and popular culture are necessarily defined in opposition to one another. In fact, the continuing expansion of commodity culture has often been linked to a blunting of political and theoretical direction. A common version of this argument, familiar in theoretical critiques of "postmodern" culture such as Jameson's, Baudrillard's, and Debord's, suggests that it has become increasingly difficult to maintain one's bearings—politically and otherwise—amid the constantly shifting, yet ultimately stagnant, profusion of images, signs, and data that makes up contemporary cultures. From its beginnings, in fact, mass culture has been associated with frenetic movement, but these movements are generally seen as leading nowhere, continually circling, recycling, repeating. For Horkheimer and Adorno, for instance, the figure of recurring, mechanical motions comes to define cultural production within the culture industry:

> The machine rotates on the same spot. While determining consumption it excludes the untried as a risk. The movie-makers distrust any manuscript which is not reassuringly backed by a bestseller.
> . . . Tempo and dynamics serve this trend. Nothing remains as of old; everything has to run incessantly, to keep moving. For only the universal triumph of the rhythm of mechanical production and reproduction promises that nothing changes, and nothing unsuitable will appear. (134)

Lacking direction or aims beyond momentary consumption, the movements of mass culture churn unceasingly, but without arriving anywhere in particular. Any movement toward social or political change is therefore forestalled, caught up in the endless iterations of the culture industry. It is this seeming inability to "move forward," to "progress," that explains why what is variously represented as mass, popular, commodity, postmodern, or late capitalist culture is so often seen as inimical to politics or theory, as lacking the vision, direction, and goals that define "meaningful" theoretical or political movements.

In such critiques, mass culture is often cast as a form of capitalist contagion, a virus that infects the body—and the subject—of politics with its repetition, transience, and diffusion. Indeed, a similar critique is often extended to contemporary theory, where the multiplicity, iterability, and mixture emphasized in antifoundationalist theories are often viewed, at least implicitly, as symptomatic of a loss of theoretical and political direction. Thus, theory and politics, like mass culture, come to be figured as fickle, constantly shifting movements, governed, if they are governed at all, by the currents of the cultural marketplace, by the flows of capital.

This figuration of a loss of theoretical direction or political will is inseparable from the idea that the traditional notion of the subject has also, in some sense, become "lost." The idea of an active subject—whether individual or collective, whether historical, political, or theoretical—has been founded on its ability to move, either literally or figuratively, toward a chosen end, in a chosen direction. Fredric Jameson, for example, highlights this linkage between subjection and direction when he argues that, amid the unsettling currents of late capitalism, we must "again begin to grasp our positioning as individual and collective subjects and regain a capacity to act and struggle which is at present neutralized by our spatial as well as our social confusion" (54).

As Judith Butler has noted, however, "For the subject to be a pregiven point of departure for politics is to defer the question of the political construction and regulation of the subject itself" (13). She therefore suggests that the direction of political, and presumably theoretical, movement also cannot be taken as preexisting, determined in advance. Indeed, Butler, borrowing from Foucault, argues that "the actions instituted via [the] subject are part of a chain of actions that can no longer be understood as unilinear in direction or predictable in their outcomes" (10). Here, the actions or movements of a subject are determined within the context of a cultural-political "chain of actions" that, although it may constrain or even direct these movements, remains multiply determined and unpredictable. In other words, culture, politics, and theory—like the subject—cannot be taken for granted. For they too are performative, determined not before, but *through,* their complex, interactive movements.

Butler's arguments suggest that a sense of political or theoretical direction cannot preexist, or stand outside, culture. The direction of theoretical or political movements can often only be determined in the aftermath of the complicated, at times chaotic, cultural movements through which theory, politics, and culture are constituted. This is not to say that the movements of culture—particularly mass or commodity culture—are not frequently restrictive, directive, and oppressive, or to argue that culture is not political. On the contrary, it is to suggest that politics and theory are inevitably implicated in the same multifarious movements and diversions through which culture is enacted. Rather than judging cultural phenomena simply in terms of some preexisting political or theoretical direction, then, we might do well to imagine a theory of cultural politics that would include diversion and unpredictability, that would emphasize its own ongoing performativity. Such a theory need not be seen merely as lacking direction or purpose. Indeed, it may simply involve recognizing that the movements of politics, theory, and even history are much more like the wayward movements of culture than is generally allowed. They instead tend to diffuse and spread, replicating themselves in different ways and places, reappearing in strange new permutations that nevertheless echo the old. It is this complex, somewhat chaotic range of movements that we hope to evoke in the subtitle of this collection: *From Marx to Madonna.*

For some, *From Marx to Madonna* may suggest that a historical shift has taken place, a movement from "political" theories to "culturally oriented" theories or from theories that rely on figures of direction, navigation, and positioning to theories that stress indirection, dissemination, deterritorialization, fluidity, and the like. And certainly, this title is intended to acknowledge the increasingly important role that both cultural studies and theories of indirection have played in rethinking concepts of politics and theory. Indeed, an emphasis on these areas and approaches has been a hallmark of the work published in *Strategies.* Yet, the title *Strategies for Theory: From Marx to Madonna* is also intended to bring into question the opposition between directed and directionless movements on which many formulations of theory, culture, and politics have been founded. In other words, the "from" and "to" in this title should serve to suggest not a unidirectional movement or narrative, but a *range* of possible vectors and combinations, in which multiple directions, partial and ambiguous moves, diversions, reverberations, stops-and-starts, and other intricacies of motion would not be considered simply as failures of theoretical direction or political will. Thus, the essays that are gathered here under this title should suggest how complex, diverse, and also how diverting, cultural, political, and theoretical movements can be.

We have grouped the chapters in this collection into two parts that emphasize, respectively, the relations of politics to theory, and the relations of theory to culture. The chapters in "From Politics to Theory" move across the usual lines of the political and the theoretical, examining not only how theory can elucidate the political but also how theory is itself a political act of some consequence. Ranging from broad questions about how to conceive or theorize the political to considerations of the "politics" of particular theorists, these chapters nevertheless share a common interest in the interactions of Marxist and leftist thought with poststructuralist theories. Many of these chapters are concerned with what John Leavey refers to as "questions of post*.*": from Leavey's own reflections on the temporal assumptions and responsibilities implied by "post" theories to Ernesto Laclau's discussions of post-Marxist politics, from Keith Topper's consideration of "the politics of postmetaphysics" in the work of Richard Rorty to Donald Preziosi's critique of Fredric Jameson's notions of postmodern space. The idea of "postness" itself implies a certain temporal or historical direction, a "movement beyond" that can never entirely be achieved. Conventional figures of direction or movement are, in fact, brought into question in many of these chapters, whether they deal with issues of temporal movement, spatial direction, or political agency.

Thus, for example, Samuel Weber explores the relation of politics and deconstruction by way of the figure of piecework, derived from Marx's use of the German expression *aus freien Stücken* (literally: out of free pieces) in his description of the famous image of the dancing table. Following from Derrida's dual reading of the ghosts in Marx and *Hamlet,* Weber discusses how the spectral, "out-of-joint," or piecework quality of the table is related to Derrida's notion of iterability. Thus, the idea of piecework provides a model for a political "movement" that would not simply attempt to "put things in their proper place," to reunify the "disjointedness" of contemporary commodity culture and its emphasis on the present. As Weber argues, "politics may have to at least explore the possibilities of what might be called *piecework:* a series of disjointed, but not necessarily unifiable *programs, projects* responding as much to the ghosts of the past as to the phantoms of the future."

Like Weber, Teresa Brennan also plays on Derrida's use of the phrase "the time is out of joint" in her examination of contemporary commodity culture in "Why the Time Is Out of Joint: Marx's Political Economy without the Subject." Brennan focuses, however, on radically rethinking Marx's theory of value, moving away from Marx's subject-oriented emphasis and toward a reconsideration of value in terms of time. For Brennan, the reason that time is out of joint is that capital imposes "a direction on physical processes which is other than their own." Against this imposition, Brennan attempts to open up ecologically *sensitive*—indeed *sustainable*—positions and movements, in which not only technological production, with its emphasis on speed, but also the less frenzied temporality of natural reproduction, would be seen as contributing value to the world.

In "Time Signatures: Post*.* Responsibilities," John Leavey also explores questions of temporal and political direction and of one's responsibility to the past. In a critique of unilinear, "naively historical" narratives and approaches, Leavey employs a fragmentary, aphoristic style that moves in many directions at once as it explores the complex range of issues involved in one's relation to the past and in issues of political and ethical responsibility. Moving from Derrida, de Man, Nancy, and Blanchot to critics of deconstruction and poststructuralism, and from Marx to Marxism and post-Marxism, Leavey seeks not simply to delineate or explain the bases on which political and ethical responsibilities have conventionally been posed, but to be responsive—and "responsible"—to the full range of complexities inherent in any notion of responsibility. Much like Samuel Weber, Leavey attempts to avoid taking these responsibilities for granted.

In a now famous interview, "Building a New Left,"[1] Laclau revisits his classic work with Chantal Mouffe, *Hegemony and Socialist Strategy* (1985), and elaborates on their post-Marxist position. Commenting on the relation of post-Marxism to poststructuralism and deconstruction, Laclau points out that "there is nothing that can be called a 'politics of poststructuralism,'" since "the idea that theoretical approaches constitute philosophical "systems' with an unbroken continuity that goes from metaphysics to politics is an idea of the past." Rather, Laclau notes, poststructuralist approaches have opened a variety of possibilities for "those political practices that go in the direction of a 'radical democracy.'" In this context, Laclau observes, "the disaggregation of essentialist paradigms is not simply a critique *of* Marxism, but a movement *within* Marxism."

In "Foucault's Fallacy," Michael Ryan draws on the provocative ideas raised by Antonio Negri's autonomist Marxism in order to critique Foucault's famous thesis that power engenders resistance. Taking issue with Foucault's reading of sexuality in Greek society, Ryan observes that Greek philosophy was bound to a "system of sexual subordination," in which "effeminacy" was necessarily excluded.

Ryan therefore points to "the threat that homosexuality poses to constructed heterosexuality, a danger of indeterminacy that elicits a violent response because it suggests how ungrounded and unstable the dominant heterosexual construction is." In this sense, "resistance is primary" and points to the instability and contingency on which discourses of power/knowledge are based.

Donald Preziosi's "La Vi(ll)e en Rose: Reading Jameson Mapping Space" provides a critique of Fredric Jameson's views of politics and of postmodern culture and space, pointing to the difficulties raised by Jameson's reliance on linear historical narratives and figures of mapping. As Preziosi argues, the "untranscendable History that Jameson would have us see, that grand master narrative plot which 'goes outside the postmodern paradigm,' is itself revealed as a romantic fiction . . . for in order to make that story visible, representable, and 'mappable,' we must ultimately position ourselves *outside* or beyond not simply 'postmodernism' itself, but outside of time, space and *history*."

In "The Politics of Postmetaphysics," Keith Topper explores Rorty's efforts to portray a "postmetaphysical culture," only to find that Rorty's radical historicist/pragmatist position leaves much to be desired in terms of understanding the embedded nature of our practices and self-understandings within a context of power and privilege. As Topper argues, "moving 'beyond metaphysics' involves something more than just overcoming foundationalism or theoretical hegemony"; it also requires combining "postmetaphysical insights" with "detailed histories of practices and power."

The chapters in the second part of this collection, "From Theory to Culture," focus on the relationship between theory—and here again, with particular emphasis on deconstruction, poststructuralist, and "postmodern" theories—and cultural phenomena. These chapters do not, however, simply follow the usual procedures of cultural studies, where cultural products and representations tend to be judged in terms of their complicity with or resistance to capitalist, patriarchal, or racist ideologies. Although many of these chapters focus on issues of racism, of gender or sexual bias, or of bourgeois ideology, they emphasize the multivalent complexity of cultural formations, from William Chaloupka's discussion of the media representations of Rodney King, to Kelly Dennis's analysis of photography, voyeurism, and "the beaver shot," to Marilyn Manners's consideration of the representation of women's sexuality in popular culture and in cultural criticism. Indeed, most of cultural phenomena explored here are treated not simply in terms of their relation to some "larger" political or theoretical issue, but as fully theoretical in themselves. Thus, for example, Iain Chambers, in looking at how diasporic and migrant movements have come to constitute contemporary metropolitan cultures, suggests the dependence of theory on cultural phenomena. The dispersive, migrant movements of culture and media are, in fact, emphasized in many of these chapters, from Gregory Ulmer's views of the dissemination of theory in popular media to Laurence Rickels's playful foray across a range of theoretical and cultural icons. In all of these chapters, an awareness of the mixed, complex, and at times undecidable status of culture prevails over critiques that seek merely to apply theoretical or political models to culture.

In, for example, "Rodney King and the Awkward Pause," William Chaloupka scrutinizes media representations of King's words and silences, finding in them an expression of a DuBoisian "double consciousness" that cannot be reduced to fixed or essentialist notions of identity or politics. Moving from examples of television interviews with King to Paul Gilroy's *The Black Atlantic* and Nathan McCall's *Makes Me Wanna Holler,* Chaloupka underscores McCall's tendency to avoid easy categorizations of identity and Gilroy's emphasis on "tropes of movement and circulation" in theorizing black identity and politics. Thus, Chaloupka argues for, in Gilroy's words, "the inescapability and legitimate value of mutation, hybridity, and intermixture en route to better theories of racism and black political culture."

Gregory Ulmer also explores the interactions between popular media and contemporary theory in "The Making of 'Derrida at the Little Bighorn.'" Arguing that video and electronic media provide a way of enacting the insights of post-structuralist and Derridean theory, Ulmer outlines a "program" for linking theory, personal history, and popular media representations, as demonstrated in his project for a video entitled "Derrida at the Little Bighorn" (included in Ulmer's book *Teletheory: Grammatology in the Age of Video*). Ulmer's playful extensions of Derridean grammatology are echoed in the form of his piece, in which he mimics the interview format so commonly employed in popular culture. Yet, the interview is itself a fiction, written entirely by Ulmer himself for publication in *Strategies.*

In "Migrant Landscapes," Iain Chambers traces the hybrid, diasporic movements that have come to form the "secret, though invariably unacknowledged, heart" of contemporary metropolitan cultures. In these migrant movements, Chambers sees "the break-up of ideological essentialism" and "the fragmentation of a homogeneous and transcendental sense of the 'other.'" Miming the hybridity of these cultural movements, Chambers mixes extensive quotations and personal history with his own trenchant commentary, so that, as he observes, "writing becomes a travelogue, a constant journeying across the threshold between fact and fiction, taking up residence in that border country where histories dissolve into narrative."

Marilyn Manners's "All the Stupid 'Sex Stuff'" examines claims that the political and theoretical ends of feminism have degenerated into pop-cultural "fluff" and "sex stuff." Moving across a range of cultural representations of female sexuality, from Madonna and Roseanne to riot grrrls and *Ally McBeal,* Manners critiques the tendency of some contemporary feminists "to categorize rigidly, to underplay (or deplore) heterogeneity, or to mourn a lost golden age and view change and divergence apocalyptically." In these terms, Manners argues, those who parodically explore sexuality and who "split identities into more than two neat halves" are necessarily cast as inauthentic, insubstantial, and lacking in depth.

Kelly Dennis's "Leave It to Beaver: The Object of Pornography" takes another approach to representations of women's sexuality, from Dürer to Courbet to *Hustler,* in her analysis of "the politics of pornography." In the process, Dennis brings into question traditional readings of the place of voyeurism and the constitution of the "fixed" subject. As Dennis argues, "'normal' sexuality is that which maintains the fiction of the unified subject while perverse or marginal sexuality problematizes the homeostasis of the unified subject *in its willful identification as object rather than the object-disavowal of the subject.*"

In "Heretical Marxism: Pasolini's *cinema inpopulare,*" Kriss Ravetto engages the cinematic and theoretical work of Pier Paolo Pasolini, showing the contradictory, but potently political, significations of his portrayal of Medea, particularly as they relate to orthodox notions of Marxism. For Pasolini, as Ravetto observes, this departure "beyond Marx's and Gramsci's critiques of capitalism" is marked "as a movement toward the prehistoric (the prebourgeois)." Yet, Pasolini's turn toward a "mythic past" is not cast as a return to stability; rather, this past, in which "he expands the subproletariat to include the third world, homosexuals, woman," is itself presented in terms of "a fluidity of bodies and sensations that resist interpretation."

In "Missing Marx; or, How to Take Better Aim," Laurence Rickels moves playfully among a host of seemingly disparate theoretical and cultural topics—from Marx to Freud, from vampirism to AIDS, from "cultural critique" to "California culture"—in his consideration of the "politics" of groups, crowds, and masses, and their relation to electronic media. As Rickels points out, displacement and transmission have come to be crucial figures to any understanding of contemporary technological cultures: "AIDS, drugs, homelessness, and TV confront us with an uncanny truth; namely, that in an era of universal and global transmissions all of us (humans and machines alike) form one body—the tech-no-body of the group."

As is perhaps obvious in these summaries, the distinction that is implied in these parts of the book—between theory and politics on the one hand and culture and theory on the other—is, to some degree, arbitrary. One might easily argue that, for example, the chapters included in "From Theory to Culture" are every bit as "political" as the chapters in the first part. Ultimately, then, these two parts must be read in the same spirit as the title *Strategies for Theory: From Marx to Madonna:* that is, not as representing separate realms (or a movement between those realms), but as aspects of a range of intimately related, interactive phenomena. As the chapters in this volume amply demonstrate, the study of theory, culture, and politics cannot be confined within disciplinary boundaries nor reduced to a set of fixed, taken-for-granted perspectives or categories. These essays cross boundaries, mix categories, and combine perspectives.

It is precisely this movement across boundaries, this refusal to take for granted predefined categories, to be confined to a particular theoretical or political approach, that "defines" this volume. It can also, perhaps, be said to define "theory" itself. For if theory is foregrounded here, if these essays can all be said to be emphatically theoretical, it is not because they employ the arguments and ideas of well-known philosophers and theorists, nor because they follow a particular theoretical direction. Rather, they are theoretical because they commit themselves to an incessant movement, to a continual questioning of "how and why and what we tend to take for granted." Here, in other words, theory is not simply a matter of applying existing theory to cultural or political phenomena, but of performing or enacting theory, of theorizing. Theory, in this sense, becomes a matter of *moving,* not simply *from* one theoretical, historical, or political locus *to* another, but in multiple, interdisciplinary, and often unforeseen directions. *From Marx to Madonna* is dedicated to this sense of theoretical movement.

Notes

    1. Originally published in the first issue of *Strategies* in 1988, this interview was republished in Laclau's *New Reflections of the Revolution of Our Time* (1990).

References

Butler, Judith (1992). "Contingent Foundations: Feminism and the Question of 'Postmodernism.'" In Judith Butler and Joan W. Scott, eds., *Feminists Theorize the Political.* New York and London: Routledge, 3–21.

Horkheimer, Max, and Theodor W. Adorno (1989). *Dialectic of Enlightenment,* trans. John Cumming. New York: Continuum.

Jameson, Fredric (1991). "The Cultural Logic of Late Capitalism." In *Postmodernism, or, The Cultural Logic of Late Capitalism.* Durham, N.C.: Duke University Press, 1–54.

PART I
FROM POLITICS TO THEORY

1

Piece-Work

Samuel Weber

Granted . . .

We have come together to discuss problems designated by two words, "decon-struction" and "politics." They are familiar words; one is tempted to add: all too fa-miliar. It is not that familiarity breeds contempt—although that can easily be the case—but familiarity, a certain kind of familiarity, can easily breed overconfidence. Overconfidence that we know, or have a pretty good idea, of what those two words mean. And that there is sufficient consensus about what those words mean to make any sort of caution in their regard unnecessary. Why spend precious minutes wor-rying about words when the things they designate are so urgent?

And yet, do we all agree on what those two words mean, or at least in what direction they point us? Is "deconstruction" a synonym for the writings of a sin-gle author, Jacques Derrida, or can it be understood to designate a more general body of writing not limited to Derrida's work? Although it has become very easy to invoke—to mention—the word, which one finds virtually everywhere these days, does this widespread usage indicate that there is an equally widespread un-derstanding of just what the word entails? Or, on the contrary, is the generalized use of the word often a means for exorcising its specificity and its complexities? Exorcising them precisely by conjuring up the word and then, with a wink, dis-patching it as the empty cliché it has in many cases become in the hands (and mouths) of those who regard its use as self-evident.

Why take time—valuable time—to mention all of this? Because our collo-quium, our speaking together, will be all the more pertinent if we follow a rule that seems to be rapidly going out of style: namely, to take as little for granted as possible. And least of all, that which seems most self-evident, such as the words "deconstruction" and "politics." This is not to say that we will ever be entirely able not to take some aspects of those words—any words—for granted, as though we could arrive at some all-encompassing a priori definition of all the terms we use. It is, however, to argue for an incessant vigilance about how and why and what we tend to take for granted. Not thereby to eliminate the "givenness" of the words and concepts we use, but rather to retrace how that givenness inevitably exceeds anything we can *take* of it or from it. The problem, in taking things for granted, is that the *taking* tends to obscure the *granting*. Despite the constraints of time, let us therefore not be in too great a hurry to take "deconstruction," much less "politics," for granted.

"Deconstruction"

Before we can even begin to discuss the relation implied in the phrase, "deconstruction and politics," we must first deal with a preliminary question: Is *Specters of Marx* a deconstructive text and if so, in what way? This book, as virtually all of Derrida's writings, is intricately related to his previous work—of that there can be no doubt, and the massive citations and allusions to earlier writings are only the most manifest indication of this relatedness. But the question remains: in what way can *Specters of Marx* be said to be a deconstructive essay? A comparison of this book to one of the earliest and clearest instances of deconstruction, Derrida's reading of Husserl in *Speech and Phenomena,* is in this context illuminating. One of the major "deconstructive" moves Derrida makes in *Speech and Phenomena* is to demonstrate how one of Husserl's most central arguments—his resort to the notion of *repetition* in order to establish the "ideality" of meaning—implies that this ideality can never be entirely present to itself or self-identical, that it cannot come full circle. Repeating or reinscribing Husserl's appeal to repetition in this way, Derrida reveals it to be at odds with the use to which it is put by Husserl: that of establishing the "living present" as the founding category of phenomenology (Derrida 1967, 111). Repetition, because it entails alteration as well as recurrence of the same, introduces an irreducible element of "non-presence" which, Derrida argues, is the reason that Husserl seeks to subordinate the semiotic dimension of language in his analysis of the process of "idealization" and the categories that depend on it—of which the most important, as we have said, is that of the "living present."

Translated into the language with which we began, one can say that Derrida's deconstruction of the Husserlian notion of ideality consists in showing how, specifically, Husserl takes repetition for granted whereas, in fact, it is far more involved in *granting*: it is repetition that makes ideality possible, and with it, the determination of being as presence. But in granting that possibility, repetition also overdetermines it, as it were: makes it both more and less than itself, that is, more than merely being-present. If "absolute ideality is the correlative of a possibility of indefinite repetition" (Derrida 1967, 58), then no determination of that repetition can exhaust or arrest its implications, which necessarily exceed all such attempts at definition or identification. "This relation to non-presence . . . does not overtake, surround, even dissimulate presence . . . it allows it to emerge and . . . to renew itself afresh. But it radically destroys all possibility of self-identity being something simple" (Derrida 1967, 73). Please note that here—as elsewhere—Derrida's "deconstruction" of identity does not simply deny it outright or say that it is simply a sham: what it does do is to call into question a conception of identity as being essentially *simple:* that is, as being self-contained. Any discussion of the relation of deconstruction and politics will have to remember this nuance. Deconstruction re-situates and reinterprets identity and presence—it does not simply deny or oppose them. The question, then, is *how:* how does deconstruction resituate identity as something irreducibly *complex?*

This brings me to the second point I want to make in recalling the deconstruction of *Speech and Phenomena:* the introduction of an irreducible moment of nonpresence into the determination of ideality as repetition means that the linguistic statements no longer can be referred to a speaking subject as the principle of their intelligibility. It pertains to the structure of language as signification that the pronoun, "I," is intelligible independent of the actual presence of a speaker pronouncing it. "My death," Derrida writes, "is structurally necessary to the pronouncing of the *I*" (Derrida 1967, 108). "The meaning (*Bedeutung*) 'I am' or 'I am living' [. . .] only has the ideal identity proper to all meaning if it is not rendered unintelligible (entamer) by being-false, that is if I can be dead at the moment when it functions. [. . .] The statement 'I am living' is accompanied by my being-dead and its possibility requires the possibility that I am dead; and inversely. This is no extraordinary story by Poe: it is the ordinary history of language" (108).

Anyone who has had the opportunity of listening to a radio program in which the recorded voice of someone who is dead speaks with the same acoustical "presence" as other voices emanating from living persons—anyone who has had that uncanny experience will know that what Derrida is describing here is indeed part of "the ordinary history of language," although it has taken the development of modern recording technology to provide a sensory demonstration of the spectral powers of language.[1]

What emerges from this brief review of Derrida's rereading of Husserl is that the deconstructive strategy consists of two indispensable elements. First, a demonstration that all identification depends on a process of infinite, or at least of indefinite, repeatability. Second, that such repeatability makes every self-relationship dependent on the possibility of its radical nonpresence: "I am" must be intelligible even if the "I" is no longer presentable. "And vice versa." It is this little supplementary phrase that allows us to jump from *Speech and Phenomena* to *Specters of Marx* (1994)—and simultaneously, from the question of deconstruction, to that of its relation to politics.

"Politics"

"And vice versa—*Et inversement.*" Not only does the possibility of my saying "I am alive" require the possibility of being dead in order to function: *inversely,* the possibility of my being dead presupposes the possibility of my saying "I am alive." I must confess that for a long time I puzzled over that "Et inversement." Was Derrida yielding—uncharacteristically—to the temptations of mere rhetoric? *Specters of Marx,* some thirty years later, provides a response. The Ordinary-Extraordinary Story of Language has become the Ghost Story of Marx, theoretical-political Hamlet, "borne to set it right," this time of ours, "out of joint." Given the dependence of time in general, and our time in particular, on what in the meanwhile Derrida has come to call *iterability,* the disjointed, "out-of-joint" quality can no longer be considered as something that can simply be "set [. . .] right." Instead, such disjointedness calls for patient examination, analysis, exploration. Derrida's rereading of Marx takes place under the sign of such an exploration.

But Marx is not merely an explorer: he is also something of a medium. His analysis of the political economy of nineteenth-century Europe, designed to identify its dysfunctionalities and thus to prepare the way for "setting it right"—this analysis becomes inextricably associated with ghosts, phantoms, phantasms. To be sure, there is in Marx's work a familiar, reassuring way of dealing with the question of ghosts; namely, by apprehending it critically through the theory of ideology as the objectively false social consciousness spawned by the spread of commodity production. The more economic and social reality is determined by exchange-value, the more its relational aspects clash with a prebourgeois tradition of perception and conception marked by the categories of substance and of object. The result of that clash is the ghostlike objectivity of reality in a world of commodities.

But not just the commodity appears as a kind of specter: Communism itself, as the beginning of the Manifesto declares, also manifests itself as a kind of ghost, haunting Europe. And it is this self-characteristic that ignites Derrida's interest, particularly at a time when Communism itself is declared dead and buried. *Specters of Marx,* then, is an effort to call attention to the ghostlike quality of Marxism, history, and politics, but not as something tied to false consciousness, not as an illusion that could be ultimately done away with, but as something like a return of the repressed: of an alterity repressed by the metaphysics of presence in its specifically modern form: to wit, the metaphysics of subjective self-reflection.

The specter is the embodiment—and its corporal dimension is essential, distinguishing its unfinished finitude from the infinitude of pure spirituality—(the specter, then, is the embodiment) of that "vice versa" tacked on ostensibly to a discussion of repetition, life, and death in *Speech and Phenomena.* For who or what can demonstrate that the utterance "I am dead" is a condition of saying "I am alive" better than a ghost. The appearance of the ghost says it even without the words: "I am dead and yet I am among you, the living. I am gone and will go and yet I can always come again. I am your past but as the past, also your future, a future you can never fully control. And you can never put me in my place."

Putting things in their place is surely *one* of the essential functions of what we call "politics." About the meaning of this word there is probably as little agreement as about "deconstruction." Which is probably why it is easier to pretend, to discuss as though all were agreed about what precisely was meant, than to raise the question of just what is intended by the term. To at least raise this question— I have no illusions about being able to answer it decisively, much less definitively—

I will briefly recall the incisive definition of the term articulated by Carl Schmitt, in order then to compare and contrast the inscription of the political in this text of Derrida's.

Why Schmitt? First, because he is the political thinker who probably more than any other has occupied Derrida (as he did Walter Benjamin before him). One of the reasons for this can be simply stated: Schmitt's conception of the political, like Derridean deconstruction, is fueled by a concern with the other. At the same time, this common concern also points to a very sharp divergence, from which the distinctive relation of deconstruction to "politics" can begin to be discerned.

Schmitt's definition of the "political" is well known. First of all, it is the definition of a *concept:* the relation of Schmitt to Hegel is anything but merely external. If Hegel can be seen as the philosophical culmination of an entire tradition, that tradition comes to a head, as it were, in Schmitt's determination of the political. The essence of the political, according to Schmitt, resides in "the antithesis of friend and enemy" (Schmitt 1996, 26). Why? Because, as Schmitt writes: "The distinction of friend and enemy denotes the utmost degree of intensity of a union or separation, of an association or dissociation. [. . .] The political enemy need not be morally evil or aesthetically ugly; he need not appear as an economic competitor, and it may even be advantageous to engage with him in business transactions. But he is nevertheless, the other, the stranger; and it is sufficient for his nature that he is, in a specially intense way, existentially something different and alien, so that in the extreme case conflicts with him are possible" (27).

This "antithesis" of friend and enemy is also a relation of *negation:* the enemy, Hegel had written, is the "negated other" and it is this relation of negation that for Schmitt permits the determination of any and every political grouping. If *omni determinatio negatio est,* then the political consists in the negation of the other through the same. The generic name of that same may vary: People, State, Nation, Class, Party, Community. The "same" as a political entity results, so Schmitt says, in and through this negation of the other—through its relation to the "enemy."

Politics thus entails—and here Schmitt indeed summarizes a long tradition—the determination of identity and unity through the negation of alterity and the incorporation of difference. Difference and alterity thus are determined as moments of an antithetical or oppositional relationship. But politics does not simply exist as a logical or dialectical relationship. It is also a question of life and death. The constitution of the polity through the relationship to the enemy ultimately involves a determination of life and death that is no less antithetical than that of friend and enemy. The political entity lives through its power to kill its enemies. The political emerges as the power to decide over life and death: "The friend, enemy and combat concepts receive their real meaning precisely because they refer to the real possibility of physical killing. War follows from enmity. War is the existential negation of the enemy" (33).

The *concept* of the political, then, as Schmitt defines it, is the construction of identity through the effort to kill the other, the enemy. The killing of the enemy, of the other who is different from the same, is the not so hidden telos of the polit-ical. This is why the relation to the enemy can be privileged by Schmitt over all other relationships, because of its distinct *intensity:* it is *intense* because it consti-tutes a self-relationship, a space of inwardness (collective, to be sure), through the projection of mortality and finitude upon the other, defined as external, as foreign, as different from the same. Nothing is more *intense* than the idea of killing the other. This is, to be sure, not a very nice theory, nor does Schmitt pretend that it is: "The concern here is neither with abstractions nor with normative ideals, but with inherent reality," and whether one likes it or not, "it cannot be denied that nations continue to group themselves according to the friend and enemy antithe-sis, that the distinction still remains actual today, and that this is an ever present possibility for every people existing in the political sphere" (28). Schmitt wrote these words in 1932, but nothing that has happened since then, and above all much of what has taken place in recent years, makes it easy to regard his assertion as definitely dated.

In what way, now, can Schmitt's definition of the concept of the political cast light on the political implications of *Specters of Marx?* First of all, both Schmitt and Derrida derive, in a certain sense, identity—whether political or not—from a re-lationship to the other, the alien, the foreigner. But they do it, of course, in radi-cally different ways. For Schmitt, the "intensity" of the friend-enemy relationship is tied to its being an *antithesis,* a binary relationship in which the negation of the "other" as "enemy" allows the non-other to be, or rather, become, negation of the negation, which is to say, the same. This process of negation also determines "death" as the negation of "life," since ultimately it is the death of the other as en-emy that secures and maintains the life of the same.

It is precisely this sort of antithetical, oppositional structure that decon-struction has challenged from its very inception, and which is dramatized in the motif of the ghost. The return of the ghost—the specter *as* revenant—describes the impossibility of neatly separating life from death, same from other, presence from absence, past from future. The ghost is the past always capable of returning in the future. Which is why the ghost can never be put in its proper place, once and for all.

Deconstruction and Politics

How can a book that takes its cues from ghosts possibly have anything to do with politics? Politics is a science of the real, of the present, of power, and of the possi-ble. The ghost, we all know, is impossible, unreal, not really *present* and hence, not *really* powerful. Except in our heads, perhaps, except as "representation," except on the stage. Could there be a serious relationship between the representations of this stage, between its theatricality, and the *polis?* If Marx's writings function as a medium in which ghosts make their apparition—what then of the political significance of the *medium,* and of the *media?* Do they simply fill up the space *in between* borders whose perenniality we can continue to take for granted?

If, however, the identity of individuals no less than of groups depends on a process of iterability in which recurrence is the condition of recognition—this word says it all—as that which it is, then recurrence, repetition, representation are, in all of their irreducible complexity, the condition of simplicity. Of a simplicity that therefore will never be simply self-contained. If this is so, then what we have long known as politics may have to be radically rethought: no longer the art of the possible, if possible and impossible are held to be mutually exclusive, it will also no longer be sufficient to construe it as the maintenance of collective identity through exclusion, subordination, and domination of the other, whether as enemy or as alien.

Our societies may not be accustomed to acknowledging ghosts—which of course doesn't mean that these are not close by—but there is another "apparition" that is not so very far removed and that is, indeed, all too familiar. It is the "homeless," growing and in our midst. Those of us with jobs and homes are increasingly haunted by the specter of the growing homeless, and the impossibility of finding an adequate response to their solicitations (which are not always for money, far from it). They remind us of our past—and of our future. Once they were probably not so different from us. Once, we may not be so different from them. How can we continue to believe that we are "at home" in a society that confronts us with the increasing specter of homelessness?

Are they our "enemies," these homeless? Are they others, foreigners, aliens whom we can negate in order to confirm our own self-identities? Can we put them in their place, through economic, psychological, political analyses? Or is their uncanny apparition symptomatic of a change in the structure of social relations that challenges us to rethink our notions of home, polity, identity? And if so, how can a deconstructive text such as *Specters of Marx* help us to recognize and respond to that challenge?

"Politics" as Piecework

My time is already up and I have not even gotten to a point where I could really begin—begin the properly political discussion of *Specters of Marx.* Let me jump then to the two passages that I would have rather approached gradually. The first is in *Capital,* where Marx demonstrates how an ordinary object, a table, takes on supernatural qualities when it is considered from the perspective of commodity production. The demonstration is exemplary, not just for *Capital,* but also for Derrida's strategy of rereading Marx from the point of view of a certain spectrality. You will doubtless remember—and even if you don't, it doesn't matter all that much, since you need only open your eyes today to find the same tendencies prevailing everywhere—(you will doubtless remember how) the production of commodities, as Marx interprets it, has the curious effect of *derealizing* reality, at least in its immediate, sensuous material dimension. Curious for anyone who has been identified with "materialism," but the fact remains that Marx's account of how an object exists as a commodity displays a decidedly unmaterialistic aspect. The value of a commodity is not deducible from its material substance or properties, not directly at least. Nor is it directly related to its "use value" either. Rather, it is constituted by a social relation that in itself is invisible and that takes place elsewhere: the relation of "social labor" required to produce the object. The more one tries to *focus,* as it were, on the individual commodity qua material, sensible object, the less one can account for its strange behavior as commodity. In the passage from *Capital* that Derrida comments on and that I want to discuss, this "unreal" aspect of the commodity is exemplified using the instance of the table, which is usually considered as an "ordinary, sensuous thing" but which, once submitted to the bifocal phenomenality characteristic of commodity production suddenly appears to be invested with magical, mystical properties and begins to "dance."

It is this dance that interests me, as it interests Derrida and doubtless many readers before him. A dance is never totally chaotic; it consists of a series of more or less ordered movements and gesture. The dance of the table is thus by no means entirely arbitrary. But it does come entirely unexpected, indeed, it *breaks upon the scene* with a force that is in direct proportion to its unpredictability. This unpredictability, we should add, is historically determined: it is strongest in the nineteenth century, with the shift from a precommodity-production, substantialist, and object-oriented mode of perception, to one determined by exchange-value and therefore more relational than substantial in its orientation. From Balzac and Gogol ("The Nose," for instance, or *Dead Souls*) to Francis Bacon to *Alien* and *Terminator II,* this shift from substance to relation, from object to movement, plays itself out on, in, and around the body: what is put into question, more or less magically, is the unity and coherence of the body and in particular, of the human body, which has traditionally stood as the privileged exemplification of the discrete and individual *object*.

To return to Marx and Derrida: to be sure, the body or object of question is not manifestly a human body. It is both more and less than human: human, insofar as it is the product of labor and an object of use; human also, insofar as it serves as a gathering point for human society—people meet at and around the table, be it the dining table, the table of the medium, or even (to recall Derrida's exploitation of the word) around and before the tables of the Law. Tables have been and remain an ordering figure of human activity. Anyone in doubt need only consult the most recent word-processing programs (which many of us use) or spreadsheets and do a search under the term "table." A "table," whether material or symbolic, is a means of imposing order on a manifold, and thereby, a symbol of order itself. The key to all order is the imposition of stable and enduring *limits:* the table thereby functions as a *frame,* allowing things to be assigned to a place where they may be found when necessary.

Much more could and should be said about the table. But to get to the point: Marx's table is so interesting, as example, because precisely it violates, *in a certain sense,* this traditional expectation of order and stability. Instead of providing a focal point around which to organize a multiplicity of things, the table forgets itself as it were, and behaves in a most extraordinary way:

> The form of wood [. . .] is altered if a table is made out of it. Nevertheless the table continues to be wood, an ordinary, sensuous thing. But as soon as it emerges as a commodity, it changes into a thing which transcends sensuousness. It not only stands with its feet on the ground, but, in relation to all other commodities, it stands on its head and evolves out of its wooden brain grotesque ideas, far more wonderful (*viel wunderlicher: far more marvellous, bizarre*) than if it were to begin dancing of its own free will.[2]

One can see here how and why such a passage would be of great interest to Derrida, even apart from the question of ghosts and specters: as commodity, the table is both more and less than a simple table. It is anything but present-to-itself: whereas generally its existence qua table could be taken for granted, suddenly, abruptly, a space opens up: the space of a dance, but also—and I think this is crucial for the question, "deconstruction and politics" and in particular for *Specters of Marx*—the space that opens up to make way for the dance of the table is a stage, a scene. It is a *theatrical* space: the space of a *spectacle,* however *spectral* it may be. A spectacle may be considered *spectral* when it can no longer be anchored in a self-present reality: that which is *represented,* but also that which is *representing* (normally: the actors, actresses, properties, etc.).

The spectrality of this dancing table, then, is inseparably bound up—implicitly in the text of Marx, explicitly in Derrida's—with *a certain theatricality.* Theatricality is an inevitable consequence or, rather, correlative of *iterability,* that is of a repeatability which incites, originates but is never itself original or an origin (since, qua repetition, it entails the dislocation of all originality).

At this point, Derrida's ghost story becomes clearly not just a story but a *scenario:* the element of narrative is supplanted or, rather, resituated as part of a *staging.* Deconstruction, as practiced by Derrida at least—and this may well differentiate it from other versions—always entails a staging: the disposition of a theatrical space that is at once both spectacular and spectral: not just in the sense of nonpresent, the way a spirit or ghost can be said to be nonpresent, but spectral also in the sense of not just being the object of spectators but also regarding them as well. The reader is always inscribed, convoked, conjured by Derrida's stagings, although the place to which one is summoned is anything but simple or straightforward. This is perhaps the ultimate reason why those texts are as difficult to read as they are compelling: they make it difficult to "take a position," to occupy a place from which one could pronounce univocal verdicts or unequivocal judgments.

If "politics" is inseparable from propositional discourse, from the assumption of positions and the declaration of decisions, then it is clear that the relation of "deconstruction" and "politics" is going to be a troubled one. If however politics is to take its cue from Marx's analysis of the dancing table, and from what it implies for a society based on the production of commodities, then the relationship, I submit, will not be much easier. To illustrate what may appear to be a rather cryptic assertion, I suggest that we look at the precise wording that Marx uses in this passage, in order then to prematurely but necessarily conclude with a few remarks that might be developed in our discussion.

First, the wording. The English translation I quoted designates the table as suddenly "dancing *of its own free will.*" This is indeed along the lines stressed by Derrida, who when introducing this passage speaks of the Marxian table as a "theo-anthropomorphic figure of indeterminate sex" (Derrida 1994, 151). In other words, the spectator projects certain human properties on the commodity-table by ascribing to it the movements of a dance. But this is not just any old dance: what is particularly significant is the manner in which this dance is described. What we have already seen is its sudden, surprising emergence: it can be said to *break upon the scene,* since it interrupts the continuity of transformation referred to by Marx at the outset of the passage quoted; that is, as an object of labor, the table is also transformed from wood into table, but the transformation does not fully break with the past. The table is still an object of wood. The second transformation, however, does break with the past by investing the table with a property—that of dancing—that wood qua inanimate material did not have. Nevertheless, if one reads Marx literally, one discovers that this "break" is anything but absolute. It is not simply that the table, previously regarded as an inanimate object of wood, suddenly emerges as an animate being capable of dancing, "of its own free will." There is no will in the text of Marx, and certainly not any free will. Instead, there is a figure of speech that curiously retains the reference to that which is being transformed: the inorganic quality of the table. The German expression Marx uses to describe the unpredictable appearance of the table as it begins to dance is: *aus freien Stücken.* Literally: *out of free pieces.* "Free" here means unbound: precisely what is excluded by any conception of organic unity. To be sure, the ordinary meaning of the phrase was, and is, that of a certain spontaneity, "all by itself," "on its own," "takes it upon itself," and so on. But in this particular context, where the subject of the phrase is a table, the mentioning of "pieces" that are unbound brings with it a strong connotation of disunity. In a word, the human, animate property of "freedom" is grotesquely countered by the plurality of "pieces" that define the subject of that freedom and that, in the particular context, recall that the table is not an organic unity but a *composite* being, an entity composed of *joints:* which is to say, of relations between more or less disparate elements.

In short, not only "the time is out of joint," but the dancing table is similarly out of joint. Except that the dance of the table suggests that being out-of-joint is not necessarily a sad or deficient way to be. A table, at least, can only dance to the extent that it is out-of-joint. But who says that a table *should* dance. One might interpret Marx as implying that this dance may be inevitable, as long as we have commodity production, but that it should be abolished by a society oriented by the production of use-values rather than of exchange-values. But this would only hold if the disjointedness manifested by the dance of the table would not apply to "use-value." Derrida—also haunted by time—has no time to argue this but only asserts that this must be the case, by appealing to "the originary principle of iterability," which holds for use-value no less than for exchange-value. And there is also no doubt that there are elements of Marx's writings that seem to argue for a return to use-value, as though this could be considered a realm of pristine self-identity where objects were objects and subjects. But at the very outset of *Capital,* in his second paragraph, Marx states clearly, unmistakably, and yet all too forgettably, that this is not the case:

> A commodity is in the first place an external object, a thing whose properties satisfy human needs *of no matter what kind. Whether these needs originate in the stomach or in the imagination, their nature has nothing to do with it. (Le Capital,* vol. 1, 41, my italics, S.W.)

Marx has a structural, relational, rather than anthropomorphic conception of "need," and hence, of use-value, which is a function of a socioeconomic system that owes at least as much to imagination and desire as it does to physical need. And once imagination and desire are determining factors of use-value, the latter can no longer be exempted from the dislocating effects of iterability. Indeed, what the passage just quoted from the beginning of *Capital* indicates is that the very distinction between "need" and "desire" has little pertinence in Marx's notion of political economy.

It is this refusal to allow an anthropological bias to determine his analysis of capital that allows Marx to describe the derealization of reality in a way that is both theatrical and mediatic. For, as Derrida emphasizes, the texts of Marx are singularly "lucid about the progressive globalization of politics, about the irreducibility of technics and of the mediatic" (Derrida 1994, 13, trans. altered).

What can this lucidity tell us that might help us think the radical—and dangerous—changes that mark political movement as the twentieth century approaches its end? First of all, that the principle that has long been said to provide the cohesion of modern society, *work,* may no longer be sufficient to accomplish this task. The contamination of use-value by exchange-value that Derrida sees as an irreducible effect of "originary iterability" undermines any attempt to conceive of social justice in terms of distributive justice, as the undoing of exploitation and the restitution of "value" to those who produce it. If justice, as Lévinas and, after him, Derrida have stressed, consists in the impossible task of giving the other its due, then the notion of "expropriation" would have to be radically rethought and, above all, extricated from any dialectic that has restitution as its ultimate term.

This means that the archaeo-teleological model of *work*—with its dialectics of production and consumption—no longer sets the horizon of social relations. Indeed, the very notion of "society" needs to be rethought, and with it, the associated notions of the state and the individual. What is required is a different concept of synthesis, one that would allow an irreducible dimension of disparity to persist at the heart of all association. Derrida's foregrounding of the *spectral,* on the one hand, and of the *messianic,* on the other, suggests a way of thinking the relationship of past, present, and future that is not based on the ontological priority of the present, of sameness over alterity. Take them together, in a disjointed union, and they result in a hybrid that could be called either *spectral messianicity* or *messianic spectrality.* Both of these formulations are far less alien to the political sphere that one might have thought prior to the manifest intrusion of the media in politics. If, toward the end of *Specters of Marx,* Derrida enjoins us to rethink the "everything which *today* links Religion and Technics together in a singular configuration" (Derrida 1994, 167), then I would add that a decisive element in that singular configuration is precisely the media, and in particular, television. Dancing tables and other commodity objects have become the stock in trade of a medium that increasingly flaunts its spectrality and iterability through the digitizing of images, contemporary successor to cinematic animation. But if the image of a table can be digitized into dance, what then of televisual images "with a human face"? Society today is haunted by the media, which, like the ghost and the commodity, deprives the distinction between representation and that which is represented of its sensory plausibility. But in contrast to that "messianic hesitation" of which Derrida writes at the end of his book, the media, in their current form at least, allow no such deferral. Or at least, in its private capitalist form that predominates in the United States, it *channels* such deferral immediately and incessantly, making of iterability the recurrence of the same. The more its representations are the same, however, the more they are haunted by what they refuse and exclude. It is this that gives the media, and television in particular, their peculiar fascination. By making good on the promise to provide yet another image, yet another face, they confirm the uncanniness of an alterity that no face and no image can ever fully cover or conceal. It is in the curious half-light of such an alterity that what we still call "politics" will increasingly have to be measured. Far from being the actualization or totalization of a representation—what has hitherto been known as "work"—politics may have to at least explore the possibilities of what might be called *piecework:* a series of disjointed, but not necessarily unifiable *programs, projects* responding as much to the ghosts of the past as to the phantoms of the future. Of course, one could argue that it has long since become this, and it would probably be correct. But only in part. What characterizes the monetary logic of modern capitalist societies is still very much dominated by the *present;* that is, by the representation of the present, usually the short-term present, but where future and past are invoked, it is still largely as projections of that present. It is here that "deconstruction" *perhaps* can help to transform the perspective, by demonstrating how and why that present is both more and less than itself—by teaching it how to *respect* the ghosts that haunt it and the messianic hopes that drive it.

A Politics of the Future

In *Specters of Marx,* Derrida returns again and again to the first act of *Hamlet.* He focuses on the figure of the Ghost, the helm that hides his face, the reaction of Marcellus, Horatio, Hamlet. In what follows, I want to add a short gloss inspired by this reading, but which seeks to address the distinctive theatricality of those scenes, in relation to the problems already discussed. Act I begins with a question, uttered by the sentinel, Bernardo, who thereby states, as clearly as possible, just what is at stake perhaps in the play as a whole:

BERNARDO: Who's there?

The response this seemingly straightforward question elicits, from Francisco, another sentinel, suggests the response may not be quite as easy to provide as one might have expected:

FRANCISCO: Nay, answer me. Stand and unfold yourself. (*Hamlet,* I. i)

The question "Who's there?" is suspended between two moments. First, someone has been located. Second, that someone must now be identified. Francisco's response indicates just what is understood by identification. First, a proper name. This Francisco refuses to provide, replacing the demanded response with a command of his own (thus raising the stakes): "Nay, answer me." Second, he in turn insists not on a name, but on something more complicated: "Stand and unfold yourself." Stay in one place, so I can keep an eye on you, he tells his interlocutor; and then "unfold yourself," show what you are composed of, deploy yourself.

This is precisely what will happen in the coming scenes of act 1. But in happening, questions will not be answered so much as proliferated. And other orders, or injunctions, will be given.

In the process, all three terms making up Bernardo's initial question—*who, is, there*—will be reshuffled and reworked, precisely by virtue of the kind of spectrality that according to Derrida, is "always *there*": "Ils sont toujours là, les spectres . . . ils nous donnent à repenser le 'là' dès qu'on ouvre la bouche . . ." – and, who knows, maybe even *before* we open our mouths.

It is this task of rethinking the "there"—which includes not just the nature of *place,* but also "our" relationship to it and its relationship to "us"—that act 1 of *Hamlet* helps us to advance.

When *Hamlet* begins, the ghost has already been there. And of course it will reappear. For the moment, however, the ghost is invisible. If, then, there are good grounds for asserting that this ghost, like all ghosts, is *"toujours là"*—"always" there, to be sure, but *also "still there."* The spectral is in a very special way both temporal and spatial. It is temporal in the sense of *persisting, insisting,* of *remaining*—the ghosts are *always* there—but above all in the sense of *surviving,* of living in time and in spite of time, as the medium of passage and of evanescent. They presuppose death and at the same time relativize its relation to life. From the standpoint of the spectral, death is not simply the other of life, its opposite, but rather its uncanny repetition or recurrence. What makes this occurrence emphatically *unheimlich,* however, is that it is tied to a certain *localization,* to a certain *"là."* The ghost is always an object of indication, its "there" also a pointing ("there it goes"). It is thus "there" in a double sense: both located in a distinguishable place and at the same time in movement, from place to place, but also *of the place.* Thus, it can "stand" and at the same time "unfold itself," and still not be *identifiable* with certainty. For its "unfolding" reveals that the "places" where it takes its "stand" are not necessarily very *stable* or *constant.*

This is what the "unfolding" of the act, the series of apparitions, disappearances, and reappearances of the ghost will dramatize. It is hard to pin down a ghost, and this is doubtless what makes those whose bread and butter is inseparable from just such a project very uneasy. Scholars, for instance, as Derrida reminds us, are rarely on good terms with specters, and Marcellus confirms this a few lines later when he recounts how Horatio has reacted to the report of the ghost's sighting:

> Horatio says 'tis but our fantasy,
> And will not let belief take hold of him
> Touching this dreaded sight twice seen of us. (I. i. 23–25)

The stock and trade of scholars is knowledge, not belief. Horatio warns against "fantasy" and "will not let *belief take hold* of him." When, however, moments later the ghost makes its appearance and Horatio is thus obliged to respond—"Thou art a scholar; speak to it, Horatio"—his response seeks to disqualify the apparition:

> What art thou that usurp'st this time of night
> Together with that fair and warlike form
> In which the majesty of buried Denmark
> Did sometimes march? By heaven I charge thee, speak. (46–48)

The scholar, Horatio, charges the ghost with usurping both the time of his appearance and the "fair and warlike form" of the dead king. As a scholar, Horatio questions the ghost's *legitimacy* and insists not just that it speak, but that it *account for itself.*

No such accounting is forthcoming. The ghost remains silent. Marcellus suggests that "It is offended." Small wonder: the ghost of the murdered King finds itself greeted as a usurper! Faced with this nonresponse, Horatio does what scholars often do: he provides an historically grounded, general theory of spectral apparition:

> In the most high and palmy state of Rome
> A little ere the mightiest Julius fell,
> The graves stood tenantless, and the sheeted dead
> Did squeak and gibber in the Roman streets;
> As stars with trains of fire, and dews of blood,
> Disasters in the sun [. . .]
> And even the like precurse of feared events,
> As harbingers preceding still the fates
> And prologue to the omen coming on,
> Have heaven and earth together demonstrated
> Unto our climatures and countrymen.
> Enter GHOST. (113–125)

According to Horatio, ghosts make their appearances at times of great social crisis, when violence, regicide, and instability disturb not just the living but the dead, empty the graves, and call forth cosmic portents of a "feared" future. Ghosts appear, in a word, when the "time is out of joint." Having just announced this general theory, Horatio is abruptly interrupted by the reappearance of the thing itself, the object of his theorizing, whom he now greets as follows:

> [. . .] Stay, illusion.
> [GHOST] spreads his arms.
> If thou has any sound or use of voice,
> Speak to me.
> If there be any good thing to be done,
> That may to thee do ease, and grace to me,
> Speak to me.
> If thou art privy to thy country's fate,
> Which happily foreknowing may avoid,
> O, speak!
> Or if thou hast uphoarded in thy life
> Extorted treasure in the womb of earth,
> For which, they say, you spirits oft walk in death
> Speak of it. (128–39)

When however all of this haranguing, concluding with a scarcely veiled threat, brings no response, the scholar has no choice but to turn to the policeman:

> HOR. Stop it, Marcellus.
> MAR. Shall I strike at it with my partisan?

HOR. Do, if it will not stand.
BER. 'Tis here.
HOR. 'Tis here. [Exit GHOST.]

The best efforts of the scholar serve only to show the limitations of the attempt of scholarship to provide a response to the ostensibly so simple question *Who's there ?* The Ghost refuses to take a stand and "to unfold itself." The apparition may be "there," but its being-*there* does not translate into a being-*here*. "There" is not the opposite or complement of "here": it designates a very different type of *place,* one that will have to be addressed in a very different way if it is to begin to unfold its secrets.

The difference involved, of course, is personified in that between Horatio and Hamlet. Hamlet, too, of course, wants to get to the bottom of the mystery, to find out "What may this mean / That thou, dead corpse, again in complete steel / Revisits thus the glimpses of the moon, / Making night hideous . . ." (I. iv. 51–54). Nevertheless, despite his desire to get to the bottom of the enigma—"What may this mean?"—Hamlet's encounter with the ghost takes a very different turn from that of Horatio. First, he acknowledges a certain legitimacy in the process of questioning itself, rather than regarding it *only* as a temporary transition on the way to an answer: "Thou com'st in such a questionable shape / That I will speak to thee. I'll call thee Hamlet, / King, father, royal Dane" (43–45). Hamlet, in short, treats the ghost with a certain respect. He describes the ghost's "shape" as "questionable," but instead of dismissing or disqualifying the question, agrees to "call thee Hamlet, King, father, royal Dane." Then, after asking after the meaning of the ghost's return, he allows that it might just involve "thoughts beyond the reaches of our souls" (56). But Hamlet's manner of addressing the ghost distinguishes itself from Horatio's not only in its *words,* but in its *gestures.* When the ghost beckons Hamlet "to go away with it," Hamlet agrees to follow the ghost "to a more removed ground," despite the efforts of Horatio and the guards to hold him back.

Unlike the soldiers and scholars, then, Hamlet responds to the ghost not by *standing his ground,* nor by *demanding* that the other take a *stand,* but by removing himself from the security of his friends and protectors and by agreeing to take on the risk of a certain *separation.* To be sure, this movement is not tantamount to an unconditional self-abandonment, for after following the ghost for a while, Hamlet finally refuses to go any further, enjoining the ghost to "speak." This the ghost then does.

Although it would be well worth reading that discourse closely, for our purposes we will go directly to the ghost's closing words, words of admonition to Hamlet: "Remember me!" Hamlet's response to this injunction defines both his particular dilemma and perhaps that involved by all who do not close themselves off entirely from the spectral:

. . . Remember thee?
Ay, thou poor ghost, whiles memory holds a seat

In this distracted globe. Remember thee?
Yea, from the table of my memory
I'll wipe away all trivial fond records
All saws of books, all forms, all pressures past
That youth and observation copied there,
And thy commandment all alone shall live
Within the book and volume of my brain,
Unmixed with baser matter. (91–104)

How does Hamlet respond here to the Ghost's injunction? First, by a dou-
ble-entendre that "recalls" the theatrical situation in which this is all "taking
place": "Ay, thou poor ghost, whiles memory holds a seat in this distracted
globe"—this "distracted Globe Theater," to be sure, as well as the world as such.
One is "seated" in a theater, such as the Globe, rather than in the globe as figure of
the world. But just how, one must ask, *does* "memory *hold a seat in this distracted
globe . . .*"? Hamlet's response gives a partial answer: Memory holds its seat in that
"distracted" globe by not allowing itself to be *distracted*. Distracted by what? By
memory. That is, by other memories, those of "trivial fond records," "all saws of
books, all forms, all pressures past / That youth and observation copied there . . ."
Hamlet thus declares that he will "forget" everything he has remembered, learned,
thought about in the past, in order that "thy commandment *all alone shall live*
within the book and volume of my brain." The command of the ghost to be remembered will live on in Hamlet's brain, but only at the cost of everything else, or
at least, all "baser matter," being purged from it. Hamlet, in short, will become *sin-
gle-minded,* to escape the danger of becoming distracted. This is how his memory
will "hold a seat in this distracted globe."

But that "globe" is, as is well known, also the theater in which *Hamlet* was
performed. And just how difficult it can be to "hold a seat" in a globe that is a theater is precisely what I would like to indicate by rereading the final scene of this
first act of *Hamlet*.

This scene brings nothing new: no new message, no new meaning. Indeed,
all it seems to do is to cast an odd light over everything that has gone before and
perhaps that will come after. Following his encounter with the ghost, Hamlet, who
has been rejoined by Horatio and Marcellus, seeks to swear these two to secrecy
about what they may have seen and heard. They are to pledge themselves to utter
secrecy, without the slightest ambiguity:

That you, at such times, seeing me, never shall,
With arms encumbered thus, or this head-shake,
Or by pronouncing of some doubtful phrase,
As "Well, well, we know," or "We could, and if we would"
Or "If we list to speak," or "There be, and if they might"
Or such ambiguous giving out, to note

That you know aught of me—this do swear,
So grace and mercy at your most need help you. (172–79)

Hamlet, in short, seeks to keep the ghost secret, in order to obey its injunction to action. The condition of effective action, here as elsewhere, is that it be kept
secret. But getting the others to pronounce the oath, to give their pledge, proves
more difficult than could be expected. For each time Horatio and Marcellus are
called on by Hamlet to swear, they are interrupted, ironically enough, by the voice
of the ghost, coming from "under the stage" and reiterating the command,
"swear." The oath cannot be pledged, the ghost cannot be obeyed, precisely because of the ghost itself. Three times the company prepares to swear, and three
times it is interrupted and prevented from doing so by the voice of the ghost, echoing Hamlet's command to "swear." And the repetition of this echo leaves no room
for a binding pledge.

At first, Hamlet tries moving to a quiet place, where he and the others can
hear themselves speak, and so take the oath:

Ghost. [Beneath] Swear.
Hamlet. Hic et ubique? Then we'll shift our ground.
Come hither gentlemen,
And lay your hands again upon my sword.
Swear by my sword
Never to speak of this that you have heard.
Ghost. [Beneath] swear by his sword.
Hamlet. Well said, old mole! Canst work I' th' earth so fast?
Once more remove, good friends. (148–161)

But no matter how much Hamlet will "shift" his "ground," he will never find a
place free from the ghost's echo. This is because every place that Hamlet moves to
is never simply the kind of "container" that Aristotle defined it as. Every place always touches on *other places,* and is never self-contained or self-containing. Thus,
from *under* every place where the three figures try to take the oath, the voice-off
of the ghost comes to echo the injunction that prevents the oath from being taken.
It is perhaps not sufficiently remarked that it is this situation, on the border of parody, that elicits Hamlet's celebrated put-down of scholarship and philosophy:
"There may be more things in heaven and earth, Horatio, than are dreamt of in
your philosophy." The voice-off of the ghost is one of those *things.* Such *things,*
however, turn out to be inseparable from the place in and around which it *takes
place.* In this specific case, it is that "distracted globe" that is *also* the *stage* of the
Globe Theater, a place that localizes, but only by at the same time *touching on other
places* and addressing itself elsewhere.

To redefine the place, and the taking place of politics, as a *stage* in this sense,
which is not simply a stage in a fixed scenario, but which touches on an elsewhere

and in turn receives echoes from it—this might begin to redefine the space of politics from a deconstructive perspective. It would be a space in which the "seat" "held" by memory is never fixed or immobile, because the ground on which it stands is like the boards of a "distracted globe": straddling a past which, in echoing the present, calls out to the future.

Notes

1. In Fritz Lang's film "The Testament of Dr. Mabuse," a phonograph is used to simulate the presence of the Doctor, who is in fact elsewhere and who is, in any case, a revenant.

2. K. Marx, *Capital,* trans. Ben Fowkes (New York: Vintage, 1977), vol. 1, ch. 1, §4, pp. 163–64. *Spectres de Marx,* pp. 242ff.

References

Derrida, Jacques. (1993) *Spectres de Marx: l'état de la dette, le travail du deuil et la nouvelle Internationale.* Paris: Editions Galilée.

———. (1994) *Specters of Marx: The State of the Debt, the Work of Mourning, and the New International.* Trans. Peggy Kamuf. New York: Routledge.

———. (1973) *Speech and Phenomena, and Other Essays on Husserl's Theory of Signs.* Trans. David B. Allison. Evanston, Northwestern University Press.

———. (1967) *La Voix et le phénomène, introduction au problème du signe dans la phenoménologie de Husserl.* Paris, Presses Universitaires de France.

Marx, Karl. (1977) *Capital.* Trans. Ben Fowkes. New York: Vintage.

———. (1985) *Le Capital.* Trans. J. Roy. Paris: Flammarion.

Schmitt, Carl. (1932) *Der Begriff des Politischen.* München: Duncker & Humblot.

———. (1996) *The Concept of the Political.* Trans. George Schwab. Chicago: University of Chicago Press.

2

Why the Time Is Out of Joint
Marx's Political Economy without the Subject

Teresa Brennan

for Liana Giorgi

In his *Specters of Marx*, Derrida runs together a rereading of Marx with evocations of *Hamlet*, especially Hamlet's understanding that "'the time is out of joint'" (Derrida 1994 passim). Derrida's general concern is with the logic of haunting, hence Hamlet and his untimely ghost. But Derrida also has a particular "haunting obsession" in mind. "At a time when a new world disorder is attempting to install its neo-capitalism and neo-liberalism, no disavowal has managed to rid itself of all of Marx's ghosts" (Derrida 1994, 37). Nor does Derrida think these spirits should be suppressed. *Specters of Marx* is a major, courageous political statement. Marx's stakes have never been lower, but the most influential philosopher of recent times has chosen this point to insist that deconstruction is only an extension of a "certain spirit of Marx." Moreover, Derrida thinks that a reworking of Marxism is the condition of subverting the easy dominance of neocapitalism. But this reworking has to be much more than a rerun.

> Marxism remains at once indispensable and structurally insufficient: it is still necessary *but* provided it be transformed and adapted to new conditions and to a new thinking of the ideological, provided it be made to analyze the new articulation of techno-economic casualties and of religious ghosts, the dependent condition of the juridical at the service of socio-economic powers or States that are themselves never totally independent with regard to capital. (Derrida 1994, 58–59)

But how, as the old question has it, is this to be done? I want to propose here that one way of doing it is by theorizing why "the time is out of joint." As I said, the refrain is the centerpiece of *Specters of Marx*. We can build on this refrain: for Marx's political economy points to why, quite literally, the time is out of joint. But it only points. While Marx himself was obsessed with time (as the chapter headings of *Capital* make plain), the time factor in his value-theory has been obscured by Marx's own emphasis on subjective human labor-power as the key factor in profit. I will try to use Marx's value-theory without this subjective emphasis. Used this way, it becomes a theory of time and speed, in which time is, quite literally, compressed in favor of distance. It is compressed by the binding of nature in the "fixed points" of commodities. These fixed points are fixed relative to the reproduction time of nature; they are fixed because they cannot reenter the natural reproduction at the same rate as that of other natural substances. Their "time" is out of joint with the reproduction time of nature.

But why the labor theory of value? It is the least used and possibly the most criticized aspect of Marx's oeuvre, yet it remains unique in its stress on the "twofold" nature of a commodity. A commodity, as Marx defined it, is always produced for exchange, and has exchange-value. But it also and always has use-value, and there can be no use-value without nature, or natural substance. Because of Marx's emphasis on the twofold nature of a commodity, the labor theory of value can become a theory whose essential contradiction is between natural energy and the time or speed of exchange. Marx himself saw this basic contradiction in terms of labor-power and technology, where labor-power alone adds value, but where value will necessarily be diminished, as more is spent on technology. Technology adds no value in itself, but more has to be spent on it, in order for capital to produce in the fastest time possible, and thus compete.

Understanding of this contradiction has been limited because of Marx's subject-centered perspective, which singled out labor for special treatment. I will briefly sketch his analysis before discussing how it can be reworked "without the subject."

For Marx, in all modes of production, across time and across cultures, labor was the subject, nature was relegated to the realm of object. More exactly: nature and technology alike are the object. Together they constitute the "means of production," which Marx defines as the "objective factors," while he defines the "subjective factor" as labor-power (*Capital* vol. 1, 179). For Marx himself, surplus value or profit is made because of the difference between what the subjective and objective factors add in production. The subjective factor or "the subject" (as he calls it elsewhere), labor-power, adds value while the objective factors or "the object," nature and technology, does not. This is because the subject, labor-power, is variable in its capacity for adding value, while the object is constant. Marx formalizes the difference between them by terming the subjective factor "variable capital" and the objective factors "constant capital." Variable capital is variable because it adds more than it costs in the production process. It does this because it adds more, within a given time in production, than the time it takes to reproduce labor-power overall. Marx dwells at length on labor-power's ability to add more than it costs. But it comes down to this: labor-power is living energy, and its livingness distinguishes it from constant capital (nature and technology), which is ostensibly dead. Its value accordingly is precisely constant. Being ostensibly "dead," nature and technology can give no more than they cost.

Despite all this, the profit maker will spend more on constant than on variable capital. This is so for the following reason. In order to compete, to get more and more products onto the market in the shortest possible time, more will have to be spent on constant capital and less on variable capital. More will have to be spent on constant capital as improved technologies make for faster production. For profit makers to stay in the race for profit, they have to produce and distribute commodities in the fastest possible time. Thus they have to spend more on constant capital, on technologies and the natural resources that feed them. At the same time, they spend less on variable capital, because the more sophisticated the technology (as a rule, and there are of course exceptions) the less labor-intensive the industry. In other words, while technological expenditure enables profit makers to compete more effectively in the short term, it leads, according to Marx, to a "tendency of the rate of profit to fall" in the long term. Profit depends on the difference a living subject makes to a dead object.

Both theoretically and politically, the subject/object distinction is no longer a tenable place to begin. At the same time Derrida was deconstructing binary oppositions and present time, the environment we inhabit was marshalling another critique of the subject-centered position. The practical critique begins with the ecological movements and environmental writings that are conscious of the diminution of certain natural substances and the degradation of the biosphere, a process wherein human beings have arrogated themselves the right to control and direct their environment for their own benefit.

Details of this practical critique are, of course, well known. The odd thing is that with the partial exceptions of Deleuze and Guattari, and Gayatri Spivak, the attention to the subject/object distinction in general, and binary oppositions in particular, has stopped short at criticizing these oppositions and their effects on Marx. Spivak analyses the use of oppositions, and the subject position, in Marx's value theory, but insists on a "materialist predication," in express distinction from Deleuze and Guattari (Spivak 1987, 154–55 and passim).

It is time to take this materialist predication further. In fact, and obviously enough now, it is not only labor or human beings that live and add energy; it is also nature, although it was easy enough to forget this, to objectify nature, when it was abundantly there to be taken for granted. If nature or certain natural forces are shown to have an energetic property in common with labor-power, and I will try to show this, Marx's "essential contradiction," between time and technology, has more explanatory power. Nature is the source of all value, and ultimately of all energy, but the inherent dynamic of capital is to diminish this value and this energy in favor of time and technology.

Energy and Time

Labor-power, as Marx said quite precisely, is energy transferred to "a human organism by means of nourishing matter" (*Capital* 1, 207 n.1); nourishing matter, in turn, is produced by other natural sources and the socially directed energy of humans (usually women).

Just as nourishing matter feeds labor-power, so is nourishing matter fed by other natural substances. Just as the reproduction of labor-power cannot take place without or outside the cycles of natural reproduction, neither can the reproduction of other natural sources and forces. So on the one hand, all these forces and sources are connected. On the other, they are not equal from the temporal perspective of capital. But for the time being, I will continue to refer to natural sources and forces without qualification, while bearing in mind the obvious point that not all of them add energy, or useful energy, to the same extent. Some of them add more energy than others, including labor-power. Some add less.

For Marx himself, energy can only be added by living labor; all other constituents of production are supposedly lifeless. As far as the behavior of capital is concerned, their livingness is irrelevant. But this does not mean that it is irrelevant to the inner workings of production, or to a value theory that is not subject centered. It is important to remember that Marx, in discovering what he thought was the source of capitalist profit, also showed how capital loses consciousness of that source; it spends more on constant capital, less on the variable capital that adds value. This source was so obscured that part of it remained hidden even from Marx.

As labor-power is precisely energy, even "tension" (*Capital* 1, 583), it has everything in common with other natural forces, capable of realizing energy as humans can. For that matter, it has a potential affinity with natural substances that are inanimate as well as animate, insofar as these can be made into sources of energy. Of course they still have to be *made* into these sources, and on the face of it, it would seem that only labor has this power of making. But our immediate concern is with their energetic dimension.

Like labor-power, natural sources and forces are commodities capable of releasing and adding energy. Like labor-power, they have a certain time of natural reproduction, which means that, potentially, the value they add in production can be greater than their reproduction time. Like labor-power, they can add more or less energy in the production process. Of course, we have to distinguish between these natural sources and forces in terms of (a) what kind of and how much energy they generate and (b) the cost of acquiring them, in relation to one another and to labor-power.

The point here is that because Marx begins from a subject/object world in which all things, artifacts and natural substances alike, are already commodities, objects for the consumption of a subject, he makes two mistakes: (1) He overlooks the affinity between labor-power and nature at the level of energy. Labor-power and other natural substances are alike in that they are living; in this, they stand opposed to technology, which really is dead. Technology can only borrow energy from natural sources. (2) Because Marx ignores the vital energetic affinity between labor and nature, he may then suppose that the only new substantial value added in the (industrial) production process is the energy newly materialized by *labor* in the product.

But once labor-power is treated as a source of energy, one form of all natural sources of energy, once the opposition between subjective and objective factors is replaced by one between living nature and the commodified dead, then value theory's logic can be extended. We can keep the logic that led Marx to break capital down into two components: constant and variable capital. We can even say that variable capital is the source of surplus-value, while constant capital is not. We can deduce too that the greater the outlay on constant as opposed to variable capital in production, the less the surplus-value extracted. We can deduce further that the imperative to produce more in the shortest possible time will lead to a greater outlay on constant capital.

But the change we will make is that we will assume that *all natural sources of energy entering production should be treated as variable capital and sources of surplus-value,* and some can be replaced by others. The logic of this replacement will encompass labor-power. If another natural substance can supply what labor supplies, it too counts as variable capital. Moreover, this series of assumptions entails that *there is no real check on the speed with which variable capital can be used up, apart from whether or not a particular form of variable capital can be replaced,* meaning its reproduction has to be guaranteed. The absence of any natural check on speed is the short answer to why the time is out of joint. But we will approach this conclusion more slowly.

If all energetic sources entering production add value, the famous tendency of the rate of profit to fall will be offset.[1] It will only fall where constant capital is really "fixed" in relation to labor-power, fixed in that no other natural force—disguised as constant capital—figures in production.[2]

The Law of Substitution

Does this mean that any natural force or source of energy will do the same profit-making job that labor-power does? Only under certain circumstances, and with many qualifications. How far one energy source will be replaced by another depends on what I will term the "law of substitution." It is necessary to explain this law before the speeding up of production time, and its disjointedness with natural time, can become apparent. (I return to time and speed in the next section.)

According to the law of substitution, capital will, all other things being equal, take the cheapest form of energy adequate to sustaining production of a particular commodity at the prevailing level of competition. Many of these energy forms will be refined; they will be—from one to many times—removed from their natural state. But this does not mean they cease to be valuable. They only cease to be this when their capacity for adding energy is exhausted. Up to this point, their value may be increased as other forms of energy (including labor-power) are mixed into them, although this mixing can also diminish energy sources overall, especially when their reproduction—time—is discounted. We will see that the reproduction time of other natural substances aside from labor-power will be discounted whenever possible; labor-power is the only source of energy whose reproduction time capital *has* to pay for—as a rule.

But our immediate concern is with qualifying "natural sources and forces." Some substances are more ready forms of energy and add more energy than others. In everyday thinking, the extent of the energy they have or add is precisely what makes them valuable. And this cuts both ways. If labor-power can stand in for another energy source more cheaply and more effectively, it will be the source chosen. The points are that at the level of substance, the material energetic level, the common denominator is energy, not labor-power, and that all energy sources, including labor-power, vary in what they cost compared to what they add. At the same time, the critical distinction Marx drew between labor and labor-power is amplified massively in the case of other natural sources and forces. Marx's critical point was that *labor* added more in production than the reproduction cost of the commodity *labor-power,* although capital did not cheat: it paid for labor-power at its value. Other natural forces and sources also add more than their reproduction costs, but capital (and for that matter state socialism) *does* cheat in relation to other natural forces; it does not pay for them at their value.

Do we have any warrant other than the direction of my argument for assuming that capital will operate by a law of substitution? In fact a similar assumption about substitution was made by Marx when he discussed the various permutations of labor-power as a commodity. Capital, he claimed, would not hesitate to force down the wage as much as possible (keeping "socially necessary labor-time" to the minimum) or import (that is, replace) labor-power from another source. This is why Marx assumed that the need to extract surplus-value could lead to the immiseration of the working class. He assumed that as the organic composition of capital changed, and a greater expenditure on constant capital meant less outlay on variable capital, then the only way to make a profit or increase surplus-value may be to keep wages down, to the extent that the level of subsistence became the level of near survival. Thus also the advantage to capital of a reserve army of labor (the unemployed, and the famous *lumpenproletariat*), whose existence in itself is a way of keeping the price of labor-power down: it weakens the bargaining power of the working class.

By the same logic, if certain natural forces capable of adding value within the sphere of industrial production are interchangeable, then capital's range of cheap options is greatly extended. It has in its back pocket not only Marx's "reserve army" but Heidegger's "standing reserve" of nature. In line with the logic of substitution that governs capital's selection of labor-power, where it will always, all other things being equal, take the cheapest option, it should be the case that capital operates by a general law of substitution where living forces overall are concerned. If one energy source can stand in for labor, and stand in more cheaply, it will be the source chosen. Thus, to pick up on Marx's famous nineteenth-century cloth example at the tail end of the twentieth century: natural fabrics cost more than synthetic ones, whose raw materials can be "reproduced" at a faster rate, unless the natural raw materials as well as the fabrics are reproduced and produced in "cost-effective" labor-intensive centers, where the cost of labor-power is so low that the fabrics can compete internationally (*100% Cotton: Made in India*).[3]

The law of substitution can offset trends toward the immiseration of the working class, to the extent that other energy sources can stand in effectively for labor. I say "to the extent" because while the immiseration of the working class did not occur in the capitalist heartlands in the manner Marx predicted, it has occurred in the global context.

The effects of the law of substitution here are similar to those wrought by imperialism, and to the creation of a labor aristocracy. When Lenin, following Marx and Engels, argued that a labor aristocracy, a richer segment of the working class, could be created through the exploitation of other sections of that class, nationally and internationally, they were drawing attention to how the rate of surplus-value extraction of one portion of the labor market could be less in one place if it were higher elsewhere.[4] We can now see how a similar "benefit" to portions of the labor market can be effected through increasing the rate of surplus-value extraction of other natural entities and things. If coal or wood or oil provide energy that labor-power would otherwise provide, if they add value in the same way, and if they can be exploited more ruthlessly, then labor-power can "benefit." Labor-power can be better off when wood, coal, and the like receive less than they need to reproduce. As a rule, the reproduction time of natural substances is not factored in to capital's costs; as I said, frequently this reproduction time is not paid for at all, let alone at its value.

In certain circumstances, and from its utterly ruthless perspective, capital might be concerned for the reproduction of natural forces, and the substances on which they depend, but it will only be concerned: (i) insofar as these sources, if replaced, provide a continual cheaper option and (ii) if they are irreplaceable and necessary to capital. While capital had to be concerned about labor-power's capacity for resistance, it only has to be concerned about resistance in relation to natural forces when they are spoken for. Needless to say, natural forces, substances, and nonhuman beings, are ununionized, unrepresented, and therefore frequently not spoken for. It is ironic that the avant garde at this point discourages speaking on behalf of the other.

The Speed of Acquisition

The question of the reproduction of natural sources returns us to time. Capital does not pay for the reproduction time of natural substances in order to make a profit. It is at this point that a value theory without the subject/object distinction reveals that capital's basic contradiction is between the time of natural reproduction and technology. By this theory, for a particular capital to stay in the race, it has to speed up the materialization of energy, the value added by natural substances in production, and so speed up the rate of surplus-value extraction. While this speeding up diminishes overall use-value in the long term, it works compellingly in the short term. It leads to speedier profit via speedier production. But this speedier production is out of joint with the time of natural production. This will be made more clear if we consider two ways in which the extraction of surface value from natural substances is intensified.

But first, we can note that if we treat all natural forces capable of materializing energy, or commodities produced naturally (agriculture) as variable capital, the problem with the idea of nature's expanding use-values, and therefore expanding the potential basis of exchange-value, would appear to be not that natural substances lack the "specific" quality of labor (for materializing energy, thereby increasing value), but that they cannot be measured according to the socially necessary labor time for, say, a plant to produce a tomato. This is a problem for agricultural capital in particular, in that agricultural commodities are more obliged to keep their natural form and, thus (it is implied), their natural time cycle of reproduction. Yet it is not an insurmountable problem.

Marx had a concept of "socially necessary labor time." This is based on the average amount of time required to produce a given object at a given level of technology. Now the average amount of time a tomato plant takes to produce a tomato can in fact be calculated with some precision. The real point is that the plant's technology *appears or appeared* to be fixed. One of the main historical limitations affecting the author of *Capital* was the assumption that the reproductive time of natural substances cannot be speeded up; that is, the tomato plant's inner working cannot be regulated or controlled. It is historically plain that this is not so, and that capital has indeed found social ways of speeding up various forms of natural reproduction.[5]

The speeding up of the natural products that need to keep their forms in order to serve as agricultural commodities takes place by regulating their conditions of production. These commodities generally are animals, animal products, trees, plants, and their produce. We have succeeded in breeding pigs without trotters that cannot walk. They lie on shelves to speed up the fattening that takes them to pork; cows are next in line for the same treatment, and wingless chickens are on the way in. "Modern turkeys have been bred with breasts so large that it is impossible for them to mate . . ." (Raines 1991 p. 341, cf. Spallone 1992).

There is no doubt about the motive, not even a coating of palaver about science for science's sake. Simply, "a wise farmer is not going to buy a patented animal, or any other item, unless it will increase profits. That is just what transgenic breeds are being engineered to do" (Raines 1991, 342). The chickens already lay eggs at several times the natural rate under battery lamps; the lactation of cows is artificially increased by BST; and the tomatoes, like a great deal else, are planted in soil that has been artificially fertilized to mean its fallow time is by-passed. For that matter the plants themselves are subject to genetic recombination guaranteed to increase their rate of reproduction.

By the processes that speed up the commodification of animals and plants (among other things), surplus-value will be increased, but the longer-term effect may well be an impoverishment of surplus-value based on use-value, to the extent that surplus-value must embody use-value. I say "may well be" because it is always possible to take account of the conditions of use-value production (for example replenishing soil fertility by natural or artificial means). However, if we keep our focus on the overall quantity of use-value, then this account taking must either diminish the overall quantity or run counter to it if it is done naturally. If it is done naturally, it will be at odds with the speed imperative. If it is done artificially, and being done at a profitable speed, it must be overdrawing somewhere else.

The price paid for speeding things up is a price paid by overall productivity, and hence overall long-term profit. There should be a decline in long-term profit to the extent that commodities embody less real substance, and this they must do as they become degraded of substance. Take the giant, airy American strawberry. Genetically recombined for improved size, and grown of degraded soil, it looks great and tastes . . . like nothing. In the medium term, even its comparative price has fallen. It is a symptomatic postmodern commodity: seeming wonderful, yet it has literally less substance, and hence less value. Nonetheless, its price increased in the short term with the speed of its deceptively luscious production.

Short-term gain and a decline in long-term productivity and profit is also evident in the second way of speeding things up, characteristic of industrial production: changing the form of natural forces and sources beyond recovery. But it is evident at an even more accelerated pace. Changing the form of a natural force or source can involve violent conversions whereby, for instance, coal is converted into electrical power or naturally occurring organic compounds are reproduced in artificial conditions, or recombined in chemical conversions to make anything ranging from plastic to CFCs.

The burden of this argument is that the reproduction time, or real value, will be and is discounted the more industrial production is centralized. Discounting the cost of reproduction, in fact, is the other side of centralization. It is not only quantitatively, in terms of use-value, that centralization demands more of nature than it can return, to support a political, juridical, and distributive apparatus additional to those essential for local production. It is also that the pathways of centralization are simultaneously the pathways of any extended acquisition. In one respect, this was anticipated by Marx:

> The *smaller* the direct fruits borne by *fixed capital,* the less it intervenes in the *direct production process,* the greater must be this relative *surplus population and surplus production;* thus, more to build railways, canals, aqueducts, telegraphs etc. than to build the machinery directly active in the immediate production process. (trans. mod., *Grundrisse:* 707–708).

Of course, energy cut off from its natural source of origin cannot continue to regenerate the natural energy that enabled it to come into being. However, as more and more natural substances assume this form, and as more and more natural substances are bound in fixed capital, they require more and more supplies of external energy to enable them to keep producing, due to two obvious facts: the binding and fixing of natural substances in the form of commodities diminishes the overall quantitative supply of nature; and these bound forms have no regenerative energy of their own. Yet as capitalism cuts back the supply of natural substances, it not only diminishes nourishing matter—one source of energy—it also diminishes the conditions for other natural sources of energy to regenerate as well. Natural reproduction time is seriously out of joint. Capital, to cope, has to speed up agricultural production, which of course makes things worse. Speeding up agriculture in turn feeds into the speed of acquisition through consumption, which depends on wide networks of distribution, as does industrial production. In fact, this is where the two forms of speeding things up are tied together. To acquire more at a faster speed for production means distributing more, and consuming more. This puts a pressure on agriculture to produce at a rate comparable with other aspects of production and distribution. As available sources of energy in either agriculture or industrial production are diminished, capital has to create routes for the old sources of energy to come from farther away, or create new sources of energy altogether, ranging from electricity to chemicals to "nuclear power."

The reproduction of natural substances and sources of energy goes according to a natural cycle taking a certain amount of time. The hyperactive rhythm of capitalism, on the other hand, means that the conversion of substances into energy leads to the further conversion of already converted substances into other energetic forms, which are more and more coming to be the basis of energy overall, with lunatic environmental consequences. As by now should be abundantly plain, the reality is this: short-term profitability depends on an increasing debt to nature, a debt that must always be deferred, even at the price of survival.

Short-term profitability, with its inflated price, must lead to a diminution in long-term profit and productivity. In that the substantial material embodiment in productivity and profit has to be reduced or rendered unreproducible by the logic of production geared to speed, capital is its own worst enemy. How this is played out in total terms should be reflected in the crisis of capital, in its "long waves" and "laws of motion." In sum, what Marx saw clearly and before all was the inherent contradiction in capital as a mode of production. He saw it in terms of labor and technology, or constant and variable capital, as he defined it, where the former, to keep pace, had to expand at the expense of the energy input of labor. The contradiction is recapitulated in this account, although its terms of reference have changed. Or rather, its terms of reference have been stripped of their phenomenal forms, so that the contradiction emerges as what it is essentially: one between substantial energy and artificial speed.

How Space Replaces Time

Yet the contradiction between energy and speed is not simple. Two forms of time are at issue: the generational time of natural reproduction, and speed, the artificial time of short-term profit. Speed, as I have already indicated, is about space as much as time as such. It is about space because it is about centralization and distance. Speed, measured by distance as well as time, involves a linear axis, time, and the lateral axis of space. In this section, I will begin by emphasizing how, in the consumptive mode of production, the artificial space-time of speed (space for short) takes the place of generational time. For to the extent that capital's continued profit must be based more and more on the speed of acquisition, it must centralize more, command more distance, and in this respect space *must* take the place of generational time.[6]

It is clear that generational time suffers because capital tends inevitably to speed up the production of all commodities, including naturally formed or agricultural ones. While there are countervailing tendencies in agriculture, and the very existence of labor-power, and in scarce or apparently irreplaceable sources, the speed imperative will override them wherever possible. As capital speeds up, it is also clear, it will diminish or degrade the conditions of the natural reproduction of natural things. But this is not the only way that generational time is short-circuited by short-term profit. As I have indicated, in relation to fixed and constant capital, capital will also bind more and more living energy in forms that cannot reproduce themselves. These fixed or bound commodities can either not be recycled at all, or they are out of time in that they can only be recycled at a pace far slower than that of other biospheric ingredients. The production of these kind of commodities is the heart of industrial production, and this industrial heart has a temporal beat: the beat of instant gratification, a beat that gets more rapid by the minute. The substances in bound commodities are cut out permanently from the generational process of natural exchange, at the same time that they are inserted, in their newly acquired objectified or bound forms, into the process of commodity exchange. Of course, it matters to some substances more than others; trees lose more than rocks or minerals.

But what these erstwhile natural things lose in their ability to go on living, to reproduce down the generations, they gain in mobility. Not much of a gain, to be sure, for the things themselves, but a big gain for capital, which certainly requires the portability of most commodities. Moreover one cannot consume more products within production without having a market for those commodities outside production. So both processes of consumption have to be speeded up. The more directly consumable a product is, the greater its use-value. Once more, the easily consumable product is the one that is most portable, and that involves the least expenditure of energy in consumption (a dishwasher is more valuable than a bucket, a shower has the edge over a pump). More time and energy are required to produce these products and make them portable; less energy to consume them, especially if they come to you, and come to you as fast as possible.

The point here is that the disjointedness of time depends on increasingly rapid movement through space. A commodity has to be shiftable, for it has to be able to come to market. Aside from pigs and their ilk, commodities can only come to market in a movable form, and this means that they have to be shifted, that is, removed from the circumstances in which they can reproduce themselves. Only labor-power and animals continue to reproduce after they have been uprooted. I noted that one of the distinctive features of the commodity labor-power is that it is portable of its own accord. Labor-power, like other animals, can be portable without losing its capacity for reproduction. But humans and animals aside, no other natural substance can reproduce itself if it is uprooted, or, more generally, removed from the earth. However, centralization requires portability and therefore uprooting; and it requires it more the faster production becomes, and the more the scope of centralized production extends. This should mean that, until and if something takes its place in a cost-effective way, the portability of labor-power becomes ever more important, both as a commodity which covers its own transportation costs, and because of the part it plays in shifting things around. And the scope of centralization must extend as the extent of acquisition depends on it.

To extend acquisition one needs means of transportation in the first instance: either to bring the desired good to you, or for you to go to it. Extending acquisition to consume more goods in the process of production automatically entails two things. The first is an alteration in the scale of production. Production ceases, to a greater or lesser degree, to be local in scale, and this means the consumptive producers are more likely to lose track of the source of value, in terms of the time of natural reproduction (cf. Shiva 1988). The second consequence of extending the means of acquisition is that the speed with which the goods have to come to the point of production also increases. That is how capital operates according to its own fantasmatic law of speed. Or rather, that is the operation of the process we are renaming "centralized consumption," a process of which capital is the greediest and most efficient exemplar. The more things are brought together from out of their habitat and locale, the more networks bringing them to the place of consumption are needed. The more they are brought together, following the paths of centralized consumption, the more they are cut out of their habitat and locale. The more they are cut out, the less they can reproduce. The less they reproduce, the less they become. The less they become, the more substitutes for them need to be found. The more substitutes need to be found, the greater the centralization needed to find and transport them. Centralization, speed, and spatial scope all increase because the newly produced goods have to be produced and distributed in accord with a time scale that at least matches that of local production in order to compete with it, a time scale that will of course aim at overtaking local production and same-scale competitors.

In other words spatial centralization creates energy demands and an energy field that can only sustain itself by extracting surplus-value from nature. It is impossible for it to do otherwise: even without the imperative to constantly speed up to stay in the races, the additional demands centralization makes on the reproduction of nature, through transportation and energy services (electricity, water, and so on), means that more has to be extracted from nature than can be returned in terms of the time necessary for natural reproduction. This form of extracting surplus-value from nature is inexorable, for it is necessary to maintain the *central-ized* apparatus of the state *and* advanced technological production, regardless of whether the *mise en scène* is capital's, or that of erstwhile state socialism.

Thus the distance of production and distribution based on increasing cen-tralization takes the place of time. Moreover distance should take the place of time in inverse proportion to it, so that generally, lateral space will more and more sub-stitute for the time of local generational production and consumption. Space will take the place of time by the denominator common to both—namely speed—and it will take time's place by increasing the speed at which the entities and substances traverse the means of transportation to the place of production, the speed with which they are consumed in production, and the speed at which they are distrib-uted, in accordance with the scale in which they are consumed in production and distributed for further consumption. The idea that space takes the place of time in modernity has been put forward by others (Jameson especially). But the fact that this takeover of time by space is integral to the process of surplus-value extraction has not been clear before now.

The speedy continuum of consumption for production and further con-sumption is the essence of why space has to override time in the CMP. In fact, the idea that centralization of itself demands that more be extracted from nature than can be returned requires a formula: the condensed distance and imposed direc-tions of spatial centralization are paid for by the time necessary for natural repro-duction.

By this analysis, we are left with a world in which centralized space, in gen-eral, is paid for by the sacrifice of reproductive time. This world is made over on a lateral axis, which uproots to a vast extent the generational or "linear" one. In this making over, capital carries on like a parody of natural production. It has to have a means to "reproduce" its products, to enable substance to turn into some-thing else. In natural reproduction, this is the energy generated by the natural cy-cles themselves. And we know that capital, like nature, uses energy to enable it to transform one substance into another. But it garners its energy by violent conver-sions, and these conversions follow rhythms that bear only an attenuated relation to the rhythms of natural production, whose temporal constraints they ignore.

In reproducing or producing its babies, capital has its own cycles and "laws of motion." Its parody of nature is almost complete. It plays God and redirects na-ture at its own speed and from its own subject-centered standpoint. It is playing with high stakes here, because it is literally altering the *physis* of the world, ad-justing the inbuilt logic of nature and the spatio-temporal continuum to suit itself. By its will, it is imposing a direction on physical processes that is other than their own. Meantime the willful subject, the agency affecting this, becomes more and more invisible in the diverse forms of power without accountability that mark the present era. The time is out of joint. We smell this around us and know it in our bodies. We console ourselves with myths of hybrids, while living the divide be-tween a speedy fantasy that overlays us, and a natural time that knows it is running out. The time is out of joint; we know this not only because of a sometimes romanticized sense of loss, but because it is the necessary economic consequence of the present course of capital.

Notes

Liana Giorgi, to whom this argument is dedicated, was responsible for persuading me to revise it when I had all but abandoned it. A longer version of it is in chapter 4 of my *History after Lacan*. The present version has been rewritten in the light of Derrida's *Specters of Marx*. See, too, my "Arbeitskraft und Naturals Reproduktionskosten," *Das Argument* 205, Spring 1994, pp. 341–57.

1. In the literature on Marxism and the environment thus far, it has been supposed that if capital has to make provision for environmental safeguards, this will increase the expenditure on constant capital and therefore exacerbate the tendency of the rate of profit to fall. Gorz's (1983) argument to this effect has been influential. There may be a minor increase, but the inflexibility of energy sources massively affects it and all other increases.

2. Other natural forces are readily disguised by Marx's original conceptual armory. We have seen that his definition of the "objective factors" elided nature and technology. So too does the definition of another key term in Marx's vocabulary: "circulating capital." Circulating capital, for Marx, refers to technological *as well as* natural forms of energy. And circulating capital, as we will see, is the measure of just how fast money can move mountains (rivers, dams, trees, and a few other things besides). The significance of circulating capital in this epoch is recognized by Marxist political economy; for Mandel, it is probably the most important factor within it, because of its increasing range and speed. See Mandel's classic and comprehensive *Late Capitalism*. My rereading of value theory will explain this phenomenon as one that is basic rather than incidental: the range and speed of circulation is one key to how surplus-value is extracted and profit made.

3. See Redclift (1984 and 1987).

4. The concept of a labor aristocracy belonged more to the previous century than this one (Hobsbawm 1964) but the logic remains the same. The labor aristocracy was more likely to perceive itself as middle class.

5. While in this section we are talking of substances that need to keep their original form and probably their ability to reproduce themselves, in order to serve as commodities, the same process applies to some natural substances capable of materializing energy as such (e.g., oil seed).

6. The same point is very well made by Altvater (1989) in the context of a discussion of thermodynamics, economics, and time. This article is in part a creative, critical discussion of Georgescu-Roegen's thermodynamics-orientated "bioeconomics" (which argues, on the basis of Newton's second law, which it applies to space, that scarcity is inevitable). Georgescu-Roegen differentiated be-

tween time "T" (a continuous sequence) and time "t," the mechanical measurement of intervals. Shades of Heidegger! Mechanical time lacks the historical sense that goes with a continuous sequence, and it is also opposed to historical time "T," because it cannot be measured and predicted mechanically. For Georgescu-Roegen, "a particular logic develops in the space and time coordinates (as in the social and economic coordinates): economic surplus production is guided by the quantitative imperative of growth by way of reducing the time spans of human activities (especially those of production and consumption). It does this by accelerating and transcending the quantitative and qualitative impediments in space in order to compress time, thus setting "T" into "t." There are thus two coordinating systems of space and time, which, in the form of two patterns of "functional spaces," are fixed on a territorial-social reality (Altvater 1989, 63). Altvater goes on to conclude that "the expansionist pressure inherent in the economic logic or surplus production has a territorial dimension (as production is necessarily always spatial). Surplus production is thus identical to the economic conquest—exploration, development, penetration, and exploitation—of space, i.e., the 'production of space'" (Altvater 1989, 69). A different distinction between two forms of time is made by Kristeva (1979), who distinguishes between cyclical and monumental time, on the one hand, and historical or linear time, on the other. Cyclical time is the natural time of repetition; monumental time is that of eternity. The problem with equating historical and linear time is that the sequential nature of generational as well as historical time is downplayed.

References

E. Altvater (1989). "Ecological and Economic Modalities of Time and Space," trans. M. Schatzscheider. *Capitalism, Nature, Socialism* 3:59–70.

T. Brennan (1977). "Women and Work." *Journal of Australian Political Economy* vol. 2, no. 1:8–30.

J. Derrida (1994). *Specters of Marx* (trans. Peggy Kamuf). New York and London: Routledge.

A. Gorz (1983). *Ecology and Politics,* trans. P. Vigderman and J. Cloud. London: Pluto.

E. J. Hobsbawm (1964). *Labouring Men: Studies in the History of Labour.* London: Weidenfeld and Nicholson.

J. Kristeva (1979). "Women's Time" (trans. S. Hand). In Toril Moi (ed.) (1986), *The Kristeva Reader.* Oxford Basil Blackwell (also trans. A. Jardine and H. Blake). *Signs* vol. 7, no. 1 (Autumn 1981): 13–34.

E. Mandel (1972). *Late Capitalism* (trans. J. De Bres). London: New Left Books, 1975.

K. Marx (1857–58). *Grundrisse der Kritik der politischen Ökonomie.* Europäische Verlagsanstalt, 1953, trans. M. Nicolaus. *Grundrisse.* London: NLR Allen Lane Penguin, 1973.

————. (1867). *Capital* vol. 1 trans. S. Moore and E. Aveling. Moscow: Progress, 1954.

L. J. Raines. (1991). "The Mouse That Roared." In F. Grosveld and G. Kollios (eds.), *Transgenic Animals*. London: Academic Press, 1992.

M. R. Redclift (1984). *Development and the Environmental Crisis: Red or Green Alternatives?* London: Methuen.

————(1987). *Sustainable Development: Exploring the Contradictions*. London and New York: Metheun.

V. Shiva (1988). *Staying Alive: Women, Ecology, and Survival in India*. London: Zed.

P. Spallone (1992). *Generation Games: Genetic Engineering and the Future for Our Lives*. London: Women's Press.

G. C. Spivak (1987). *In Other Worlds*. New York: Methuen.

3

Time Signatures
Post.* Responsibilities*

John P. Leavey Jr.

§ "Millions have been killed because they were marxists; no one will be obliged to die because s/he is a deconstructionist" (Michael Ryan, *Marxism and Deconstruction: A Critical Articulation* [Baltimore: Johns Hopkins University Press, 1982], p. 1).

§ **To the reader 1.** Before considering the responsibilities of the above, whether it is an epigraph, a statement of a theme, or a responsibility, I want to indicate the law of this text: the strategy of the fragment. I choose for my text what might be called an irresponsible discourse, a series of notes or fragments to an essay never to be written. Lyotard would say I have begun a modern discourse on the postmodern, an impossible discourse then, at best a naively proleptic or apocalyptic one: "It seems to me that the essay (Montaigne) is postmodern, while the fragment (*The Athaeneum*) is modern" (Jean-François Lyotard, *The Postmodern Condition: A Report on Knowledge,* trans. Geoff Bennington and Brian Massumi [Minneapolis: University of Minnesota Press, 1984], p. 81).

§ **To the reader 2.** De Man warns against a too simple analysis of the questions of post*.*: "The difficulty for me is that the 'postmodern approach' seems a somewhat naively historical approach. The notion of modernity is already very dubious: the notion of postmodernity becomes a parody of the notion of modernity. . . . It is a bottomless pit that does attempt to define the literary moment in terms of its increased modernity. . . . It strikes me as a very unmodern, a very old-fashioned, conservative concept of history, where history is seen as a succession, so that the historical model that is being used at that moment is very dubious and, in a sense, naive, very simple" (Paul de Man, *The Resistance to Theory* [Minneapolis: University of Minnesota Press, 1986], pp. 119–20).

§ **To the reader 3.** I am reticent about the proposed topic. The questions of post*.* have a long history of writing, a corpus I am only now becoming acquainted with. My first reaction to titles of time schemas (e.g., ancient, medieval, modern) is to add a note that makes me laugh: although wrong, since the term is so diverse, it will still be used for purposes of discussion or demonstration. A variant of this is Andreas Huyssen's note (no. 42), in "Mapping the Postmodern," *New German Cri-*

Figure 3.1

tique, No. 33/11:3 (Fall 1984): 37: "A cautionary note may be in order here. The term poststructuralism is by now about as amorphous as 'postmodernism,' and it encompasses a variety of quite different theoretical endeavors. For the purposes of my discussion, however, the differences can be bracketed temporarily in order to approach certain similarities between different poststructuralist projects." My second reaction is to remember, as Habermas points out by referring to Jauss, "The term 'modern' has a long history. . . . The word 'modern' in its Latin form 'modernus' was used for the first time in the late 5th century in order to distinguish the present, which had become officially Christian, from the Roman and pagan past. With varying content, the term 'modern' again and again expresses the consciousness of an epoch that relates itself to the past of antiquity, in order to view itself as the result of a transition from the old to the new" (Jürgen Habermas, "Modernity—An Incomplete Project," in *The Anti-Aesthetic: Essays on Postmodern Culture,* ed. Hal Foster [Port Townsend, Washington: Bay Press, 1983], p. 3). When post- is added to the modern, too much or too little is possible. My third reaction concerns history. The various histories (of literatures, philosophies, art forms) rarely seem in sync in the application of the terms, particularly those in post*.*. However (to use the rhetoric of the cautionary note), in reading over many of the "current" debates on the post*.* terms, I noted that the politics of deconstruction has been the source of numerous complaints, sometimes personal, sometimes theoretical, at times overt, at times implied. To respond to such complaints in fragments (to call them complaints already begins a rhetoric of jeremiad and of the future as disaster) is to assume an impossible responsibility: the impossible responsibility of one's writing (even as I deny a defense, the very broaching of the complaint as complaint can be read as a defense) and of the subject (my own, the other's, the topic of the complaint).

§ **"Mark the first page of the book with a red marker.** For, in the beginning, the wound is invisible.—Reb Alcé" (Edmond Jabès, *The Book of Questions,* trans. Rosmarie Waldrop [Middletown: Wesleyan University Press, 1976], p. 13).

§ **Author's Note.** This series of fragments for an essay yet to be written, a series that remains prefatory (to the essay, to the post*.*), examines the possibilities and responsibilities of the signature as an approach to "those questions which have gone under the names POST-MARXISM, POSTMODERNISM, POST-STRUCTURALISM." (This citation with its odd hyphenation is the subtitle from the call for papers on the topic of "Beyond the Modern" for the inaugural issue of *Strategies: A Journal of Theory, Culture and Politics.* Centering the call is an image of a computer keyboard before a screen with a reflection of an industrial plant in the background and in the foreground three women carrying baskets on their heads. In this image, who's bearing responsibility? And is responsibility a matter of bearing? Only the women bear here. Are they in opposition to the industry of the background and the technology of the foreground, since they occupy the middle of this indistinct image?)

§ Another Signature Event. I want to recall the "prefatory" signature event of *Notes from Underground*. Like those notes, the order here will be without order (intentional or not, like cities, but like Petersburg, "this most abstract and intentional city on earth," order is the result of any discussion of disorder). And insofar as the signature is an autobiographical event, it lies, as the remarks ending the first part of *Notes from Underground* indicate in recalling Heine on autobiography's lie. In that sense, the signature must always be of interest to the signer of the dated entries of "Télépathie," the one for whom "discourses in which the lie is impossible have never interested me" ("13 July 1979," in Jacques Derrida, *Psyché* [Paris: Galilée, 1987], p. 256). In addition, *Notes from Underground* extends the problematic of the signature. Dostoyevsky signs a note to the *Notes,* a note attesting the fictionality of "the author of these *Notes* and the *Notes* themselves" and the fact that such a personage "must" exist, a note that comes in certain English translations within the first part, as a note to the title "Underground," or in others as a separate "Author's Note" before the first part. In either case, the "I" signed Fyodor Dostoyevsky, on the edge of the text within the text, the "I" that "wished to bring before the public, somewhat more distinctly than usual, one of the characters of our recent past," is not the "I" that begins, "I am a sick man . . ." (Ginsburg trans.). The signer on the edge of the text testifies to the truth—that text is fictional, this signature is not from the signer of the narrative, the two I's "must" not be confused in the signature Fyodor Dostoyevsky that signs on the edge within the text— an edgy signature between the truth and the lie, on the edge between the title and the text, in the time of the edge. (I leave aside that end signature of the second part, often read as the frame for this fiction.)

§ Sériature. ". . . only after a series of words that are all faulty and that I have as it were erased [*raturés*] in passing, in tempo [*en mesure*], regularly, one after the other, while leaving them their tracing force, the trail [*sillage*] of their tracing, the force (without force) of a trace that the passage of the other will have left. I have written while marking them with, while letting them be marked by, the other. That is why it is inexact to say that I have erased these words. In any case I shouldn't have erased them, I should have let them be entrained in a *series* (a tied-up suite of twisting *erasures*), an interrupted series, a series of interlaced interruptions, a *hiatus* series (wide-open mouth, a mouth open to the cut-in word or to the gift of the other and to-the-bread-in-his-mouth), what I shall call from now on to formalize economically and to dissociate no longer what is no longer dissociable in this fabrication [*fabrique*], *sériature*" (Derrida, "En ce moment même dans cet ouvrage me voici," in *Psyché,* p. 189). I translate this term as seriature.

§ Fragmented Responsibility. Can I be responsible for my writing if I only use fragments? or citations? Is a fragment a *Vor-schrift,* a law of writing as preface, as writing before the book, before the essay, as writing before responsibility? Blanchot writes that the "responsibility with which I am charged is not mine and causes me not to be I." That responsibility is the responsibility of the fragment, whose language is "the language of shattering, of infinite dispersal." But fragmentation is not fragmentation of a whole, of a previous totality now absent, of a responsibility once mine but now dispersed and dispersing me. Fragments are fragments, incomplete, "written as unfinished separations" and "destined partly to the blank that separates them," a blank that does not end them, but prolongs them, "makes them await their prolongation" that "has already prolonged them, causing them to persist on account of their incompletion." There is in responsibility, prolonged, "the silent rupture of the fragmentary" (Maurice Blanchot, *The Writing of the Disaster,* trans. Ann Smock [Lincoln: University of Nebraska Press, 1986], pp. 18–19, 58, 14; *L'écriture du désastre* [Paris: Gallimard, 1980], pp. 35–36, 96, 30).

§ **Aphoristic Essay.** "*Il y a toujours plus d'un aphorisme*" (Jacques Derrida, "Cinquante-deux aphorismes," in *Psyché,* p. 517). There is always more than one aphorism and no more of an aphorism. And there is always more than one use of the aphorism and no more use of the aphorism. For Adorno, would the aphorism be the briefest of essays? The aphorisms of his *Minima Moralia* proleptically recall the form of the essay. "In the emphatic essay," Adorno writes, "thought gets rid of the traditional idea of truth" ('The Essay as Form," trans. Bob Hullot-Kentor and Frederic Will, *New German Critique* no. 32/11:2 [Spring–Summer 1984]:159).

§ **Seriature 1.** "Aphorism is a name, but every name can take on the figure of aphorism" (Derrida, "L'aphorisme à contretemps," in *Psyché,* p. 519). Then the aphorism is a fragment, the fragment an aphorism. Seriature of the fragment: essay, aphorism, fragment.

§ **Seriature 2.** The signature is an aphorism of the name, the name an aphorism of the signature. Second seriature of the fragment: aphorism, name, signature.

§ **Modalities of the signature.** The signature rethinks the regulation of the referent, the manners in which the text refers to the one who signs, who takes responsibility for the text, and finally to the text itself within the general text. In *Signsponge* Derrida isolates three modalities of the signature: (1) that of the signature proper, of the representation of the proper name of the signer (e.g., the antonomasia of the signature: Hegel as *aigle,* eagle; Genet as *genêt,* broomflower, or *genet,* horse; this modality might be labeled the aphorism of the proper name); (2) that of what is more commonly called "style": "the set of idiomatic marks that a signer might leave by accident or intention in his product" and which "would have no essential link with the form of the proper name as articulated or read 'in' a language"; and (3) that of the signature's signature, the general signature, of how the text signs itself: the abyss of the fold when "writing (un)signs itself, designates, describes and inscribes itself as *act* (action and archive), signs itself before the end by affording us to read: I refer to myself, this is *some* writing, *I* am writing, this is *writing*" (Jacques Derrida, *Signéponge/Signsponge,* trans. Richard Rand [New York: Columbia University Press, 1984], pp. 52–55). The signature in all three modalities fragments reference and in that fragmentation makes reading impossible and irresponsible (the responsibility of the fragment).

§ **Tempo.** What is the tempo of a signature? The time of the signing? For a very brief measure, since "what counts in post cards, and moreover in everything, is the tempo, say you" (Jacques Derrida, *The Post Card,* trans. Alan Bass [Chicago: University of Chicago Press, 1987], p. 247), I want to read one of *Glas*'s time signatures, the time signature of the "philosopher," of the one that signs for philosophy, if such a case is possible. I want to countersign Hegel and Derrida in a brief series on how and if one can sign according to *Sa* (the siglum in *Glas* for *savoir absolu,* absolute knowledge), according to *Sa*'s annulment of time in the concept.

(I take up only to leave open the relation of this brief measure to the colossus rising up in tempo, *en mesure,* to Kant, to the *"philosophos kolossos"*: "not the 'great philosopher,'" but "the one who calculates almost too well the approaches to the 'almost too' in his text" [Jacques Derrida, *The Truth in Painting,* trans. Geoff Bennington and Ian McLeod (Chicago: University of Chicago Press, 1987), pp. 119 and 125].)

§ **Countersignature.** I countersign. What is it to countersign? The signature requires it. In truth, speaking in the name of truth, I cannot countersign, but I want to, I must, as a philosopher. Philosophically, I want to sign the truth, but only the truth can sign for the truth (Hegel's desire at least). I want to verify their signatures—Hegel's and Derrida's—I ask to take responsibility for them, and so I sign, beloved warrior (*Leof-wig*) of truth, and in signing do not sign for truth.

§ **Tempo of the Signatures.** Adami signs the tempo of Derrida's signature in annotating their signing of the posters of the *ICH* serigraph. This dated (i.e., signed) entry from Adami's journal, extracts of which formed the text for the 1976 exposition of his paintings at the Galerie Maeght, repeats the split sex and time of *Glas,* the mother of Genet, the father of Hegel—the mother of Adami, the father of Derrida.

"19.1 [1976]. . . .

"Lunch with Jacques Derrida in a restaurant, place Denfert-Fouchereau, then the whole afternoon together in the studio of rue Danville, we sit side by side for the signature of 500 posters.

"He evokes his father.

"He focuses himself [*se concentre*] before signing, and then it's a rapid gesture as if he was not writing.

"As for me, I speak of my mother, my writing at present resembles hers. When I was a child I spent hours copying her writing.

"I reread a text I had written in '60 for the exposition '*Possibilità de relazione.*' I copy it on a notebook like this one. I note in passing how my writing was different then" (Valerio Adami, "Les règles du montage," trans. from the Italian by Giovanni Joppolo, *Derrière le Miroir,* No. 220 [October 1976]: 9). Derrida signs with a rapidity of writing without writing ("as if he was not writing") and with the evocation of the father. Unlike Adami and Genet, whose evocation will be of the mother, as Genet writes in *The Thief's Journal,* but forgets he had written, according to the "latest intelligence" (Jacques Derrida, *Glas,* trans. John P. Leavey, Jr. and Richard Rand [Lincoln: University of Nebraska Press, 1986], p. 206b; *Glas* [Paris: Galilée, 1974], p. [231b]), here Derrida evokes his father as he signs without writing.

§ **Evocation.** In *Glas* the evocation of the father is the word *Derrière.* The judas on the Genet side (68bi [80bi]) states: "*Derrière:* every time the word comes first, if written therefore after a period and with a capital letter, something inside me used to start to recognize there my father's name, in golden letters on his tomb, even before he was there."

§ **The Philosopher's Signature.** How does the philosopher sign, here in particular Hegel? In *The Ear of the Other,* Derrida says that Hegel's signature was hard to read, that Hegel wanted it to be illegible, subtracted from the system to show the system's "truth" and "autonomy": "Hegel presents himself as a philosopher or a thinker, someone who constantly tells you that his empirical signature—the signature of the individual named Hegel—is secondary. His signature, that is, pales in the face of the truth, which speaks through his mouth, which is produced in his text, which constructs the system it constructs. This system is the teleological outcome of all of Western experience, so that in the end Hegel, the individual, is nothing but an empirical shell which can fall away without subtracting from the truth or from the history of meaning." Not only is this fall possible, it "is even necessary in his own system because it will prove the truth and the autonomy of that system. Thus, my exclusion from what I am saying—the exclusion of my signature from the text produced through me—is absolutely essential and necessary if my discourse is to be a philosophical, ontological one. It appears, then, that Hegel did not sign. . . . Yet, in fact, Hegel signs just as clearly. One could show, as I have tried to do elsewhere, in what way it was difficult to dispense with the name of Hegel in his work, to withhold its inscription—call it personal or biographical—from his work. It implies a reelaboration of the whole problematic of the biographical within philosophy" (*The Ear of the Other,* trans. Peggy Kamuf [New York: Schocken, 1986], pp. 56–57).

§ **Hegel.** *Of Grammatology* sets up the edginess of Hegel: "And he reintroduced . . . the essential necessity of the written trace in a philosophical—that is to say Socratic—discourse that had always believed it possible to do without it; the last philosopher of the book and the first thinker of writing" (trans. Gayatri Spivak [Baltimore: Johns Hopkins University Press, 1976], p. 26). *Dissemination* continues on this edginess: "Hegel is thus at once as close and as foreign as possible to a 'modern' conception of the text or of writing: nothing precedes textual generality absolutely. There is no preface, no program, or at least any *program* is already a *program,* a moment of the text, reclaimed by the text from its own exteriority. But

Hegel brings this generalization about by saturating the text with meaning, by *teleologically* equating it with its *conceptual tenor,* by reducing all absolute dehiscence between writing and wanting-to-say, by erasing a certain occurrence of the break between *anticipation* and *recapitulation:* a shake of the head" (trans. Barbara Johnson [Chicago: University of Chicago Press, 1981], p. 20).

§ **Circumstantials.** In the discussion of Ponge on the unclean Hegel, Derrida elaborates the stakes of the philosopher's signature: "In explaining this, I must also refuse to be the philosopher that, in the light of some appearances, I am thought to be, and above all I must make a scene in which I oblige him not to wash his hands any more of the things I say here, be they proper or improper. And to do this, I have to have it out with the signature, with his, with mine, perhaps, and with the other's, since one of the reasons (perhaps) that philosophers as such are a little disgusting is that none of them, as philosophers (this being a part of philosophy), will have known how to cut short to a decision, to stop (whence the 'volumeinseveraltominous' character of their work), or to cut, and thereby to shorten and to sign. In order to sign, one has to stop one's text, and no philosopher will have signed his text, resolutely and singularly, will have spoken in his own name, accepting all the risks involved in doing so. Every philosopher denies the idiom of his name, of his tongue, of his circumstance, speaks in concepts and generalities that are necessarily improper" (*Signéponge/Signsponge,* pp. 32–33). Derrida here refuses to sign as the philosopher, refuses to sign as the one who denies the idiom of the name. Derrida signs, signs in the properness of his name, signs in what might be termed the circumstantials of the name. The impropriety of the philosophical signature—in one sense the *aigle* of Hegel and what makes the philosopher disgusting—is the denial of circumstantials.

§ **Aphorism of the Name.** "Those who still pronounce his name like the French (there are some) are ludicrous only up to a certain point: the restitution (semantically infallible for those who have read him a little—but only a little) of magisterial coldness and imperturbable seriousness, the eagle caught in ice and frost, glass and gel" (*Glas,* 1a [7a]). Hegel: *aigle*: eagle.

§ **Poet-Philosopher.** If the signature is improper circumstantiality for the philosopher, for the poet would the signature be improper generality? These two options of signing, poet or philosopher, are not exclusive, but seem to be a series, more properly, *seriatures.* Both sign in (ex)clusion, in the exclusion of inclusion and in the exclusion of exclusion (a series abundantly explored in *Glas* in relation to Hegel and Genet and in *The Ear of the Other* on the signature in Nietzsche).

The philosopher never coincides with work, tongue, circumstances.

§ **Circumstantial Space—Hiatus.** The space of the signature is the space of the preface. In "Hors livre: Outwork" (in *Dissemination*), Derrida examines the prefatory within Hegel. The preface "belongs to the inside and to the outside of the concept," is "necessarily opened up by the critical gap between the logical or scientific development of philosophy and its empiricist or formalist lag" (p. 11). The tempo of the signature is that of the preface, that of the book: "A certain spacing between concept and being-there, between concept and existence, between thought and time, would thus constitute the rather unqualifiable lodging of the preface.

'Time is the time of the preface; space—whose time *will have been* the Truth—is the space of the preface. The preface would thus occupy the entire *location* and *duration* of the book" (pp. 12–13).

§ **The Writer.** According to Blanchot, the writer too shares in the philosopher's noncoincidence. Blanchot takes his clue, as he says, "in a simplified manner," from "the teaching of Hegel and even the Talmud: doing takes precedence over being, which does not create itself except in creating": "before the work, the writer does not yet exist; after the work, he is no longer there. . . .

"From the 'not yet' to the 'no longer'—this is the path of what we call the writer, not only his time, which is always suspended, but what brings him to life through an interrupted becoming [*un devenir d'interruption*]" ("After the Fact," in *Vicious Circles,* trans. Paul Auster [Barrytown, New York: Station Hill, 1985], pp. 59–60).

The writer-philosopher signs only in the interruption of the *not yet* and the *no longer*—all (the) time—*tempus interruptum.*

§ **Not-There.** The *not yet* and the *no longer* are complicated even further in *Glas*'s reading of absolute knowledge, of *Sa.* ". . . the absolute of the already-there of the not-yet or of the yet of the already-no-more . . . to abbreviate this syntagm and to de-temporalize it, let us simplify it to *not-there* [*pas-là*] (the being-there (*da*) of the *not* [*pas*] that, being there, is not, *not there*)" (*Glas,* 219a [245a]). The philosopher signs(,) not there.

§ **The signature and the signer.** Derrida signs, in his rhythm, after focusing himself, rapidly as if not writing and evokes the father, in a series of signatures that erase the series, hiatus in the signature itself—*seriatures* of the philosopher's signature as improper to the properness of truth. The writer can never sign as writer. The signature and the signer never coincide. This would be, then, the tempo of the signature—seriatures of a jerky rapidity seemingly without writing, suspended in time, whose "Intermittence—jerking rhythm—is an essential rule" (*Glas,* 147a [166a]).

Glas has indicated how the signature is lost on the inside or the outside. Filiation, the aphorism of the signature, is lost in both cases, philosophical or literary. What is the time of this loss, the time signature of the signature? And how is that tempo to be read across the *not yet* and the *no longer,* or in the *not there* (the de-temporalization of the not-yet-no-longer), of its signing?

§ **The Edge.** The edgy signature—neither inside nor out, on the edge, parergonal in a sense—is Judas's.

In the last supper scenes—of which in Italy I saw so many—the iconography tries to indicate *exin*clusion by darkening the halo (see for instance Fra An-

gelico's *Betrayal of Judas,* cell 35, or his *Institution of the Eucharist,* same cell, in San
Marco Museum, Florence) or by subtracting it (Ghirlandaio's *Last Supper* in the
Hall of the Last Supper, where Judas sits opposite the others, or Fra Angelico's
Christ in the Sepulchre with the Virgin and St. Thomas, cell 26, both in San Marco
Museum).

The thirteenth, always one too many, is the inverse double of Christ, since
he sits apart and like Christ signs differently. He is the signature: JUDAS. Thus,
Hegel's discourse (the discourse of the eagle) is the *ex*inclusion, in Derrida's and
Gasché's terms, the *quasi* transcendental to the very system it refuses to (or says it
cannot) sign. Exinclusion, the fragment.

§ Sa. Still fascinated by JUDAS as the place of the signature: the betraying peephole (and so no peephole at all, just the (con)striction of seeing). The burnished
halo. A dark circle signs JUDAS, at least at the last supper scene that at once fore-
tells and commemorates the future—what the signature must do—and what
Hegel seems to say he desires least of all—that is the philosopher's task: to make
this desire possible in its impossibility, to write as if the I is the We outside time,
in *Sa.—*

Is Hegel's signature the *Aufhebung*—that process that negates and preserves
(the signature) and raises to replace—Hegel signing?

As signature, doesn't Hegel's *Aufhebung* try to sign for all of philosophy, in
the name of philosophy, in philosophy's name? As such, the *Aufhebung* con-
sum(mat)es all in the holocaust of its signing and its sacrifice to its signing. *Sa*—
the holocaustic fragment of the encyclopedia.

§ Autograph. There is a JUDAS in *Glas* (257a–58a [286a]) on the request to Hegel
for his autograph, a request we learn about from a letter of Hegel, 6 July 1827. The
letter says that Hegel would have requested "'some kind of content to be dic-
tated,'" but to write that now would be superfluous, "'So allow the superfluity of
having submitted the request and thereby at once annihilated it suffice. . . . H.'"
The signature for Hegel is this superfluity and annihilation, the superfluous going out to be annihilated in order to return to the same, to "*remain present*" (258a
[286a]). The *Da* of *Sa* is its time (in the contagion of language, the language of the
fragment).

§ Ciné vérité. *Sa's* tempo's slow; it moves slowly ("*der an die Zeit entäußerte Geist
. . . eine träge Bewegung . . . von Geistern . . . eine Galerie von Bildern*"—Hegel,
Phänomenologie des Geistes, last ¶; see *Glas,* penultimate page). The philosopher
wants to sign *Sa's* tempo, the tempo of the slow-moving gallery of images, in other
words, history, and in the desire of such a signature, whose content is truth, the
signature is superfluous and annihilated in that superfluity. *Not there* (the *sine qua
non* without which there is no signature), the signature, always philosophical in its
tendency to the generality of its iterability, montages the slow-moving *Sa* with a

philosophical riff—a *ciné vérité* of philosophy's truth as it signs, the undeniable *circumstantials* of truth's signature (*signé vérité*).

§ **Strategy.** Generalship, the leadership of an army, strategy's signature indicates this.

§ **Post*.* strategy.** Not there, who signs in such a strategy? What is the strategy of a text on post*.*? Doesn't the not-there raise questions about deconstruction and politics (for an informative but overdetermined beginning on this topic, see Nancy Fraser, "The French Derrideans: Politicizing Deconstruction or Deconstructing the Political?" *New German Critique* no. 33/11:3 [Fall 1984]: 127–54), about the subject and responsibility, about the signer and history?

§ **Complaint.** ". . . the poststructuralist notion of endless textuality ultimately cripples any meaningful historical reflection on temporal units shorter than, say, the long wave of metaphysics from Plato to Heidegger or the spread of *modernité* from the mid-nineteenth century to the present. The problem with such historical macroschemes, in relation to postmodernism, is that they prevent the phenomenon from even coming into focus" (Andreas Huyssen, "Mapping the Postmodern," p. 10).

§ **The strategy of the general text.** What is the general text? It "is not reduced to a book or a library," or to what can "be governed by a referent in the classical sense, that is, by a thing or by a transcendental signified that would regulate its movement" (Jacques Derrida, *Positions,* trans. Alan Bass [Chicago: University of Chicago Press, 1981], p. 44). The maxim from *Of Grammatology,* that there is nothing outside the text ("*il n'y a pas de hors-texte,*" p. 158), indicates the difficulties the general text raises. As Derrida explains, it is generalized "almost without limit, in any case without present or perceptible limit, without any limit that is" ("But, beyond . . . [Open Letter to Anne McClintock and Rob Nixon]," trans. Peggy Kamuf, *Critical Inquiry* 13 [1986]: 167). If no referent, no thing, no transcendental signified regulates the general text, how is reading to proceed, reading that in the classical sense is anchored by the referent? One might conclude that in the classical sense, without the referent's regulation and governance, reading does not take place, the general text is unreadable. However, in another sense, the general text is read, is read otherwise, that is, (one) reads the play "of forces: heterogeneous, differential, open, and so on." "That's why," Derrida continues, "deconstructive readings and writings are concerned not only with library books, with discourses, with conceptual and semantic contents. They are not simply analyses of discourse. . . . They are also effective or active (as one says) interventions, in particular political and institutional interventions that transform contexts without limiting themselves to theoretical or constative utterances even though they must also produce such utterances" ("But, beyond . . . ," p. 168). One might say then—in a language that would immediately have to be questioned, since the statement must be made from *beyond* the general text, either before or outside of what has no limits—that

Derrida delays or sidesteps discriminating politics and philosophy until after he
has generalized the text, or that the discriminations and relations of politics and
philosophy are to be understood from the general text, and not the general text
from the relations of politics and philosophy.

§ **Strategy of the name.** The battle continues, as "strategies" suggests in its name.
Marxism seems able to claim, even as it provides the philosophical work, it is not
reduced to such a restricted role. Ryan says, "Marxism . . . is not a philosophy. It
names revolutionary movements, based among other things on Marx's critical
analysis of capitalism, the theory and practice of which aim at the replacement of
a society founded on the accumulation of social wealth in private hands with one
in which freely cooperating producers hold social wealth in common" (*Marxism
and Deconstruction,* p. 1). Or Smith: "a mode of thought which—for all its faults—
is eager to propose that it is human beings who make history; I refer, of course, to
Marxism" (*Discerning the Subject,* p. 50). Such statements, whether accurate or not,
underlie the value system of the opening fragment. The death of millions labeled
by a name (Marxist) stamps Marxism with validity, with significance, with importance. Millions have also died in opposition to that name (here in criticism and
to the contrary I reiterate the value system). The name Marx is a name to battle to
the death for. What is this rhetoric of the sums of death, a rhetoric that opens an
"academic" text on Marxism and deconstruction? What is it to die in the name of
one who does not die in the name of? Is the validity, significance, or life of X, or
of its name, to be judged by the number that have died in its name? The trump
card death is too frequently played in the name of removing something from life
(Marxism's millions of deaths outplay deconstruction's lack of deaths). In the name
of the name: disaster.

§ **"Apocalypse of the Name."** "You will say: but all wars are waged in the name
of the name, beginning with the war between God and the sons of Shem who
wanted to 'make a name for themselves' and transmit it by constructing the tower
of Babel. This is so, but 'deterrence' had come into play among God and the Shem,
the warring adversaries, and the conflict was temporarily interrupted: tradition,
translation, transference have had a long respite. Absolute knowledge too. Neither God nor the sons of Shem (you know that Shem means 'name' and that they
bore the name 'name') knew absolutely that they were confronting each other in
the name of the name, and of nothing else, thus of nothing. That is why they
stopped and moved on to a long compromise. We have absolute knowledge and
we run the risk, precisely because of that, of not stopping. Unless it is the other way
around: God and the sons of Shem having understood that a name wasn't worth
it—and this would be absolute knowledge—they preferred to spend a little more
time together, the time of a long colloquy with warriors in love with life, busy writing in all languages in order to make the conversation last, even if they didn't understand each other too well" (Jacques Derrida, "No Apocalypse, Not Now [full

speed ahead, seven missiles, seven missives]," trans. Catherine Porter and Philip Lewis, *Diacritics* 14:2 [Summer 1984]: 31).

§ **Post-Marxism.** Ernesto Laclau and Chantal Mouffe are concerned with rereading the Marx texts: "Is it not the case that, in scaling down the pretensions and the area of validity of Marxist theory, we are breaking with something deeply inherent in that theory: namely, its monist aspiration to capture with its categories the essence or underlying meaning of History? The answer can only be in the affirmative. Only if we renounce any epistemological prerogative based upon the ontologically privileged position of a 'universal class,' will it be possible seriously to discuss the present degree of validity of the Marxist categories. At this point we should state quite plainly that we are now situated in a post-Marxist terrain. It is no longer possible to maintain the conception of subjectivity and classes elaborated by Marxism, nor its vision of the historical course of capitalist development, nor, of course, the conception of communism as a transparent society from which antagonisms have disappeared. But if our intellectual project in this book is *post*-Marxist, it is evidently also post-*Marxist*. . . . The surpassing of a great intellectual tradition never takes place in the sudden form of a collapse, but in the way that river waters, having originated at a common source, spread in various directions and mingle with currents flowing down from other sources. This is how the discourses that constituted the field of classical Marxism may help to form the thinking of a new left: by bequeathing some of their concepts, transforming or abandoning others, and diluting themselves in that infinite intertextuality of emancipatory discourses in which the plurality of the social takes shape" (*Hegemony and Socialist Strategy: Towards a Radial Democratic Politics,* trans. Winston Moore and Paul Cammack [London: Verso, 1985], pp. 4–5.

§ **Marx's Legacy.** Is there any relation of Marx to Marxism? And must one take into account all the diversities of interpretation to which Marx gives rise or to which Marx is submitted, not as an aberration to a true interpretation, but as the possibility of reading. (This recalls the reading of Derrida on Nietzsche's appropriation by Nazism in *Otobiographies* in *The Ear of the Other.* See also Christopher Norris, *Derrida* [Cambridge: Harvard University Press, 1987], pp. 194–213.) Robert D'Amico, in *Marx and Philosophy of Culture* (Gainesville: University of Florida Press, 1981), writes of Marx: "Marx is finally a characteristic modern thinker. He had hoped to destroy the enterprise of traditional philosophy but in no way wanted to deny the significance of the questions asked by philosophy. He offered instead of a system, which is what Marx meant by metaphysics, a symptomology, to use Nietzsche's phrase, of the modern world. But in constructing his 'social hieroglyphics' Marx had to represent speculatively what it was to act, know, and live as social beings. The dilemmas he leaves us with in his speculation are worth considering. On the one hand, Marx gave a sobering demonstration, between Hobbes and Freud, of the cost in terms of oppression and repression that have made society possible and that our culture serves in turn to justify and legitimize with its refinements. But, on the other, in the vast work carried on by humanity Marx always saw more of a promise than a curse" (p. 93).

§ **Complaint.** "Nor has Derrida done much better, whether darkening counsel with equivocations on 'property,' 'representation,' and 'copyright,' or muddying the waters of feminism. I think this rhetoric [of de Man and by implication Derrida] in bad taste, but my point is not to reproach de Man and Derrida for not doing what they never intended to do. It is simply that if we wish to ask about 'modernism and politics' or even 'deconstruction and politics,' we are on our own and can't expect simply to read off what to think from their pronouncements" (Donald Marshall, foreword in Stephen Melville, *Philosophy beside Itself: On Deconstruction and Modernism* [Minneapolis: University of Minnesota Press, 1986], p. xx). In other words, Derrida and de Man, because of their rhetoric, cannot simply be "read off" on politics and deconstruction. "We are on our own." But can any rhetoric be read off? Is not the rhetoric of the general text precisely the argument that rhetoric is not simply a rhetoric for the reading?

§ **Modernity as postmodernism.** ". . . what, once again, is called 'modernity' in France or, more problematically in the United States, 'post-modernism.' . . . It is the word 'postmodern,' as commonly used in the United States, that perhaps most accurately applies to the specific set of writers important here: those writing, self-consciously, from within the (intellectual, scientific, philosophical, literary) *epistemological* crisis specific to the postwar period. To put it simply, they are those writers, whom we may call our 'contemporaries,' who, in John Barth's caustic formulation, do not try to pretend that the first half of the twentieth century did not happen" (Alice A. Jardine, *Gynesis: Configurations of Woman and Modernity* [Ithaca: Cornell University Press, 1985], pp. 22–23).

§ **Exemplum of complaint.** Derrida's use of "invaginated text" at Columbia University in 1978 and a woman's question are "a single exemplum" for Jardine of how the "'feminine' has become—to use an old expression of Roland Barthes— 'a metaphor without brakes'" and what "allowed the philosopher to speak for another twenty minutes" (p. 34).

§ **Complaint: responsibilities.** "It seems clear that the minimum requirement for elaborating any political usefulness for deconstruction, or for deconstructive tactics, is to reinstall within it some discussion of the subject/individual as the agent within the discursive machinery of which deconstruction both treats and is part. This might have the effect of recalling deconstruction to responsibility, and of having it answer for its interpretative practices" (Paul Smith, *Discerning the Subject* [Minneapolis: University of Minnesota Press, 1988], p. 55). What is it to take responsibility here? Smith, whose "'post-Marxist' claim" is "that Marxist theory has perhaps more to gain from an investigation of subjectivity than it currently admits" (p. 4), would appear to argue that I must ask, what is it for me to take responsibility here? In other words, how can I *discern(e)* responsibility, where *discern(e)* for Smith is the disruption of the surrounding and inheritance of the subject? To discern(e) what is the agent responsible for this text is to find a subject of tactics, the agent Smith unable to discern a strategy for reading, even as he points out the essentials of any *discerning the subject*. In the chapter on "Responsibilities," under the sixth of "his" responsibilities, Smith reiterates the handicaps of "contemporary theory": "I think it worth reiterating here that the era of what is commonly called poststructuralism has perhaps brought with it a tendency to problematize so much the 'subject's' relation to experience that it has become difficult to keep sight of the political necessity of being able to not only theorize but also *refer* to that experience. Any claim to the specificity of experience is foreclosed upon—or at least severely debilitated—by the theories of language, representation, and subjectivity which poststructuralism has conventionalized. In other words, poststructuralism's skepticism, its radical doubt, about the availability of the referent has been canonized, even exaggerated, to the point that the real often disappears from consideration.

"This is not quite to say that contemporary theory is never politically motivated or politically useful. Rather, I want merely to suggest that it often shows itself unable to approach the political dilemmas left open by its own consistent and elaborate privileging of a view of difference which can best be described as *indifference*. My sense is that this theory is especially handicapped by its own theses about the nature of language and the relation to the real. However, I think that it's still not too late to claim that an articulation of the political based on the principles of heterogeneity *is* possible to theorize; but only if it is accepted that

"(a) the 'subject's' relation to its own history must be involved in the necessary articulation of self-interest;
"(b) such an articulation demands a recognition of the 'subject's' experience in all its specificity;
"(c) this recognition can take place only if the 'subject's' ability to refer to real conditions is unblocked by theory" (p. 159).

§ **The legal subject.** ". . . a *legal* 'subject,' a mere nominee, the signatory to a metaphysical pact with the sign and its functions of *arraisonnement*. Derrida's tactic of debarring any more complex notion of the 'subject'—in particular, his 'reticence' in employing the psychoanalytical theory of the 'subject' and the unconscious—leaves only one 'subject,' which is quite specifically the legal 'subject,' the one with responsibilities" (Smith, *Discerning the Subject,* p. 49). "Derrida furthermore identifies such a legal 'subject' by its characteristically having to use a legalizing signature, and by its ensuing presumption that it can hold the copyright on its own utterances" (p. 48). What is a responsible reply here? To assert that Smith seems unable to read, that Derrida is not "reticent" about employing the unconscious—unless employment would entail a mastery and domination of that "uncon-

scious"—in fact, Derrida seems to want its full employment, such assertions fail
to realize the unconscious desires here. Possibly Smith unconsciously wants to
point out the difficulty of understanding the signature, that Derrida does not so
much reduce the "subject" as complicate the signature and its copyright. Smith
goes further, saying what he does not want to say, slips with his pen (possibly computer or typewriter, or even with his eyes if there is a misprint), that the legal subject, to which Derrida has reduced all subjects, is the subject "with responsibilities." So Smith, even in his criticism, renders responsibilities to the signing subject.
But have I been responsible? Am I to take Smith seriously? Am I taking him too
seriously? On the unconscious and the serious, I refer to Derrida's "Limited Inc."

§ **Complaint.** But I am not being serious. Or responsible. Smith "ends" his chapter on "Deconstruction" with a note (p. 167) appended after writing the chapter, a
note concerning Derrida's recent articles on apartheid. Without rehearsing much
of what was exchanged, Smith states his interest not in what was said, but in the
self-defense of these articles (of which his own note takes part): "What Derrida actually says is perhaps much less interesting tha[n] the ruthless, almost hysterical
way in which he defends himself (and it is without question *himself* whom he defends). But it strikes me as signal that (even while he seems obsessed with the kindness of the editors of *Critical Inquiry* in letting him take up sixteen pages of their
space) Derrida chooses to demolish the two students [Anne McClintock and Rob
Nixon, from Columbia University] rather than say anything—howsoever
vaguely—which could lead one to believe that deconstructive thought in any way
entails, causes, or is even related to his own personal opposition to apartheid.
     "Alex Argyros, in an unpublished article which I am grateful to have read,
'The Vulgar Difference: Deconstruction and History,' argues to a similar conclusion about 'Racism's Last Word'; he successfully questions 'whether the deconstructive posture that underlies Derrida's arguments could ever in fact be the theoretical reason for his opposition to apartheid.' Given the continued absence of any
clear relation between deconstruction and Derrida's personal 'beliefs,' there seems
little point in amending anything in the present chapter which is, after all, directed
against deconstruction more than against Derrida the man." Smith-Argyros calls
for, makes an appeal for, theoretical reason as the basis for the personal position,
here concerning the opposition to apartheid. In other words, deconstruction must
be theoretically responsible for Derrida's personal opposition to apartheid (no
other reason could suffice), even though he is not, proportionally speaking, the focus of the attack. And if deconstruction is not the theoretical reason for his opposition to apartheid, deconstruction is of little merit, remains one of the theories that
blocks "the 'subject's' ability to refer to real conditions" (p. 159). Rather than a heterogeneity of the "subject," Smith insists on a singular homogeneity, the homogeneity of a subject in "real" conditions, with the ability, "unblocked by theory,"
to refer to those "real" conditions. The homogeneous, real subject founds the heterogeneity of the political. I repeat without responsibility, against him and with

only a name change from "Derrida" to "Smith," his critical claim: "My claim is that such a conception of 'the subject' is limited indeed, but that Smith is forced to surpress any other conception" (Smith, p. 50).

§ **Community: post-Communism or beyond.** Smith's question on the relation of deconstruction and the person, while misreading the texts of Derrida and misunderstanding the general text, does raise the problem of community, of the relation of the individual to the community's *clinamen.* As Jean-Luc Nancy argues, "no theory, no ethics, no politics, no metaphysics of the individual is capable of envisaging this *clinamen,* this declination or decline of the individual in the community" (*La communauté désoeuvrée* [Paris: Christian Bourgois: 1986], p. 17). Nor can "*Communism*" any "longer be our impassable horizon. It is, in fact, already no longer our horizon—but we have passed beyond no horizon. . . . While positing that communism is no longer our impassable horizon, it is also necessary to posit, with as much force, that a communist exigency communicate with the gesture by which we are going to have to go further than all horizons" (p. 28). This movement, this double positioning, might be designated as the step beyond that does not step beyond: Blanchot's *pas au-delà.*

Till now, Nancy argues, community has been the ground for thinking history, but always as a community "lost—and to be found again or reconstituted" (p. 29). However, in its *pas au-delà,* the community is not a collection of subjects, of self-conscious subjects, but "*is* the ecstatic consciousness of the night of immanence, insofar as such a consciousness is the interruption of self-consciousness" (pp. 52–53). Not "a work to be done," the community is a "task," "an infinite task in the heart of finitude" (p. 89). The political (*le politique*) of such a community, if it "is not to be dissolved in the socio-technical element of forces and needs (in which, in effect, it seems to dissolve itself in our eyes), . . . must inscribe the community's *partage,* its sharing division. Political would be the line [*tracé*] of singularity, of its communication, of its ecstasy. 'Political' would mean a community organizing itself to the worklessness [*désoeuvrement*] of its communication, or destined to this worklessness: a community consciously experiencing its sharing division," the writing of "the singular line of our being-in-community [*être-en-commun*]" (p. 100), the writing of our disaster.

In *La communauté inavouable* (Paris: Minuit, 1983), Maurice Blanchot takes up certain issues of Nancy's text (the first version appeared in 1983), for example, the reading of Bataille and the reading of the *pas au-delà,* the step beyond that is no passage. "Thus, there is the sense that the community, in its very failure, is intimately tied up with a certain sort of writing, a writing that has nothing else to seek than the last words: 'Come, come, all of you come, you or you whom the injunction, the prayer, the waiting could not suit'" (p. 26). Here the "come" that has come from beyond the community, the call of the community's shared division, its writing, repeats the passing without passage beyond, repeats the passing without passage of all post*.* in their writing, the *pas au-delà* of post*.*.

§ Fragment of a fragment: beyond responsibility. Responsibility is beyond responsibility, is irresponsible, if responsibility is understood as belonging "to consciousness." "Not an activating thought process put into practice, nor . . . even a duty that would impose itself from without and from within," responsibility fragments me. Responsible, I am not me, but displaced "in time and perhaps in language." Requiring "that I be responsible for the impossibility of being responsible, an impossibility to which this responsibility without measure has always already pledged me in sacrificing me and setting me astray," responsibility "comes as though from an unknown language which we only speak counter to our heart and to life." Responsibility beyond responsibility, then, "would have . . . to turn toward some language that never has been written—a language never inscribed but that is always to be prescribed—in order that this incomprehensible word be understood in its disastrous heaviness and in its way of summoning us to turn toward the disaster without either understanding it or bearing it. That is why responsibility is itself disastrous . . ." (Blanchot, *The Writing of the Disaster,* pp. 25–27 [modified]; *L'écriture du désastre,* pp. 45–47), is beyond responsibility. Disastrous responsibility, the responsibility of the community beyond, responds to and is responsible for the "Come" that summons beyond in the *pas au-delà,* in the fragment written without writing, signed, prescribed.

4

Building a New Left
An Interview with Ernesto Laclau

Strategies Collective

Strategies: Before we ask you about your notion of post-Marxism, we would like to inquire about the genealogy of these ideas. It is clear in your early essays published in *Politics and Ideology in Marxist Theory* that you are approaching the various issues—feudalism and capitalism in Latin America, the specificity of the political, the origins of fascism, and the notion of populism—from the viewpoint that most theorists have approached these topics with theoretical terrorism, if we may use that term. That is, you seem to argue that, in the name of paradigmatic clarity and logical consistency, there has been a tendency to overlook the historical specificity of the phenomena under question. This strategy seems to point toward your more general critique of essentialist discourses you now hold. In your introduction to *Politics* you even raise the whole problem of "class reductionism" in Marxist theory, an issue that takes on central importance in your recent work with Chantal Mouffe. At the same time, your early studies are still within the parameters of the Marxist tradition—your homage to the theoretical and practical riches of Althusser and Della Volpe are indicative of this tentative stance. What was the intellectual history behind your current theoretical position? What brought you from these first hesitant steps toward your later conception of post-Marxism?

Ernesto Laclau: Let me tell you, in the first place, that I do not think there is such a radical discontinuity in my intellectual evolution. In some way or another I think that evolution has been but a process of deepening some intuitions that were already there. The idea of politics as hegemony and articulation, for example, is something that has always accompanied my political trajectory. I remember that in 1984, after many years, I traveled to Buenos Aires with Chantal Mouffe and we were able to consult early works of mine. Chantal was surprised to read my leading articles in *Lucha Obrera* (of which I had been the editor) of twenty years earlier, in which socialist struggle was already spoken about as the struggle of the working class for the hegemonization of democratic tasks.

In that sense, I have never been a "total" Marxist, someone who sought in Marxism a "homeland," a complete and harmonic vision of the world, to use Plekhanov's terms. The "language games" I played with Marxism were always

57

more complicated, and they always tried to articulate Marxism to something else. In my first works published in England—the critiques of Poulantzas and Gunder Frank, for example—people were inclined to see a more rigorous reformulation of Marxist orthodoxy, but I do not think this has been a correct interpretation. The critique of Frank, for example, was an attempt to define capitalism as a *mode of production* to prevent the concept from losing all analytical validity; on the other hand, it is also stated that the modes of production are not a substratum or foundation, but are articulated into larger totalities, that is, *economic systems*—and at that time many already observed that the category of "economic system" is not a Marxist category. And I do not think you can find in my writings at any time the reduction of nonclassist components to the role of superstructures of classes. My critique of Poulantzas's conception of fascism was based precisely on stating the irreducibility of the "national-popular" to classes.

As for the influence I received from thinkers like Della Volpe and Althusser, the answer is similar: it is only insofar as they allowed me to start a gradual rupture from the totalizing character of Marxist discourse—Althusser's overdetermined contradiction, Della Volpe's antidialectical trend—that I felt attracted by their works. In the case of Della Volpe, I think my enthusiasm for his work was, at a given point, considerably exaggerated. His reduction of historicism to teleology, his insistence on the validity of Marxism's abstract categories vis-à-vis their articulation to concrete traditions, his lack of comprehension of Gramsci's thought, go exactly in the opposite direction to what I have intended to do in the last few years. But in the case of Althusser I think a good deal of my later works can be seen as a radicalization of many themes already hinted at in *For Marx* (much more than in *Reading Capital*). I think that the sudden disappearance of the Althusserian school can be explained, to a great degree, by two factors: in the first place because it had little time to mature intellectually in a post-Marxist direction—the '68 wave created a new historical climate that turned obsolete all that analytical-interpretative lucubration around Marx's holy texts; but in the second place—and this is linked with what I said before—it is also necessary to remember that the Althusserian project was conceived as an attempt at an internal theoretical renewal of the French Communist Party—a project that gradually lost significance in the seventies.

At any rate, as far as I am concerned, the deconstruction of Marxist tradition, not its mere abandonment, is what proves important. The loss of collective memory is not something to be overjoyed about. It is always an impoverishment and a traumatic fact. One only thinks *from* a tradition. Of course, the relation with tradition should not be one of submission and repetition, but of transformation and critique. One must construct one's discourse as *difference* in relation to that tradition and this implies at the same time continuities and discontinuities. If a tradition ceases to be the cultural terrain where creativity and the inscription of new problems take place, and becomes instead a hindrance to that creativity and that inscription, it will gradually and silently be abandoned. Because any tradition may die. In that sense Marxism's destiny as an intellectual tradition is clear: it will either be inscribed as a historical, partial, and limited moment within a wider historical line, that of the radical tradition of the West, or it will be taken over by the boy scouts of the small Trotskyist sects who will continue to repeat a totally obsolete language—and thus nobody will remember Marxism in twenty years' time.

Strategies: If we may follow up on this line of inquiry for a moment—it seems clear that your theoretical position in some way reflects the concrete and practical developments in "radical" politics in the post-1968 climate of Western democracies. Not only does one perceive an awareness in your work of the importance of those struggles associated with women's rights, gay rights, nuclear disarmament, and the ecology, but one also senses the "presence" in your text of those "anticapitalist" movements (e.g., the Autonomy movement in Italy) that were inspired by Marx, but were antagonistic to conventional Marxist discourses and practices. How have these and other political developments affected your present theoretical position?

EL: In the sense that they created the historical and political terrain that allowed me to deepen certain intuitions which up to then I had only been able to base on my Argentinean experience. The 1960s in Argentina had been a period of fast disintegration of the social fabric. After the 1966 coup d'état there was a proliferation of new antagonisms and a rapid politicization of social relations. All I tried to think theoretically later—the dispersal of subject positions, the hegemonic recomposition of fragmented identities, the reconstitution of social identities through the political imaginary—all that is something I learned in those years in the course of practical activism. It was evident to all of us that a narrowly classist approach was insufficient. The roots of my post-Marxism date back to that time. Well, in these circumstances the 1968 mobilizations in France, Germany, and the United States seemed to confirm those intuitions and made it possible to place them in a wider political and historical terrain. Later on, already in Europe, the study of the new social movements you are referring to enabled me to advance theoretically in the direction you know through *Hegemony and Socialist Strategy*. In that sense an important role was played by my collaboration with Chantal Mouffe, who made very important contributions to the problematic we were trying to elaborate together. (The formulation of politics in terms of radical democracy, which appears in the last part of the book, is basically her contribution.)

Strategies: In the first two chapters of *Hegemony and Socialist Strategy,* you and Chantal Mouffe construct a genealogy of the concept of hegemony as it developed out of the Marxist tradition since the Second International. In this narrative, the most striking feature is your argument that, even for Gramsci, the "new political logic" of hegemony could not be theorized because of the dominance of essentialist categories. What are the inherent discursive limitations of the Marxist tradition?

EL: More than about an inherent discursive limitation of the Marxist tradition I would speak about limitations that Marxism shares with the ensemble of the nineteenth-century sociological tradition. The main limitation in this respect is the "objectivism" in the comprehension of social relations, which is ultimately reduced to the "metaphysics of presence" which is implicit in sociological categories—that is, the assumption that society may be understood as an objective and coherent ensemble from foundations or laws of movement that are conceptually graspable.

Against this, the perspective we hold affirms the *constitutive* and *primordial* character of negativity. All social order, as a consequence, can only affirm itself insofar as it represses a "constitutive outside" which negates it—which amounts to saying that social order never succeeds in entirely constituting itself as an objective order. It is in that sense that we have sustained the *revelatory* character of antagonism: what is shown in antagonism is the *ultimate* impossibility of social objectivity. Now Marxism constituted itself as an essentially objectivist conception, as an assertion of the rationality of the real, in the best Hegelian tradition. The radically *coherent* history constituted by the development of productive forces and their combination with various types of production relations is a history without "outside."

Of course, from the beginning this history had to postulate a supplement not easy to integrate into its categories: this supplement is class struggle—that is, the element of negativity and antagonism. If history is an objective process, negativity cannot occupy any place in it; on the other hand, without negativity there is neither theory nor revolutionary action. Class struggle thus plays in Marxist theory the role of what Derrida has called a hymen: the theory both requires it and makes it impossible. But we do not have to regret this inconsistency: it is thanks to it that there has been a *history* of Marxism. And this history has consisted in the progressive erosion of the main body of the theory on the part of that supplement which cannot be integrated. What is positive and retrievable in Marxism is the set of categories—hegemony, in the first place—that it elaborated in the course of its distancing from its originary objectivism. As regards the latter, it is necessary to relegate it where it belongs: the museum of antiquities.

Strategies: While you argue quite convincingly for the problem of the "double void" in Marxism from the Second International onwards, you never sufficiently deal with Marx's theory itself. Given this omission, the inevitable comment from Marxist quarters would be that although you have shown the necessity of going beyond Marxism, you have not shown the necessity of going beyond Marx. We need only look to the historical and political texts of Marx—*The Civil War in France, The 18th Brumaire of Louis Bonaparte,* even *The Critique of the Gotha Programme*—to see a theoretical opening for a "logic of the contingent," discussions of the materiality of ideology, etc. Thus, it would seem that your argument might lead one not to become post-Marxist, but rather to study Marx more thoroughly, to become more Marxist. How would you respond to this type of comment?

EL: By saying that the conclusion is highly optimistic. It is true that in our book we have dealt with Marx's work only marginally, the reason being that the trajectory of Marxism we put forward there, as from the Second International, is conceived not as a "general" history but as a genealogy of the concept of hegemony. But it would doubtless be wrong to assume that Plekhanov or Kautsky, who devoted a considerable part of their lives to the study of Marx's work—and who were certainly not hacks—have simply misread Marx. Finally, the one who said that the most advanced countries show those which are less so the mirror of their own future, or the one who wrote the preface to *A Contribution to the Critique of Political Economy* is not an economistic commentator of the Second International, but Marx himself. That such a duality between the "rational and objective" history—grounded on the contradiction between productive forces and relations of production—and a history dominated by negativity and contingency—grounded, consequently, on the constitutive character of class struggle—can be traced back to the work of Marx himself is something of which I am well aware. And it is evident that it is in the political and historical writings that the second moment naturally tends to become more visible. I have never said that Marx's work should be abandoned *en bloc* but deconstructed, which is very different. But precisely because that duality dominates the ensemble of Marx's work, and because what we are trying to do today is to eliminate it by asserting the primary and constitutive character of antagonism, this involves adopting a post-Marxist position and not becoming "more Marxist" as you say. It is necessary to put an end to the tendency to transvest our ideas, presenting them as if they belonged to Marx, and proclaiming *urbi et orbi* every ten years that one has discovered the "true" Marx. Somewhere in his writings Paul M. Sweezy says, and very sensibly at that, that instead of attempting to discover what Marx meant to say, he will make the simplifying assumption that he meant to say what he actually said.

Strategies: In chapter 3 of *Hegemony,* you attempt to fill in the theoretical space left open by your deconstruction of Marxism. Central to this theoretical reconstruction is the introduction of the notion of the "impossibility of the social," and the concepts of "articulation" and "antagonism." What exactly is meant by each of these terms or concepts, and how do they provide a basis for theorizing the new political logic of hegemony?

EL: The three concepts are interrelated. By "impossibility of the social" I understand what I referred to before: the assertion of the ultimate impossibility of all "objectivity." Something is objective insofar as its "being" is present and fully constituted. From this perspective things "are" something determinate, social relations "are"—and in that sense they are endowed with objectivity. Now in our practical life we never experience "objectivity" in that way: the sense of many things escapes us, the "war of interpretations" introduces ambiguities and doubts about the being of objects, and society presents itself, to a great degree, not as an objective, harmonic order, but as an ensemble of divergent forces which do not seem to obey any unified or unifying logic. How can this experience of the failure of objectivity be made compatible with the affirmation of an ultimate objectivity of the real? Metaphysical thought—and sociological thought, which is but its extension—respond by opting for the reaffirmation of the objectivity of the real and for the reduction of their failures to a problem of incorrect or insufficient apprehension—that is, to a problem of *knowledge*. There is a "being" of objects—and of history and society among them—that constitutes its ultimate reality and that remains there, waiting to be discovered. In the "war of interpretations," what is at stake is not the construction of the object, but its correct apprehension; society's irrationality is mere appearance for, behind its phenomenal forms, a deeper rationality is always at work. In that sense, the progress of knowledge is the discovery of a gradually deeper stratum of objectivity, but objectivity as such is not a point at issue.

This is the point where our approach differs (and not only ours: it is but the continuation of a multiple intellectual tradition which becomes manifest, for example, in a philosophy such as Nietzsche's). The moment of failure of objectivity is, for us, the "constitutive outside" of the latter. The movement toward deeper strata does not reveal higher forms of objectivity but a gradually more radical contingency. The being of objects is, therefore, radically historical, and "objectivity" is a social construction. It is in this sense that society does not "exist" insofar as objectivity, as a system of differences that establishes the being of entities, always shows the traces of its ultimate arbitrariness and only exists in the pragmatic—and as a consequence always incomplete—movement of its affirmation.

The radical contingency of the social shows itself, as we have stated, in the experience of antagonism. If the force that antagonizes me negates my identity, the maintenance of that identity depends on the result of a struggle; and if the outcome of that struggle is not warranted by any a priori law of history, in that case *all* identity has a contingent character. Now, if, as we have shown, antagonism is the "constitutive outside" that accompanies the affirmation of all identity, in that case all social practice will be, in one of its dimensions, *articulatory*. By articulation we understand the creation of something new out of a dispersion of elements. If society had an ultimate objectivity, then social practices, even the most innovative ones, would be essentially repetitive: they would only be the explicitation or reiteration of something that was there from the beginning. And this applies, of course, to all teleology: if the "for itself" was not *already* contained in the "in itself," the transition from one to the other would not be teleological. But if contingency penetrates all identity and consequently limits all objectivity, in that case there is no objectivity that may constitute an "origin": the moment of creation is radical—*creatio ex nihilo*—and no social practice, not even the most humble acts of our everyday life, are entirely repetitive. "Articulation," in that sense, is the primary ontological level of the constitution of the real.

And this shows why the category of "hegemony" is something like the starting point of a "post-Marxist" discourse within Marxism. Because Marxism was well rooted in the traditional metaphysics of the West, it was a philosophy of history. The dénouement of history was the result of *"objective* laws" which could be rationally grasped and which were independent of the will and consciousness of the agents. The Stalinist conception of the "objective sense" of actions is but the coarse expression and the *reductio ad absurdum* of something that was implicit in Marx's theoretical project. But "hegemony" means something very different; it means the contingent articulation of elements around certain social configurations—historical blocs—that cannot be predetermined by any philosophy of history and that is essentially linked to the concrete struggles of social agents. By *concrete* I mean *specific,* in all their humble individuality and materiality, not insofar as they incarnate the dream of intellectuals about a "universal class." Post-Marxism is, in this sense, a radicalization of those subversive effects of the essentialist discourse that were implicit from the beginning in the logic of hegemony.

Strategies: If we were to look again at your early studies, it is clear that you were influenced by Althusser. In your essays on fascism and populism, for instance, you argue for the importance of Althusser's conception of ideology, especially the notion of "ideological interpellation," for understanding the specificity of these social phenomena. What is interesting is the way in which these formulations bear a close resemblance to your notion of "discourse" in *Hegemony and Socialist Strategy.* What are the defining characteristics of your notion of discourse, and in what way does it differ from Althusser's concept of ideology? More generally, how does your notion avoid the status of an essentialist category?

EL: The concept of discourse in *Hegemony and Socialist Strategy* is in no way connected with the category of "ideology" as it was formulated by Althusser. To be more precise: while the concept of ideology was the terrain where Althusser started to *recognize* some of the problems that have become central in our approach, he could not radicalize them beyond a certain point, as his analytical terrain was limited by the straitjacket of the base/superstructure distinction. This already establishes a clear line of demarcation between the two perspectives. For Althusser, ideology, despite all the recognition of its "materiality," is a superstructure, a regional category of the social whole—an essentially topographical concept, therefore. For us, "discourse" is not a topographical concept, but the horizon of the constitution of any object. Economic activity is, consequently, as discursive as political or aesthetic ideas. To produce an object, for instance, is to establish a system of relations between raw materials, tools, and so forth, which is not simply given by the mere existential materiality of the intervening elements. The primary and constitutive character of the discursive is, therefore, the condition of any practice. And it is at this point where the fundamental watershed takes place. Confronted with the discursive character of all social practices, we can follow two courses: (a) conceive those practical-discursive forms as manifestations of a deeper objectivity that constitutes its ultimate reality (the cunning of Reason in Hegel, the development and neutrality of productive forces in Marx); or (b) consider that those practical-discursive structures do not conceal any deeper objectivity that transcends them, and, at the same time, explains them, but that they are forms *without mystery,* pragmatic attempts to subsume the "real" into the frame of a symbolic objectivity that will always be overflown in the end. The first solution only has a sense within the frame of traditional metaphysics, which, insofar as it asserted the radical capacity of the concept of grasping the real, was essentially idealistic. The second solution, on the contrary, implies stating that between the real and the concept there is an insurmountable asymmetry and that the real, therefore, will only show itself in the distortion of the conceptual. This path, which is, in my view, the path of a correctly understood materialism, involves asserting the discursive character of all objectivity; if the real were transparent to the concept, then there would be no possible distinction between the objectivity of the conceptual and the objectivity of the real, and the discursive would be the neutral medium of presentation of that objectivity to consciousness. But if objectivity is discursive, if an object *qua object* constitutes itself as an object of discourse, in that case there will always be an "outside," an ungraspable margin that limits and distorts the "objective," and which is, precisely, the real.

　　This, I hope, clears up why a category like that of "ideology," in its traditional sense, has no room in our theoretical perspective. All topography supposes a space within which the distinction between regions and levels takes place; this implies, therefore, a closure of the social whole, which is what allows it to be grasped as an intelligible structure and which assigns precise identities to its regions and levels. But if all objectivity is systematically overflown by a constitutive outside, any form of unity, articulation, and hierarchization that may exist between the various regions and levels will be the result of a contingent and pragmatic construction, and not an essential connection that can be recognized. In that sense, it is impossible to determine a priori that something is the "superstructure" of anything else. The concept of ideology can, nevertheless, be maintained, even in the sense of "false consciousness," if by the latter we understand that illusion of "closure" that is the imaginary horizon that accompanies the constitution of all objectivity. This also shows why our concept of "discourse" does not have the status of an essentialist category: because it is precisely the concept which, by asserting the presence of the "constitutive outside" that accompanies the institution of all identity, points to the limitation and contingency of all essences. Finally, let me point out that the concept of "interpellation" is the phenomenon of "identification" which Freud described at various points of his work, especially in *Group Psychology.* In its Lacanian reformulation, it presupposes the centrality of the category of "lack." In my own analyses, the important issue is also the reconstitution of shattered political identities through new forms of identification. The limits of the symbolic are, therefore, the limitations that the social finds to constitute itself fully as such. But in the Althusserian formulation—with all its implicit Spinozanism—the central point is the production of the "subject effect" as an internal moment of the process of reproduction of the social whole. Instead of seeing in "identification" an ambiguous process that shows the limits of objectivity, the former becomes precisely the opposite: an internal requirement of objectivity in the process of its self-constitution (in Spinozan terms, the subject is substance).

Strategies: In your final chapter, you argue that what underlies political struggles for radical democracy is the "democratic imaginary." There are a number of questions that arise from the use of this concept: first, does not this symbolic discourse become an essentialist category in your narrative of the history of radical democracy? Secondly, it seems as if your characterization of the origin of the democratic imaginary in the French Revolution might be open to the charge of Western-centrism. Do you see this democratic discourse as universal? If so, why? And, if not, what imaginary functions for non-Western societies?

EL: No, the democratic imaginary is the opposite of any form of essentialism. To affirm the essence of something consists in affirming its *positive identity*. And the *positive identity* of something, insofar as all identity is relational, consists in showing its *differences* from other identities. It is only insofar as the lord is *different* from the bondsman that his identity as lord is constituted. But in the case of the democratic imaginary, what happens is different. What is affirmed are not *positive* and *differential* identities but, on the contrary, the *equivalence* between them. The democratic imaginary does not constitute itself on the level of the (differential) positivity of the social, but as a transgression and subversion of it. Consequently, there is no essentialist assertion involved. A society is democratic, not insofar as it postulates the validity of a certain type of social organization and of certain values vis-à-vis others, but insofar as it refuses to give its own organization and its own values the status of a *fundamentum inconcussum*. There is democracy as long as there exists the possibility of an unlimited questioning; but this amounts to saying that democracy is not a *system* of values and a *system* of social organization, but a certain inflection, a certain "weakening" of the type of validity attributable to any organization and any value. You must notice that there is no skepticism here; "weakening" the foundation of values and forms of organization also means widening the area of the strategic games that it is possible to play, and therefore, widening the field of freedom.

This leads me to your second question. The universality of values of the French Revolution lies not in having proposed a certain type of *social order* grounded on the rights of man and citizen, but in the fact that these rights are conceived as those of an abstract universality that can expand in the most varied directions. To affirm the rights of the people to their self-determination presupposes the legitimacy of the discourses of equality in the international sphere, and these are not "natural" discourses, but they have conditions of possibility and a specific genesis. That is why I think it is illegitimate to oppose the "universality" of Western values to the specificity inherent in the various cultures and national traditions, for asserting the legitimacy of the latter in terms different from those of an unrestricted xenophobia involves accepting the validity of discourses—for example, the rights of nations to self-determination—which can only be put forward in "universalist" terms.

The problem of "ethnocentrism" thus presents itself as considerably more complex than in the past. On the one hand, there is a "universalization" of history and political experience that is irreversible. Economic, technological, and cultural interdependence between nations means that all identity, even the most national-istic or regionalistic, has to be constructed as specificity or alternative in a terrain that is international and that is penetrated, to a great extent, by "universalist" val-ues and trends. The assertion of a national, regional, or cultural identity in terms of simple withdrawal or segregated existence is nowadays simply absurd. But on the other hand, that same pluridimensionality of the world we live in implies that, for instance, the link between capitalist productive techniques and the sociocultu-ral complexes where they were originally developed is not necessary, that there may be absolutely original forms of articulation that construct new collective iden-tities on the basis of hegemonizing various technological, juridical, and scientific elements on the part of very different national-cultural complexes. That there has been throughout the last centuries a "Westernization" of the world through a tech-nological, economic, and cultural revolution that started in Europe is an obvious enough fact; that those transformations are intrinsically Western and that other peoples can only oppose a purely external and defensive resistance by way of de-fense of their national and cultural identity, seems to me essentially false and re-actionary. The true ethnocentrism does not lie in asserting that the "universaliza-tion" of values, techniques, scientific control of the environment, and so forth, is an irreversible process, but in sustaining that this process is linked by an essential bond, immanent to the "ethnia of the West."

Strategies: One of the more salient topics in recent critical literature is that of post-modernism. Do you consider the topic an important one? And if so, how would you define this constellation of discourses and practices? Also, in what way do you feel your own theory is linked to the logic of postmodernity?

EL: The debate around postmodernity has embraced an ensemble of loosely inte-grated themes, and not all of them are relevant to our theoretico-political project. There is, however, a central aspect common to the various so-called postmodern approaches to which our theoretical perspective is certainly related, and that is what we may call a critique of the fundamentalism of the emancipatory projects of modernity. From my point of view this does not involve an abandonment of the human or political values of the project of the Enlightenment, but a different mod-ulation of its themes. Those that for modernity were absolute essences have now become contingent and pragmatic constructions. The beginning of postmodernity can, in that sense, be conceived as the achievement of a multiple awareness: epis-temological awareness, insofar as scientific progress appears as a succession of par-adigms whose transformation and replacement is not grounded on any algorith-mic certainty; ethical awareness, insofar as the defense and assertion of values is grounded on argumentative movements (conversational movements, according to Rorty), which do not lead back to any absolute foundation; political awareness, insofar as historical achievements appear as the product of hegemonic and contingent—and as such, always reversible—articulations and not as the result of immanent laws of history. The possibilities of practical construction from the present are enriched as a direct consequence of the dwindling of epistemological ambitions. We are going into a world that is more aware than at any other time in the past of its dangers and the vulnerability of its values but which, for that same reason, does not feel limited in its possibilities by any fatality of history. We no longer regard ourselves as the successive incarnations of the absolute spirit—Science, Class, Party—but as the poor men and women who think and act in a present that is always transient and limited; but that same limitation is the condition of our strength: we can be ourselves and regard ourselves as the constructors of the world only insofar as the gods have died. There is no longer a Logos, external to us, whose message we have to decipher inside the interstices of an opaque world.

Strategies: Since you have described hegemony as a field of articulatory practices and antagonisms grouped around various nodal points, it would seem that *cultural* struggles would become an extremely important area in your theory. Yet you seem to concentrate in your examples of democratic struggles on explicitly "political" struggles. What place do you see for the struggle within, for example, the arts? In particular, what about the role of mass cultural forms?

EL: Yes, you are right. The field of cultural struggles has a fundamental role in the construction of political identities. Hegemony is not a type of articulation limited to the field of politics in its narrow sense, but it involves the construction of a new culture—and that affects all the levels where human beings shape their identity and their relations with the world (sexuality, the construction of the private, forms of entertainment, aesthetic pleasure, etc.). Conceived in this way, hegemony is not, of course, hegemony of a party or of a subject, but of a vast ensemble of different operations and interventions that crystallize, however, in a certain configuration—in what Foucault calls a *dispositif.* And in an era when mass media play a capital role in the shaping of cultural identities, all hegemonic offensives must include as one of its central elements a strategy concerning them.

Let me go back at this point, apropos of cultural strategies, to certain aspects related to the question of postmodernity. The aesthetic dimension—the dimension of desire that is fulfilled in the aesthetic experience—is fundamental in the configuration of a world. Plato had already understood this: beauty is for him the splendor of truth. And his "aesthetic" project consisted in showing, behind the imperfections of the world of sensible experience, the forms or paradigms that made up their essence. There is a very clear mechanism of identification here: Platonic aesthetic experience lies in this passage from limitation, from imperfection, to that which is conceived as pure or essential form. But this essential form is also the universal, and if in aesthetic experience the individual *identifies her- or himself* with the universal, identity is achieved through repetition—of what is in me identical with other individuals.

I think this is important for the subject we are speaking about, given that the culture of the left has been constructed in a similar way. It has been, to a large extent, a culture of the elimination of specificities, of the search of that which, behind the latter, was regarded as the universal. Behind the various concrete working classes was *the* working class, whose historical destiny was established outside all specificity; the 1917 revolution was not a *Russian* revolution, but a general paradigm of revolutionary action; the activist had to reproduce in his or her behavior all the imitative automatisms of a "cadre." As in many other things, Gramsci represents, in this respect, an exception and a new beginning that had few followers. Well I think that the main task of a new culture—of a postmodern culture, if you like—is to transform the forms of identification and construction of subjectivity that exist in our civilization. It is necessary to pass from cultural forms constructed as a search for the universal in the contingent, to others that go in a diametrically opposite direction: that is, that attempt to show the essential contingency of all universality, that construct the beauty of the specific, of the unrepeatable, of what transgresses the norm. We must reduce the world to its "human scale." From Freud we know that this is not an impossible task, that the *desire* from which this venture, or rather this constellation of cultural ventures, can be started is present there, distorting the essentialist tidiness of our world. It is necessary to pass from a culture centered on the absolute—that therefore denies the dignity of the specific—to a culture of systematic irreverence. "Genealogy," "deconstruction," and other similar strategies are ways of questioning the dignity of the "presence," of the "origins," of the form.

Strategies: We would like to ask you a question on both the role of poststructuralism in your own work and about the politics of poststructuralism in general. It is clear in your recent book that there are close affinities between some of your ideas and those of poststructuralists (in particular, Foucault and Derrida). However, poststructuralists have long been accused of promoting views of language, history, and so forth, that are implicitly nihilistic and apolitical; or if political, they have been interpreted as either anarchistic or even authoritarian. While it is hard to believe that all of these charges are true, it does raise questions about the politics of poststructuralism. Given your own commitment to radical democracy, what do you see as the political possibilities and limits of poststructuralism (especially deconstruction) as a way of furthering this project?

EL: In the first place, let us clear up a point: there is nothing that can be called a "politics of poststructuralism." The idea that theoretical approaches constitute philosophical "systems" with an unbroken continuity that goes from metaphysics to politics is an idea of the past, that corresponds to a rationalistic and ultimately idealistic conception of knowledge. At the highest point of Western metaphysics it was asserted, as you know, that "the truth is the system." Today we know, on the contrary, that there are no "systems"; that those that appear as such can only do so at the cost of hiding their discontinuities, of smuggling into their structures all types of pragmatic articulations and nonexplicit presuppositions. It is this game of ambiguous connections, not the discovery of underlying systematicities, that constitutes the true terrain of an intellectual history. What the currents that have been called poststructuralist have created is a certain intellectual climate, a certain horizon that makes possible an ensemble of theoretico-discursive operations arising from the intrinsic instability of the signifier/signified relation. The correct question, therefore, is not so much which is *the* politics of poststructuralism, but rather what are the *possibilities* a poststructuralist theoretical perspective opens for the deepening of those political practices that go in the direction of a "radical democracy." (And here we should not actually limit ourselves to poststructuralism *sensu stricto:* postanalytical philosophy as from the work of the latter Wittgenstein, the radicalization of the phenomenological project in Heidegger's work, go in an essentially similar direction.)

If we then concentrate not on a so-called—and mythical—essential connection between poststructuralism and radical democracy, but on the possible articulation, on the *possibilities* that poststructuralism opens up to think and deepen the project of a radical democracy, I think we should basically mention four aspects.

Firstly, the possibility of thinking, in all its radicality, the *indeterminate* character of democracy, which has been pointed out in numerous recent discussions, especially in Claude Lefort's works. If in a hierarchical society the differential character of the positions of the agents tends to establish a strict fixation between social signifiers and signifieds, in a democratic society the place of power becomes an empty place. The democratic logic of equality, therefore, in not adhering to any concrete content, tends to become a pure logic of the circulation of signifiers. This logic of the signifier—to use the Lacanian expression—is closely related to the growing politicization of the social, which is the most remarkable feature of democratic societies. But thinking of this democratic indetermination and contingency as constitutive involves questioning the metaphysics of presence, and with that, transforming the poststructuralist critique of the sign into a critique of the supposed closed character of any objectivity.

Secondly, going more strictly into the problem of deconstruction you refer to, the possibility of deconstructing all identity is the condition of asserting its historicity. Deconstructing an identity means showing the "constitutive outside" that inhabits it—that is, an "outside" that constitutes that identity, and, at the same time, questions it. But this is nothing other than asserting its contingency—that is, its radical historicity. Now, if something is essentially historical and contingent, this means that it can always be radically questioned. And it also means that, in such a case, there is no source of the social different from people's decisions in the process of the social construction of their own identities and their own existence. If history were the theater of a process that has been triggered off outside people's contingent decisions—God's will, a fixed world of essential forms, necessary historical laws—this would mean that democracy cannot be radical, as the social would not be constructed politically but would be the result of an immanent logic of the social, superimposed on, or expressed through all political will. But if the case is the opposite one, then this deconstruction, in showing the contingent character of all identity also shows its political character, and that radical democracy, insofar as it is based on the reactivation of the ultimate character of the social (that is, its political character), beyond its sedimented forms becomes the first historical form of what we might call *post-society.* And please note that with this I am not contraposing the essentialism of an immanent law to the essentialism of a sovereign chooser. The same contingency that is constitutive of all social identity is also constitutive of the subjectivity of the agent. These will *always* be confronted by a partially opaque and hostile society and by a *lack* that will be constitutive of their subjectivity. What I am stating is that these decisions, taken while partially ignoring the circumstances, the consequences, and one's own motivation, are the *only* source of the social, and it is through them that the social is constituted. If in the traditional conceptions of a radical democracy the transparency of the social was a condition for full liberation, what I am stating now is the opposite; that it is only insofar as the social is radically contingent—and does not therefore obey any immanent *law*—that the social is on the same scale of agents that are historical, contingent, and fallible themselves. True liberation does not therefore consist in projecting oneself toward a moment that would represent the fullness of time, but, on the contrary, in showing the temporal—and consequently transient—character of all fullness.

Thirdly, the systematic weakening of all essentialism paves the way for a retrieval of the radical tradition, including Marxism. Antiessentialism, as a theoretical perspective, has a genealogy that also passes through the various radical political traditions. In the first chapters of *Hegemony and Socialist Strategy,* we have tried to show how the disaggregation of essentialist paradigms is not simply a critique *of* Marxism but a movement *within* Marxism. The Sorelian conception of myth, for example, is based on a radical antiessentialism: there is no "objectivity" *in itself* of the social outside the mythical reconstitution of identities and of the relations that take place through the violent confrontations of groups. And "hegemony" in Gramsci goes in the same direction: the notion of historical bloc, which replaces in his vision the base/superstructure duality, is entirely grounded on pragmatic and contingent hegemonic articulations. We should therefore start off from the new awareness that allows us practices such as deconstruction or "language games" to trace a political genealogy of the present. And this genealogy is the construction of a *tradition,* in the strictest sense of the term. The danger that haunts us now is not so much the continuity of the essentialist discourses of classical Marxism, which have been totally shattered and in which nobody believes, but their nonreplacement by any alternative discourse—that is, the collapse of *all* radical tradition. But true loyalty to a tradition lies in recognizing in the past its transient and historical character, its difference with the present (a difference that involves continuities and discontinuities at the same time), and not in transforming the past into a model and an origin to which one tries to reduce the present through more and more absurd and less credible theoretical manipulations.

Fourthly and finally, there is the question of the relation between the "superhard"—the transcendentality, the apodicticity, the algorithmic character of decisions—and democracy. An apodictic decision, or, in a more general sense, a decision that claims for itself an incontestable "rationality," is incompatible with a plurality of points of view. If the decision is based on a reasoning of an apodictic character it is not a decision at all: a rationality that transcends me has *already* decided for me, and my only role is that of recognizing that decision and the consequences that unfold from it. This is why all the forms of radical rationalism are just a step away from totalitarianism. But if, on the contrary, it is shown that there is no ultimate rational foundation of the social, what follows is not a total arbitrariness, but the weakened rationality inherent in an argumentative structure grounded on the *verisimilitude* of its conclusions—in what Aristotle called *phronesis*. And this argumentative structure, precisely because it is not based on an apodictic rationality, is eminently pluralistic. Society only possesses the relative rationality—values, forms of calculation, argumentative sequences—that it collectively constructed as *tradition* and that can therefore always be transformed and contested. But in that sense the expansion of the areas of the social that depend less on an ultimate rational foundation, and that are based, therefore, on a communitary construction, is a condition for the radicalization of democracy. Practices such as that of deconstruction, or Wittgenstein's language games, accomplish the function of increasing our awareness of the socially constructed character of our world and open up the possibility of a foundation through collective decisions of what was before conceived as established forever by God, or by Reason, or by Human Nature—all those equivalent names that function by placing the destiny of human beings beyond the reach of their decisions.

Strategies: In the Marxist tradition, there has been substantial debate concerning the role and place of the intellectual in furthering human liberation. Given your conception of hegemony, it seems clear that the intellectual can play neither the role assigned to it by those theorists of the Second International, nor that which Gramsci signified by the term "organic intellectual." What is the role of the intellectual in furthering the project of radical democracy?

EL: I don't know why you say that our conception is incompatible with the Gramscian idea of the "organic intellectual." On the contrary, I think that it is, to a great degree, an extension of the latter. The "organic intellectual" in Gramscian thought depends on a double extension of the function of intellectual activity, which is perfectly compatible with our approach. In the first place, the "intellectual" is not for Gramsci a segregated social group but that which establishes the organic unity of a set of activities, which, left to their own resources, would remain fragmented and dispersed. A union organizer, in that sense, would be an intellectual, since s/he welds into an organic whole activities such as the channeling and representation of workers' demands, the forms of negotiation with employer organizations and with the state, the cultural activities of the unions, and so on. The intellectual function is, as a consequence, the practice of articulation. And the important thing is to see that this practice is recognized as more and more important insofar as there is a decline of the image of an historical evolution dominated by the necessary movements of the infrastructure. I would like to remind you that Kautsky himself had to admit that socialism does not arise spontaneously from the working class, but has to be introduced into it by the radical intellectuals; that is to say, the unity between *Endziel* and immediate demands depends on the mediation of an organic ideology—that is, on an articulation. And the Gramscian conception of the intellectual is, in that sense, but the extension of this articulatory function to growing areas of social life. Well what, then, is our approach but an antiessentialist conception of the social whole based on the category of articulation?

In the second place, it is precisely because the "organic ideologies" in Gramsci play this central role that the intellectual function extends immeasurably with respect to what it had been in the various debates of classical Marxism: if a historical bloc cements its organic unity only through an ideology that founds *the unity* between base and superstructure, then hegemonic articulations are not a secondary or marginal effect but the ontological level itself of the constitution of the social. And please note that there is no "superstructuralism" or "idealism" here: economic practices themselves depend on social relations constructed through hegemonic articulations. Well what is this moment of "intellectual" mediation that gives its relational character to all collective practice and identity, but that which in our works we have called "discourse"?

In both respects our work can therefore be seen as an extension of Gramsci's work. With this I can answer your last question about the role of the intellectual in furthering the project of radical democracy. The function of the intellectual—or rather, the intellectual function, since the latter does not concentrate on a caste—consists in the invention of languages. If the unity of the historical blocs is given by "organic ideologies" that articulate into new projects fragmented and dispersed social elements, the production of those ideologies is the intellectual function par excellence. Note that those ideologies are not constructed as "utopias" proposed to society; they are inseparable from the collective practices through which social articulation takes place. They are therefore eminently practical and pragmatic—which does not exclude *certain* utopian or mythical (in the Sorelian sense) aspects, which is given by their dimension of *horizon*.

It is to this latter dimension that I would like to refer, with some final remarks. If intellectuals—now regarded in their traditional restricted sense—are to play a positive role in the construction of the new forms of civilization that we are starting to glimpse, and are not to be responsible for a new *trahison des clercs,* they must construct the conditions of their own dissolution as a caste. That is, we should have fewer "great intellectuals" and more "organic intellectuals." The idea of the "great intellectual" was linked to a function of *recognition;* the task of the intellectual was inseparably bound to the classical concept of *truth.* Because it was thought that there was an intrinsic truth in things that *revealed itself* to certain particular forms of access that were the private hunting ground of the intellectual. This is why the latter received the set of privileges that established him as a member of a caste. But if we consider today that all truth is relative to a discursive formation, that all choice between discourses is only possible on the basis of constructing new discourses, "truth" is essentially pragmatic and in that sense becomes democratic. It is because we know today that the social is articulation and discourse that the intellectual dimension cannot be conceived as *recognition* but as construction; but it is for that same reason that intellectual activity cannot be the exclusive hunting ground of an elite of great intellectuals: it arises from all points of the social fabric. If the "system" was the characteristic expression, the highest point and the ideal of knowledge of the traditional intellectual, the new forms of thought are not only asystematic but essentially *anti*-systematic: they are constructed out of the recognition of their contingency and historicity. But in this general movement of the death of gods, ideologies of salvation, and high priests of the intellect, aren't we allowing each man and woman to fully assume the responsibility of their own contingency and their own destiny?

5

La Vi(ll)e en Rose
Reading Jameson Mapping Space

Donald Preziosi

Is it not possible that the doctrine of "History," so arduously cultivated
by the Western tradition of thought since the Greeks as an instrument
for releasing human consciousness from the constraints of the Archaic
age, is ready for retirement along with the "politics" that it helped to
enable? And could not the death of "History," politics, and narrative all
be aspects of another great transformation, similar in scope and effect to
that which marked the break with Archaism begun by the Greeks?
Marx thought that the communist revolution would release humankind
from the conditions of pseudo-historical existence and usher in a
genuinely historical one. The problem may be not how to get into history,
but how to get out of It. And in this respect, modernism in the arts may
be . . . an impulse to get beyond the myth-history distinction, which has
served as the theoretical basis for a politics that has outlived its usefulness,
and into a post-political age insofar as "politics" is conceived in its
nineteenth-century incarnations.
> —Hayden White, "Getting Out of History"[1]

You will therefore note in passing that a certain unifying and totalizing
force is presupposed here—although it is not the Hegelian Absolute
Spirit, nor the Party, nor Stalin, but simply Capital Itself; and it is on the
strength of such a view that a radical Jesuit friend of mine once publically
accused me of monotheism.
> —Fredric Jameson, "Cognitive Mapping"[2]

Beginning with the founding of the journal *Social Text* in 1979 and the publication of *The Political Unconscious* in 1981,[3] Fredric Jameson has increasingly argued
for a certain subsumption of contemporary critical theory into an extended, absolute horizon of a "new" Marxist hermeneutics that would frame the former as
second-order critique(s) capable (despite all appearances to the contrary) of being
rescued and reoriented in the service of the latter. Like a referee on the Homeric
battlefield of contesting poststructuralist players, Jameson would like to blow his

whistle on all those "great themes and shibboleths of post-Marxism"; it is time, he has argued, for us to leave the field and come home to the long nightmare of History and the untranscendable Real(ities) waiting impatiently on the sidelines.

Jameson himself is clearly not unaware that the turn he has taken in recent years has caused a certain amount of astonishment:

> ... in a Marxist conference in which I have frequently had the feeling that I am one of the few Marxists left (like some antediluvian species momentarily spared the extinction of the postmodern)—I take it I have a certain responsibility to restate what seem to me to be a few self-evident truths, but which may seem to you some quaint survivals of a religious, millenarian, salvational form of belief.[4]

Enough has been written elsewhere over the past years about Jameson's Utopian and totalizing resolutions as Imaginary wish-fulfillments of resounding religiosity to require little comment here,[5] except perhaps to observe in passing that his revised agendas for history and criticism may well comprise a stunning (and to not a few, a surprising) example of plain old-fashioned countertransference, a case of the analyst losing his place amid the scenographies generated by his analysand.[6] The Jameson of the eighties, as someone noted recently, seems fully in tune with the Age of Reagan.

There may now perhaps be a certain distance from the critical astonishments greeting *PU* in the early eighties, as well as from Jameson's reactions to that astonishment, to begin to assess what has happened with some degree of circumspection. While a full-scale reassessment is beyond the scope of these pages, a beginning might be made by addressing some of the consequences of his "new" agendas for history and criticism. I will focus here on some of Jameson's work in the mideighties on the question of postmodernism by attending closely to a theme increasingly foregrounded in the writings: the question of *space*—the space of the city, or, as Jameson has put it, the *hyperspace* of the (postmodern) city.[7]

La vi[ll]e en rose

Although Jameson has written a good deal about various arts under modernism and postmodernism, it is clearly *architecture* which occupies a privileged place in his lectures and essays on the relationships he has projected between postindustrial, "late," or multinational capitalism and postmodernism:

> Architecture is . . . of all the arts the closest constitutively to the economic, with which, in the form of commissions and land values, it has a *virtually unmediated relationship:* it will therefore not be surprising to find the extraordinary flowering of the new postmodern architecture grounded in the

patronage of multinational business, whose expansion and development is strictly contemporaneous with it. That these two phenomena have an even deeper dialectical interrelationship than simple one-to-one financing of this or that individual project we will try to suggest later on.

The latter remarks, taken from a celebrated essay of 1984 entitled "Postmodernism, or the Cultural Logic of Late Capitalism,"[8] prefigure a lengthy discussion of what Jameson terms a *"mutation in built space itself"* into a "hyperspace" of postmodern architecture, an emblem of which he presents as the 1977 Bonaventure Hotel in Los Angeles, designed by John Portman. Further on in the same essay he again accords to architecture a primacy of place in the *figuring* of postmodernism:[9]

> [Postmodern texts] afford us some glimpse into a *postmodern or technological sublime,* whose power or authenticity is documented by the success of such works in evoking a whole new postmodern space in emergence around us. Architecture therefore remains in this sense the *privileged aesthetic language;* and the distorting and fragmenting reflections of one enormous glass surface to the other can be taken as *paradigmatic* of the central role of process and reproduction in postmodernist culture.

Postmodern writings (and painting) afford us only "glimpses" into this postmodernist "sublime"; they merely "evoke" the space of multinational capital: postmodern building, however, *figures* that space powerfully, directly, and paradigmatically. If you want to understand the force and power of multinational capitalism, *look* at the musculature and sinewy skeleton of contemporary building, which has a "virtually unmediated relationship" to the latter.

It is not enough to merely look, however, and Jameson avers that such figurations may nonetheless remain opaque for human subjects "who happen into this new space," for the "mutations" in this (new) object have been unaccompanied as yet by any equivalent "mutation in the subject." We do not, he claims, "possess the perceptual equipment to match this new hyperspace . . . in part because our perceptual habits were formed in that older kind of space I have called the space of high modernism."[10] This postmodern hyperspace, he asserts, induces us to "grow new organs" and "expand our sensorium and our body."

Leaving aside the question of who precisely the "we" might be in all this hyperspatial bewilderment, or for that matter just *which* "high modernism" "our" perceptual habits were formed under, let us press on to consider Jameson's "analysis of a full-blown postmodern building." Before sketching out that "analysis," however, he takes pains to say that the Bonaventure Hotel is "in many ways uncharacteristic" of that postmodern architecture of Venturi, Moore, Graves, or Gehry, yet to his mind nevertheless it "offers some very striking lessons about the originality of postmodern space."

In the first place, the Bonaventure confirms a claim similar to many other postmodernist works that it is, in Jameson's words, a popular or populist structure in contrast to the elite and "Utopian" austerities of the great architectural modernisms: it "respects the vernacular of the American city fabric" and seeks to "speak the very language" of the "tawdry and commercial sign-system of the surrounding city." It has in fact "learned from Las Vegas."[11]

However, despite its "populist insertion into the city fabric," the hotel in fact "transcend[s] the capacities of the individual human body to locate itself, to organize its immediate surroundings perceptually, and cognitively map its position in a mappable external world."[12]

The building accomplishes this generation of confusion in four ways: by means of (1) the complexities of its multiple *entrance systems* on several levels: "these curiously unmarked ways-in . . . [which] seem to have been imposed by some new category of closure governing the inner space of the hotel itself"; (2) *escalators and elevators*: "here the narrative stroll has been underscored, symbolized, reified, and replaced by a transportation machine which becomes the allegorical signifier of that older promenade we are no longer allowed to conduct on our own"; (3) the complex shape of the *atrium* or lobby: "it is quite impossible to get your bearings in this lobby;" "hanging streamers indeed suffuse this empty space in such a way as to distract systematically and deliberately from whatever form it might be supposed to have"; and, the visitor is "in this hyperspace up to [its] eyes and body"; (4) the reflective *glass skin* or cladding of the building: "the glass skin achieves a peculiar and placeless dissociation of the Bonaventure from its neighborhood" for on the outside "you cannot see the hotel itself, but only the distorted images of everything that surrounds it."

Jameson does not mention the hotel rooms themselves in his remarks, except to observe that "one understands that the rooms are in the worst of taste,"[13] nor does he dwell on the shopping mall boutiques grouped on several levels above the central atrium lobby except to note that

> I will take as the most dramatic practical result of this spatial mutation the notorious dilemma of the shopkeepers on the various balconies: it has been obvious, since the very opening of the hotel in 1977, that nobody could ever find any of these stores, and that even if you located the appropriate boutique, you would be most unlikely to be as fortunate a second time; as a consequence, the commercial tenants are in despair and all the merchandise is marked down to bargain prices.[14]

Our analyst finds this all the more remarkable, since one must "recall that Postman [sic] is a businessman as well as an architect, and a millionaire developer," an artist who is also "a capitalist in his own right." He notes laconically that "one cannot but feel that here too something of a 'return of the repressed' is involved."[15] All of which leads Jameson to conclude, finally, that this alarming disjunction point between the body and its built environment—which is to the initial bewilderment of the older modernism as the velocities of space craft are to those of the automobile—can itself stand as *the symbol and analogue* of that even sharper dilemma which is the incapacity of our minds, at least at present, to map the great global multinational and decentered communicational network in which we find ourselves caught as individual subjects.[16]

This is all truly astonishing: is he kidding? Is this intended as a hilarious parody of that lugubrious and vulgar art historicism that fills the pages of the "Art" or "Style" or "Living" or "Entertainment" section of American newspapers? Is the author simply universalizing his own (non)narrative strolls in the place during the annual MLA convention held in part at the Bonaventure shortly before this "analysis" appeared in print? But let us press on, for shortly a grim realization will set in that in fact this is no intended parody:

> But as I am anxious that Portman's space not be perceived as something either exceptional or seemingly marginalized and leisure-specialized on the order of Disneyland, I would like in passing to juxtapose this complacent and entertaining (although bewildering) leisure-time space with its *analogue* in a very different area, namely the *space of postmodern warfare*.[17]

Jameson goes on to discuss and quote at some length a book by Michael Herr on the Vietnam experience, *Dispatches,* which, as he claims, opens up "the place of a whole new reflexivity."[18] In the machinery of this "first postmodernist war," "something of the mystery of the new postmodernist space is concentrated."

His analogy rests in part on his view of the Bonaventure that it is a whole world in itself: "for it does not wish to be part of the city, but rather its equivalent and substitute . . . the Bonaventure aspires to being a total space, a complete world, a kind of miniature city," for in his view to this new total space corresponds a now collective practice, "something like the practice of a new and historically original kind of hypercrowd."[19] And corresponding to this new hyperspace (with its new hypercrowd) are a certain number of other characteristic postmodern buildings, notably the Centre Pompidou in Paris and the large Eaton Centre shopping mall in Toronto. And what is a "hypercrowd"?

Jameson's discussion thus has taken a reverse turn: where at the beginning the Bonaventure was a popular or populist structure "speaking the language" of its ambient urban fabric, now it is seen as its replacement and repudiation. The postmodern hyperspatial Bonaventure contrasts with the spaces of "the great monuments of the International Style" of high modernism—that is, for Jameson, Corbusier's buildings on *pilotis*: both are Utopian gestures, but whereas the latter "explicitly repudiates" a degraded and fallen older (Victorian) city fabric, the former "is content to let the fallen [older] city fabric continue to be in its being."[20]

Moreover, the Bonaventure rises against "its referent, Los Angeles itself," which spreads out breathtakingly "and even alarmingly" before it. (Alarmingly?)

Once again, Jameson insists, we are no longer in a cognitively mappable position in a mappable external world. This "new and virtually unimaginable quantum leap in technological alienation" is for him exactly equivalent to the world of the Vietnam War:

> This first terrible postmodern war cannot be told in any of the traditional paradigms of the war novel or movie—indeed that breakdown of any shared language through which a veteran might convey such experience ... open[s] up the place of a whole new reflexivity.[21]

As it is equally consonant with the world of postmodernist writing or painting, with a brief sketch of which Jameson prefaces his discussions of architecture and war, along lines familiar from some of his other essays.[22]

It is abundantly clear that the chief problem with what he construes as postmodernism is its "unmappability" for the traditional instruments of Jameson's nostalgically Lukacsian perspective: "the luxury of the old-fashioned ideological critique, the indignant moral denunciation of the other, becomes unavailable." For in its apparent abolishment of critical distance, the world of the postmodern creates (for Jameson) a dilemma for a certain Left politics that

> has [not] been able to do without one notion or another of a certain minimal aesthetic distance, of the possibility of the positioning of the cultural act outside the massive Being of Capital, which then serves as an Archimedean point from which to assault this last.[23]

He reflects that his own analyses of literature, painting, and (above all) architecture have demonstrated that

> distance in general (including critical distance in particular) has very precisely been abolished in the new space of postmodernism ... our new postmodern bodies are bereft of spatial coordinates and practically (let alone theoretically) incapable of distantiation; meanwhile, it has already been observed how the prodigious expansion of multinational capital ends up penetrating and colonizing those very pre-capitalist enclaves (Nature and the Unconscious) which offered extraterritorial and Archimedean footholds for critical effectivity.[24]

Jameson is in effect claiming that the "demoralizing and depressing original new global space" is the *moment of truth* of postmodernism. If there is to be any hope left for a Marxist or a socialist *position* in the realities of this "new space"— any "Archimedean point" as he remarkably puts it[25]—then that must be thought in a manner analogous to (a) Marx's move vis-à-vis "the newly unified space of the national markets," or (b) Lenin's move with respect to "the older imperialist global network."

What could such an Archimedean, panopticist position conceivably *be* in a global matrix where "critical distance" is apparently now abolished? Jameson's answers turn out be as problematical as his "analyses" of postmodernist hyperspace and its congruent cultural acts are stunningly impressionistic, reductive, and, to perhaps restate the obvious, ahistorical.

The Subject in Hyperspace

But if society has no form, how can architects build its counterform?
—Aldo van Eyck (1966)[26]

To understand Jameson's proposals for resolving the dilemmas he has projected, one must turn to the last section of the essay under discussion, along with a paper presented at the important major conference on Marxism and the interpretation of culture held at the University of Illinois in 1983 (published 1988).[27] The latter paper also appeared in typescript for a conference held the following winter at Santa Cruz in honor of Henri Lefebvre.[28] Also of pertinence here is an interesting interview in an international art-market magazine published in 1987, conducted with Jameson by a *Social Text* colleague.[29]

Throughout the above, Jameson is concerned with "cognitive mapping," and bases his understanding of this on the research of MIT urban planner Kevin Lynch nearly thirty years ago: the text Jameson references is Lynch's famous *The Image of the City* of 1960. And Jameson's strategy, or rather his desire, is to somehow combine and reconcile Lynch's empirical research with Althusser's concept of ideology and its Lacanian underpinnings.[30]

Lynch conducted research into the ways in which residents of particular American cities conceptualized and internally represented their native habitats; in essence he found that individuals develop cognitive maps of their urban environments which enabled them to negotiate, navigate, and conceptualize their urban spaces. In classic studies of residents of Boston, Los Angeles, and Jersey City, Lynch, in Jameson's words,

> taught us that the alienated city is above all a space in which people are unable to map (in their minds) either their own positions or the urban totality in which they find themselves: grids such as those of Jersey City, in which none of the traditional markers (monuments, nodes, natural boundaries, built perspectives) obtain, are the most obvious examples.[31]

Urban alienation is thus taken by Jameson to be "directly proportional" to the mental unmappability of local cityscapes. He suggests that a city like Boston, then, with its monumental perspectives, its markers and monuments, its combination of grand but simple spatial forms, including dramatic boundaries such as the Charles River, not only allows people to have, in their imaginations, a generally successful and continuous location to the rest of the city, but in addition gives them something of the freedom and aesthetic gratification of traditional city form.[32]

Leaving aside for the moment the obvious questions with such a claim (for *whom* is a cityscape "successful"—which classes, races, economic or neighborhood or age groups? Or for that matter whether "traditional city form[s]" inevitably evoke "freedom and aesthetic gratification"?), let us press on. Jameson does not consider any of the enormous body of research and writing spawned by or stimulated by the work of Lynch and his colleagues and students since the early sixties (and continuing unabated today).[33] He simply notes in passing that *The Image of the City* "spawned a whole low-level subdiscipline (why 'low-level'?) that today takes the phrase 'cognitive mapping' as its own designation."

In short, he wishes only to take this research as *"emblematic"* since "the mental map of city space . . . can be *extrapolated* to that map of the social and global totality we all carry around in our heads in variously garbled forms." Jameson's agenda becomes apparent in his subsequent words:

> I have always been struck by the way in which Lynch's conception of city experience—the dialectic between the here and now of immediate perception and the imaginative or imaginary sense of the city *as an absent totality*—presents something like a spatial analogue of Althusser's great formulation of ideology itself, as "the Imaginary representation of the subject's relationship to his or her Real conditions of existence."[34]

For Jameson, cognitive mapping would involve such extrapolations to "the totality of class relations on a global (or . . . multinational) scale." Thus,

> the incapacity to map socially is as crippling to political experience as the analogous incapacity to map spatially is for urban experience. It follows that an aesthetic of cognitive mapping in this sense is an integral part of any socialist political project.[35]

The connection with his analyses of postmodern texts, paintings, and buildings (such as the Bonaventure) thereby becomes clear, and Jameson closes his essay as follows: "The political form of postmodernism, *if there is any,* will have as its vocation the invention and projection of a global cognitive mapping, on a social as well as a spatial scale."[36]

And yet he gives us no easy clues as to what this might be; as to what *forms* such a "new aesthetic of cognitive mapping" might take (surely not the return of a repressed social realism?). Instead, he provides us with a suggestive "historical" analogue, one drawn from the evolution of cartography itself. He suggests earlier in his essay that Lynch's "cognitive maps" elicited from his research subjects were really, in effect, *pre*-cartographic, being essentially subject-centered itineraries or sketches of existential journeys. These he compares, in his narrative stroll, to the old nautical itineraries or *portulan* sea charts foregrounding coastal features, of the type developed by Mediterranean navigators who in ancient times seldom ventured out into the open sea.

Next, he observes that the historical introduction of the magnetic compass utterly transformed the problematic of the itinerary. Together with the sextant and the theodolite, this new technology introduced a whole new coordinate—that of a relationship to a uniform *totality*. At this point, Jameson claims, "cognitive mapping in the broader sense comes to require the coordination of existential data (the empirical position of the subject) with unlived, abstract conceptions of the geographic totality."[37] Such coordinations, it would appear, correspond to his earlier observations on "the imaginary sense of the city as an absent totality." He then goes on to speak of a *third* age of cartography, ushered in during the last decade of the fifteenth century by Mercator projection and the invention of the globe. This "third dimension" of cartography involved, according to Jameson, a whole new fundamental question of the languages of representation itself, which now becomes a pressing practical and empirical problem—the dilemma of the transfer of curved space onto flat charts. It becomes clear at this time, he asserts, that there can no longer be "*true* maps" as such. Any map, it might be added, is always already a partial perspective, coexisting with other perspectives which may or may not be directly transcodable or in some way compatible.

Obviously, Jameson is projecting here an analogy with his problems with postmodernist "hyperspace" and its "unrepresentability" as he sees it. Just before concluding the essay, he notes that

> an aesthetic of cognitive mapping—a pedagogical political culture which seeks to endow the individual subject with some heightened sense of its place in the global system—will necessarily have to respect this now enormously complex representational dialectic and invent radically new forms to do it justice.[38]

A "new political art," he writes, must hold firm to "the truth of postmodernism" while at the same time achieving a breakthrough to "some as yet unimaginable new mode of representing . . . in which we may again begin to grasp our positioning as individual and collective subjects" because our inabilities to act or struggle are at the moment "neutralized by our spatial as well as our social confusion." It is not that the new totalities of hyperspatial postmodernism and multinational capitalism are un*know*able: it is that they are "unrepresentable," unmappable.

Jameson presents this as *the* dilemma of contemporary socialist vision (to the consternation of some of his colleagues)[39]—the problem of *repositioning* individual/collective subjects in such a way as to allow for the perspectival clarity of "cognitive mapping" (of the spatial and the social) *without* "returning to some older kind of machinery . . . some more traditional and reassuring perspectival or mimetic enclave."[40]

The dilemma of course is Jameson's own, and is in fact part of a complex matrix of double binds informing his work since the publication of *The Political Unconscious*. In order to understand more clearly the makeup of these contradictions and the *position* Jameson has propelled himself into, we must begin to consider more explicitly his perspectives on history, periodicization, and signification, all of which are necessarily interrelated.

The Subject in [Hyper]History

Jameson's dilemma is in fact a nexus of intersecting and coimplicative double binds of classic configuration. Consider first the following oft-quoted passage from *PU*:[41]

> These matters can recover their original urgency for us only if they are re-told within the unity of *a single great collective story;* only if, in however disguised and symbolic a form, they are seen as sharing a *single fundamental theme*—for Marxism, the collective struggle to wrest a realm of Freedom from a realm of Necessity; only if they are grasped as vital *episodes* in a single vast unfinished *plot*. . . . It is in detecting the traces of that uninterrupted *narrative,* in restoring to the surface of the text the repressed and buried reality of this fundamental *history,* that the doctrine of a political unconscious finds its function and necessity. History is thus a story "waiting to be told once and for all, in the one and only way."[42]

Necessity, moreover, is no mere "content," but "rather the inexorable *form* of events." History, then, as the experience of Necessity, is what he would call that *space* which includes and comprehends all things. For Jameson, his version of Marxism is a place *coextensive* with the space of History. To arrive in that space, it is necessary to "pass through" texts, and above all the texts and hyperspaces of postmodernism, in order to grasp the latter's "absent causes": their History.

The obvious problem of course is how to distinguish Marxism in Jameson's version from "ideology" itself? If we construe ideology (as Jameson does) on the order of Althusser's formulation—"the Imaginary representation of the subject's relationship to his or her Real conditions of existence"—and if that Real is coterminous with History as, in Jameson's words, "ground and untranscendable horizon," then of necessity this History must in fact be a "text" or narrative which is *at the same time Real*.

Weber has astutely delineated the Jamesonian double bind at work here in one of the more penetrating critiques of *PU*, entitled "Capitalizing History":[43] the

Marxism of *PU* would criticize its competitors as being ideological (in the sense of being partial and partisan, of practicing strategies of containment). Yet at the same time, its own claim to offer an alternative to such ideological containment must itself be based on a strategy of containment, only a radically more total and comprehensive one.[44] In addition, it might be noted, this places the individual in precisely the position Jameson wishes to avoid: a position of unmappability. For structurally and systemically, there would be no criteria by which to *distinguish* a "false" ideology from the "truth" of (Jameson's) Marxism, apart, ultimately, from teleological faith.[45]

Another double bind is folded into this envelope: an oscillation between two contradictory notions of signification or semiosis, two variations on the nature of the relationships between signifier and signified. On the one hand, a distinction is made between a text (narrative, space) and its referent or "absent cause." On the other hand, they are collapsed together: History is not merely any text, but *the* text, a *Real* text. In a curious way, Jameson's dilemma resonates with that of the Port Royal grammarians whose agenda necessitated an accounting for the central Christian mystery (*hoc est corpus meum*) within a system of signs simultaneously necessitating distantiation between signifier and signified, sign and referent. For the believing Christian, the host could not be construed as mere sign or symbol of the body of Christ: it must be (*est*) that body.[46]

The "flotation" of contradictory versions of semiosis is, as I have argued elsewhere at some length, at the foundation of modern disciplinary knowledge and critical practice in art and architectural history;[47] within such a framework, Jameson can be seen as projecting a subsumption of contemporary poststructuralisms by what might be characterized as a *eucharistic modernism* that seeks to restore a singular point of view (and a self-identical individual subject capable of cognitively mapping the spatial and social). By naming that a "collective subject," we remain in the realm of hocus-pocus.

Yet Jameson is often at great pains to eschew an individualistic and expressive modernism. Both in the recent "space" essays and in the older *PU*, the category of individuality is a highly contested space—a place that must be exploded in favor of a collective unity.[48] He explicitly asserts that

> one of the most urgent tasks for Marxist theory today is a whole new logic of collective dynamics, with categories that escape the taint of some mere application of terms drawn from individual experience (in that sense, even the concept of praxis remains a suspect one).[49]

But the assertion might raise not a few eyebrows for readers of his architectural or art historical musings. As Sam Weber notes, ultimately Jameson simply universalizes the individual by construing the collective as a "self-sufficient, intelligible unity": what, additionally, could be more individualistic than a notion of History as a "single, vast, unfinished plot"?[50] What remains unanswered is how this scenario differs fundamentally from the plot structure of the realist novel: despite his portrayal of literary history in *PU* as a play of sedimented and conflictual realities (each age of which might be characterized by a "dominant"), a nostalgia for a linearist and totalizing "history" remains strong.[51]

Jameson's writings on art and architecture have elicited no substantive reaction from the community of historians and critics of those fields.[52] On the face of it, this remains somewhat surprising, given that a fair amount of his writings have appeared within such disciplinary contexts.[53] I suspect this may have less to do with any explicit aversion to Marxist interpretations of artworks or cultural practices—not that such aversion is nonexistent; indeed, far from it.[54] Rather, it may well be that his observations on modernist and postmodernist art and architecture have seemed to offer little more than an inflection on what has been a commonplace, totalizing historicism central to art historical discourse since its nineteenth-century institutionalizations on both sides of the Atlantic.[55]

Indeed, despite the contemporary contexts of his discussions and analyses of the modernist/postmodernist problematic in the arts, in many ways the closest analogue to Jameson's writings on painting and "space" is not the rich body of contemporary criticism, but rather the work of Erwin Panofsky in the 1950s, and in particular the Panofsky of the celebrated essay *Gothic Architecture and Scholasticism* of 1951,[56] "An inquiry into the analogy of the arts, philosophy, and religion in the Middle Ages."

In his vision of the period of High Scholasticism, Panofsky elegantly wove together a complex series of historical phenomena to demonstrate the existence of a striking homology between the logical and systemic structure of Scholastic texts and arrangement of parts and divisions within the space of Gothic design. The principles of homology that controlled the entire process of architectonic organization corresponded, for Panofsky, to the "visual logic" evident in Aquinas's system of *similitudines:*

> . . . the membrification of the edifice permitted [one] to re-experience the very process of architectural composition just as the membrification of the *Summa* permitted [one] to re-experience the very processes of cogitation . . . the panoply of shafts, ribs, buttresses, tracery, pinnacles, and crockets was a self-analysis and self-explication of architecture much as the customary apparatus of parts, distinctions, questions, and articles was . . . a self-analysis and self-explication of reason . . . the Scholastic mind . . . accepted and insisted upon a gratuitous clarification of function through form just as it accepted and insisted upon a gratuitous clarification of thought through language.[57]

In Jameson's terms, the era of High Scholasticism would be a supremely "mappable" age, and its space(s) would (in Panofsky's analysis) emblematize an "endow[ing of] the individual subject with some heightened sense of its place in the global system," assuming that subject to be an educated Schoolman. Such mappability was necessarily promoted and enhanced by the perfection into a fine art of the reconciliation of opposites or of the (seemingly) irreconcilable, through the public rituals of the *disputationes de quolibet,* wherein every topic (as in every *articulus* in Aquinas's *Summa*) had to be formulated as a *quaestio,* the discussion of which, as Panofsky notes,[58] was staged dialectically, setting one set of authorities against another. What is of interest is that apparently contradictory propositions—for example different views on, say, the permissibility of suicide among several authorities—could not simply be sorted out between a correct and an incorrect view; rather, both had to be worked through to the limit, and reconciled at some distant theoretical point or end.

Panofsky then takes pains to demonstrate how such reconciliations evolved in the history of French Gothic cathedral building, and he cites architectural sources referring to discussions about design that proceeded along the Scholastic *videtur quod—sed contra—respondeo dicendum:*[59]

> And what is the result of this *disputatio?* A chevet which combines, as it were, all possible *sics* with all possible *nons.* It has a double ambulatory combined with a continuous hemicycle of fully developed channels, all nearly equal in depth. The groundplan of these chapels is alternately semi-circular and—Cistercian fashion—square.

Panofsky saw in Gothic space what Jameson cannot find in postmodern hyperspace. There is a complex double-reversed irony in this juxtaposition of Jameson and Panofsky, for their particular insights are the result of a certain blindness.

In the case of Panofsky, the "mutual inferability of parts" in "Gothic" space was in no small measure the projection (by no means Panofsky's own) onto a diverse and complex historical age of a "High Scholastic" order which was in fact itself a pastiche of philosophical and rhetorical contradictions and differences held together by "reconciliations" beyond reason—that is, by faith. A faith, it should be observed, that would reconcile contradictions among equally venerable authorities on a far rhetorical horizon: an "untranscendable horizon" isomorphic to that projected into the future by Jameson.

Panofsky himself was careful to admit that his reader might very well find his schemata "fanciful" or even rather Hegelian, for his architectonic "reconciliations" and unities were momentary and fleeting. The homologies projected between Gothic cathedral design and Scholastic philosophy were limited to a few examples looked at in a certain light—the light of (as he says) a "single scrap of evidence" from a sketch plan in the *Album* of Villard de Honnecourt.[60]

In Jameson we find little appreciation of such ironies. And what he fails to see in "postmodern space" is in fact an important characteristic feature of recent design that pastiches earlier formations by means of quotation, historical allusion, and the juxtaposition and abruptly surprising sedimentation of styles of different ages, places, and peoples—the effective *ironicization* of the unities and "mutual inferability of parts" of the received historical canon of forms.

In short, recent design (whether "postmodernist" or more recent "deconstructivist") frequently works to foreground the usually repressed *ficticity* of those very unities which Jameson, in his nostalgia for what is not here and now, patently longs for—as indeed we have seen in his rhetorical overcomplications of the relatively simplistic Bonaventure Hotel.

What is in fact highlighted by a good deal of recent design—from the hilarious multilevel pastiche maze of the Horton Plaza urban mall in San Diego, to Eisenman and Trott's Wexner Center for the Visual Arts in Columbus, to the thirty fragmented "follies" of Bernard Tschumi for the Parc de la Villette in Paris (which will also include a garden designed jointly by Eisenman and Derrida)—is a metacommentary on architectonic representation itself, directed equally to the past and the present. In such an address, the unities of the historical canon(s) are themselves revealed as having always already been fictive, as pastiches of contradictions, and as suppressions of difference.

What Jameson would have us see as "dehistoricizing" is in fact supremely historical. In precisely the same way, that untranscendable History which Jameson would have us see, that grand master narrative plot which "goes outside the postmodern paradigm,"[61] is itself revealed as a romantic fiction and an anamorphic fable.[62] For in order to make that story visible, representable, and "mappable," we must ultimately position ourselves *outside* or beyond not simply "postmodernism" itself, but outside of time, space, and *history.* Jameson's Real(ism) is finally just another realist, modernist novel, a collapsing together of the "three ages" of cartography into the "reassuring perspectival or mimetic enclave" he is at pains to go beyond: a world before Mercator.

This is a dangerous game which, perhaps not so ironically, is itself one of the emblems of the "politics" we have inherited.

Notes

1. Hayden White, "Getting Out of History," *Diacritics,* vol. 12, no. 3 (Fall 1982): 13.

2. Fredric Jameson, "Cognitive Mapping," in C. Nelson and L. Grossberg, eds. *Marxism and the Interpretation of Culture* (Urbana & Chicago: University of Illinois Press, 1988), 348 (written 1983).

3. Jameson, *The Political Unconscious* (Ithaca N.Y.: Cornell University Press, 1981). *Social Text,* eds., Stanley Aronowitz, John Brenkman, and Fredric Jameson, began publication in 1979. In its opening Prospectus (vol. 1, p. 3), the following appears: "Our position is that the valuable interpretative and theoretical work done in these various schools [semiotics, Lacanian psychoanalytic theory,

Althusserian marxism, deconstruction, etc.] is often accompanied by a strategic containment or delimitation of the field being interrogated. This . . . takes the form of suppressing or repressing history and the historical perspective. It is this which the Marxist framework seeks to restore."

4. "Cognitive Mapping," typescript, p. 1, from the Conference on Urban Ideologies, Politics and Culture in Honor of Henri Lefebvre, University of California at Santa Cruz, Feb. 29–Mar. 4, 1984. In its essentials, this version is identical to the citation in n. 2 above, except for the phrase reproduced here in parentheses.

5. Of the great many responses and critiques of *PU*, the most important are to be found in the special fall 1982 issue of the journal *Diacritics* (vol. 12, no. 3), with essays by Hayden White, Terry Eagleton, Geoff Bennington, S. P. Mohanty, Jerry Aline Flieger, and Michael Sprinker; the issue includes an interview with Jameson conducted by Jonathan Culler and Richard Klein; see also Sam Weber, "Capitalizing History: Notes on *The Political Unconscious,*" *Diacritics,* vol. 13, no. 2 (Summer 1983): 14–28; Timothy Bahti, "'Mastering' Mastery: A Critical Response," in *Enclitic,* vol. V, no. 1 (Spring 1981): 107–23; Dana Polan, "Above All Else to Make You See; Cinema and the Ideology of Spectacle," *boundary 2* vol. II, no. 1/2 (Fall 1982/83): 129–44; Cornel West, "Fredric Jameson's Marxist Hermeneutics," in *boundary 2:* 177–230 (this entire issue is devoted to Marxism and Postmodern Criticism); John Brenkman, review of *PU* in *SubStance,* vol. 37/38 (1983): 237–39; Alice Benston, review of *PU* in *SubStance* vol. 41 (1983): 97–103; Cornel West, "Ethics and Action in Fredric Jameson's Marxist Hermeneutics," in Jonathan Arac, ed., *Postmodernism and Politics* (Minneapolis: University of Minnesota Press, 1986), 123–44. While this list does not exhaust the citations for reviews of Jameson's *PU,* it will provide a good representative sample. On the subject of postmodernism and Marxism more generally, useful introductions to basic issues and debates may be found in many places, among them the vol. 2, no. 3 issue of the journal *Theory Culture and Society* (Special Issue on The Fate of Modernity, 1985), and vol. 20 of the Australian journal *Leftwright* (1986).

6. The penetrating critique of Jerry Aline Flieger in *Diacritics,* vol. 12, no. 3 (1982), entitled 'The Prison House of Ideology: Critic as Inmate," elaborates on this point in discussing Jameson's "imprisonment in the maze of intersubjective desire" by his failure to "relinquish any claim to a position outside ideology." Flieger's essay (pp. 47–56) is largely devoted to the "blindness" in *PU* which undermines Jameson's claim to have assimilated the lessons of deconstruction in his totalized historical methodology.

7. The principal texts are: "Postmodernism, or The Cultural Logic of Late Capitalism," *New Left Review,* vol. 46 (July/August 1984): 53–59; "Cognitive Mapping," cited above, nn. 2 and 4; "Postmodernism and Consumer Society," in Hal Foster, *The Anti-Aesthetic* (Port Townsend, Wash.: Bay Press, 1983), pp. 111–25 (originally delivered as a lecture at the Whitney Museum in New York, Fall 1982); "An Interview with Frederic Jameson" with Anders Stephanson, in

Flash Art no. 131 (Dec. 1986/Jan. 1987): 69–73. See also Jameson's "Reification and Utopia in Mass Culture," *Social Text,* vol. 1 (1979): 130–48, and various film reviews in the same journal in subsequent issues [esp. Vol. 2, no. 1, *Social Text,* no. 4 (1981)].

    8. "Cultural Logic," p. 46, p. 56 (1984). Italics mine here and subsequently.

    9. "Cultural Logic," p. 79.

    10. "Cultural Logic," p. 80.

    11. "Cultural Logic," p. 81; the reference is to the seminal study *Learning from Las Vegas* by R. Venturi, D. S. Brown, and S. Izenour, (Cambridge: MIT Press, 1972). There is an enormous body of literature spawned by the latter; see especially the critiques of M. Tafuri in *The Sphere and the Labyrinth: Avant-Gardes and Architecture from Piranesi to the 1970s* (Cambridge: MIT Press, 1987), esp. chapter 9 "The Ashes of Jefferson"), p. 291ff.

    12. "Cultural Logic," p. 46, p. 83 (hereafter "Cultural Logic").

    13. "Cultural Logic," p. 83.

    14. "Cultural Logic," p. 83.

    15. "Cultural Logic," p. 83.

    16. "Cultural Logic," pp. 83–84.

    17. "Cultural Logic," p. 84.

    18. "Cultural Logic," pp. 84–85; the reference is to Michael Herr, *Dispatches* (New York, 1978), pp. 8–9.

    19. "Cultural Logic," p. 81.

    20. "Cultural Logic"; Jameson suggests that the architecture of [Corbusier's] "high modernism" would wish to "fan out and transform [the older urban fabric] by the virulence of its Novum," whereas the postmodern Bonaventure implies "no further effects, no larger proto-political Utopian transformation." By contrast, see M. Tafuri's *Architecture and Utopia: Design and Capitalist Development* (Cambridge: MIT Press, 1976), esp. p. 125ff.

    21. "Cultural Logic," p. 84.

    22. See especially *Flash Art,* no. 131 (Dec. 1986/Jan. 1987): 69–73. In "Cultural Logic," pp. 58–64, Jameson discusses Van Gogh's famous printing of the "pair of peasant shoes" focusing primarily on Heidegger's reading. Remarkably, he omits any mention of the Heidegger-Meyer Schapiro controversy regarding the painting's interpretation, discussed by Derrida in his *The Truth in Painting* [(Chicago: University of Chicago Press, 1987), esp. pp. 257–382] except to note that "Derrida remarks, somewhere, about the Heideggerian *paar Bauernschuhe,* that the Van Gogh footgear are a heterosexual pair, which allows neither for perversion nor for fetishization." As has become familiar in Jameson's discussions of the visual arts, individual artistic impressionism stands in for historical and theoretical analysis, which may in large part explain the rather pregnant silence regarding Jameson's writings on art among art historians and critics.

    23. "Cultural Logic," p. 87.

    24. "Cultural Logic," p. 87.

25. On the problematic of Archimedean *Ansatzpunkten,* see D. Preziosi, *The Coy Science: Rethinking Art History* (New Haven & London: Yale University Press, 1989), chapter 3, "The Panoptic Gaze and the Anamorphic Archive."

26. Quoted in Kenneth Frampton, *Modern Architecture: A Critical History* (New York: Oxford University Press, 1980), p. 276.

27. See above, n. 2. Jameson's essay, "Cognitive Mapping" was followed by a discussion session with questions by Nancy Fraser, Darko Suvin, and Cornel West (p. 358).

28. Jameson's participation in that conference (see above, n. 4) also included an outline of the problematics of the conference, consisting in part of summaries of Henri Lefebvre's books *Le droit a la ville* and *The Production of Space,* which (along with the writings of Ernest Mandel) Jameson draws heavily upon in formulating his approach to postmodern "hyperspace." A somewhat different approach to the dialectics of spatiality and sociality is given in two essays by E. W. Soja: see his "The Socio-Spatial Dialectic," *Annals of the Association of American Geographers* vol. 70, no. 2 (June 1980): 207–25, and "The Spatiality of Social Life: towards a Transformative Retheorization," in typescript for that conference. Soja's essays give an excellent introduction to the various strains of Marxist writings (both anglo and francophonic) on the problematic of social space. In the first essay, Soja criticizes what he terms "an increasingly rigidifying orthodoxy [which] has begun to emerge within Marxist spatial analysis that threatens to choke off the development of a critical theory of space in its infancy"—an observation that prefigures Jameson's own later writings on "cognitive mapping," as we shall see. A fine discussion of the "space" debate and the ramifications of Lefebvre's writings may be found in Mark Gottdiener, *The Social Production of Urban Space* (Austin: University of Texas Press, 1985), pp. 110–56 and pp. 157–94.

29. See above, n. 7.

30. K. Lynch, *The Image of the City* (Cambridge: MIT Press, 1960). See Louis Althusser, *For Marx* (London: NLB/Verso, 1977), *Pour Marx* (Paris: Maspero, 1965), esp. chapter 7, "Marxism and Humanism," pp. 219–47, which originally appeared in June 1964 in the journal *Cahiers de l'ISEA.* On the Lacanian underpinnings of Althusser's conception of ideology, see the suggestive discussion in R. Coward and J. Ellis, *Language and Materialism: Developments in Semiology and the Theory of the Subject* (London: Routledge & Kegan Paul, 1977), pp. 61–121. See also D. Preziosi, *The Coy Science,* chapter 3, section 3. See also n. 62 below.

31. "Cultural Logic," p. 89.

32. "Cognitive Mapping," p. 353.

33. A representative bibilography would be beyond the scope of these pages; for useful general introductions, see R. M. Downs and D. Stea, eds. *Image and Environment: Cognitive Mapping and Spatial Behavior* (Chicago: Aldine, 1973), K. Lynch, *A Theory of Good City Form* (Cambridge: MIT Press, 1981).

34. "Cognitive Mapping," p. 353.

35. "Cognitive Mapping," p. 353.

36. "Cultural Logic," p. 92.

37. "Cultural Logic," p. 90.

38. "Cultural Logic," p. 92.

39. See the responses to the "Cognitive Mapping" essay (pp. 358–60), and especially the remarks of Cornel West: "I think that holding on to the conception of totality that you invoke ultimately leads toward a Leninist or Leninist-like politics that is basically sectarian, that may be symptomatic of a pessimism." See also West's critique of *PU* cited above, n. 5, where he observes (p. 188) that "[Jameson's] viewpoint rests upon an unexamined metaphor of translation, an uncritical acceptance of transcoding"; "[Abram's] attempt to recuperate the humanist tradition and the bourgeois conception of history, and . . . Jameson['s] to recover the Marxist tradition and the political meaning of history all ultimately revert to and rely on problematic methodological uses of various notions of analogy and homology."

40. "Cultural Logic," p. 92.

41. *PU*, p. 18.

42. In the words of Sam Weber, "Capitalizing History: Notes on *The Political Unconscious*," *Diacritics* vol. 13, no. 2 (Summer 1983): 24. Weber's critique also appears as chapter 4 in his *Institution and Interpretation* (Minneapolis: University of Minnesota Press, 1987), pp. 40–58.

43. See above, n. 42. Weber notes (p. 25): "To determine History as totalization, as a single, selfsame narrative, as a process of unification and of integration—ultimately, in short, as a movement of *identity* and *presentation*—is to assume a point of view from which the whole can be comprehended, a position, therefore, that must be essentially detached from and outside of what it seeks to contemplate." On Panopticism and disciplinary knowledge, see D. Preziosi, chapter 3, section 2, "The Eye(s) of Power," and Michel Foucault, "The Eye of Power," in *Power/Knowledge: Selected Interviews abd Other Writings 1972–1977,* ed. Colin Gordon (New York: Pantheon, 1980), pp. 146–65.

44. See Weber, "Capitalizing History," p. 22.

45. Weber, "Capitalizing History," pp. 20–21. As Weber observes, it has been precisely the persistent suspicion of the "teleological perspective of totalization in which historical 'development' has traditionally been conceived" that has constituted the "poststructuralist" challenge to the linearist Marxism which Jameson would wish to revive. "Capitalized" History, then, in Derrida, Lacan, and Foucault has been subjected to a reexamination that has problematized the attributes of self-identity, universality, and objective "necessity" hitherto attributed to it, redefining such attributions as part of a strategy that sought to impose itself precisely by masking its own strategic and partisan character. See also Eagleton's critique of *PU* in *Diacritics* vol. 12, no. 3 (Fall 1982): 14–22, entitled "Fredric Jameson: The Politics of Style," which observes (p. 22), "there is no resting place in criticism for those who take their poetry from the future."

46. Discussed in detail in D. Preziosi, chapter 4, section 5; see also L. Marin, *Le portrait du Roi* (Paris: Minuit, 1981), and M. Doueihi, "Traps of Representation," *Diacritics* vol. 14, no. 1 (Spring 1984): 66–77.

47. See above, n. 46, and "That Obscure Object of Desire: The Art of Art History," *boundary 2* vol. 13, no. 2/3 (Winter/Spring 1985): 1–41.

48. See the *Flash Art* interview (above, n. 7), p. 70ff: "I always insist on a third possibility beyond the old bourgeois ego and the schizophrenic subject of our organization of society today: a *collective subject*, decentered but not schizophrenic."

49. *PU,* p. 294.

50. Weber, p. 25ff. See also Cornel West's comments in his *boundary 2* critique (p. 189ff.) on Jameson's mistaken presupposition that analogous and homologous relations obtain between ethics and epistemology. He observes that Jameson misreads the Marxist perspective wherein all metaphysical, epistemological, and ethical discourses are construed as complex ideological affairs of specific groups, communities, or classes in particular societies, with their collective dynamics. Jameson, he argues, misreads Marx's own rejection of bourgeois ethics, resulting in an unnecessary call for a "new logic" of collective dynamics.

51. Weber (p. 23) astutely notes that "to hear [Jameson's claim] that 'History as ground and untranscendable horizon needs no particular theoretical justification' is doubtless music to the ears of many scholars and critics for whom recent theoretical discussion has rendered the ground upon which the discipline has been based less than solid, and its horizons anything but clear and 'untranscendable.'" Compare the remarks made recently by a prominent Marxist art historican (O. Werckmeister) to the effect that "If we can qualify our techniques of investigation and pursue them with consistency, we won't need the abstraction of current theories in order to write a straightforward social and political history of art," quoted in the "Announcement and Call for Papers: 1988 Annual Meeting" of the College Art Association of America.

52. See however the interesting critique of *PU* by film critic and historian Dana Polan (cited above, n. 5), who observes in the course of his discussion that "[Jameson's] nomination of certain practices as aesthetic and others as economic is itself reificatory of their potential imbrications and conjunctural exchange" (p. 136).

53. Such as the *Flash Art* interview; the appearance of his "Postmodernism and Consumer Society" first as a 1982 lecture at the Whitney Museum and then as an essay in the important *Anti-Aesthetic* anthology; the presentation of "Cognitive Mapping" in the "Urban Ideologies" conference at Santa Cruz. An exchange between Rosalind Krauss and Jameson at the Kansas symposium on the postmodern in 1987 is unpublished. Jameson's essay "Progress versus Utopia; or, Can We Imagine the Future," appearing in the anthology *Art after Modernism: Rethinking Representation,* eds. Brian Wallis and Marcia Tucker (New York: New Museum of Contemporary Art, 1984), pp. 239–52, originally appeared in *Science-Fiction Studies* vol. 9, no. 2 (July 1982): 147–58.

54. For example, the notoriously anti-Marxist journal *New Criterion,* edited by retired *New York Times* critic Hilton Kramer. The 1988 College Art Association meetings in Houston included a major symposium on the Marxist tradition in U.S. art history (as yet unpublished).

55. The question is taken up in the final chapter of D. Preziosi, *The Coy Science* (New Haven & London: Yale University Press, 1989); see also Hayden White's discussion of *PU* referred to above in n. 1.

56. E. Panofsky, *Gothic Architecture and Scholasticism* (New York: World, 1957), delivered as a lecture six years earlier at St. Vincent College.

57. *Gothic Architecture and Scholasticism,* pp. 59–60.

58. *Gothic Architecture and Scholasticism,* p. 68.

59. *Gothic Architecture and Scholasticism,* pp. 87–88.

60. *Gothic Architecture and Scholasticism,* p. 87 and n. 62. Cf. H. R. Hahnloser, ed., *Villard de Honnecourt: Kritische Gesamtausgabe* (Vienna, 1935), p. 69, plate 29. The inscription recording a *disputatio* between Villard and the master Pierre de Corbie was in fact added by the former's disciples. Panofsky notes at the end of his essay (p. 88), "Here Scholastic dialectics has driven architectural thinking to a point where it almost ceased to be architectural."

61. At the end of the *Flash Art* interview (p. 71), the interviewer observes that "The historical dimension counteracts the postmodernist immersion in the present, the dehistoricizing or nonhistorical project. In that sense it goes outside the postmodern paradigm." To which Jameson responds: "That is essentially the rhetorical trick or solution that I was attempting: to see whether by systematizing something which is resolutely unhistorical [i.e., postmodernism], one couldn't force a historical way of thinking *at least about that.* The whole point [is] about the loss in postmodernism of the sense of the future."

62. On the subject of the "anamorphic" perspectivism of ideology, see D. Preziosi, "Reckoning with the World: Figure, Text, and Trace in the Built Environment," *American Journal of Semiotics* vol. 4, no. 1/2 (1986): 1–15; and "Structure as Power: The Mechanisms of Urban Meaning," *Espaces et Sociétés* no. 47 (1985): 45–55. Some of the implications of an Althusserian position on the "space" of the subject in ideology are delineated therein, within the contexts of a specific historical analysis.

6

Foucault's Fallacy

Michael Ryan

crescens publicus cinaedus[1]
 —Pompeiian graffito

'In high school, when students would poke fun at faggots or sissies, I wouldn't speak up,' he said. 'I'd go along with the crowd.' The facade he kept up included disguising what he considered potentially effeminate mannerisms.
 —*The New York Times,* June 28, 1993

Foucault's fallacy consists of assigning power priority over resistance when in fact resistance constitutes power. By resistance I mean such things as incoherence, interference, dissonance, and the like that seem irreducible components of social regimes organized around exclusion, subordination, and unequal distribution. Such resistance represents a permanent and irreducible danger to such regimes. While active resistance requires intermittent applications of force on the part of those in power, this implicit resistance elicits more elaborate and more constant forms of social and psychological policing. It is this exercise of power that Foucault so brilliantly analyzes in *Discipline and Punish.* However, he conceives of power as a primary and productive activity when it should be seen as a response to the dangers posed by implicit resistance, dangers that must be permanently stabilized if the society is to survive. The strategies of power that Foucault sees as producers of resistance are in fact responses to it.

The fallacy has two corollaries. The first is Foucault's claim that subjects are constructed by power when in fact there would be no power, no relation of authority, force, or discipline, if there were no subjects whose acts of subordination or insubordination in regard to each other produce or elicit power. The European discourse of imperialism, for example, did not invent "the native"; rather, the encounter with indigenous peoples evoked a discourse of power that allowed the dangerous impediment they represented to be resignified within legal and religious codes and translated into European categories of identity, thus transforming them from either dangerous others or quaint pastoralists to moral evils or exploitable bodies. Their dangerous and already constituted subjectivity—itself discursively mediated within the terms of their own religious and social codes—provoked this response. (The term "subject" here should be understood in an historical sense to mean a temporary and contingent sculpting of physical material into social and psychological forms that can fall apart or assume other shapes in other contexts and in accordance with other codes.)

The second corollary is Foucault's assumption that power/discourse posits or constructs positive realities when, in fact, the positive discourses of power are themselves constructed in reaction to negativities whose immunity to discursive capture underscores the indeterminacy and contingency of all such positive realities. What cannot be understood or known, what cannot be rendered in the discursive terms that apply consistency, order, and predictability to the world, is always dangerous from the perspective of power. It cannot become a positive reality to which a term of comprehension can be assigned, and it threatens the very notion of a positive reality purged of indeterminacy by offering an example of a different discursive determination of the world. North American notions of property allocation were incomprehensible to the European invaders because land was not held but used in a functional economy of subsistence and minimal trade. Those notions were dangerous because they proposed a different ordering of acquisition, holding, and distribution than the one practiced by the Europeans, one that followed in the tracks of a coarsely commercial and imperially acquisitive Roman legal system.

Within a regime of power, such alternatives must either be banished from the reigning positive reality or else be somehow accounted for within the discourse of power. While power usually neutralizes danger by processing negativity—the resistance to functional consistency and order—into accountable positivities, in many cases, the danger is undiscoursable. The alternative constructions of reality or identity remain immune to categorical subsumption, the process by which dangers are incorporated and neutralized by being translated into the figures, tropes, and terms of power. They can therefore register in the discourse of power only in the form of reactive figures that invert, displace, or disavow their danger without granting them positive existence.

One such figure, until recently, has been the homosexual. Foucault claims that homosexuality was invented by the discourses of knowledge/power in the late nineteenth century.[2] At that point in time, the homosexual was first constructed as a positive object of knowledge and as the subject of a sexual identity. Prior to that time, there was no subject of sexuality that was homosexual. There were only a variety of sexual practices, some of which, like sodomy, were enjoined or criminalized. The invention of scientific "homosexuality" at this time is indisputable, but homosexuality also exists as an invisible object, an undiscoursable silence, in the discourses of power prior to the nineteenth century.

Foucault is aware of the problem silence poses for a Structuralist history based exclusively on discourse.[3] But he does not take into account the possibility that discourse might be constituted as a response and resistance to things that are silent—that is, unavailable to discursive positivity—precisely because they are undiscoursable. They are so negative or dangerous that they threaten the very vocabulary that constructs positive things. As a result, he does not entertain the possibility that homosexuality might have constituted a point of resistance and a danger to the gender codes in place before the nineteenth century. It might have had no name because its existence destabilized the available codes of social ontology.

If this is true, homosexuality, rather than being an effect of heterosexist power, would be its unstated occasion. The regimes of sexual power that seem not to have known homosexuality before the nineteenth century would need to be seen as coming into being as defensive responses to the dangers posed by such undiscoursable material—the danger of gender indeterminacy, for example, or of practices of nonreproductive sexual pleasure.

In describing Foucault's fallacy, I will be particularly concerned with his discussion of homosexuality in the second volume of his history of sexuality—*The Use of Pleasure*.[4] There, Foucault mistakes a heterosexual hazing ritual and initiation rite in classical Athens for male homosexuality or "the love of boys."[5] While that initiation rite contained an erotic component—at least for the adult males—it also constituted a systemic form of child abuse perpetrated on young boys by older men.

My analysis will be enabled by a critical reexamination of Foucault's theories of power, subjectivity, and discourse.

Power, rather than being transsubjective or systemic as Foucault claims, is a response by a threatened subjectivity to the danger another subject or subject possibility poses. It is a dynamic relation of forces, of danger and defense, that particulates one subject's fears and desires regarding other subjects. Rather then produce subjects, power is constructed by subjects as a way of constituting themselves and their values as normative in relation to other subjects who endanger their values and identities.

For example, Foucault claims that the emergence of homosexuality into discourse was a move within power. Expressive sexual self-identification and the pursuit of "perverse" pleasure, rather than being independently constituted moves against power, played into the hands of technologies of control that thrive on exposure, knowledge, and visibility. Those resistances made themselves available to examination by acting out processes of implanted micropower that work precisely through greater expressivity and perversity. Power, in other words, produced resistance as a secondary term.[6]

But while the new scientific discourses of the late nineteenth century may indeed have advanced the techniques of social control, many of those techniques of scientific dominance, at least in the U.S. experience, were themselves responses to dangers that can be said to have provoked those exercises of scientific power—the danger of a developing countersociety of recently freed blacks, for example, or of the early women's movement or of the recently arrived and "alien" immigrant working-class cultures. These new subjectivities constituted "resistances" within the social system, blockages to efficient functioning and impediments to the circulating currents of managed social energy that demanded and provoked an empowered response, often scientific, to the dangers they posed. Without dirt, without crowded movie theaters where smells and classes mixed, there would have been no personal hygiene movement.

Similarly, the invention of homosexuality in the late nineteenth century as a term of scientific knowledge allied with the technologies of social control can be read as a response to the emergence out of the closet of homosexuals in post-Romantic western Europe. The growth of "perversions" in the nineteenth century that Foucault sees as an effect or product of the discourses of power in fact provoked the emergence of those discourses. Homosexuals, especially in cultural movements like Romanticism, pre-Raphaelitism, and Decadence, began to assume discursive positions that had been denied them and to enter discourses that had denied their existence. If they were discovered at this point, it was because the closet doors had begun to be pried open—not by the scientific agents of power but by homosexuals themselves—usually "scandalous" homosexuals like Byron, Swinburne, and Wilde.[7]

Foucault's concept of power is monological to the degree that he ignores the necessarily double nature of power, the fact that it is always a response to resistances that are an irreducible part of any society that requires power in order to function. Social ontology is always indeterminate, always a matter of the temporary authorization and stabilization of contingent categories (such as heterosexual and homosexual). That indeterminacy will be exacerbated as the levels of inequality and subordination in the society increase, and those increases augment the resistant potential of suborned subjects—the danger they pose. In responding to such dangers, power, rather than originating attempts at liberation or de-repression as moves always already contained within its strategies, resists these ineradicable resistances with the instability of its structures, the indeterminacy of its categories, and the displacement of its privileged subjects.

Such a reconsideration of Foucault's concept of power has implications for his notions of subjectivity and discourse.

Foucault follows Structuralist protocols in his history of sexuality by treating subjective identity as a symptom of power, a delusory construct that is either determined by more important discursive structures or else manufactured in order to better control people. But subjects may not so much be the effect of power/discourse as one of the dangers that summons it into existence. In order to pursue that possibility, we need to envision a more relational and social concept of subjectivity than the one Structuralism offers, one that would see both the other and representation as intricated in the constitution of subjectivity.

According to those schools of psychology that emerge after Structuralism and that largely eschew Structuralist (neo-Freudian) assumptions regarding subjectivity, the self is a relational entity that comes into being through the establishing of boundaries that are malleable and far from absolute in their demarcations. Relations to others shape the self through care or abuse in childhood, as well as through the social processes of aggression, shaming, friendship, eroticism, and the like in adult life. Especially in regard to dangerous gender possibilities like exclusive homosexuality, the self is a social scene, traversed, until recently, by the psychological violence of shame and stigmatization and recently, by pride. The self, in such theories, is a much more indeterminate entity than Structuralism credits it with being. Relations assume different configurations, and there is no identity outside such relations. In place of the static model Structuralism offers of a self shaped by unchanging laws such as castration, the more recent model sees the self as dynamic and evolving, its being a mixture of determinations that are as much social and historical as instinctual.

From the perspective of cultural history, perhaps the most interesting dimension of the new psychology is the emphasis on the constitutive role of representation in the making of the self. Childhood relations implant the self as a mental representational system; in the adolescent passage into adulthood, external representations of ideals are internalized and shape behavior; and in adult life, one lives one's desires through internal representations of the external objects of others one either desires or fears. The self emerges through the acquisition of a capacity for representation that distinguishes an object world apart from subjective processes. The self, in other words, is made up of image surfaces that demarcate identity from alterity and are the synapses of the self's constitutive social relations.

These insights allow the Structuralist division between determining discourse and determined and, hence, false subjective identity to be transcended. Others exist for the self as representations, and the inchoate self becomes a subject by acquiring its own power of representing. The crucial problem for subjectivity is no longer its subjection to determining laws such as castration or incest and is instead its dynamic, indeterminate, changable, and representationally mediated relations to others distributed along a variety of axes, with fission into bounded individuality and fusion with a lost other being two of many possible poles of self-construction.

Because Foucault's work remains mortgaged to the Structuralist notion of the systemic determination of subjectivity, he is incapable of seeing the subjectivity in power, and he fails to be sufficiently attentive to the ways in which subjects-in-power representationally constitute themselves in reaction to threatening subjective alternatives in the dominant discourses of an era. Power is a relational term between subjects, not a system of nonsubjective strategies that operate without allegiance. If the various subjects-in-power in Euro-American society—whites, males, heterosexuals, capitalists, and so forth—subcontracted the exercise of power to institutions like schools in the nineteenth century, it was not because they abdicated subjectivity in favor of nonsubjective systems; it was because the threats and dangers to their power had become so diverse and widespread that they required new kinds of systemic vigilance. Those dangers often assumed the form of new subjective possibilities—young people in the eighteenth and nineteenth centuries, for example, who defied adult forms of social discipline and rejected the narratives of career and marriage offered to them.[8] Those alternatives assumed the cultural form of such new representational modes as the picaresque novels of the era, from *Lazarillo* to *Huckleberry Finn,* which celebrated those rejections. Those new possibilities were not any the less subjective because the most appropriate means of managing them were systemic.

Because subjectivity and representation are intricated one with the other, the empowered responses to these resistances are always themselves representational. They are efforts to reconstruct a threatened privileged subjectivity. It has become a commonplace of American cultural history to note, for example, that the great male literary discourses of the nineteenth and twentieth centuries, from Emerson to Hemingway, are attempts to representationally reconstitute masculine ideals of identity and authority laid to waste by emerging representational counterideals of female subjective autonomy and power.

The intrication of subjective representational dynamics with systems of power calls for an interpretive strategy that locates the origin of seemingly positive discourses in negativities they attempt to accommodate or to redress. Discourse defends against danger by mobilizing therapeutic exaggerations of the very things danger threatens—placidity, stability, identity, authority, and so on. In consequence, a theory of discourse that conceives of discourse as a producer of positive realities will fail to see the dangers that evoke discursive mobilizations; indeed, the invisibility of those dangers, their absence from discursive positivity, is one effect of those mobilizations. A legion of white blood cells advertises disease as much as health, even if the disease has been rendered undetectable.

This is the blind of power: anything that so threatens power that it cannot be granted positivity will be eliminated from view and remain unnamed. But such silence frequently means that the other against which discourse mounts a defense is invisible precisely because it is immune to discursive appropriation; it is that which lies outside discursive capture, while nevertheless calling forth discursive mobilizations. What can be seen, therefore, is often of less evidentiary value than what is banished from view in a discursive history of systems of domination.

This reconsideration of Foucault's theory of discourse imposes a different reading strategy than the one Foucault practices. Instead of taking discourses at face value, we should instead interrogate their relation to nondiscoursable elements to which they respond. We should ask how the tropes of power are apotropaic, how they turn away from danger. For example, when Aristotle declares the Good to consist of a particular mean between extremes or of a certain purity that avoids mixture, we must ask—what qualities of the so-called extremes are so dangerous and threatening and for what reasons? How is the mean itself extreme in relation to alternative norms that might see virtue in certain forms of banished extremity? How might the social subjects and activities tainted by association with extremity themselves constitute an alternative norm?

Such questions undermine the evidentiary value of discourse, while outlining an alternative method to Foucault's interpretive strategy, which reads acceptingly the texts of those in power in fifth-century Greek society as if those texts were uninflected by relational dynamics. He treats those texts in a semiotic version of positivism (just the words, instead of just the facts) and assumes they align with positive realities in a straightforward manner undisturbed by the distortions that are one effect of the interpretive frames of power.

An alternative reading strategy would begin by asking what elicits discourse? Is discourse a positive naming of objects or does it respond to dangers, wounds, and instabilities that require the healing, patching up, smoothing over, concealing, and bandaging of things that can never, as a result, appear within discourse in a recognizable or undistorted form? When we read Plato or Aristotle on Greek sexuality, are we reading words aligned with positive realities or observing plaster beneath which, were we to scratch hard enough, we would find somewhat more negative, dangerous, and perhaps horrifying materials?

One can usually discover what power resists or responds to by inverting its premises. Where the discourses of power treasure purity, masculine ideals of Reason, and moderation understood as the taming of the potential excesses of desire and as the subordination of the materiality of the body to ideals such as Beauty or the Good, one can assume that the danger power responds to consists of impurity or mixture, emotional forces associated with effeminacy, and the body and bodily desire considered as sites of potentially uncontrollable forces that transgress and undermine the balance and the boundaries established by phallogocentric Reason. Such is the case with the classical Greek discourses that Foucault privileges in *The Use of Pleasure*. Because his concept of power is monological, his concept of the self nonrelational and nonrepresentational, and his concept of discourse numb to the undiscoursable dangers that frequently are the occasions as well as the violent objects of otherwise apparently nonviolent discourses, Foucault does not read the Greek texts as responses to instabilities and indeterminacies within the social ontological and categorical system of classical Athens, nor does he fully note just how deeply rooted in the Greek system of thought was the violence done to women and young boys in that society.

To take one very pertinent example: there is no apparent mention of male homosexuals—in the modern sense of someone whose consistent and exclusive sexual object is other men—in the surviving discursive evidence from fifth-century Athens. But does that mean that there were no male homosexuals in Athens? Or does the consistent stigmatization of effeminate men (*kinaidoi*) in Athenian discourse suggest that Greek culture was as homophobic as our own, that the coerced submission of boys to sex with older men as part of their initiation into the power elite was perfectly compatible with an animus regarding men who would have preferred to spend their entire sexual lives with other men?

I will suggest that homosexuals—people whose sexual object choices are consistently and exclusively of the same biological sex—were a group whose existence in ancient Athens is only scarcely detectable in the surviving discursive evidence because they were victims of the blind of power. They posed a threat to the dominant highly masculine heterosexual paradigm, and as a result, they appear most visibly in the occasional acts of discursive violence aimed in their direction. Given the power of the reigning ideal of aggressive masculinity, male homosexuals especially were undiscoursable and had to be converted into highly displaced, even inverted figures (man = woman) in order to be comprehensible to the ruling intellectual elite. Furthermore, the dominant discourses privileged by Foucault—those of Plato and Xenophon most notably—which seem to celebrate homosexual love, in fact provide an ideological justification for an abusive system of male heterosexual power that turned boys into sexual servants of older heterosexual men until those older men reached the age of marriage. If American prisons resemble Athens, it was because Athens resembled an American prison.

Foucault claims that before the nineteenth century there were no homosexuals as such; there were only people who engaged in certain sexual practices—"sodomy"—without identifying themselves as homosexual or being identified within knowledge regimes as possessing a homosexual identity. One implication of this description is that sexuality before the Victorians was more plural, especially in fifth-century Athens. This Romantic ideal recalls the "inconsequential bucolic pleasures," themselves frequently laden with child abuse, that Foucault attributes to premodern agrarian life. And it seems as distant from reality.

The sexual sciences of the nineteenth century may have invented the concept of homosexuality, but they did not bring into being a new genre of males who decided, upon reading *Psychopathia Sexualis* after 1846, that it was high time to have done with women altogether and to begin having erotic relations exclusively with other men. For one thing, the sexual figures that Foucault claims were "scarcely noticed in the past" were in abundant display during the Renaissance. In England, homosexual men were pervasively labelled as "catamites"—a derivative of *kinaidoi*. James II may not have thought of himself as a "homosexual" in our modern sense of someone who possesses and is possessed by a particular sexual identity. But his very consistent catamitic practices, especially his penchant for young male lovers, scandalized sensibilities unused to having a Court known widely to be a gathering place of catamites and mimes—either transvestites or actors—many of whom, like Shakespeare, were homosexuals parading as heterosexuals. For James, homosexuality, once the task of fulfilling national expectations by producing a mandatory heir was complete and the obligatory wife shifted to a separate abode, was something more than an external, ancillary, and contingent practice. It had all the marks of an exclusive interest whose origins were subjective and rather deeply felt, not socially imported or discursively appended. While deep feelings are always effects of representational construction, they must also, if there are no determining scientific discourses in sight, be given some weight as counters to the idea that no realities exist that are not somehow discursively recorded. Moreover, one can probably safely surmise that before science caught up with the phenomenon in the late nineteenth century, much as it caught up with, though did not "invent," gravity in the seventeenth, homosexuality preexisted the science that discovered it.[9]

Moreover, while sexual practices need not imply sexual identities (sodomy = homosexuality?), neither does the absence of evidence regarding identity necessarily imply an absence of identity. The relation between sexual practices—sodomy, for example—and sexual identity is contingent enough for sodomites to be either heterosexuals or homosexuals. But when the object of concern (or stigmatization) is consistency and exclusivity of object choice, one can safely assume that it is identity, not practice that is at issue. Such was the case in Greece.

Male homosexuals—men whose consistent and exclusive sexual object choices are other men—were visible enough in classical Greece to elicit a fair amount of scorn and derision.[10] Such figures as the *kinaidos,* the effeminate male who exclusively prefers the passive or female sexual position with other men, look all too familiar in the context of our own homophobic culture,[11] and in the surviving literary documents they are treated with the kind of scorn that until recently consistently attached to homosexuals in Western societies.[12] Foucault risks siding with the silencing procedures of past heterosexual power regimes when he downplays the importance of such a figure. He also ignores the possibility that homosexuals may simply have found it impossible to speak about themselves in contexts that were so violently homophobic. That this discursive violence is not scientific in our modern sense (it is scientific if one credits texts like Aristotle's *Problems* as "science" and accepts that the action of the buttocks is instrumental in propelling sperm) does not diminish its usefulness as a strategy of power.[13]

Foucault's primary concern in *The Use of Pleasure* is the ideal of moderation regarding sexuality and desire in Greek classical discourse. According to that ideal, the upper-class men who dominated Athenian political life were supposed to exercise control over their emotions and appetites and to tame the revolts and excesses of the body. In Aristotle, this ideal takes the form of a mean, or balance, between extremes; in Plato, of the subsumption of the body to reason, materiality to ideal forms like Beauty. Foucault describes this ideal of moderation as a technique or an aesthetics of the self. Men were called on to dominate themselves, especially in regard to sexuality. Because, before moving on to marriage in their thirties, upper-class men in their twenties used adolescent boys as sexual partners[14] (girls were kept within the home until marriage, and one reading of intermale sexuality is that it resulted from the scarcity of alternatives),[15] the ideal of moderation is often elaborated around iso-male erotic and amorous relations particularly. In the *Symposium,* Socrates boasts of having spurned Alcibiades, a beautiful young boy who offers himself to the older man. In its extreme form the ideal of moderation consists of abstention, but it also takes the form of moderate practices of pleasure with both boys and women.

Upon first reading, Foucault's description of this discursive system is disconcerting. He speaks of "the Greeks" as if that general term did not conceal differences and exclusions. But then he notes in addenda and caveats that he is of course referring to free men, not to women and slaves, who occupied subordinate positions in Greek society. Still, in the organization of his own discourse, central issues are relegated to the position of additions. For example, after describing the ideal of moderation as self-domination, he adds that it is "shown" in the domination of others. Foucault's wording consistently places moderation as self-domination in a primary, even a private position, something which originates and concludes within the self without any reference to others; it might also, as an addition to what it is, be exercised in regard to others, or it might be done "in order to" dominate others, but it stands essentially on its own as a technique of the self.

I have evoked the relational concept of the self because it suggests that something like self-domination in the ideal of moderation is constitutively the domination of others. By dominating one's feelings regarding others, one in effect dominates others by preventing oneself from assuming a dependent position in relationship to them. Moreover, by dominating those feelings in oneself that are repellent because they pertain to a feared other in one's society, one also dominates that other. One reinflects subjectively the communal rules that mandate the marginalization of that feared and perhaps dangerous genre of person. The process of self-domination—by empowered men particularly over feelings and bodily forces associated with effeminacy—was itself therefore constitutive of and inseparable from the domination of women in classical Greece. The putative characteristics of women (emotional excess, genre mixture, etc.) in the male self represented a danger to male rule. Because women were associated with weakness, mixture, impurity, lack of control, and the like in Greek male thought,[16] those characteristics in the dominant male group, whose interactions were characterized by a violent competitiveness organized around shaming relations of domination and subordination,[17] had to be purged.

What Foucault—following Greek ideology—calls "moderation as self-domination" is in fact the domination of others, especially women, through the assurance that those in dominance are clearly sealed off from traits associated with enforced subordination. Ruling Greek men did not practice moderation so that they would be better qualified to exercise political power over the subordinated groups in Greek society; in dominating their bodies and emotions, they were dominating those subordinated groups.

Rather than being an ethics of the self, moderation was a practice of subordination designed to make a boundary between those who both control and are in control and those who because they do not control are more likely to be out of control. By designating the characteristics of one group—heterosexual males—as an ideal (dissociation from bodily and emotional processes), the Greek ideological discourses assured that the characteristics of the other groups such as women particularly, who were associated with impurity and emotional excess, were excluded from qualification for power; those discourses thus excluded those groups from power. The domination of the feminine, rather than being an addition in the realm of social practice to a "self"-contained psychological process, was internal to male power and essential to the attainment of moderation. By keeping women out (of themselves), men could obtain public power, and by having power, they could keep women out (of public life).

Moreover, the system of subordination that Foucault sees as an addendum to the ethics and aesthetics of sexual moderation in fact determined and made necessary those practices. That system of subordination was the frame within which such things as moderation acquired meaning. There would have been no need to speak of moderation, to make it a crucial issue of male rule, if there were not in place a system of subordination which created dangers that took the form of immoderation—the revolts and excesses of feeling that are also the excesses of femininity as the Greek ideologists conceived of it.[18] Subordination cannot therefore be described as something appended to the practice of moderation. Moderation was enacted *because* of subordination. The dangers of excess and revolt solicited a response in the form of a discourse of psychological self-control.

Feminine qualities were also assigned to and condemned in effeminate males or *kinaidoi.* Foucault chooses to ignore the possibility that this figure might represent one segment of the wide array of nonheterosexual gender possibilities, and he is particularly careful to make certain readers do not entertain the idea that the *kinaidoi* might be homosexual men with a penchant for effeminate styles of dress and behavior. Instead, he embraces the myth of Greek homosexuality. According to that myth, the hazing rituals by which older, empowered males took adolescent boys who aspired to enter the realms of power as sexual servants and thereby initiated them to the highly aggressive and competitive male heterosexual social system of Athens[19] constituted homosexual practices in our modern sense of that term; that is, Greek intermale eroticism consisted of freely chosen love relations, and while these relations began with an asymmetry between adult and boy, person-in-power and person-without-power, they developed into the "convergence" of "true love" and "friendship."[20]

To maintain this myth, Foucault must pass quickly over the issue of the figure of the *kinaidos,* ignore the evidence—some of which he cites—that exclusively homosexual men were objects of shame and scorn, and accept as true the self-justifications of those in power. Of the scorn levelled at *kinaidoi* in Aristophanes' plays, Foucault writes: "It would be completely incorrect to interpret this as a condemnation of love of boys, or of what we generally refer to as homosexual relations; but at the same time, one cannot fail to see in it the effect of strongly negative judgments concerning some possible aspects of relations between men, as well as a definite aversion to anything that might denote a deliberate renunciation of the signs and privileges of the masculine role. The domain of male loves may have been 'free' in Greek antiquity [but] the fact remains that one sees the very early expression of . . . forms of stigmatization that will extend well into the future" (p. 19). Foucault suggests that adult males who were condemned for effeminacy were vilified not for being homosexual, but for renouncing the masculine role. Yet if the so-called free, homosexual, man/boy sexual practices of Athens were male heterosexual initiation rites and hazing rituals designed to elicit subordination from a new threatening group of young males and to create alliances between older and younger power figures, a different reading of the *kinaidos* becomes mandatory.

At issue here is the possibility that Greek males were so different from modern males that none of them were either homosexual or heterosexual in our modern sense of those terms; instead, all of them freely practiced both homosexuality and heterosexuality.[21] I have noted that the construction of the masculine heterosexual ideal at the time was defensive; it resided on the expulsion of feminine traits associated with women. Those traits are even more threatening or dangerous when they are present in someone whose biological identity would seem to call for other, more "masculine" modes of behavior. Women could at least be locked away in the home and covered with veils; effeminate biological men, on the other hand, had to be kept "out" of the home and unveiled. Otherwise, the entire logic of gender division and subordination that allowed Greek society to function would be put in question. Queer queens—assuming that is one possible meaning of *kinaidos*—thus posed a particularly vexing problem for "the Greeks." If femininity was condemned because it was a characteristic of women, it was also condemned because it raised the real possibility that "men" might be "women" and that gender traits did not necessarily align with physiology.

Because that very simple point undermined all the values, ideals, and role assignments of classical Greek culture, the effeminate male homosexual was probably more threatening than women, who at least possessed a recognizable identity that could be talked about. He brought the dangerous qualities of femininity closer to home, which is to say, closer to the home turf of physiological masculinity. If women had to be foreign, the homosexual male was the foreign agent who threatened to subvert the state from within. One reading of Greek sexual practices and institutions is that they were derived from an all-male military culture and were designed to assure courage and loyalty in war.[22] The ideal of masculinity was thus very much a military and patriotic value, and any threat to it had significant political consequences.

The absence of discursive evidence regarding male homosexuals—people with an exclusive preference for other men—might thus be read not as a sign of the absence of such people but rather as a sign of the greater danger they posed. They were quite literally unspeakable. If the state was to survive, if men were to be masculine at home and at war, male homosexuals could not exist. The condemnation of *kinaidoi* may therefore have less to do with effeminacy than with the possible dislocation of the founding gender equations (male = masculine, female = feminine) of Athenian society that the *kinaidoi* represented. It was not so much that they were condemned for being effeminate, as that effeminacy was condemned because it was associated with such men. It summoned the possibility of exclusive homosexuality, of (in this particular version of such homosexuality) men-that-would-be-women. That alternative gender possibility suggested an abandonment of the central masculine ideal of sexual domination over women and boys (whose figures in Greek homoerotic vase paintings always resemble women).[23] It rendered indeterminate the foundational and supposedly noncontingent identification of males with active, "masculine" sexual domination.[24]

Women might therefore have been as much suborned because they represented the potential effeminacy of men as for any more inherent defect. Effeminacy, in other words, may not have been the quality that gave catamitism its meaning; rather, catamitism—the crossing of female and male in biological men—may have been the normative danger that qualified effeminacy as a threat to male heterosexual rule. The technique of the self, the ideal of moderation, was directed at this "other" particularly, and it was an other that inhabited the self as the very real possibility that a man might be a woman, that the characteristics of women such as emotional excess might be found in men. The danger that technique addressed was that a man might always be "one" himself. And that is why it was so important to be vigilant regarding oneself. It kept the wrists straight.

While Foucault is therefore correct to suggest that the figure of the *kinaidos* does not reflect negatively on the taking of boys as sexual partners, the figure does suggest that the adoption by dominant males of homosexual practices in order to build philic power alliances does not exclude the possibility that those males had an investment in the exclusion and denigration of men whose exclusive sexual object choices would have been other men. Indeed, everything about Greek culture suggests that the need for intermale power alliances in an aggressive, masculinist setting mandated the elimination of such a threat to the ideals of masculinity.

The *kinaidos* may therefore be a figure worth more than a few dismissive pages at the beginning of a book that then goes on to suggest that the Greeks were more liberal than we benighted moderns because they could experience a variety of homosexual and heterosexual relations. That evasion speaks to a larger evasion that nags at Foucault's argument, much as he attempts to push it away. And that is that all Greek men were expected to marry women. Heterosexuality was mandatory.

Foucault notes that "the Greeks" did not require another nature in order to love a man. Greek men could either be attracted to a boy or to a girl. While the ideal of plural sexual practices is a laudable one, the utopian dimension of this assertion becomes evident when one considers that adult males could only engage in sexual relations with boys during a certain period of both of their lives—teens for the boys, twenties for the young adult males. Both were expected to "graduate" to heterosexuality and marriage.[25] If they didn't, Foucault rightly notes, they became an object of criticism, although shame and disgrace would be more accurate terms.

The implications of this heterosexual mandate for male homosexuals in Athens—assuming, again, that there were men around, like Timarchus in Askhines' *Against Timarchus*, who exclusively preferred other men—were onerous. If one were unlucky enough to be an adult male homosexual, that is, if one would have preferred to have sex only with other men rather than with women, one could have sex with boys during a certain period of one's life. But one had to pass on to one's reproductive responsibilities with women, and one could never have sex with other adult men unless one frequented male prostitutes, all of whom were slaves or foreigners. Similarly, one could not as a boy remain in intermale relations; one had to "grow up" and marry. And while as an adult one might still have sex with boys, one could not establish a household with another adult male without risking being accused of being a prostitute, and one could not establish a household on a long-term basis with a boy.[26] If one were an adult male homosexual with effeminate characteristics—or a queen or a transvestite—one was treated with scorn. The best one could do, apparently, was to become a male prostitute, but that excluded one from participating in the political life of the city and one risked becoming an object of the kind of abuse Askhines levels at Timarchus in his famous oration.

That oration suggests just how difficult it was to be a male homosexual in Athens. Askhines accuses Timarchus of prostituting himself to other men. Prostitution as he describes it consists of living in the homes of those other men and of being maintained like a courtesan. This is an important point, since the certified sexual relations between adult males and boys seem to have been organized around the gymnasia. Classicists like Dover focus on the citation of the law against male prostitution in the oration and argue that it implies that sexual relations between free male citizens that were not mediated by money were legitimate. Yet the depiction of prostitution in the oration can also be read as suggesting that adult men who chose other adult men as exclusive sexual partners or who lived together (there is no mention that Tirmarchus was ever married) ran the risk of being publicly vilified and denied the rights of citizens. Askhines accuses Timarchus of squandering his fortune, yet he seems to have been "prostituting" himself—that is, living with other men—for some time before his fall from economic grace. In other words, he scarcely needed the money, so prostitution hardly seems to be the issue. What all of this suggests is that prostitution in the oration may be a metaphor for male homosexuality and especially for what today would be called gay marriage.

The adoption by Athenian males of sexual practices normally associated with homosexuals (though not exclusively practiced by homosexuals, as Justice Marshall's law clerk noted regarding *Bowers v. Hardwick*)[27] should be associated not so much with homosexuality in our modern sense of the term—that is, with freely chosen sexual relations—as with ritualized domination and subordination of the kind practiced by victorious Greek armies on their prisoners.[28] Because entry into the upper-class male power circles was not guaranteed, boys allied themselves with powerful males who would later be able to grant them political favors in return for the sexual ones the boys had to offer. It is doubtful that this system of exchange and resource distribution was as "free" as Foucault claims. He himself notes that one could be punished for life if one refused the "good advice" of an elder. If older males could help, they could also, no doubt, hurt, and there seems to have been an unstated set of rules that ritualized the practices of domination and subordination that grew up around man/boy sexual relations. Those who did accept advice seem to have done well for themselves; at least, Socrates taunts Aristophanes in the *Symposium* by pointing out that boy lovers turn out to be the most manly public servants, a remark that probably should be read as indicating that those who gained political favors and power by submitting sexually as boys turned out to be most well situated to give evidence of "masculine" political traits as adults; that is, they were the ones who had acquired the most power. Moreover, by undergoing a ritualized submission to older males, the boys were separated from the female realm of the household and initiated into the male public world. In order to enter, they were obliged to acknowledge the dominance of empowered males by submitting sexually. Such submission no doubt diminished intergenerational competitiveness by establishing a recognized order of rank.

Foucault points out that boys could not identify with the feminine role that was assigned them in the hazing ritual (and the intercrural or between-the-legs nature of the sex—essentially mutual masturbation—further diminished the possibility that the boys would be excessively feminized through anal penetration).[29] To do so was to risk being described as a *kinaidos.* Consequently, one of the most commented-on features of the celebrated Greek vase paintings of intermale sexual conduct is the disinterest of the boy, his appearance of detachment from what is being done to him. But this disinterest also invites another reading. If we assume that homosexuals were a minority in Athens, then most of the boys obliged to submit to the heterosexual initiation rite by adult males were not homosexual; that is, they would not as adults be, like Tirmarchus, inclined to seek out male sexual partners exclusively. The famous detachment of the *eromenos* or boy lover may therefore have been a response to the systemically coercive nature of the intermale sexual contact imposed by young adult men. By "systemically," I mean that the ground rules were unstated but that they were such that one could not really avoid playing the game if one wished to survive politically.

This reading of the boys' detachment allows one to account for the ideology of abstention or moderation in Greek philosophic discourse of the period in a manner somewhat different from Foucault's. Both the avidity of the adult engaging in coerced (one might say, sadistic) sexual domination and the detachment of the boy object might be evidence of psychological dissociation. Foucault describes the ideal of moderation in terms that suggest such dissociation—a sense of removal from one's own body, indifference to sensations, a separation from affect, and an overemphasis on cognition. One source of dissociation is child abuse, and while the Greeks were apparently avid child beaters, one might also characterize the Greek hazing ritual as abusive.

One outcome of dissociation is detachment from others and a tendency to turn them into objects or instruments, two attitudes evident in the vase paintings.[30] The adult objectifies, while the boy detaches. Greek sexual practices may therefore form a circle of power: what initiates boys into power also makes them more capable of exercising power. Their abuse as children implants a power of dissociation, of separating cognition from affect, that makes them more capable as adults of engaging in the same kind of abusive objectification with regard to others. And by "abusive" here I mean something that, because it might not have been freely chosen, constitutes an unsolicited violation of another.

Foucault fails to recognize the role of the discourse of moderation in formulating and justifying this circle of power. In Plato's version of moderation, the soul withdraws from the body in order to enter a higher, more spiritual realm where truth becomes available. That love is thematized as the love of a boy, not because such love was for "the Greeks" a particularly "delicate" problem, as Foucault suggests, but rather because the soul's concentration of all of its energies on itself constitutes a narcissistic ideal that is best realized in a purely isomorphic romantic relation, what one might call same-subject eroticism. That ideal of purity purges the realm of male idealization of anything that might suggest impurity or the taint of the other, be that woman or *kinaidos*. Gone is all suggestion of disturbing mixture; Being in its truth can be grasped because the materiality of the body, something strongly linked to woman in Greek culture, is now subject to a control that etherizes physicality and emotionality. The mirror of the ideal of reason takes the place of the physical and the emotional, and the heterosexual male gazes, essentially, upon himself.

Included in that expulsion order is the effeminate male, the one homosexual who, like the comic figure of Agathon in Aristophanes' *Thesmophoriazusae*, stands out because he cannot conceal himself under a ruse of heterosexual masculinity. While such figures are associated with falseness, mendacity, and imposture, the Platonic ideal that imposes abstention and moderation is characterized by truth and purity. It is essentially and heterosexually male. Greek philosophy, therefore, was bound up with the Greek system of sexual subordination. It is not a way of "problematizing in thought" the "harsh system" of Greek society, as Foucault claims. Rather than being a stylish addition, it is one of the ways that harshness was constituted and sustained.

A review of the literature regarding fifth-century Athens suggests that male homosexuality was not invented in the late nineteenth century. Nor was it constituted by power as one of its strategies. When Aristotle writes in the *Problems* of "those who are effeminate by nature," he anticipates by several millenia what Foucault locates in our own era—the scientific description, as a strategy of power, of at least a certain kind of homosexuality: "[T]hose who are effeminate by nature . . . are unnaturally constituted; for, though male, they are in a condition in which this part of them is necessarily incapacitated. Now, incapacity . . . may involve . . . perversion; . . . When [desire] finds its way to the fundament only, there is a desire to submit to sexual intercourse . . . All of this is more likely to occur in the case of one who is both lustful and effeminate."[31] But heterosexual power did not invent the effeminate homosexuals Aristotle describes. They themselves summoned that scientific attention. And they did so because they evoked fear in male heterosexual hearts. They constituted a danger and a point of resistance to the normative, compulsory, and maritally anchored heterosexuality of fifth-century Athens. The danger was that the system might come undone if alternatives existed; the resistance that not everyone had to submit.

The danger still exists, and it is the danger that we might invent other possibilities, refuse the compulsory constructions. By misreading the danger of homosexuality (or of any alternative sexuality) as a strategy of power, an effect rather than a cause, Foucault was incapable of imagining any alternative other than a heterotopia that would be entirely outside the system he inaccurately described as pervasive and impermeable. As hysterical responses to danger and resistance, those systems of power are always unstable, never sufficiently naturalized to allay all anxiety or purge all indeterminacy. And it is in the forms of hysterical response that we can already glimpse the makings of alternatives, the reality of already existing possibilities.

When one reads of the brutal murder of Harold Schindler by a fellow sailor because he was homosexual, one realizes the threat homosexuality poses to constructed heterosexuality, a danger of indeterminacy that elicits a violent response because it suggests how ungrounded and unstable the dominant heterosexual construction is. One sees other versions of that violence in the snarling ferocity of a Patrick Buchanan or a Bob Dole, or in the harsh responses to Elizabeth Sussman's revolutionary 1993 Whitney Biennial. One does so because power is endangered at each one of its points of application, elaboration, or idealization—from representation, to authority, to sexuality, and so on. Gays and lesbians are indeed as bad as higher taxes or impure art. And this is the case because power, subordination, and inequality are always nothing more than the occlusion of resistance, the mobilization against danger of forms of stabilization that make power seem self-motivated and self-sustaining.

Which of course, it isn't.

So remember: resistance is primary, and indeterminacy makes all the categories of the discourses of power contingent and remakeable.

Notes

1. Roughly modernized: "Queers are coming out of the closet."

2. Michel Foucault, *The History of Sexuality: Volume One, An Introduction* (New York: Random House, 1978).

3. Ibid., p. 37. Also, "The Discourse on Language," in *The Archaeology of Knowledge,* (New York: Harper, 1976).

4. Michel Foucault, *The Use of Pleasure, The History of Sexuality: Volume Two* (New York: Random House, 1985).

5. See Harald Patzer, *Die grieschen Knabenliebe* (Wiesbaden: Steiner Verlag, 1982) for a description of so-called Greek homosexuality as a heterosex-

ual initiation rite. His view is challenged by David Halperin in *One Hundred Years of Homosexuality: And Other Essays on Greek Love* (New York: Routledge, 1990). The modern confusion of Greek upper-class male sexual practices with "homosexuality," understood as freely chosen sexual or erotic relations between persons of the same biological sex, was initiated by Kenneth Dover in *Greek Homosexuality* (Cambridge: Harvard Univ. Press, 1978). By using the modern term "homosexuality," Dover makes it seem as if Greek practices resemble or are indistinguishable from gay life today. The pervasiveness of same-sex relations among a particular class of men simply means that the Greeks were more capable of a "sympathetic response to the open expression of homosexual desire" (p. 1).

6. See especially *Discipline and Punish* (New York: Pantheon, 1979).

7. See Louis Compton, *Byron and Greek Love: Homophobia in nineteenth-Century England* (Berkeley: Univ. of California Press, 1985), and Ed Cohen, *Talk on the Wilde Side: Toward a Genealogy of a Discourse on Male Sexualities* (Minneapolis: Univ. of Minnesota Press, 1992).

8. See Lawrence Stone, *The Family, Sex, and Marriage in England 1500–1800* (New York: Harper, 1979).

9. See Alan Bray, *Homosexuality in Renaissance England* (London: Gay Men's Press, 1984), and David Bergerson, *Royal Family, Royal Lovers: King James of England and Scotland* (Columbia: Univ. of Missouri Press, 1991).

10. See D. Cohen, *Law, Society, and Sexuality: The Enforcement of Morals in Classical Athens* (Cambridge: Harvard Univ. Press, 1991), and E. Cantarella, *Bisexuality in the Ancient World* (New London: Yale Univ. Press, 1992).

11. See Maud Gleason, "The Semiotics of Gender," in D. Halperin, et al., eds., *Before Sexuality: The Construction of Erotic Experience in the Ancient Greek World* (Princeton: Princeton Univ. Press, 1990), who points out that Foucault's description "of the nineteenth-century homosexual fits the cinaedus remarkably well" (p. 411). She notes that cinaedus "describes deviance, in its most specific sense referring to males who prefer to play a 'feminine' (receptive) role in intercourse with other men" (p. 396).

12. See especially Aristophanes, *Thermosozusiae*.

13. See *Problems* in *The Complete Works of Aristotle,* ed. Jonathon Barnes (Princeton: Princeton Univ. Press, 1984). Gleason notes that there was a pseudo-science of power/knowledge in the ancient world. Astrologers and physiogomists sought signs of effeminacy in men in such things as horoscopes (*Before Sexuality,* op. cit., p. 399).

14. On relative ages, see Cantarella, op. cit., pp. 36–42.

15. See Dover, op. cit., p. 149.

16. See Ann Carson, "Putting Her in Her Place: Woman, Dirt, and Desire," in Halperin, *Before Sexuality,* op. cit.

17. See John Winkler, *The Constraints of Desire: The Anthropology of Sex and Gender in Ancient Greece* (New York: Routledge, 1990).

18. See Paige Du Bois, *Sowing the Body: Psychoanalysis and Ancient Representations of Women* (Chicago: Univ. of Chicago Press, 1988); Roger Just, *Women in Athenian Law and Life,* (London: Routledge, 1989); Sarah Pomeroy, *Goddesses, Whores, Wives, and Slaves: Women in Classical Antiquity* (New York: Schocken, 1975); and, M. R. Lefkowitz and M. B. Fant, *Women's Life in Greece and Rome* (Baltimore: Johns Hopkins Univ. Press, 1982).

19. See Patzer, op. cit., and Cantarella, op. cit., p. 7.

20. Foucault, *The Use of Pleasure,* pp. 251–54. The less idealized side of the hazing ritual—the bargain struck between sexual servant and influence-provider—is well described by Xenophon in *The Anabasis.* The two halves of Plato's *Phaedrus* describe a move from a frank description of the exchange of sexual favors for political influence to Socrates' much more idealized account of "true love." It is an ideological path Foucault follows unquestioningly.

21. Such a reading (especially in the rather stellar work of David Halperin) offers the possibility that we are victimized by both heterosexual and homosexual gender-identity constructions. What awaits us beyond these constraints is a world of plural-gender possibilities in which objects and practices might float more freely. Such an ideal is indeed worth striving for, but was a Greek male multisexual experience a glitch in history, a hundred years of homosexuality, that provides us with a glimpse of such a future?

22. See Dover, op. cit., p. 185.

23. Ibid., p. 71

24. Halperin, in *One Hundred Years of Homosexuality,* op. cit., provides the clearest exposition of this dimension of Greek sexual life.

25. See Cantarella, op. cit., p. 51.

26. Halperin argues that men could set up households, but this contention is based on a questionable reading of a legal document that stipulates that "it shall not be lawful for Philisticus (the prospective husband) to bring home another wife in addition to Apollonia or to have a concubine or boy-lover" (*One Hundred Years,* op. cit., p. 34). Halperin concludes that the passage says that a man could "set up another household with his boyfriend," but the passage seems only to say that he might bring home a lover, not that he might set up another household.

27. *The New York Times,* May 26, 1993, p. 1.

28. As recounted in Xenophon, *The Cyropaedia.*

29. Cantarella disputes the accepted account of male sex by suggesting the possibility of anal penetration. See *Bisexuality,* op. cit.,p. 25.

30. Dover, op. cit., p. 52.

31. Jonathon Barnes, op. cit., pp. 1356–57.

7

The Politics of Postmetaphysics

Keith Topper

At the start of *Contingency, Irony, and Solidarity* Richard Rorty remarks that "ever since Hegel . . . historicist thinkers have tried to get beyond [the attempt to ground our practices in some theory of a common human nature]. They have denied that there is such a thing as 'human nature' or the 'deepest level of the self.' Their strategy has been to insist that socialization, and thus historical circumstance, goes all the way down—that there is nothing beneath socialization or prior to history which is definatory of the human."[1] This "historicist turn," he adds, has proven to be extremely therapeutic, for it "has helped free us, gradually but steadily, from theology and metaphysics—from the attempt to look for an escape from time and chance" (p. xiii).

While many poststructuralist, feminist and hermeneuticist writers would no doubt agree with these unabashedly historicist and "antiessentialist" sentiments,[2] it is nevertheless a disturbing fact that the most notorious champions of this stance have themselves been accused of embracing doctrines that were every bit as "metaphysical" as those of their predecessors. Nietzsche, for example, is commonly charged with transforming the will to power into a metaphysical doctrine, while Freud and Heidegger are often criticized for doing the same with libidinal impulses and "Being." And although we might dismiss at least some of these attacks as nothing more than allergic reactions to the very ideas of history and contingency, their frequency even among those familiar with and sympathetic to historicist currents of thought might be enough to make one wonder whether there is something ominously revealing in Heidegger's own claim that "a regard for metaphysics still prevails even in the intention to overcome metaphysics."[3] Perhaps, as this remark suggests, there is something about our very preoccupation with untangling the webs of past metaphysicians that implicates us in the creation of new, equally metaphysical, webs.

Now it is clearly beyond the scope of this chapter to offer any *general* answer to these broad and perplexing questions about the meaning, possibility, and significance of overcoming metaphysics. Nonetheless, these remarks raise important questions that might be explored in a more modest and circumscribed manner; in particular, questions about how the recognition of historicity affects the way one examines, understands, reinforces, extends, challenges, and at times transforms

cultural and political practices. In what follows, I will explore one quite provocative discussion of these issues, that contained principally in Rorty's *Contingency,
Irony, and Solidarity*. In this work, Rorty sketches a picture of what he calls a "postmetaphysical culture"—that is, a culture populated by those who no longer believe
"in an order beyond time and change which determines the point of human existence and establishes a hierarchy of responsibilities" (p. xv)—This picture foregrounds the images of both the "liberal ironist" and a "liberal utopia," ideals which
he maintains can be accommodated without being fused theoretically.

In so doing, however, I will examine not only Rorty's vision of such a culture, but also the tools and language he fashions for articulating it. In short, I will
argue that although his historicist and nominalist sympathies commit him to a
form of cultural criticism that demands the construction of "narratives which con-
nect the present with the past, on the one hand, and with utopian futures, on the
other" (p. xvi), Rorty's own discussions of political and "philosophical" issues frequently do just the opposite. Instead of opening up new clearings in our present
cultural and political discourse, these descriptive narratives tend to evade or mask
issues that are essential for understanding our relationship to the past and the future, and hence also for disclosing what is at stake in current cultural and political practices. This, I will further propose, can in turn be traced back to his own
rather narrow understanding of what is involved in overcoming both metaphysics
and "systematic philosophy." Such an overcoming involves something more than
a shift away from epistemic foundationalism and toward an abstract recognition
of time and chance. It further involves a detailed description of how practices develop, what is at stake in their current configuration, and what possibilities exist
for preserving, extending and/or challenging them. Unfortunately, Rorty's own
narratives, in large part because they embrace almost exclusively a "global" rather
than "local" historicism,[4] tend to conceal crucial issues of power and privilege, issues that must be confronted if one hopes to clarify the nature of one's individual
and collective self-understandings.

I

Rorty's sketch of both the liberal ironist and liberal utopia emerges directly from
his opening chapters on the "contingency" of language, selfhood, and liberal community. He begins this discussion by noting that for almost two centuries philosophy has been divided into two competing factions, each with its own distinctive
understanding of science, truth, and philosophical discourse. One faction, which
might be called the "scientistic philosophers," remains devoted to the Enlightenment project and thus identifies philosophy with the defense of science and reason
against the forces of superstition, religion, and unreason. For them, this struggle
remains very much alive, having now taken the form of a conflict between those
who identify reason with the idea that truth is "found" rather than "made," and

those who adopt the "thoroughly misleading" view that truth is somehow "made," "invented," or "socially constructed." The other faction, which might be labelled the "proto-pragmatist philosophers," is animated instead by a recognition that the physical sciences' world picture offers neither moral instruction nor spiritual solace. These thinkers, who generally draw their intellectual and moral inspiration from figures like the innovative artist and political utopian, reject the scientistic suggestion that science is "the paradigmatic human activity," as well as the closely related idea that natural science is the place where humans encounter "a 'hard,' nonhuman reality" (p. 4). Rather, they view science as one form of human activity among many, one which is useful for some purposes—notably prediction and control—but largely irrelevant for others—for example, engagement in moral reflection, or in common civic activity.

Although Rorty's sympathies lie clearly with the latter group, he suggests that the initial attempts—principally by the German idealists—to give some "clear sense" to the inchoate notion that humans "make truth rather than find it" were derailed by the very way in which they chose to engage their opponents. Rather than challenging or simply dropping the foundationalist project of justifying beliefs and practices through appeals to some "intrinsic nature to be expressed or represented," idealists instead made the mistake of overthrowing one species of foundationalism only to enshrine yet another, one now based on the idea that "mind, spirit, the depths of the human self" have "an intrinsic nature—one that could be known by a kind of nonempirical super science called philosophy" (p. 4).

While generally hoping to avoid conventional philosophical argument—which, he tells us often, is no longer the most effective instrument of change and progress—Rorty tries to redescribe the idea that "truth is made, not found" in a way that bypasses the familiar criticisms of German idealism. The initial phase in this process involves an attack on representationalist construals of reality as well as a reformulation of the traditional vision of the relation between language, truth, and reality. Rorty begins by suggesting that we distinguish "between the claim that the world is out there and the claim that truth is out there" (pp. 4–5). "Truth," he maintains, "is a property of sentences" (p. 21), and since sentences cannot exist independently of vocabularies, nor can vocabularies exist independently of human beings, truths cannot be human discoveries, but only human creations. "The world," on the other hand, "is not our creation" (p. 5). It "is out there," it includes causes and effects that operate independently of human mental states, but the world "as such" is not a candidate for truth or falsehood. Only *descriptions* of the world are such candidates. Accordingly, since these descriptions are always necessarily descriptions-in-some-vocabulary, and since, as Wittgenstein argues, the concepts of "choice" and "criteria" are applicable only to comparisons between sentences, but not between vocabularies-as-wholes, then the idea of finding some neutral ground from which one can adjudicate the claims of competing vocabularies is equally out of place.

Rorty suggests that if this Davidsonian/Wittgensteinian account of the relation (or lack thereof) between language, truth, and world is sound, then we are further obliged to jettison not only the idea that language is a vehicle of representation, but also the even more pervasive belief that language is a "medium," and that it has some "fixed" task to perform. All of these ideas, he suggests, are offspring of our fidelity to the notion of an "intrinsic nature," one that language can and should represent and/or express. But this idea that there is something external to our vocabularies that serves as a standard for judging all possible vocabularies is just what the foregoing account seems to render incoherent. Rather, Rorty contends, we should abandon the idea that language has any intrinsic purpose or function and should regard it instead as "sheer contingency," as purely "a product of time and chance" (p. 22).

Importantly, however, this acknowledgment of the "sheer contingency" of language yields a similarly nonessentialist view of both selfhood and community. According to Rorty, there is simply no way of dropping the reality-appearance distinction without also dropping the separation of how we talk from who we are (p. 20). In the case of selfhood, dropping these distinctions issues in the Nietzschian view that selfhood should be understood as an activity of self-creation rather than a process of discovery. Instead of searching for some "universal impress" that binds one with the rest of humanity, one should strive to become what Harold Bloom calls a "strong poet": to create a language that articulates what is distinctive and contingent about oneself, thereby demonstrating that one is not a mere "copy or replica," a prisoner of inherited language games. In the case of community, dropping the reality-appearance distinction means discarding the deeply entrenched assumption "that a form of cultural life is no stronger than its philosophical foundations" (p. 53). Rather, it implies that the justification of a collective form of life is "simply a matter of historical comparison with other attempts at social organization—those of the past and those envisioned by utopias" (p. 53).

This description of the "sheer contingency" of language, selfhood, and community is undeniably attractive. It suggests that by casting aside the burdensome weight of philosophical foundationalism, we can not only become free to create our own identity, but also to preserve the benefits of a liberal society (which, not incidentally, include the freedom to engage in projects of self-creation). Moreover, Rorty's call for the invention and proliferation of new metaphors and vocabularies, for a spirit of exploration, free play, and "openness to otherness," is also extremely attractive. This celebration of the human capacity for transformation and self-creation is both appealing and potentially liberating, for it suggests that traditional limitations on personal and collective self-definition are ultimately nothing more than well-painted facades. Thus, if we acquiesce to them, we do so only because they have some significance for *us,* not because they are intrinsic to the human condition.

While I agree that the above account has a genuine allure, I submit that once one moves from this rarified sketch into more concrete issues regarding the forms of interplay between different vocabularies, the possibilities and limits of self-creation and imaginative potential, and the role, if any, that power plays in these questions, one begins to discover disturbing aporias in Rorty's account. More specifically, I shall argue that there is an unconsciously ironic element in Rorty's own narrative: that although it is designed to release us from the Procrustean bed of foundationalism and conventional philosophy, this narrative is in important ways still shaped by them. This, I maintain, accounts in part for Rorty's enchantment with a particularly problematic form of nonfoundationalism, one that is not necessarily dynamic, liberating, edifying, or even playful.

Perhaps these issues can be defined more sharply if we begin by examining what is clearly *the* connecting thread running throughout Rorty's opening chapters, if not the narrative as a whole. This is the rather elusive notion of "contingency." For Rorty, the term "contingency" typically stands at one end of a set of oppositions whose other term is variously "necessary," "essential," "universal," or "intrinsic." These latter terms, as I indicated above, are themselves tightly intertwined with notions of a common "human nature," a *telos,* a divine order or some other principle of legitimacy that is privileged precisely because its status is independent of any particular historical location or social practices. At a minimum, then, Rorty's invocation of contingency implies a denial of the idea that there is anything "'beneath' socialization or prior to history which is definatory of the human" (p. xiii).

Unfortunately, this in itself is not terribly informative, for it is at best a rather general and purely negative construal. When, however, Rorty does speak of contingency in a more specific manner, he typically uses the term in one of two ways. First, he frequently uses it in a way that links the term very closely with notions of novelty, innovation, originality, and creativity. In these instances—which are common in his chapter, "The Contingency of Selfhood"—contingency is deployed to pinpoint some domain or space that is devoid of any immanent nature or logic and therefore also open to innovation and transformation. Here contingency represents the positive possibilities inherent in the recognition of historicity: because our inherited practices and self-understandings are not ontologically fixed but are instead socially and historically constituted, they can—although never all at once—be questioned, redescribed, and transformed.

On the other hand, Rorty frequently uses the term contingency in a second, quite different manner, one where it is identified not with the powers of human innovation, but with notions of "chance," "luck," "accident," or "fortuitousness." This connection is made explicit in a number of different passages; for example, when he suggests that "progress results from the accidental coincidence of a private obsession with a public need" (p. 37), and when he borrows Philip Larkin's metaphor of the "blind impress" (ch. 2).[5] It is, however, also *implicit* in Rorty's radically decentered conception of human subjectivity, as well as in the periodic recurrence of tragic and haunting passages on the theme of human powerlessness. Whether explicit or implicit, the meaning of contingency in all of these passages remains essentially the same: it implies forces that shape our lives, yet are beyond our ability to predict or control.

What is interesting about all of this is the way in which it accents Rorty's own equivocations regarding the possibilities and limits of individual and social action. As one can see from his dual use of this term, Rorty vacillates between a vision of human action in which our transformative capacities are limited only by the powers of our imagination and one where we are every bit as incapable of directing events as we are in the most essentialist and totalizing of philosophical systems. Here Rorty finds himself locked in the same dichotomy between voluntarism and determinism that characterizes so many metaphysical and foundationalist enterprises.

In fact, however, neither of these construals are typical of those situations which characterize the better part of our everyday lives. Our capacity for imagination is *not* unlimited; rather, it is partly constituted by, and therefore also partly constrained by, our prevailing social practices and discourses. These practices and discourses not only privilege certain imaginative and creative efforts over others, but they also partly constitute the category of "novelty," thus distinguishing it both from "the old" and from eccentricity, insanity, and the like. Conversely, it may be true that there are countless unanticipated and uncontrollable events that in one way or another shape the course of our lives, but precisely *what* effect they have on us and *how* we respond to them is neither fully predetermined nor entirely a matter of "chance." Rather, these things are delimited both by material forces and by the horizons of our individual and social self-understandings, horizons which, importantly, simultaneously make meaning possible and limit the possible domain of meaning.

Rorty, of course, is not entirely oblivious to these problems. He does acknowledge at points that our creative capacities are not unlimited, and that even purely chance events can be understood and confronted in different ways. He tells us, for example, that there are "no fully Nietzschean lives . . . no lives which are not largely parasitical on an un-redescribed past and dependent on the charity of as yet unborn generations" (p. 42). Unfortunately, Rorty fails to appreciate fully the social and political implications of this insight. For if indeed novelty and imaginative capacities are themselves partly constituted by social practices and official discourses, and if, as I have indicated above, these practices and discourses place boundaries upon what is and is not intelligible, on who has the right to speak, on what counts as a problem and what counts as a solution to some problem, then questions about the pursuit of and capacity for self-creation and change are not just personal questions, nor are they just questions about whether we should "drop" worn-out vocabularies and metaphors in favor of newer, more useful ones. Indeed, precisely because what counts as a "worn-out" or "useful" vocabulary is itself partly constituted by our social practices and official discourses, questions about self-creation, change, and the usefulness of vocabularies all presuppose a specific social, political, and ideological context, one that cannot be erased even if it is not recognized.

What I am suggesting is that Rorty's construal of contingency, although intended to open up a clearing for pluralism, novelty, play, self-creation, and human solidarity, tends instead to pass over or mask just those forces that not only limit the range of possible projects, but also structure the level, quality, and possibility of participation in our cultural conversation. If we ask what features within Rorty's narrative encourage this problematic construal of contingency, we find at least two interrelated sources of significance. One, which will be discussed momentarily, derives from Rorty's understanding of politics and the political, while the second is, strictly speaking, more "methodological" and concerns the relation, or absence of relation, between theories and narratives, and those practices they seek to inform.

To begin with the second issue, one of the most puzzling features of Rorty's book is the apparent gap between, on the one hand, his *formal* pronouncements regarding the heuristic value of particular genres and, on the other hand, the *content* of his own writings. Formally, Rorty tells us that certain sorts of books are particularly "relevant to our relations with others, to helping us to notice the effects of our actions on other people" (p. 141). These are, first, those books "which help us to see the effects of social practices and institutions on others" (p. 141) and, second, "those which help us see the effects of our private idiosyncracies on others" (p. 141). Beyond these very general categories Rorty places few restrictions—apart from the stipulation that theories and treatises are *not* well suited for these tasks—on the types of books that might illuminate these issues. Apparently anything from "the reports . . . of government commissions" to novels like *Sister Carrie* and *Black Boy* are possible candidates for moral and political edification. In accordance with his antitheoretical, antiuniversalist posture, however, he emphasizes the import of narratives that focus on particular exemplars or engage in what Clifford Geertz calls "thick description." He observes, for example, that "ethnographies," "concrete examples," "detailed historical narratives," and "detailed description of what other people are like and . . . redescription of what we are like" (p. xvi) are all particularly effective ways of enlarging our moral sympathies and political understanding.

What is most significant here is not just the observation itself—which is, after all, fairly common among those who have rejected transcendental theorizing as a viable option—but rather the disjunction between these recommendations and the substance of Rorty's own work. For within the corpus of Rorty's writings there is almost *no* "detailed description" of "the effects of our social practices and institutions on others," nor any "detailed historical narratives" mapping the genesis and effects of those practices. In fact, it is striking that although Rorty acknowledges the existence of deep and disturbing social problems [he speaks, for example, of "the unending hopelessness and misery of the lives of the young blacks in American cities" (p. 191)], he never describes in any detail the broader context or "social field" in which those problems are embedded, nor does he locate particular social practices that contribute to and sustain these problems.

This failure to offer any detailed description of the social field or particular social practices leads inevitably to a number of difficulties. It sustains, for example, Rorty's problematic construal of contingency. As I have already argued, when he makes comments to the effect that "man is always free to choose new descriptions (for, among other things, himself),"[6] he seems on the verge of adopting a rather extreme form of voluntarism, one where, as one commentator has put it, we are "always free to choose *any* description."[7] This, of course, is a position that appears reasonable *if* we examine only the most palpable and formal types of social constraints. But once we begin observing in detail the role that social practices and privileged discourses play in *constraining* and *directing,* even if not *determining* and *compelling* our descriptions and redescriptions, voluntarism appears both facile and complacent.

Perhaps even more important, however, is the way in which Rorty's reluctance to examine the complicated interweavings of past and present social practices deprives him of any resources for either assessing the costs of those practices or for indicating how they might be extended, criticized, or challenged. All of these endeavors presuppose that one first has some idea of how discursive and nondiscursive practices interact, of the various privileges and distinctions they enshrine, and of the role they play in constituting individual and collective self-understandings. This, of course, does not imply a return to theory, or to totalizing conceptions of society, but it does imply an empiricism of sorts; namely, a willingness to examine closely how these practices developed, what their effects are, and how their benefits and burdens are parsed among different individuals and groups in society. In this regard, the recurring theme of powerlessness, along with the corresponding admission that we "have no clear idea of what to work for" (p. 182), should not be understood as being out of tune with the more celebratory temper of Rorty's narrative. Rather, both motifs should be seen as natural consequences flowing from the type of narrative Rorty constructs, one which—ironically—implicitly shares the theorist's and traditional philosopher's animus toward all forms of empiricism and detailed historical and sociological description.

II

Let us turn now to Rorty's postmetaphysical vision of liberalism. Rorty's reformulation of classical liberal thought proceeds, as we might expect, through a nonrationalist, nonuniversalist redescription of the hopes and aims of a liberal society. He begins by noting that this utopia is inhabited in part by a group of intellectuals whom he labels "liberal ironists." These figures are liberals because—following Judith Shklar's definition[8]—they "think that cruelty is the worst thing we do" (p. xv). They are ironists because their acute sense of historical contingency will not permit them the luxury of believing that their own "final vocabulary"—which is Rorty's chosen phrase for describing those foundationless yet authoritative (for those who share them) expressions, terms, and concepts through which we articulate and justify our own most basic goals, aspirations, and convictions—is itself anything other than contingent. Recognizing the arbitrariness and contingency of their own final vocabularies, ironists, Rorty tells us, never become too deeply infatuated with them. They have commitments, but these commitments are always wed "with a sense of the contingency of their own commitment" (p. 61). Constantly "aware that the terms in which they describe themselves are subject to change," ironists are "never quite able to take themselves seriously" (pp. 73–74). Instead, they continually entertain and experiment with other vocabularies, hoping "by this continual process of redescription, to make the best selves for ourselves that we can" (p. 80).

Now within this utopia where "ironism, in the relevant sense, is universal" (p. xv), Rorty insists on what is seemingly a very *unironic* demand: a demand for "a firm distinction between the public and the private" (p. 83). Irony, he suggests, is a useful and perhaps necessary tool in the quest for self-creation and autonomy. The ongoing process of questioning, redescribing, and reweaving our inherited vocabularies, of exploring and creating strange and novel ones, is, moreover, clearly central to the development of an ever more autonomous, self-created final vocabulary. At the same time, however, Rorty inveighs repeatedly against the suggestion that irony may have some productive *public* role to play. "Irony," he states, "seems inherently a private matter," something that "is of little public use" (pp. 83, 120). Furthermore, he warns that when figures like Nietzsche and Heidegger do seek to bring their irony into the public domain, they become "at best useless and at worst dangerous" (p. 68).

This injunction banning the ironist from the public corridors of liberal society seems at first glance oddly out of tune with Rorty's earlier glorification of irony as the principal catalyst in the process of self-creation. If irony is so crucial to the search for individual autonomy, why then is it useless if not dangerous in the public realm? In answering this question Rorty again reminds his readers of liberalism's primary vigil, suggesting that public ironism may well contravene the liberal imperative to avoid cruelty, albeit cruelty of a particular sort: the nonphysical but devastating cruelty embodied in acts of humiliation. As Rorty explains: "ironism, as I have defined it, results from awareness of the power of redescription" (p. 89). The ironist thus recognizes that even our most deeply valued convictions are at bottom only a "tissue of contingencies," and hence are at any moment susceptible to redescription. This, however, is something she does not share with most of her fellow humans. Most people, Rorty asserts, have no interest in being redescribed; they simply want to be accepted "on their own terms—taken seriously just as they are and just as they talk" (p. 89). But when the ironist proceeds to tell her fellow citizens that their final vocabularies—those fundamental words that both anchor and animate one's life—are "weightless," "quaint," "worthless," or "futile," the result is often not just discomfort, but humiliation. As Rorty explains:

The best way to cause people long-lasting pain is to humiliate them by making the things that seemed most important to them look futile, obsolete, and
powerless. Consider what happens when a child's precious possessions—the
little things around which he weaves fantasies that make him a little different from all other children—are redescribed as "trash," and thrown away.
Or consider what happens when these possessions are made to look ridiculous alongside the possessions of another, richer, child. . . . The redescribing
ironist, by threatening one's final vocabulary, and thus one's ability to make
sense of oneself in one's own terms rather than her's, suggests that one's self
and one's world are futile, obsolete, *powerless*. Redescription often humiliates. (p. 90)

In addition, Rorty holds that the ironist's redescriptions are especially hu-
miliating because, unlike the metaphysician, ironists cannot claim that they "free"
or "educate" their audience, that they bring that audience closer to their "true
selves" or "real interests." As Rorty puts it, "what the ironist is being blamed for
is not an inclination to humiliate, but an inability to empower" (p. 91). Rorty, then,
suggests that by the very act of inserting her redescriptions into the public conversation, the ironist potentially humiliates others and thus violates the liberal injunction to avoid acts of cruelty. For this reason, irony must remain a purely private affair, something that is useful for the private pursuit of individual autonomy,
but publicly inconsistent with the moral dictates of liberalism.

While Rorty is surely correct in maintaining that the ironist cannot claim
that her redescriptions are empowering in the sense of bringing us closer to our
"true selves," or in revealing some "deep truth" about a culture's social practices,
this still leaves unexplored a further possibility: that redescriptions *may* be empowering in the sense of clarifying or making explicit some issues about which one
remains inarticulate, or by offering an interpretation of one's experience that
makes a more effective practice possible. Indeed, I would submit that something
of this sort *is* at work in Foucault's genealogies, or in Pierre Bourdieu's examination of the "habitus" of the academy and other social-political institutions.[9] In both
of these cases one is shown in detail how particular institutions and practices come
to acquire widespread social acceptance or legitimacy, and on this basis inaugurate
a system of classifications, privileges, and relations of domination that themselves
tend to produce various effects; for example, certain individuals or groups are generally excluded from participation in certain discourses, from membership in certain occupations, or from access to certain positions of institutional power. Moreover, these institutions and practices, although not totalitarian in any typical sense
are nevertheless infused with power, and might be considered cruel as well.

In bringing these practices and their effects to light, writers such as Foucault
and Bourdieu are neither discovering some innate nature nor representing some
independent object. Rather, they are removing distortions embedded in com-
monsense understandings of these practices and institutions, and in this sense their

redescriptions have an educative and perhaps even empowering function. To exclude them from public conversation is thus both to exclude a possible means of identifying cruelty, and of assessing the adequacy of our institutions and practices.

Rorty, of course, would almost certainly respond that such an argument is merely another thinly disguised attempt to smuggle in some notion of "criteria" that can arbitrate between the claims of competing vocabularies. As we have seen, however, appeals to "criteria" are appropriate only within vocabularies, not between them. Thus, to say that one description is "less distorted" than another is to confuse questions about the possibility of arbitrating disputes within vocabularies with questions about the possibility of arbitrating disputes between them.

But here I want to suggest that Rorty's own account tends to confuse issues about the possibility of adjudicating such disputes. For when he examines such issues, he tends to focus only on two questions: first, questions regarding the relation between vocabularies and independent objects, and, second, questions about the possibility of arbitrating between discrete, self-contained vocabularies. Rorty maintains that in the first question issues of truth and falsehood are out of place, while in the second arbitration is impossible. Although these claims have themselves been the subject of much acrimonious dispute, what is important for my argument is that neither of these situations is typical of most contemporary social or political conflicts. In most social or political controversies the antagonists are not making claims about the status of independent objects (they are usually engaged in disputes about social practices, which clearly do not exist independently of human beings and their social self-interpretations), nor are the conflicting parties articulating their concerns in entirely discrete moral and political vocabularies—in which case it would be impossible to recognize them *as* moral or political vocabularies. For example, when nonliberal feminists reproach the rigid segregation and opposition of the public and private realms in liberal thought and practice, they do not articulate their criticisms from within a vocabulary or set of moral concerns that are entirely unconnected to liberalism. Indeed, as Carole Pateman has rightly pointed out, "neither liberalism nor feminism is conceivable without some conception of individuals as free and equal beings, emancipated from the hierarchical bonds of traditional society."[10] In this sense, both liberals and nonliberal feminists "share a common origin,"[11] one that serves potentially as a starting point for discourse about the meaning and import of the public/private dichotomy. Moreover, most liberals and feminists share other commitments as well—for example, a commitment to the principle of equal citizenship, that is, the idea that at a minimum all citizens are to be accorded certain basic rights and opportunities. Here also one finds genuine overlap between the two vocabularies, however different they may be in other respects.

While the existence of partially overlapping but nevertheless distinct vocabularies clearly offers a basis for dialogue and arbitration of social and political conflicts, Rorty equivocates on the question of how much and what kind of overlap is required for liberalism's public discourse. Sometimes Rorty suggests that only some minimal shared overlap among a plurality of different final vocabularies is required; he says at one point that shared words such as "'kindness' or 'decency' or 'dignity'" (p. 93) are sufficient for sustaining liberalism's public discourse. However, while this minimal overlap would seem to satisfy Rorty's desire for a public discourse that is highly inclusive, it is unclear what makes it specifically liberal. Certainly these minimal commitments do not logically entail fealty to the "thicker" features of Rorty's ideal liberal polity, for example, a commitment to a bifurcated conception of the public and the private spheres, or to a negative conception of liberty. After all, such words are common not only to the final vocabularies of liberals like Isaiah Berlin, but also to socialists, feminists of various stripes, the supporters of participatory democracy, conservatives, and even monarchists.

On the other hand, if a commitment to an entirely negative vision of liberty, a public/private dichotomy, nonintervention in economic affairs, and the like are taken to be constitutive of a liberal polity, then the public discourse of liberalism must unavoidably be monotone and highly exclusive. It must, in other words, be a discourse that is unreceptive to all of those voices—be they the voices of most feminists, of the proponents of participatory democracy, of Foucault, or whomever—who fail to subscribe to the basic credos of Rorty's liberalism. Indeed, as he remarks at various points, a liberal society—or indeed *any* society on Rorty's view—is not one that can be ironic about its own commitment to liberalism (p. 87). This means not only that liberalism must be taken "seriously," but also and more importantly that all public discourse must be conducted from within the vocabulary of liberalism. Competing voices are allowed to participate in the public discourse of liberal society, but only if their own voice is first "*assimilated* into a liberal, reformist political culture" (p. 64).[12]

This equivocation between two visions of liberalism's public discourse—(1) a more inclusive vision which is not distinctively liberal and which may, in the course of "free and open encounters" (p. 68), ultimately lead to a questioning of some basic features and categories of liberalism, and (2) a more exclusive vision, one which sustains those same basic features and categories at the expense of pluralism, difference, and perhaps even the minimization of cruelty—is, I believe, emblematic of a deeper conflict in Rorty's thought, namely, a conflict about liberalism itself. As I suggested earlier, Rorty's narrative is one that moves between celebratory declarations of liberalism's distinctive virtues and remarkable capacity for self-correction—he says, for example, that "contemporary liberal society already contains the institutions for its own improvement" (p. 63)—and contrapuntal passages evoking a sense of powerlessness, despair, pathos, and fear.[13] The former passages represent Rorty's conviction that whatever its cultural and institutional limitations, liberalism is not only "the best that we have done," but is also, with the death of Marxism as a concrete alternative, the only viable option available today. Any reform of liberalism must therefore start from within the vocabulary of liberalism, and must be consistent with the constitutive features of liberalism. By contrast, the latter passages reflect Rorty's acknowledgment that the gap between liberal ideals and the frequently depressing realities of life for many members of liberal states is very real and often ethically abhorrent. However, because he rejects all alternatives to classical liberalism as cures that are worse than the disease, his only option is to purify public discourse by making all nonliberal vocabularies by definition private.[14] The result, as I have argued, is a narrative that simultaneously embraces *privatized* diversity, idiosyncracy, and difference, yet excludes from *public* discourse all nonliberal idioms.

These tensions and equivocations are exacerbated by Rorty's failure to examine in any detail a term he links regularly and unproblematically with liberalism—democracy. The idea that the democratic element in liberal democracy may in some ways conflict with classical liberalism, yet must nevertheless be granted equal weight, is one Rorty never takes up, even though it may offer a promising alternative to the two visions of public discourse that Rorty shifts between rather uneasily. Democracy, understood not only as a set of institutional arrangements for insuring regular and popular elections of legislatures and executives, but as a commitment to equal participation in public discourse, is clearly something thicker and more substantial than the few shared words that Rorty points to in his minimalist conception of liberalism's shared public vocabulary. Moreover, this enlarged sense of democracy entails not only a willingness to view others as fellow human beings, but a commitment to insuring that those fellow human beings have an equal voice in articulating their public concerns and in shaping the outcome of public deliberations.

Moreover, granting equal weight to the democratic element of liberal democracy has the advantage of counterbalancing some of the weaknesses of Rorty's minimalist conception. As we have observed, Rorty's minimalist conception of public discourse is intended to insure that public discourse is indeed discourse and not simply a cacophony of separate and untranslatable vocabularies and voices. In order to insure this, people must, Rorty contends, possess some willingness and capacity to enter "into other people's fantasies as well as their own" (p. 93), and Rorty's minimalist conception is designed specifically to provide a common basis for public deliberation. The problem, however, is that while kindness, decency, and dignity may be indispensible ingredients in the shared final vocabulary of any public and democratic discourse, they are not sufficient for it. As the victims of what might be called "soft paternalism" surely understand, kindness and decency do not insure either genuine mutuality or democratic politics. Indeed, it is not at all unusual to encounter individuals who are quite kind, decent, and even magnanimous, but are nevertheless unable to treat those unlike themselves as genuine equals. To counter the effects of this soft paternalism in public discourse, it is necessary to have a shared final vocabulary that is richer than the few spare terms recommended by Rorty.

On the other hand, granting equal weight to democracy and the idea of equal participation involves the possibility that terms and categories linked conceptually and historically to liberalism may ultimately become subject to public debate and revision. This is precisely what Rorty fears, and it is for this reason that he erects barriers excluding ironists such as Foucault and Heidegger from the arena of public deliberation. While these fears are undeniably well motivated—a perusal of the history of antiliberal polities in the twentieth century is enough to make any student of politics appreciate the merits of basic liberal safeguards against the incursions of statist tyranny—it is far from obvious that the most effective way to preserve those individual liberties and freedoms typically associated with liberalism is to privilege liberalism at the expense of democracy. As Benjamin Barber has argued, "the forces that created the greatest pressures on the liberty of individuals in the twentieth century are . . . the consequence not of too much democracy and too little liberalism but of too little democracy and too much liberalism. Fascism in Germany was preceded by the Weimar Republic's wan liberalism; and the authoritarian personality would seem to be at least in part the product of deracination."[15] If this is the case, then Rorty's safeguards on liberalism's public discourse may have the uninteded effect of subverting rather than strengthening liberalism's most appealing features.

Finally, granting equal weight to the democratic element of liberal democracy allows one to view commonality itself in a different light, that is, as not only a precondition but also a product of public deliberation. As I have shown, Rorty's preoccupation with commonality revolves exclusively around questions of how one defines the boundaries of inclusion into public discourse—who can speak whose speech can (or must) be heard, and so on. In focusing solely on these particular questions, he presumes that commonality is never the offspring or aim of politics, but only a precondition of political life. Commonality, however, is never in any strong sense the starting point for politics, simply because where it already exists there is no need for politics or public deliberation. Rather, commonality is typically something that is achieved or disclosed *through* public discourse, or is a matter of what Barber has identified as *"willing common action in the absence of common ground."*[16] It is, therefore, archetypically a product of a dynamic process of collaboration in situations of conflict, not of establishing a priori limits to engagement in that process. In this respect, it is also much closer to the spirit of J. S. Mill, who recognized that without conflict and challenge, liberalism's most cherished principles would eventually become dead dogmas, neither esteemed nor understood.

III

To return to the questions posed at the outset, I hope to have shown that moving "beyond metaphysics" involves something more than just overcoming foundationalism or theoretical hegemony. It also means creating a space for the detailed description of our institutions and practices, of how they develop, of the effects they produce, and of the issues to which they give form. In addition, it means recognizing that the absence of an Archimedean point implies that issues of power are always at stake in constituting, sustaining, or transforming our social practices. Rorty's own work is a testament to the fact that one can all too easily combine sophisticated views about epistemology and philosophical foundationalism with political positions that are at best misconceived and at times self-stultifying. If we hope to avoid these problems, perhaps the approach to take would be to combine postmetaphysical insights on the status of knowledge not simply with "thin," global stories about the past, but with detailed histories of practices and power.

Notes

1. Richard Rorty, *Contingency, Irony, and Solidarity* (New York: Cambridge University Press, 1989), p. xiii. Hereafter all references to this book will be placed in parentheses directly after the relevant passage or quotation.

2. I have in mind writers such as William Connolly, Jacques Derrida, Hubert Dreyfus, Michel Foucault, Donna Haraway, Ernesto Laclau, Chantal Mouffe, Charles Taylor, and Iris Marion Young, all of whom claim links to historicist and antiessentialist traditions. While none of these figures would endorse without caveats Rorty's pragmatic and political vision, they nevertheless share his desire for a historicist, "postfoundationalist" form of social and political thought. See, for example, William E. Connolly, *Politics and Ambiguity* (Madison: University of Wisconsin Press, 1987), esp. ch. 8; Jacques Derrida, *Of Grammatology* (Baltimore: Johns Hopkins University Press, 1982); Hubert L. Dreyfus, *Being-in-the-World* (Cambridge, Mass.: MIT Press, 1991); Michel Foucault, "Nietzsche, Genealogy, History," in *Language, Counter-Memory, Practice* (Ithaca, N.Y.: Cornell University Press, 1981), pp. 139–64; Donna Haraway, *Simians, Cyborgs, and Women* (New York: Routledge, 1991); Ernesto Laclau, *New Reflections on the Revolution of Our Time* (New York: Verso, 1990); Ernesto Laclau and Chantal Mouffe, *Hegemony and Socialist Strategy* (London: Verso, 1985); Chantal Mouffe, "Feminism, Citizenship, and Radical Democratic Politics," in Judith Butler and Joan Scott, eds., *Feminists Theorize the Political* (New York: Routledge, 1992), pp. 369–84; Charles Taylor, *Philosophy and the Human Sciences: Philosophical Papers,* vol. 2 (New York: Cambridge University Press, 1985); and Iris Marion Young, *Justice and the Politics of Difference* (Princeton: Princeton University Press, 1990).

3. Martin Heidegger, *On Time and Being* (New York: Harper and Row, 1972), p. 24.

4. I borrow these terms from Ian Hacking, "Two Kinds of 'New Historicism' for Philosophers," *New Literary History* 21 (Winter 1990): 343–64.

5. For an even more explicit link between contingency and "chance events," see his "possible world" sketch of Heidegger's life in "Diary," *London Review of Books* 12 (February 8, 1990), p. 21.

6. Richard Rorty, *Philosophy and the Mirror of Nature* (Princeton: Princeton University Press, 1979), p. 362n.

7. Roy Bhaskar, *Reclaiming Reality* (London and New York: Verso, 1989), pp. 176–77.

8. For Shklar's own powerful discussion of the idea that cruelty is "unconditionally the *summum malum*" (p. 8), see *Ordinary Vices* (Cambridge, Mass.: Harvard University Press, 1984).

9. See especially Foucault's later works, such as *Discipline and Punish* (New York: Vintage, 1979) and *The History of Sexuality, Volume 1: An Introduction* (New York: Vintage, 1980). On Bourdieu, see especially *Homo Academicus* (Stanford: Stanford University Press, 1988) and *La Noblesse d'Etat* (Paris: Les Editions de Minuit, 1989).

10. Carole Pateman, "Feminist Critiques of the Public/Private Dichotomy," in *The Disorder of Women* (Stanford: Stanford University Press, 1989), p. 118.

11. Ibid.

12. Emphasis added.

13. In addition to the passages already quoted, see his comments in *Objectivity, Relativism, and Truth: Philosophical Papers,* vol. 1 (New York: Cambridge University Press, 1991), where he remarks: "This is not to say that there is any particular reason for optimism about America, or the rich North Atlantic democracies generally, in the year in which I write (1990). Several of these democracies, including the United States, are presently under the control of an increasingly greedy and selfish middle class—a class which continually elects cynical demagogues willing to deprive the weak of hope in order to promise tax cuts to their constituents. If this process goes on for another generation, the countries in which it happens will be barbarized" (p. 15).

14. This point is also made by Nancy Fraser. See "Solidarity or Singularity? Richard Rorty between Romanticism and Technocracy," in Alan Malachowski, ed., *Reading Rorty* (Cambridge, Mass.: Basil Blackwell, 1990), p. 315. Unlike the discussion here, however, Fraser doesn't accent the ways in which Rorty equivocates between two distinctive visions of liberalism's public discourse.

15. Benjamin Barber, "Liberal Democracy and the Costs of Consent," in Nancy L. Rosenblum, ed., *Liberalism and the Moral Life* (Cambridge, Mass.: Harvard University Press, 1989), p. 56.

16. Ibid., p. 63.

PART II
FROM THEORY TO CULTURE

8

Rodney King and the Awkward Pause
Interpretation and Politics

William Chaloupka

People I just want to say . . . can we all get along? Can we get along? Can we stop making it horrible for the older people and the kids? . . . It's just not right. It's not right, and it's not going to change anything.

We'll get our justice. They've won the battle but they haven't won the war. We will have our day in court and that's all we want. . . . I'm neutral. I love everybody. I love people of color. . . . I'm not like they're . . . making me out to be.

We've got to quit. We've got to quit. . . . I can understand the first upset in the first two hours after the verdict, but to go on, to keep going on like this, and to see a security guard shot on the ground, it's just not right. It's just not right because those people will never go home to their families again. And I mean, please we can get along here. We all can get along. We've just got to, just got to. We're all stuck here for awhile. . . . Let's try to work it out. Let's try to work it out.[1]

Let's try, indeed. There is quite a bit of working out to do. Rodney King's odd call to peace—added to the videotape that was, indirectly, its progenitor—forms the background for one of the signal events of the early 1990s. But what to make of it?

Judith Butler provides a useful start, at the beginning of the collection *Reading Rodney King: Reading Urban Uprising*.[2] The King events, despite striking an exceptionally immediate response in many people, and despite having a vividly graphic quality, demand, more than anything else, the skills and perseverance of a reader, an interpreter. The King matter—an unlikely candidate for such a role—confirms interpretation. That is to say, it confirms the interdisciplinary and postmodern approaches that best understand it.

Like most viewers, Butler *knows* what she *saw:* "the video shows a man being brutally beaten." And she knows that this has been an exercise in contested and negotiable interpretations, from very early on. The trial of the police officers was a festival of contested readings: "How could this video be used as evidence that the body being beaten was *itself* the source of danger? . . . [A] juror reported that she believed that Rodney King was in 'total control' of the situation" (15–16).

133

Butler knows what she saw, and it was not King in total control. But she acknowledges the other reading. "And yet, it appears that the jury in Simi Valley claimed that what they 'saw' was a body threatening the police. . . . From these two interpretations emerges, then, a contest within the visual field, a crisis in the certainty of what is visible." That crisis was no intellectual vanity; it was situated at a telling site of power, where victims are differentiated from victimizers, where a price is paid, where cities burn. Even at that focused, charged point, these readings diverged wildly: "The visual representation of the black male body being beaten on the street by the policemen . . . was taken up by [the] racist interpretive framework to construe King as the *agent* of violence" (16).

Butler asks about mechanisms; "How was this feat of interpretation achieved?" And although she understands the mechanism at work—"the inverted projections of white paranoia"—she also knows that her analysis carries its own ambiguities. "The trial and its horrific conclusions teach us that there is no simple recourse to the visible, to visual evidence, that it still and always calls to be read, that . . . an aggressive reading of the evidence is necessary" (15–17). In short, Butler knows there is more than one crisis here.

In this chapter, I want to raise the stakes of that crisis, in order to inquire how modernity in general interacts with the events of race and racism. Departing from essays in the Gooding-Williams volume, from Paul Gilroy's *The Black Atlantic: Modernity and Double Consciousness,* and from a popular autobiography, Nathan McCall's *Makes Me Wanna Holler,* this chapter considers how the interruptions, pauses, and fissures in talk about (around, in the context of) race and racism amount to calls for a kind of politics that might fairly be called "postmodern." Such a politics would take issues of interpretation and representation seriously. Then, because this political approach has made this move, it would also be uniquely situated to respond to racism and power.

I

Rodney King's visibility is a strange instance of our conventional understanding of politics and their primary media of transmission, television news. Television's extraordinary combination of density and shallowness—and its concomitant lack of modernist "meaning"—forms the crucial instance of emerging cultural and political possibilities. Television is, by definition, a moving image. As such, televised politics becomes a moving target, oddly marked by characteristic absences—cultural gaps and indeterminacies, or preferences oddly marked by their tendency to dissolve.

King deployed an astute minimalism amid the riots, when he invoked a sense of community based on confinement.[3] "Can't we all get along? . . . We're all stuck here for a while." In context, this utopian sentiment seems terribly unlikely. But it is also carefully modest, even exhausted. Perhaps King spoke with ironic understatement, exposing forces that prevent such "getting along." Other readings abound. Privileged property owners knew that passivity works to their advantage. Their opportunistic reading was supported by (the rhetoric of) a basic desire for safety. Their poorer neighbors understood that "getting along" implied more than the indefinite passivity of victims; King couldn't possibly have intended permanent submission. A few listeners heard the words and hoped for the reverse; no, we can't simply "get along." King's phrase evoked all these— and more— interpretations. King's little talk was a masterpiece of minimalist hope, a romantic plea pared down to the point where it cannot be romantic anymore.

NBC's John Chancellor, always willing to grasp at even the shortest straw of community, emphasized another part of King's plea. King paused repeatedly in his brief statement, perhaps most notably when he said, "I love [pause] people of color." Hastening to his apology, Chancellor easily concluded that King must have meant, "I love people of all colors." Even if that is clearly not what King said. Others, more attuned to LA's landscape, heard the phrase differently. Both of the Korean-Americans represented in *Reading Rodney King* focus on that line. Sumi Cho quoted the "I love people of color" line (if without the pause), noting that "almost all the mainstream edited out this statement."[4] Elaine Kim noted that the "we all can get along" line has "been depoliticized and transformed into a Disneyesque catch phrase for Pat Boone songs and roadside billboards in Los Angeles."[5]

What if King had been thinking about dissension between blacks and Koreans? This might have been the case. He might have started to say, "I love black people," then altered his course to include Koreans, in an act of compassion no less magnanimous than the one Chancellor invented. Like every other commentator, Chancellor would sift through the rubble, finding only the shards that point back toward community. No piece is too small, if it conjures up a lost unity. No occasion is too ambiguous. This is the sign of his urgent concern.

II

Of course, this is not the only way to express concern. And, as Paul Gilroy explains in *The Black Atlantic,*[6] some expressions now emphasize circulation, complicity, interchange, and the borrowing and mixture of genres and themes as entry points to the politics of the most marginalized contemporary citizens.

> The cultures . . . of the European settlers and those of the Africans they enslaved, the "Indians" they slaughtered, and the Asians they indentured were not, even in situations of the most extreme brutality, sealed off hermetically from each other. . . . This seems as though it ought to be an obvious and self-evident observation, but its stark character has been systematically obscured by commentators from all sides. (2–3)

Gilroy's call differs wildly from Chancellor's vacant appeal to unity; but it also differs from calls to essentialism, exceptionalism, or black nationalism. Gilroy sees opportunity for a politics around racial experiences and difference arising precisely at the points of combination, appropriation, and expression across any number of lines. "[G]roups have fallen back on the idea of cultural nationalism, on the overintegrated conceptions of culture which present immutable, ethnic differences as an absolute break in the histories and experiences of 'black' and 'white' people. Against this choice stands another, more difficult option" (2).

That "more difficult option" involves a theorization of hybridity. But while Gilroy criticizes the language of absolutism and essentialism, the language of hybridity is just as unsatisfactory a way "of naming the processes of cultural mutation and restless (dis)continuity that exceed racial discourse and avoid capture by its agents." Gilroy thus shifts to tropes of movement and circulation, emphasizing "the stereophonic, bilingual, or bifocal cultural forms originated by . . . blacks," forms that are "dispersed within the structures of feeling, producing, communicating, and remembering" (2–3).

"The black Atlantic" refers to a field of circulation—a crossing and recrossing that Gilroy argues is central to the modernist roots (routes) of our current racial predicaments, and central to effective political responses to continuing oppressions. The "popularity of ideas about the integrity and purity of cultures" have been precisely tragic in their appeal to "crude and reductive notions of culture . . . clearly associated with an older discourse of racial and ethnic difference . . . entangled in the history of the idea of culture in the modern West" (7). Categories that have seemed somehow permanent and immutable are in fact vital to the extent that their contingency is acknowledged. As Gilroy understands, this is the best basis on which to refute popular charges of politically correct multiculturalism.

Gilroy's discussion of the double consciousness forced upon (and adopted by) American and European blacks is particularly useful. The concept of double consciousness comes from Du Bois, as well as Richard Wright. This doubleness "follows from being both inside and outside the West," and affects the politics of opposing racial oppression and encouraging black autonomy. While conservative critics of PC ideology try to impose essentialism, the actual experience of black communities is precisely the opposite. Both PC conservative and black nationalist essentialism are dangerous because they overlook "the development and change of black political ideologies and [ignore] the restless, recombinant qualities of the black Atlantic's affirmative political cultures" in their rush to privilege moralistic denunciation (30–31).

But if essentialism is dangerous, there are problems with an excessively bland and modernist pluralism, too. The banal "can't we all get along" approach exemplified by mainstream readings of King's speech risks missing the forcefulness of the idea of black community. For a pluralist, modernity functions as opportunity, as a clean break with a past. For Gilroy, the pluralist break is excessively abrupt, depriving pluralists of a crucial political identity.

The conceptualization of the modern and postmodern, so often dismissed as an intellectual irrelevancy or even a political evasion, becomes, in Gilroy's treatment, a development of "the most profound importance," in part because of the way it maps "the shifting relations of domination and subordination." But it is most relevant "in elaborating an interpretation of the origins and evolution of black politics" (44). Postmodernism's "ambivalences towards modernity" underscore the double consciousness crucial to the black Atlantic. That double consciousness both inhibits and points toward freedom (73).

Gilroy's best examples involve popular music, especially hip hop (which combines Caribbean, "the sound system culture [with black American] soul and hip hop styles . . . , as well as techniques like mixing, scratching, and sampling") and reggae—"a supposedly stable and authentic category" that nonetheless has moved, concealing "its own hybrid origins" and ceasing, at least in Britain, to signify an exclusively ethnic, Jamaican style (82). The "special power" of black cultural expressions "derives from a doubleness, their unsteady location simultaneously inside and outside the conventions, assumptions, and aesthetic rules which distinguish and periodise modernity" (73).

Against the criticism that black popular music is insufficiently attentive to a necessary black purity, Gilroy cites its liveliness and efficacy. Nelson Mandela responded to "the Africentric expectations" of his Detroit audience (during his first U.S. visit) "by confiding that he had found solace in listening to Motown music while in jail on Robben Island." In Gilroy's story, Mandela's appropriation of Motown revealed the "purist idea of one-way flow of African culture from east to west" as absurd. The improbable emblem—a pop genre from industrial America—was revealed to have participated in the "global dimensions of diaspora dialogue." But Motown's gesture is always just a gesture; it cannot be mistaken for ideology or modernist completion and hegemony. "The value of music as the principal symbol of racial authenticity was simultaneously confirmed and placed in question" (96). Marvin Gaye's syncopated pause and cry both exclaimed and denied itself, at the same time.

III

This gets us back to Rodney King, whose pauses have often taken the forms of silences that, as Houston A. Baker argues in *Reading Rodney King,* could be interpreted to the soundtrack of popular music, especially rap.[7] The most extraordinary silence, in this case, is the lack of a soundtrack to the tape of King's beating. As Baker notes, that lack follows a timeworn form, relying on a central fact of oppression and slavery: slaves lack "interpretive power or authority." This often was also the case among the white opposition to slavery. "At northern abolitionist rallies . . . the fugitive becomes the 'Negro exhibit.' She silently turns her naked back to the audience in order to display the stripes inflicted by the southern overseer's whip. Blacks in white-abolitionist employ were required always to earn the right—by silent display—to tell their stories" (39–40).

As Baker explains, "King was always already *silent,*" even after his situation became pervasively visible. His protests went unheard at the scene, and that silence spread. "It is as though he is sickeningly caught forever in the graceless heaviness of his attempts . . . to escape the next crushing blow." King's silence continues in the long period of preparation for the first trial. "And—stunningly—to the amazement of so very many—he is not called to . . . testify in his own behalf" in that first trial. "King is *silent,* and barely seen outside the repetitive scene of video violence" (43).

There is yet more to this silence. As in the case of William Horton (who Bush operatives renamed Willie) and Lee Oswald (who police renamed Lee Harvey Oswald),[8] Rodney King, too, has been renamed in the process of a thorough identity graft. His family and friends use his middle name, Glen, not the clunky (and perhaps, to white editors, the black-identified) "Rodney." And the surname "King"—the inversion of "slave," and a reminder of Martin—is almost not a name at all.

When King first breaks through this silence, with his extraordinary midriot statement, it is only an attempt to end the immediate firestorm. Baker prefers to imagine King speaking through the tough, assertive rap favored in the streets, so he derogates the riot statement; "It *was* moving. But no heroic interpretation is available after we learn that the main lines of the broken, sweated King plea for pacification were supplied by . . . his lawyer" (45).

I prefer to read Baker's judgment literally; "no *heroic* interpretation is available." But heroism is a classical game, and originality a modernist ruse. I would hear King's actual statement in his breaks, stutters, reluctances, and pauses. He appropriated, if just briefly, the silence imposed on him. Each of these verbal strategies invites us to locate double meanings—to hear King in a polyphonic mode. The potentially disastrous wait for heroic leadership, clear and rationalistic, is called into question. As is the entire political apparatus that ensnares bigots and, too often, their opponents, too.

IV

There is one possibility Baker did not consider; we might keep on not hearing "Rodney" King, over and over again. Or we might keep getting opportunities for polyphonic readings. In 1993, shortly after the second trial's conviction of two of the officers who beat him (but before their strangely light sentences were announced), King was on television again. King and his lawyer, Milton Grimes, were interviewed by Paula Zahn.[9] The occasion for the interview (a CBS "exclusive," as viewers were reminded throughout) was death threats King had received from local skinheads.

ZAHN: "Mr. King, you've really tried to stay out of the public eye . . . , [W]hat did it feel like, to live with the knowledge that someone might be out to get you?"

This seems an odd question to ask someone who has long lived amid the LAPD, with disastrous consequence. King answers about discomfort and sleeplessness. He starts twice, "I've always . . . I've always. . . ." We wait for him to dismiss the ridiculous query; I've always lived that way. He rights himself, ending, "It's not easy." The viewer with a taste for postmodern doubles might finish his sentence for him—it's not easy, talking about these things, with white Americans.

But Zahn was just warming up. She wants a reprise of the riot speech, another repetition of the anthem she heard then.

ZAHN: "After the first trial and after the . . . riots, you said at a news conference, 'why can't we all just get along.' How do you think your trial has changed Los Angeles, and do you think it has done anything at all to improve race relations in the city?"

Having commanded a performance, she gets one, though not the one she had requested. As if to prove that there are many, many ways to mute this King, his lawyer takes full advantage of the slightest pause and answers for him, with standard rhetoric about what African Americans think.

Seemingly undaunted that Grimes has answered the question, Zahn then asks King how stiff a sentence the two convicted officers should get. Again Grimes intervenes: "Excuse me, we informed the studio that we would talk about the threat to Mr. King from the skinheads." He then said that "we" (a "royal we," one is to presume) would not comment on the sentencing.

Zahn presses on: "I'm wondering, can you share any feelings at all, though, with us this morning about your client's reaction to the convictions?" She has stopped even trying to talk to King, satisfied instead to repeat resistance rituals with the lawyer—a humiliation routine familiar to every TV journalist.

After Grimes talks about the "skinheads . . . and rogue cops of the world," expressing cliched hopes that race crimes will diminish, Zahn tries, "in closing," to push King about the state of his lawsuit against the city. Of course, the lawyer interrupts again.

Still seemingly intent on rehearsing every method by which an interviewer can mute her subject, Zahn tries once more before the quickly approaching break. "And in closing [again], Mr. King, do you have any message for any of those skinheads who are still in hiding out there?" The rhetorical form of the question seems intent on drawing some response like, give yourselves up, it's hopeless—an answer King, who had repeatedly experienced the LAPD's touch, probably would not rush to give. Surely, Zahn could not be imagining that King would ask the skinheads to just get along. King, silenced so many ways, now grounds to a stop a Derridean could love:

KING [long pause]: "Don't have any words, I don't have any words for 'em, no. I don't have, I don't have any words for 'em."

Zahn rushes to cut King off, to make the station break. Her hurry seems to push her into yet sillier territory: "You still simply see this as an alleged hate crime?" How does one *simply* see a death threat from skinheads as a hate crime? Is there some chance it could be *personal?* And why the "still"? Has someone been trying to dissuade King? Does she doubt its (obvious) sense? And besides, King never got to say anything about hate crimes. In a fitting ending, Zahn gives King just enough time to start saying one word before she interrupts, reinserting that falsely familiar name; "Rodney King, thanks for joining us this morning."

This was a sufficiently odd and unsatisfactory "interview" that CBS brought Grimes and King back after the break. In the interim, the lawyer had obviously been advised to let his client speak. Zahn asks King if he is concerned about the threats, and King manages a natural answer to this, the first straightforward question of the interview. King ends again with "it's not easy."

Immediately, the craziness resumes. Zahn asks King when he thinks he will return to a "normal life." King eventually refers to a life of "some decency." But each of us viewers inserts an answer of our own; what can you possibly mean by "normal"? The possibilities range from the obnoxious to the profane.

Zahn then asks King about the mayor's settlement negotiations. As we hear an off-camera King sigh heavily, Grimes interrupts, after asking Zahn's permission. Yet another black man, silenced. But this spectacle is not over yet; one imagines it may never end.

Now sounding like a prosecutor or a detective, Zahn tries again:

> Mr. King, whether you like it or not, you have, over the last year or so, become a symbol of heightened racial tensions in this country. Does that create pressure for you, to live up to a certain standard? Do you feel people . . . are looking to you to do something, maybe, that you hadn't ever thought about doing, in terms of trying to bring the community together?

This is, of course, what Zahn herself had been doing, just minutes before, when she tried to prompt a reprise of the "live together" anthem. And where did the "whether you like it or not" come from? The listener, in heavy antiphonal call-and-response with Zahn by now, imagines how it must be, to be black, and be interviewed on national television by a white woman who uses the phrase "whether you like it or not." King struggles to respond, just as he has struggled throughout the interview. Ethereal electronic music finally ends the scene.

V

There are correctives to issue. All of this sounds pathetic, but in other interviews (notably, one conducted by CNN's Bernard Shaw several months later), King comes off as neither pathetic nor silenced. It is time to leave Glen King alone. The pattern of articulate pauses and silences extends far beyond him as does the double consciousness Gilroy champions.

More examples can be found in Nathan McCall's *Makes Me Wanna Holler: A Young Black Man in America,* a book that received high profile publicity treatment from Random House when it was released in 1994, and was optioned to John Singleton (director of "Boyz N the Hood") before its publication. *Holler* is autobiographical, which is unusual enough, since the author is still in his thirties and is not an athlete or media star. McCall is a journalist for the *Washington Post,* but that's just the end of the story. The book recounts McCall's serious gangsta youth. He made a mark in his Norfolk, Virginia, 'hood with shootings, rapes, robberies, and muggings. Eventually, he did three years in Virginia prisons before earning a journalism degree and beginning the career that quickly took him to the top of his profession.

McCall avoids every trap of easy explanation or apology. This is not a religious jeremiad in which a prisoner transports himself out of a previous life; in many ways, McCall is clearly the same person now as he was on the streets. Nor is the book an exercise in the psycho-babble now used to explain personal change. McCall's story is focused by his experience, and that experienced life had a core— he was and is, as the subtitle says, a young black man in America—an angry black man who has found a number of ways, throughout his life, to express that anger. And who has now begun to learn from his anger—not by discarding it, but by articulating it.

Lives are lives because of their specificity. A "self" is unified by experience in a historical and social context. As a result, autobiography—the most anecdotal telling possible—has a function for social and political analysis. The self unifies, then tells, creating a space for dialogue and reflection. In McCall's story, what we know, abstractly or statistically, emerges in a way that must be confronted. His story refutes the oblivious assumption that criminals are stupid, or that only broken families produce crime—McCall's family was stable and caring. Even the supposed weakness of community is at issue here; it is, in part, a commitment to the brotherhood he shares with other young black men that propels McCall's early life.

More than anything else, it is the gulf between black and white that made McCall's early life so insular, hateful, and transgressive. After prison, the gulf did not miraculously close; McCall's uncertainty about how to handle his three-year resume gap almost stunts a brilliant career; white employers did not know what to do with a black man who had been to prison. (Black employers, who would understand the way life works for young black males, had no jobs to offer at a good salary.)

McCall's story does not end with wonky policy recommendations, nor with anything else that might let his readers off the very sharp hook this country finds itself on. Having described his life as the consistent, if frightening, life of a contemporary black man, McCall's narrative insists that the madness was not entirely his. Thus, the "double consciousness" of Gilroy's argument permeates McCall's story, too. There is one mode of living in black America, another in white America. And there are doubles to negotiate within black America, too.

McCall recounts a search for alternate ways to mediate middle-class professionalism, on the one hand, with the lively, polyphonic black culture, on the other. Friends drop in from his old life. A son, born shortly before he went to prison, ties his experiences into a continuum. Religious options present themselves as essentialist, fundamental resolutions of the doubleness, but McCall finds them only temporarily diverting. None of the escapes fit. Each are somehow already exhausted.

But modernism is nimble. The authenticity that essentialist positions wish to deploy in response to authority can be co-opted, too. Gilroy promotes popular music "as a model that can break the deadlock between the two unsatisfactory positions [essentialism and pluralism] that have dominated recent discussion of black cultural politics." Gilroy is not just taking the pluralist side. The "two loosely organised perspectives . . . in opposing each other, have become locked in an entirely fruitless relationship of mutual interdependency" (99–100).

The experience of the black life, lived, gives signals of a solution—that is the point where Gilroy meets McCall straight on. As Gilroy explains, "black identity is not simply a social and political category to be used or abandoned according to the extent to which the rhetoric that supports and legitimises it is persuasive or institutionally powerful" (102). This is McCall's point, expressed in a conversation recounted in the book, with a white journalist friend who would pry him away from his focus. Gilroy's warning seems largely internal, but it has external utility as well; this is what white America cannot quite get. The singular, if constantly doubled, mixed, and at tension, experience of black life in the modern world is never optional. But it is also the basis for a strong sense of self and community, of possibility.

Gilroy summarizes: black identity "is lived as a coherent (if not always stable) experiential sense of self. Though it is often felt to be natural and spontaneous, it remains the outcome of practical activity: language, gesture, bodily significations, desires" (102). In his book's last pages, McCall invokes a kind of antiphony that Gilroy would appreciate. He recalls visiting a convenience store that had been the site of many of his earlier adventures. He greets old friends, still there. But he then feels menaced by a younger group of toughs, out to make their rep, the way he once made his. He beats a quick retreat, leaving us without any comparable way out, but still leaving us with his title, a phrase from a Marvin Gaye song about the frustration and madness of the black experience in this country. This is the reference to actual black culture that Gilroy celebrates. Made me wanna holler, throw up both my hands.

VI

Gilroy's book marks an attempt to break with politics based on essentialisms that "reify the concept of race," replacing them by efforts "to figure the inescapability and legitimate value of mutation, hybridity, and intermixture en route to better theories of racism and of black political culture than those so far offered by cultural absolutists" (223). The lesson Gilroy wants to draw at the end of his argument may well be surprising to both the nationalists and pluralists: "At its most valuable, the history of contending racial identities affords a specific illustration of the general lessons involved in trying to keep the unstable, profane categories of black political culture open. Equally importantly, it can reveal a positive value in striving to incorporate the problems of coping with that openness into the practice of politics" (223).

It is not an easy message to incorporate. Addressing the King riots, Mike Davis suggested similar possibilities (in a widely circulated interview, reprinted in the Gooding-Williams book). The rebellion amounted to a postmodern bread riot, he argues. It was not nearly as clearly defined, racially, as it seemed on the television. Nor was it well contained geographically (or, as we well know, in terms of duration, either).

It cannot be a model, but the openness Gilroy uses to intervene into the current political impasse does not necessarily search for well-formed and coherent models. It will do, instead, to find ways to talk about the pauses, gaps, and breaks that are both forced upon American blacks, and at the same time serve as an opportunity. Glen King's pauses were awkward, but awkwardness can be associated with openings, too.

Notes

1. *Los Angeles Times* (2 May 1992) printed the text of King's statement. Also in Robert Gooding-Williams, ed. *Reading Rodney King: Reading Urban Uprising* (New York: Routledge, 1993), 235 n. 19.

2. Judith Butler, "Endangered/Endangering: Schematic Racism and White Paranoia," in Gooding-Williams, 15–22.

3. The confinement theme is suggested by Thomas L. Dumm, "The New Enclosures: Racism in the Normalized Community," in Gooding-Williams, 178–95.

4. Sumi K. Cho, "Korean Americans vs. African Americans: Conflict and Construction," in Gooding-Williams, 196–211, quoted from 197.

5. Elaine H. Kim, "Home Is Where the *Han* Is: A Korean American Perspective on the Los Angeles Upheavals," in Gooding-Williams, 215–35, quoted from 228.

6. Paul Gilroy, *The Black Atlantic: Modernity and Double Consciousness* (Cambridge: Harvard University Press, 1993), further references in parentheses.

7. Houston A. Baker, "Scene . . . Not Heard," in Gooding-Williams, 38–48.

8. On the Horton instance, see Kathleen Hall Jamieson, *Dirty Politics: Deception, Distraction and Democracy* (New York: Oxford, 1992). On the Oswald case,

see Don Delillo, *Libra* (New York: Penguin, 1988). King's preferred name is seldom mentioned, but was made evident in a CNN special, narrated by Bernard Shaw. That special showed King in black contexts, with a self-assurance not visible elsewhere.

9. 7–21–93 *CBS This Morning.*

9

The Making of
"Derrida at the Little Bighorn"
An Interview

Gregory L. Ulmer

Strategies: Your new book, *Teletheory: Grammatology in the Age of Video,* continues your research on the implications of critical theory and the electronic media for academic discourse. When we asked you to contribute to this special issue on pedagogy we considered the possibility that you might want to avoid being typed or pigeonholed as "the one who does pedagogy."

GREGORY L. ULMER: Not at all. I was pleased to have this opportunity to talk about *Teletheory,* which started out trying to be a book about television. *Applied Grammatology* also wanted to be on television (that *on* is important) but I wrote five hundred pages of orientation and wasn't even close so I stopped. When I finished *Teletheory* I was surprised by the extent to which it is a sequel to the first book, elaborating on what is named there as the *mana*-word of post(e)-pedagogy—"invention." I remember being taught that novelists write the same book over and over again, so perhaps I write like a novelist. Or thought may be like a homing pigeon—no matter in what territory it is released, it will head for its nest. A pigeon is able to do that because of its sensitivity to the earth's electromagnetic field. The homing pigeon is electronic, in a way. So I homed in on your issue.

Strategies: Why did you insist on the interview format? Why not something like "Barthes to the Third Power" as a way to discuss your books?

GLU: I admire Barthes's review of his own work; there ought to be more of that kind of thing. One of the features of the age of video, however, is the emergence of the interview as a dominant mode of communication, exemplifying the new relationship between writing and speaking that is reorganizing knowledge in our time. The social sciences, along with the helping professions, as they are sometimes called, rely on it, as does television. The interview is the form that crosses the boundary separating the institutions of knowledge and entertainment, and has a major role to play in mediating and renegotiating the jurisdictions of these institutions. I am thinking, too, of the increasing use of this form in magazines, challenging the essay form that dominated that medium. Andy Warhol's *Inter-*

view is a salient example, but many other magazines at all levels of sophistication are using it.

Strategies: The interview form isn't featured in *Teletheory,* is it?

GLU: No, or only to the extent that the psychoanalytic session is used to suggest the complexity of conversation. The link for me is in the teaching situation—the nature of the conversation that carries disciplinary thinking, as distinct from both writing and everyday life talking. Many of my students are much better writers than they are speakers. There has been considerable attention given in recent years to the artificial divisions organizing the language and literature disciplines—the separation of writing from literature, of one literature from another, of literature from other modes of writing across the curriculum. To these should be added the separation of literature from speech. These divisions are institutionalized, which makes any reform of pedagogy a political question as well. I try in my classes to give attention to the spoken as well as to the written representations of knowledge in academic discourse. It turns out, as the study by Gilbert and Mulkay shows (*Opening Pandora's Box*), that scientists (but I think the same results would occur with specialists in any discipline) tend to give quite different, even contradictory, accounts of their fields of knowledge in interviews than in writing.

Strategies: The link with *Teletheory* would be your exploration of the way the discourses of daily life, both private and public, the discourses of the family and the community, interact with the discourses of expert knowledge? Is this orientation an attempt to respond to Habermas's criticism of Derrida, whom he accuses of forgetting the different functions of literary criticism and of philosophy as mediators separating the discourses of daily life and expert discourse?

GLU: In part, yes. The pigeon in Habermas's thought prevents him from understanding this aspect of Derrida's work as a grammatologist, theorizing the new relationship among the cultures of orality, literacy, and electronics that is emerging today. This despite Habermas's insight into the way in which magazine journalism mediates the exchange of knowledge across specialized borders. Habermas noted that specialists in one division of knowledge often rely on something like *Time* magazine for their understanding of expert work in the other divisions of knowledge. Indeed, such journalism is a primary means of dissemination of ideas, facilitating the invention process. Derrida should not be upset about the total misrepresentation of deconstruction in the popular press, since it is the nature of dissemination to work in this way; I would go so far as to say that it is precisely the misrepresentations that allow the ideas to spread. Journalism passes along primarily the myth of a theory, which is just the part that is fertile, that is capable of fertilizing another field. Derrida knows this better than anyone, and has theorized it fully in his appropriation of the very term "dissemination." The myth of a theory is to culture what the seed is to nature (with a multitude of variations on the transmittal of the seed).

Strategies: Dissemination would be another term, then, for the invention/*inventio* that is the organizing issue of *Teletheory.* Which brings us to the chief question we have about that book. At one level it is an account of your invention of a new genre for academic writing, to be used by teachers and students alike, we presume, as the essay is now—the "mystory." Perhaps we can clarify what you mean by "the myth of a theory" by asking you to explain the properties or purposes of a mystory.

GLU: A mystory is to learning, to the experience of a person as learner, what history—historiography—is to the collective experience of a people, or what herstory is to the political experience of women. It is a representation of the exchange across discourses that happens in the invention process. Invention depends on a "popcycle," or circulation of ideas through the principal discourses and their institutions organizing our culture, without being able to identify any one level as "origin."

Strategies: In what sense are you using "invention"?

GLU: I mean it to include both the rhetorical sense of *inventio*—finding something to say, getting up materials for a presentation—and the sense of innovation, as in revolutionary science. The popcycle includes expert knowledge (institutionalized in university disciplines), explanatory knowledge (the level of Hirsch's cultural literacy, already institutionalized in K–12 schooling), everyday life common sense (family discourse), and myth (entertainment industry, popular culture). My notion of the popcycle is adapted from a general observation in the history of discovery that when someone invents or innovates it is done not only by means of elements from public and private stocks of stories and images. The genre of mystory is designed to allow students to represent for themselves, as part of their preparation for working in the discipline of their choice, the peculiar, even unique, interaction of that discipline with the other disciplines they inhabit. Against the conventions of knowledge now ordering academic research, which separate expert knowledge from myth and anecdote, mystory requires the student to bring these dimensions of culture together.

Strategies: Your mystory is entitled "Derrida at the Little Bighorn." How are we supposed to respond to it as a text? By what standard might it be evaluated? Is it possible to write a bad mystory?

GLU: How *did* you respond to it?

Strategies: Let's not get into that now, since it is your interview, except to say that we noted the risk of the experiment. Three-quarters of the book at least is devoted to laying out the theoretical rationale for the genre, along with the models for it that already may be found on the contemporary scene, in the works of Mary Kelly, Ross McElwee, Francis Ponge, or N. Scott Momaday for example. We were reminded here of the strategy of *Applied Grammatology,* in which you showed that Derrida had theorized a writing that was already practiced in the teaching of Eisenstein, Beuys, and Lacan. Then, in the final section, there is your experiment. By that time our expectations have been raised; we expect something significant.

GLU: The difficulty of the mystory is that it is not necessarily a text that is written for publication; not at all. It is produced for oneself, to bring into awareness the pattern of that pigeon we mentioned earlier. I guess I should change that image to another electromagnetic device—the compass. The mystory will show its author the direction of his or her personal invention in a "pure" incarnation, but, like a compass, which always points north, it can be used to go in any direction, to assist in the solution of any problem. Another way to look at it is as the simulation, before the fact, of inventive thinking. This aspect is especially important, given the pedagogical function of the mystory. The knowledge as institutionalized now puts the student in the position of acquiring what others already know. The pedagogy and curriculum we have now is designed to reproduce the discipline, not to change it. It prepares students to repeat the given, the *inventio* without the innovation.

Strategies: Would you say that theory is changing that relationship now?

GLU: Yes, and the mystory is a genre that will allow students to work theoretically, that is, without knowing what they are doing in advance. It is possible to solve the problems of normal science entirely within the boundaries of disciplinary knowledge, without the support of the stories and images derived from the family and community. It is not possible to think theoretically that way. One can learn *about* theory as if it were another topic of normal science (which at one level it is). But to reason and write theoretically requires one to draw on the kinds of resources that usually are associated with the making of art. What distinguishes theoretical texts from works of criticism in the language fields is just this added dimension of "literature" that theory possesses. It has been assumed that theory itself can't be taught, except at the most advanced levels of graduate school, because it requires a mastery of methods and objects of knowledge of the discipline. That would be true if theory were only a matter of normal science (to use Kuhn's distinction as a shorthand for now). Mystory evades this obstacle by allowing the student to manipulate bodies of information without having to understand them (the way a child learns its native language by practicing it).

Strategies: Is this the "heuretics" you refer to, as the alternative to hermeneutics?

GLU: Exactly. "Heuretics" (related to Eureka! and heuresis) concerns the "subject" of knowledge, and takes up texts for the purpose of making something else out of them. (Barthes said the only way to relate to a *text* is to make another text, which may be generalized as the inventive relationship to cultural materials.)

Strategies: Do you think it was a mistake to stress the separation, even the opposition, between heuretics and hermeneutics? Isn't there an unacknowledged hermeneutics at work in the selection and combination—the montage—of the three discourses in the mystory?

GLU: The mystory learns from the psychoanalytic interview the strategy of suspending critical analysis, temporarily, in order to bring into appearance, into representation, the pattern that inevitably arises when texts are juxtaposed. "Derrida at the Little Bighorn" is classified as a "fragment" in *Teletheory* because it remains to be interpreted. It was generated euretically by juxtaposing the three discourses that constitute my "life story." In fact, the main purpose of this interview is to begin the interpretive process. I would like to at least identify what the experiment produced that I had not anticipated, and that calls for analysis and evaluation.

Strategies: Could you say something first about the principle of selection for your text?

GLU: To complete something I was saying earlier, a mystory has value primarily, perhaps exclusively, for its author. I'm not sure that it can be evaluated qualitatively, but only formally. Or, as is the case with therapy, the author will know if it is any "good," because the juxtaposing of these levels of sense should produce another dimension of pleasure, what Lacan punningly named "bliss-sense" (punning on *jouissance*). When the discourses of the family and community are brought into contact with a discipline, there should arise a certain number of contingent coincidental parallels or homologies. A discursive illusion is created in which one level turns out to be a kind of allegory of the others, albeit in a most elusive way. The effect of a mystory is a combination of nonsense and destiny at once.

Strategies: In your case the experiment brings together your experience working at your father's sand and gravel plant (that would be the family story, the history of Custer's Last Stand, which you say is the public story of your home town, Miles City, Montana, in Custer County) and Derrida's writings—obviously the disciplinary register. Would other particulars have served as well? What is the procedure for finding the parallels?

GLU: After quite a few false starts I narrowed the range of possibilities down to the ones you noted, and I suggest that these categories can be generalized, at least for the purposes of experimentation, by others who want to use the genre. The book explicitly invites others to experiment further with the genre, or to invent another one—that would be the greatest compliment to teletheory as a disciplinary movement, as distinct from my book, since what is called for is the engagement by academics with the academic institutionalization of video. Mystory is a genre designed to bring into relationship, or to make it possible to think the relationship, among oral, literate, and electronic cultures. As it stands now the categories are, first, gendering stories from the family level. I recount several anecdotes about going to work for my father at the Miles City Sand and Gravel, a place of machinery, heavy equipment, common laborers—a completely masculine environment. The purpose of the anecdotes is not to do an oral history of the place, but to evoke it, to put it in position, as the situation that made me the most self-conscious about needing to play the role expected of me as a male. I experienced gendering as a problem. Secondly, the category of the public story, a story that informs my community (however one might define "community"—it needn't be a hometown), is a tale of "disaster" or "catastrophe." The Custer massacre in my case. This level is introduced by citing various materials. I used Evan Connell's *Son of the Morning Star* along with a number of other sources, again evoking the whole historical issue by means of a few documents, metonymically. The problem of gender and of the public disaster are joined finally with the problem of a discipline, represented in my text by Derrida.

Strategies: Could you give an example of the bliss-sense that was generated by this convergence?

GLU: The example that comes to mind at once, with which I begin the text, can be appreciated best if you keep in mind the origins of my strategy in Derrida's signature project, which is a new means of moving between the particular and the general by punning across languages, translating proper names as common nouns, and other linguistic play. The idea for mystory began as a test of the replicability of the coincidences that Derrida keeps producing in his texts between the lives and the writings of various thinkers such as Hegel or Freud (the "oto-biography"). I was looking at a map of the Custer Battlefield, marking the positions of the companies that perished with Custer, companies identified by letters of the alphabet. It occurred to me, given the strategy, that the letters might spell something. C, E, F, I, and L. They spelled "LIFE-C"! That was my first impression, as if in support of my decision to use the format of the VITA to arrange the mystory. The "C" was Custer: "Custer's Life"? Or, it was Custer assigning a grade to life.

Strategies: You don't use that reading in *Teletheory.*

GLU: No, I went with the French version, which really stunned me. "FICEL." The letters of the cavalry companies spelled a French word, appropriately for my mystory, with considerable significance in critical theory. There is a gender problem with it too, since its critical usage is feminine (*ficelle*), whether in Henry James, or Lacan—his *ronds de ficelles,* the loops of string tied into knots, theorized in the "Encore" Seminar. This *thread* led me to the whole topic of French poststructural psychoanalysis and the various discussions of the *kernel* of the unconscious (the shell and the kernel with the messenger moving between, Freud's image, picked up by Lacan and Derrida, as well as by Nicolas Abraham). This *kernel* became the COLONEL of my story, Lt. Colonel being Custer's actual rank at the time of his death. Custer represents the unconscious in "Derrida at the Little Bighorn." The Colonel of the Unconscious.

Strategies: What do you do with this? Do you identify with the Custer story? Certainly the culture no longer considers him a hero. Or is *that* your point, the internalization of Custer being similar politically to the masculine gendering you experienced working for your father? The discourse of the fathers that formed your personality in childhood, a process that continues now with Derrida? The experiment as it stands does not make clear your point of view on these stories. The logic you set in motion thus sets up an expectation that the problems of gendering and colonization will find some equivalent at the disciplinary level.

GLU: This logic is one of the points that calls for interpretation. My response to "Derrida at the Little Bighorn" is that it *identifies* for me the problem most in need of a Derridean solution—the colonization of the life world, as formulated by Habermas and the Frankfurt School. Habermas posed the issue well, but, in my terms, his Enlightenment assumptions may not be the most suitable for dealing with the problem. Since finishing *Teletheory,* therefore, I have been working on a Derridean redescription of instrumentalization, which opens onto the whole question of cognitive jurisdiction, the distribution of life-world problems among the disciplines. The Institute for European and Comparative Studies (of which I am co-director, along with Robert D'Amico) at Florida is taking up the matter of institutional invention, the deconstruction of the opposition between pure and applied research.

Strategies: Is Custer the model for your strategy as a warning or as an example to be followed? He was not much of a military strategist, was he? Not to mention the political and moral implications of what he stands for.

GLU: The first step of heuretics is to avoid the self-critical censor, in order to let come into representation whatever is actually at work (the unconscious *in* discourse). I might now intellectually reject the values of the men at the gravel plant, and the colonialism of my community, but it is important for me to recognize that a large part of my imagination and cultural understanding was formed in these registers. A foreclosure of those discourses reproduces in discipline formation the same schizophrenic effects that result from repression in ordinary life. Once the stories have been gathered, they make available through evocation an encyclopedia, a semantic domain, which may then be gleaned critically for new possibilities. The real victims of the Custer story are the Native American Indians, and it may be that Indian culture might offer new resources for the problem of the colonization of the life world. Indeed, the various descriptions of the thinking of all the "others" of Western reason, including "the savage mind" topos, that have appeared within the human sciences, provide the best intuition about the nature of a cognition that might be specifically electronic.

Strategies: Your awareness of gender and colonialism as ideological problems is a feature of your disciplinary training, which directed your attention to those aspects of the life story. Why were you surprised when these concerns appeared also in your theoretical discourse? Isn't it a self-fulfilling prophecy?

GLU: I knew it intellectually, in principle only. I had been trying to develop a teaching strategy for helping students recognize the interdependence of what they know and what they believe. I found that their intellectual sophistication about the categories of ideology—class, gender, race, and the like—was never applied to themselves. Their *opinions,* at the level of emotional engagement, remained largely untouched by the theory or the knowledge. Alexander Kluge and Oscar Negt have theorized this persistence as the "obstinacy" of experience. It is the obstinacy of stereotypes that seem to be invulnerable to critique, at least in the register of common sense. To see that the very theories we were working with were themselves informed by the ideologies in question required a shift of levels, to find another discourse within which the discourse of knowledge could itself be made an object. Having in mind Wittgenstein's suggestion that nothing is hidden, along with Lacan's axiom that the hiding place is in plain sight, I looked for a way to materialize the theory of ideology. In this context I thought about my high school, Custer County High, and realized that many of the seemingly invisible pressures that formed my "self" were manifested clearly in the story of Custer. Not that Custer's story is unified; there is more than one Custer. But the story in all its versions carries the contradictions of the belief system in the heads of the citizens of Miles City.

Strategies: Custer's story is not localized to Montana, of course. It is on E. D. Hirsch's list of national culture.

GLU: Right, and there are any number of other communities named after Custer. The pedagogical value of shifting the research to the discourse of public history, however, comes from the student recognizing the relevance of the story to his or her cultural formation. It is not that the individual accepts or believes consciously in the story itself, but that the story brings into representation the historical and social situation in which the person was constructed as a self. One's imagination comes into formation around such stories, for better or worse. The point I want to stress is that, once formed, that imagination is not limited to thinking in terms of that story, although there may be some outer, Whorfian boundary. The students have to find their own disaster story, which is done simply by using Barthes's notion of the *punctum* or sting. What is in your memory? Think about it or reflect. One will occur to you.

Strategies: Does it have to be a disaster story?

GLU: Not at all. It's just that such stories tend to remain in memory, when we hear about them as children. They put down roots or foundations that permit an imagination to develop. Any affecting story will do, but disasters also are often monumentalized, even if not so obsessively as in the Custer example.

Strategies: Once you have identified the stories how do you use them? What is the method for composing the text?

GLU: It is a collage text, of the synthetic sort, in which fragments of each of the three discourses are included to evoke the whole paradigm from which it is drawn. The actual format is what I called the "minor vita" (alluding to Deleuze and Guattari's minor literature, minor science). The categories of the vita are filled in the mystory with "credentials" from childhood, to represent the achievement of a "self," which is ignored later on the professional resume. The vita format avoids the traps of narrative teleology and also identifies categories that assist with the invention process.

Strategies: How does this arrangement allow the contact across discourses needed to create bliss-sense?

GLU: Part of the selection principle for those fragments to be included comes from the search for coincidences between the discourses. Let me give as an example the other main surprise that emerged from "Derrida at the Little Bighorn" that remains to be interpreted. Using the puncept that I had observed in Derrida, as an alternative way to bring items into a set—alternative to the concept that gathers items based on similarity of properties—I found that the information generated by the vita converged on a very few names. The most striking in my case was the word "gall," and I organized part of my text into a "gall series," bringing into relation information from each level of discourse based on an association with *gall.* My father had gall bladder cancer, in the family story. I knew from childhood that Crazy Horse led the attack on Custer. But when I researched the battle I learned that there had been three field chiefs, one of whom was named Gall. This repetition of "gall" called attention in the disciplinary discourse to the Frenchness of Derrida as a gallic philosopher, living in what was once Gaul. The three of these led me to think about the humour "gall," one of the four elements of alchemical psychology. There is considerable luck in this connection, in that the logic of mystory as invention is that of the joke (the interference of unrelated semantic domains)—the pun on *humor.* A whole cloud of possibilities for making a text arose out of the gall puncept, and I am still curious about what it might mean. Or rather, what it can be made to mean, since it is an experiment in invention. What struck me in the way of bliss (which is not necessarily pleasure) was the insistence in the text of "gall" as an emotion of bitterness. Reading a history of Miles City I learned that the name of the sheriff, during the 1880s, was Wormwood! So there it was— "gall and wormwood." I included dictionary definitions of this emotion and personality type, contrasting this emotion with the melancholy—black bile—associated traditionally with scholarship (Robert Burton). My immediate impression was that the new emotion of theory, motivating scholarship in our time, is not melancholy but anger. Anger is to gall what melancholy is to black bile. There is plenty of evidence to support this link between anger and theory in the area of critique coming from the groups victimized by patriarchy.

Strategies: Is this the link motivating the references both to Hamlet and to the H-bomb?

GLU: Both of these stories carry lessons of revenge, as does the Custer story. Wounded Knee was the revenge the Seventh Cavalry took on the Indians for the

Custer defeat. I still don't know quite what to make of the predominance of those themes in my text. The conceptual pun is on madness, in any case. To be mad is to be angry and/or crazy. Custer's pseudonym for his articles about hunting was "Nomad," alluding to his fabled identification with the Indians he fought. The H-Bomb was generated out of another series, which I should mention just to indicate that the link or gram coupling one discourse to another is often found in some quite minor detail of the scene or situation evoked. The "H" series, for example, joins the three discourses at the following points: The "H" pattern on the gearshift knob of the trucks I drove for my father; the "H" of the goalposts in football; the "H" of the H-Bomb (total war waged on the Indians, genocide) and the *aitch* in Derrida's *Signsponge,* the missing "H" from the hatchet that cut the tree. Gall was famous for having fought only with a hatchet at the Little Bighorn. Add then Derrida's essay on Nuclear Criticism.

Strategies: To accept the possibility that these items have anything to do with one another assumes, does it not, the validity of Derrida's linguistics? Isn't this an obstacle to any general use of the mystory genre?

GLU: The mystory is an experimental extension of the Derridean Writing (picto-ideo-phonographic) I first outlined in *Applied Grammatology.* But it is entirely experimental, composing according to its terms in order to see what happens. The mystory should be acceptable regardless of one's theoretical commitments because it does not replace hermeneutics, critique, criticism, or any other mode of analysis, but supplements them in an area—invention—that until now has not had much if any place at all in our pedagogy. It is a form of artificial memory, showing the kind of short-circuits between discourses that occur at a subconscious level in the process of discovery/invention. Which is not to underestimate its capacity to function directly as critique in its own terms—self-critique, especially, in showing to its author his or her ideological formation. The genre also has problem-solving applications, in areas in which disciplinary methods have been blocked, requiring a shift to other levels of discourse in order to overcome the obstacle to thought.

Strategies: You have stressed three levels of discourse. What about the fourth one included in your "popcycle"? The discourse of entertainment doesn't seem to figure in your mystory, yet it obviously could, considering all the movies made about Custer. Or is that the way it works?

GLU: You're right. I do mention *They Died with Their Boots On,* I think, but I don't develop that register in "Derrida at the Little Bighorn," except to allude to the continuity of the frontier myth through my vita, linking the history of my hometown in Montana, with its frontier values, to my work on the vanguard arts and theory, mediated by the new frontier, the race for space (the American project was named "Vanguard"), which indirectly paid my way to graduate school (Sputnik and our response—the National Defense Education Act that included grants for language study). Mind you, I don't claim any causality in these relationships. But to observe them emerge in the text produces an uncanny effect (which is why I am eager for others to try the genre). Why don't you-all make one? *Strategies* is a perfect place to publish that kind of experiment.

Strategies: We'll think about it. Meanwhile, there is still the question of the pop-cycle.

GLU: Yes. That is another direction I am taking up after *Teletheory*, continuing the experiment in dissemination. I am conducting a seminar this spring in which we are attempting to adapt the mythical discourse of entertainment to the representation of disciplinary knowledge. Bernard Tschumi mentions in *Cinégramme Folie* (the *folie* relates to that strange madness that turned up in "Derrida at the Little Bighorn"; the *folie* that Derrida helped design, with Peter Eisenman, has the same structure as the washer in a sand and gravel plant!) that structuralism today has value primarily as a heuristic device, that is, a device for invention. The relation of structuralism to poststructuralism is turning out to be that the former described various rhetorics or higher-order language systems, which the latter is learning to practice. Lévi-Strauss showed this possibility when he produced a new version of a myth that his informant then accepted as "native" while admitting that he hadn't heard that particular version before. The discourse of television, for example, has already been described, although so far exclusively for the purposes of critique. Deconstructive artists have demonstrated that it is possible to mount a critique of the media without going to a metadiscourse of hermeneutics (the theory and practice of deconstructive art is documented in Brian Wallis's anthology, *Art after Modernism,* and demonstrated in the situationist poetics of *Cultures in Contention*). They use the representations found in the media of all our ideological categories the same way Derrida uses, paleologically, the terms of the philosophies of consciousness, which are turned back on themselves to produce a countermyth, or counterconcept, thus revealing the constructed nature of the system. This process may be extended to solve the problem of how to put academic discourse on television, which I believe is necessary to the survival of the university in the age of electronics.

All these charges made against contemporary theory—that it is elitist, exclusionary, without relevance to the life story, and so forth—are made by people whom I suspect have made no effort to find out if that is really the case. Like the person who said during a job interview at Florida that contemporary theories of language, such as Derrida's, had no applicability to actual composition courses. Having just completed *Text Book,* with Robert Scholes and Nancy Comley, which does just this "impossible" thing, I had to object. The assertion turned out to be an assumption, reflecting one of the extraordinary aspects of the debate over theory in the literature disciplines, which is that many of our colleagues simply do not want to have a theoretical component at all. They want to leave our work untheorized, and refuse to use the theory that does exist, despite the fact that such theory is one of the ways the liberal arts or humanities might in fact achieve parity with the other divisions of knowledge in the university hierarchy.

Strategies: In *Teletheory* you emphasize that mystory is not medium specific. Could you say a bit more then about how mystory relates to your point about television and education?

GLU: In writing *Teletheory* I realized that I am becoming less interested in making individual products myself, and more interested in designing collective activities that are "writing machines"—groups cooperating to produce work that no one individual could make alone. In short, teaching. The classroom has always been a writing machine. Oddly, teachers who advocate revision as the key to good writing often don't revise their pedagogy—their writing machine—when the work the class produces is unsatisfactory. Perhaps this is too "auteurist" a view of teaching, with the professor as the "director" and hence praised or blamed for the class product.

In any case, I was working on a video version of "Derrida at the Little Bighorn," exploring the possibilities of low-tech compilation assignments for composition classes. I wanted to push the explanatory effect that results from emphasizing in writing classes that literacy is a technology by doing comparative projects, working across the apparatuses of literacy and electronics. About that time an extraordinary convergence of events pushed me into rethinking my relation to video. As an advisor to the Southern California Consortium's telecourse project, I had experienced the frustrations of trying to influence the conception of big-budget educational television, which for obvious reasons is quite conservative. I was invited to do a program with Paper Tiger Television, the New York cable access collective. As a way to think about my treatment of their format, dealing with media critique, I assigned my classes to do a Paper Tiger project, but using the docufiction genre invented by Alexander Kluge. Then, during John Hanhardt's visit to Gainesville, as part of the IECS study of literacy and orality (as curator of video at the Whitney, he was speculating on the implications of electronics for literacy), he noted that Kluge had agreed to do a Paper Tiger project himself, which I had not known at the time I gave the assignment. The students liked the idea of working out how Kluge would do a Paper Tiger critique before he did it himself.

The next step was that Paper Tiger suggested they come to Gainesville to do a workshop to help us start our own collective for cable access TV. And that is what we did, sponsored by an alliance (but why not think of ourselves as a "consortium") of the English Department's Cultural Studies program, the Architecture School, and Santa Fe Community College. "InvestiGATORS TV" is experimenting with the apparatus of an electronic university, hypothesizing a situation in which video is the dominant means for representing knowledge in all disciplines, just as the book is now in the apparatus of literacy. We invite experts in various fields to work with our group, to find ways to do research in their field *directly* in video.

Strategies: Directly? Is this where mystory comes in?

GLU: Exactly. So far at least, and we are still only at the earliest stages, our premise is that the current divisions of the university may make sense in terms of justification or verification of knowledge, but not in terms of the invention or discovery of knowledge. Mystory is a useful way for teachers in any field to represent their inventive thinking—to bring their disciplinary discourse into relation with the discourses organizing the public and private spheres.

Strategies: How are you going to get around the copyright problems, assuming you want to distribute these tapes?

GLU: Our position is that we are not using the signifieds of the footage we use (off-air taping, documentary archives, and all the graphic paratexts of the textbook industry), but only the signifiers, since we almost always recontextualize borrowed items in an allegorical text. We are saying something entirely other, different from whatever the fragment said originally. Again, however, the goal is not a "product," but a situation—to devise a prototype in our community for how to institutionalize video other than as entertainment television. One intention, once we get both the organization and the format worked out a bit more, is to invite the local public schools to work with us, to help us demonstrate that one way to improve the education of our children is not by dropping summer vacation, adding still more science courses, and aping the Japanese, but rather by ending the curricular and pedagogical segregation of the arts and sciences in our schools at all levels. Given the institutional obstacles to cooperation across the levels of schooling (primary through graduate), InvestiGATORS TV is exploring television as the place for intereducational cooperation.

Strategies: Is it likely that colleagues in the sciences are going to take your new academic genre seriously? Will they want to assign their apprentices to make a text holding together a bunch of irrelevant nonsense with a few puns?

GLU: Well said. You have come to the crux of the problem. No one will be persuaded that a mystory "works" by listening to me or anyone else explain it to them. It does not convince at the level of argument, but only at the level of practice. Making one of these is what convinces the maker. How to get people to try it? Perhaps the metaphoric vehicle for dissemination should not be plants but disease—the plague, to use Freud's image for psychoanalysis. I have used Dan Sperber's epidemiology notion elsewhere to conceptualize the spread of ideas. The host/parasite metaphor has already organized some of the debate surrounding deconstruction. The intense concern about immunology now is probably relevant to this question of the resistance of bodies of knowledge to new ideas, with rather negative implications. But, if teletheory is right, it suggests a reorganization of the relationships among the disciplines—a more direct connection between the humanities and the sciences, for example, to replace the "general education" curriculum that persists in the name of "humanism," in which the arts are to be appreciated in the domain of leisure rather than work. Since the humanities, seen from the outside, are disciplines of entertainment, anyway, we should take advantage of this association to intervene much more aggressively in that institution.

10

All the Stupid "Sex Stuff"

Marilyn Manners

Scene: Early 1990s

A band member flings her bloody tampon into an appreciative crowd;[1] songs are titled "Suck My Left One" (Bikini Kill) and "Shaved Pussy Poetry" (Huggy Bear). Mixed-gender and all-female band names go beyond the mere underscoring of gender (e.g., Lunachicks, Babes in Toyland, Throwing Muses, Ringling Sisters) to proclaim an assertive and often parodic female sexuality: Hole, Bikini Kill, Yeastie Girlz, Hammerbox, Dickless, Breeders, Fetus Production, 7 Year Bitch. Employing an increasingly typical pastiche of reappropriation, anger, and irony, female singers bare their flesh and scrawl on it "Slut," "Rape," or "Fuck You."

In musical realms and beyond, female sexuality was everywhere represented—often figured as ironic hyperbole or parodic lack. Self-conscious presentation, as well as consciousness of representation, prevailed—from Annie Sprinkle's "porn" performances to musicians who transformed the "nothing-to-see" (Irigaray, 26) into anthem, or vaginal poetics:

> We are the very first of the Vagina Core bands
> So if you want to join us gotta do one thing
> Grab onto your vagina and shout and sing:
> Yeast Power! Yeast Power!
> —(Yeastie Girlz)

> Some have teeth, some have hair, some have soft
> sweet petals, some look like Cher, some make you
> sweat, some make you run, some will even eat their
> young: The Power of Pussy.
> —(Ann Magnuson, of Bongwater)

While Madonna and Roseanne publicly grabbed their crotches, Sandra Bernhard displayed hers parodically in *Playboy*. And some women simply queered everything in their paths, from fashion to Freud— memorably k.d. lang: "I have a little bit of penis envy. Yeah, they're ridiculous, but they're cool" (Bennetts, 144).

Susie Bright has claimed that "A woman's allure is only made more striking when she counterpoises masculine costume or gestures against her feminine
body" (56). This has generally worked well for Madonna, for example, but it did
prove a sticking point for Roseanne, whose crotch grabbing and pulling provoked
public and media outrage, including death threats. Whereas her promotion of
bi/queer sexuality in the realm of televisual representation (Martin Mull's and Sandra Bernhard's characters on *Roseanne*) was more or less taken in popular stride,
Roseanne's own transgression of male/female boundaries in her National An-
them-baseball player parody was met with rage. (Her performance probably did
not, however, shock anyone familiar with her monologues' gendertwists: to those
who accuse her of not being feminine enough, she responds, "Well, I say—suck
my dick!") Screechingly bad renditions of the National Anthem do not in themselves necessarily lead to public condemnation; they are so common as to be exactly (part of) what Roseanne was parodying. What pushed this performance piece
over the line, of course, was its warping not *just* of gender but of male (sports) heroism. Roseanne's rendition was not just off-key but off-kilter: in part, outrage may
have erupted because her body has not always been perceived as feminine, or even
quite female. Aging, hefty, far too powerful in a too-powerful business—
Roseanne has often provoked anxiety because perhaps she *is* tugging at her balls.
A related possibility: the baseball-player parody was such an excessive example of
the butch-femme gender flipping she had been performing for quite some time
that it finally forced itself into a shocked public's awareness.

Madonna's sex parodies evoke rather different responses. bell hooks (who
was from early on one of the few feminists to read popular feminisms both seriously and with attention to irony) has charged that Madonna's earlier, more resistant and feminist presentations gave way to facile and traditional
dominance/submission manifestations; she argues that Madonna's own admission
in *Sex* that she has a "dick in her brain" underscores her inability to think and act
beyond male structures (79–80). While a good deal of hook's point-by-point criticism of *Sex* is indeed convincing, I find it more difficult to agree that things overall are quite so clear cut. Even if we leave aside Madonna's intriguing assertion that
Sex is her version of Cindy Sherman's genre of "self"-representation (Handelman,
393) or her disclaimers about wanting "one" between her legs (in *Sex*), we may still
find a way out of the limiting oppositions so often noted:

> This book [*Sex*] is about having a penis but I wish she had a big pussy in her
> head and worked that. . . . But see pussy is not quite as marketable. . . . And
> that's the sad thing because if anybody could make a female erotic agenda
> available it would be her. (Harris, 44–45)

If we take, just for example, Madonna's role in *Body of Evidence* (whatever
the merits or lack thereof of the film itself), it is difficult not to be struck by how
it plays with and off the staple crop of psychotic female killer/revenge roles. But

Madonna's character, Rebecca Carlson, is decidedly *not* psychotic: she is instead *at once* a sexual succubus of rather mythic proportions *and* a "real dick" in the best colloquial sense. Some might read this combination as the mark of a true bitch, but the connotations of "bitch" do not approximate either her frightening, engulfing sexuality or her complete disregard of bitchy behavior in doing and getting what she wants.

One major objection to *Body of Evidence's* narrative,[2] that Madonna's Rebecca Carlson is too powerful sexually and must then certainly and stereotypically be punished for it, preferably by death (Che, 30, and compare Califia, 177), seems accurate as far as it goes, but perhaps does not go far enough. The "climax" of the film, which reveals Rebecca's culpability and ensuing extrajuridical punishment, strikes me instead as unmistakable parodic allusion (whether intentional or, equally likely, unintentional) to other texts having to do with "excessive" female sexuality. First, we encounter the male characters' discovery of the woman's absolute duplicity and disregard for men, through her own telling (the classic reference is, of course, the film *Rebecca*). Then, the at-last-dead female body floats, face up, hair spread wide, in a conveniently located body of water: *Fatal Attraction* comes to mind, as does Ophelia, of course (as represented in the popular imaginary, if not in the actual text of *Hamlet*)[3]—and once again *Rebecca*. Rebecca de Winter is indeed everywhere in *Body of Evidence*: her nonprocreative and "dangerous" sexuality; her use and abuse and exchange of men; her bodily purchase of big money; her death in a boat house (Rebecca Carlson lives and dies in a house boat, for heaven's sake) and her watery "grave." This is not the first time that Madonna has taken on the persona of Rebecca de Winter, has given her "presence," brought her back to life (*Desperately Seeking Susan* in many ways parodies *Rebecca*)—although Rebecca as a character was never really "alive" but would not stay "dead" either: "And yet that woman-thing speaks. . . . It speaks 'fluid,' even in the paralytic undersides of that [phallocratic] economy" (Irigaray, 111).

The extreme excess of *Body of Evidence,* including but not limited to Madonna's performance, is difficult to read *straight,* in part because the film's major characters are in fact so resolutely heterosexual and so self-importantly serious. It's the kind of film that makes the "good guy" seem sadly silly in his masculinity: in response to the defending attorney's (Willem Dafoe), "It's not a crime to be a great lay," the prosecutor (Joe Mantegna) retorts, "Well sure, I'd have to have *myself* indicted." *Body of Evidence* also abounds with lines that seem always to be nudging its viewers, saying two things at once, often something about itself and/or its audience: "The state's case is built on fantasy, not fact," or "I always thought the message on the answering machine was a little over the top . . . but you even bought that." Whether by "truth or dare" or by hit or miss then, Madonna remains part of an ongoing feminist process (often parodic, which does not necessarily mean dismissive or belittling) of "writing the body" (Cixous) as well as a "'mechanics' of fluids" (Irigaray), and her often-noted physical metamorphoses are but one part of this process.

However much Madonna's actions defined "pushing the envelope" in the early 1990s, she was nonetheless far from the only voice on the sex line. Consider, for example, those (generally, but not exclusively, younger) women who also intentionally intermixed "masculine costume or gestures" (associated with the Whole) and their "feminine bod[ies]" (associated with the Hole). There were a number of young female bandmembers who dressed un-femme, downright butch in fact, or sometimes both femme *and* butch. And a great deal was made—in both the mainstream and alternative media—of the new angry young women: riot grrrls (including bands, fans, and 'zines);[4] "lipstick lesbians"; the politically aware pierced and tattooed. National media attention to riot grrrls permeated the strangest places (including *Cosmopolitan*) and was overall positive, though generally uncomprehending, while in the alternative press there emerged at times a rather divisive backlash (France, McConnell). While this backlash routinely posited a homogeneity that simply did not exist,[5] many commentators finally had to admit not really knowing exactly who riot grrrls were or where to find them. And indeed, they were not exactly where you might have expected: working a discourse in contradistinction to Madonna's, just for the most spectacular example, they were not "speaking out" in *Rolling Stone;* they were "silent" right under your nose—out in *Out,* for example. And "truly," how much could they be hiding when riot grrrl phone numbers and addresses were everywhere to be found, not only in 'zines but in *Cosmo?* (Bernikow, 212).

Yet it was not only (or so much) that the major weeklies and glossies were quick (relatively speaking) to pick up on the riot grrrl and lipstick lesbian "phenomena," it was also that more openly (pan)sexual women began taking their acts on the road. Susie (Sexpert) Bright's advice moved from the pages of the lesbian sex 'zine *On Our Backs* to *Elle;* Annie Sprinkle not only displayed her cervix in "alternative" performance venues, but offered as well a course in the Learning Annex (whose courses in sexuality were themselves covered on *Hard Copy* [July 1993]). Nor was it simply that body piercing became common enough to be parodied in Matt Groening's *Life in Hell* in 1992 ("It's disfigure-iffic!"), or (and involving an interracial lesbian couple) on a show notorious for its disregard of race and gender issues, *Saturday Night Live* (March 1995), but that perhaps more obscure, certainly more graphic, tableaux—such as the clang of tongue stud on clit ring—rapidly became narrative clichés, although perhaps only in limited circles.

The sex-power link that so constituted the figure "Madonna" in the early 1990s, and that came to a head, as it were, with the publication of *Sex* and the releases of *Erotica* and *Body of Evidence,* was not the unique phenomenon it was generally presented to be. And for all the flap at the time over Madonna's "overexposure," or Roseanne's parodic "blasphemy," or, for that matter, Courtney Love's supposedly poisoned womb (and mouth and mind), *Sex* sold out, *Roseanne's* ratings remained at the top, and Hole signed a bigger contract than Nirvana's. All were part of a growing popular feminist discourse which was quite conscious of itself *as* discourse— aware of itself as both transgressive and yet always caught up in other, less "liberating" networks.

In this emergent feminist discourse, the speech uttered was sometimes eerily attentive to the silences that constitute it. For all the showing and telling in *Truth or Dare,* for instance, the only two doors actually shut in the cameraman's face were those that would have exposed not Madonna's bared body but Madonna as body-product and as producer: the doors of her home gym and her business meetings. Similarly, Bikini Kill, as prototypical riot grrrl band, more than once imposed an interview ban, preferring instead to distribute information through concerts and 'zines—small wonder when this choice for relative self-representational control was reported, in an article trying very hard to be objectively sympathetic, as "hat[ing] the media's guts," "a movement that apparently seeks to alienate," and "not exactly breaking through" to major labels (France, 23–24). Such willful female mutism is far from traditional female silencing; rather, it actively inscribes the self-conscious *process* of current discourses of female sexualities (*The Piano* is but one obvious manifestation). Such attention to silence as discursive process begins to enact Trinh Minh-ha's provocative suggestion: "Silence is so commonly set in opposition with speech. Silence as a will not to say or a will to unsay and as a language of its own has barely been explored" (73–74).

The question of silence in ambivalent relation to speech could also be usefully compared to the troubling relation of the untrue to the true, and Kirsten Marthe Lentz has argued that such "problems" may be intimately related to the "problem" of bisexuality:

> The double move Madonna makes as she promises "truths" and delivers "untruths" has long been the central and defining aspect of her work. But questions of truth and untruth, authenticity and inauthenticity become very problematic when one considers the way in which bisexuality figures into Madonna's sexual ethos. . . . even if we could decide that Madonna is "truly" bisexual, thus conferring a stroke of authenticity upon her, it would be fruitless. Bisexuality is already caught up in ideologies of inauthenticity and stereotypes of opportunism and sexual excess. (158)

Madonna may only have "played" with the undecidability of bisexuality, but others have been more explicit. Kathleen Hanna (of Bikini Kill) "came out" as bisexual in a national glossy, albeit that glossy was *Out* (Aug./Sept. 1993). She poses for a photo in which her face is covered by her hands, themselves covered by a scrawled "IDE/N/TI/TY"—the word itself split more than doubly: by her two hands, by her fingers, and by the scrawled word's position this one time on her concealing hands rather than, more typically, on her exposed belly. An early nineties joke concerning queers being the only national political movement that would (over)use the word "liminal" seems apropos here. And those who cross and recross borders distort all sorts of boundaries, split identities into more than two neat halves, cannot be trusted to be where or do what they're supposed to. Like the clitoris, inside and outside, difficult to put to "use."[6]

Scene: Late 1990s

A lack of proper seriousness, particularly as concerns feminism, is still often seen as a very big problem. *Time* magazine's "Is Feminism Dead?" issue (June 29, 1998) provides an example of widespread tendencies, in the media and elsewhere, to attribute the decline of feminism itself to "frazzled, self-absorbed girls," such as Ally McBeal (Bellafante, 58). Ally McBeal is, of course, a television character, but one whom *Time* nonetheless chose to depict on its cover along with the historical figures of Susan B. Anthony, Betty Friedan, and Gloria Steinem. Yet it seems somehow perversely appropriate that Ally McBeal provides evidence that "much of feminism has devolved into the silly" (58) in an essay that closes with Friedan's own scornful dismissal of much current feminist activity: "All the sex stuff is stupid" (60).

I have no particular interest in defending *Ally McBeal*—or Ally McBeal, or Calista Flockhart, or David E. Kelley—indeed the producer and cast have themselves already critiqued *Time*'s (and others') misreadings of the show: "This is a comedy about an exaggerated character, and to compare her to Susan B. Anthony is outrageous. To say that our generation has no feminists, that all we have is Ally McBeal is just crap" (Flockhart, cited in De Vries, 26). A subsequent episode of the show parodied *Time* itself, with Ally dreaming "that they put my face on the cover of *Time* magazine, as the face of feminism," as well as a feminist (dream) character who insists Ally drop "that skinny, whiny, emotional slut thing and be exactly who we want you to be" (January 18, 1999).

Ginia Bellafante, in *Time*'s cover article, insists on a stark conflict between the good old days of 1970s feminism and the bad girls of the late 1990s: "In the '70s, feminism produced a pop culture that was intellectually provocative.... Today it's a whole lot of stylish fluff" (56). And this dead-feminism issue of *Time* worries anxiously that somehow all this "stylish fluff" is destroying feminism, a nightmare vision of bad feminists eating up good like deranged (but fashionable) vagina dentatas. Bellafante decries the flighty superficiality of "pseudo-feminists of today" (58) as set against the earnest depth of the (presumably real) feminists twenty years earlier, employing a tired enough, though certainly traditional, strategy: inauthenticity/truth, surface/depth, silly/serious (woman/man).

Ally McBeal is not Bellafante's sole example of the end of feminism, of course: her essay opens, predictably, with a Courtney Love anecdote and goes on to criticize the Spice Girls, an assorted grab-bag of writers dubbed post-Paglian feminists, the novel *Bridget Jones's Diary* (a satire, misread à la *Ally McBeal* as an earnest piece of work), nonsocial–science feminists in the academy, and the magazine *Bust*. As I happened to have on hand a copy of *Bust* contemporaneous with

Time's "Is Feminism Dead" issue (Summer/Fall and June 29, 1998, respectively), it seemed appropriate to take a look at that "peekaboo view of the world of sex that leaves one feeling not like an empowered adult but more like a twelve-year old sneaking in some sexy reading behind her parents' back [sic]" (Bellafante, 60). Comparing the two issues proved quite fascinating, as it turned out. On the cover of *Bust* is Missy (Misdemeanor) Elliott—with one extremely foregrounded, latex-gloved hand extended toward the spectator, while, inside, her interview focuses on the supportive relationships of women in hip hop. Thus far, *Bust* does not much resemble what Bellafante would have led one to expect. (I can only wonder whether Missy Elliott's parodic performance strategies irritate Bellafante also, as she doesn't mention her—nor does the following article, by Nadya Labi, which addresses "the future of feminism" [61].) Indeed, that particular *Bust* publication reads like the world of '90s feminism that *Time* forgot, although it does include an article in which a young lawyer answers questions people pose her about the "realism" of *Ally McBeal*. Elsewhere, *Bust* addresses issues and figures from both ends of *Time*'s great generational feminist divide: the "Media Whore" page sharply reads ads and other media, much as the (then) young *Ms.* magazine did; and Nancy Friday (then) is interviewed, as is Eve Ensler, the (now) author of *The Vagina Monologues.*

The point here is not to beat the dead cultural relic that *Time* surely is, nor to castigate Ms. Jones, in this case Bellafante, for not knowing what's been happening. Rather, I should like to draw attention to a number of tactics that commonly emerge in such criticisms of contemporary feminism—including their typical tendencies to categorize rigidly, to underplay (or deplore) heterogeneity, or to mourn a lost golden age and view change and divergence apocalyptically. But also commonly found in such critiques is an overarching implication that "all the sex stuff is [indeed] stupid"—often alongside a strong preference for Truth (authenticity, depth, earnestness, realism) matched by an equally strong distrust of (or blindness to) humor, irony, or parody. Indeed, when Roseanne stretched the limits of the realistic domestic sitcom beyond common recognition on her show's often parodic last season, *Roseanne* was criticized on precisely those grounds: "Remember how wretched her ABC sitcom got in its final year when she turned away from realism?" (Roush, 12).[7] (By the way, wasn't the former problem-with-feminism the "fact" that feminists had no sense of humor?)

Finally, one might begin to suspect that it is sometimes female sexuality *itself*—particularly when unmoored from reproductive issues and "lost" in realms of pleasure or desire or performativity— which is read as fluffy, superficial. Is it really still just the hole, the "nothing-to-see," which is in and of itself considered to be "silly" or "stupid," "a whole lot of stylish fluff"? Bellafante's argument suggests as much: "The glitziest affair in recent months was a reading of *The Vagina Monologues,* a performance piece about female private parts. . . . The actresses had come to raise money to fight domestic violence, but the cause seemed lost amid the event's giddy theatrics"—the latter referring to performances about pubic hair, "an homage to an obscene word for female genitalia," and "three solid minutes of orgasmic moaning." She bemoans "Fashion spectacle, paparazzi-jammed galas, mindless sex talk—is this what the road map to greater female empowerment has become?" (56). "Giddy theatrics" and "mindless sex talk." Does the problem-with-feminism-these-days seem to emerge precisely when women take their sexuality quite seriously but also stop taking it so *seriously* —that is, when they represent it with irony or humor or—worse—parody? Is that the point at which "the cause seem[s] lost"?

Notes

1. There are different versions of the audience's reaction to Donita Sparks's tampax tossing, although Sparks herself has narrated that someone threw it back on stage when the audience discovered what the lobbed object actually was (Crist, 33).

2. More than one critic has also remarked on the homophobia of her character's courtroom revelation that she broke off with a previous (wealthy, older) lover because she discovered him in bed with a man and therefore didn't feel she could "compete" (Crimp and Warner, Champagne in *Madonnarama*). While this is, narratively speaking, "true" (the man so accused nods in agreement and slinks from the courtroom), Rebecca's motivation (besides sexual domination and satiation—the succubus persona) is that everything she says and does is a web of self-serving lies (the dick persona—which this character shares with Sharon Stone's in *Basic Instinct*, with the very significant exceptions of (1) *Basic Instinct's* bisexuality and (2) a narrative insistence on the absolute difference between truth and lies in *Body of Evidence*). Rebecca's "true" character motivation in rejecting a bisexual lover, therefore, seems to me almost irrelevant (I shall return to the issue of truth as it intersects with sexuality shortly).

3. Consider whether you remember Ophelia's hair "spread wide," then check *Hamlet* IV.vii.175. Ophelia's problematic sexuality, of course, consists of the possibility that she may have (had) one.

4. A useful overview is provided by Gottlieb and Wald.

5. *Rolling Stone* conveniently "exposed" such charges in list form, while reproducing a number of them in the same article (France, 23):

> 1. They can't play.
> 2. They hate men.
> 3. They're fakers.
> 4. They're elitist.
> 5. They aren't really a movement.

6. See Gayatri Spivak on the excess of the clitoris relative to the economy of reproduction:

even as we reclaim the excess of the clitoris, we cannot fully escape the symmetry of the reproductive definition. One cannot write off what may be called a uterine social organization . . . *in favor of* a clitoral. The uterine social organization should, rather, be "situated" through the understanding that it has so far been established by excluding a clitoral social organization. (152)

7. And, once again, the more powerful she became, the more she was envisioned as out of control (or touch): "When we asked Roseanne to pick her all-time favorite episodes, she named, with typical defiance, five from this [final] season, which most critics and fans agree has been a disaster" (*TV Guide* Editors, 51).

References

Bellafante, Ginia (1998). "Who Put the 'Me' in Feminism?" *Time* (June 29): 54–60.
Bennetts, Leslie (1993). "k.d. lang Cuts It Close." *Vanity Fair* (August): 94–98, and 142–46.
Bernikow, Louise (1993). "The New Activists: Fearless, Funny, Fighting Mad." *Cosmopolitan* (April): 162–65, 212.
Bright, Susie (1992). *Sexual Reality: A Virtual Sex World Reader.* Pittsburg, Pennsylvania and San Francisco, Calif.: Cleis Press.
Califia, Pat (1993). "*Sex* and Madonna; or, What Did You Expect from a Girl Who Doesn't Put Out on the First Five Dates?" In Frank and Smith, *Madonnarama:* 169–84.
Champagne, John (1993). "Stabat Madonna." In Frank and Smith, *Madonnarama:* 111–38.
Che, Cathay (1993). "Wannabe." In Frank and Smith, *Madonnarama:* 21–34.
Cixous, Hélène (1981). "The Laugh of the Medusa." (1975). In *New French Feminisms.* Ed. Elaine Marks and Isabelle de Courtivron. New York: Schocken, 1981: 245–64.
Crimp, Douglas, and Michael Warner (1993). "No Sex in *Sex.*" In Frank and Smith, *Madonnarama:* 93–110.
Crist, Renée (1993). "The Magnificent 7." *Spin* (July): 32–35, 90.
De Vries, Hilary (1998). "Ally Chat." *TV Guide* (September 26): 18–20, 23, 26.
Editors (1997). "Our View." *TV Guide* (May): 51.
France, Kim (1993). "Grrrls at War." *Rolling Stone* (July 8–22): 23–24.
Frank, Lisa, and Paul Smith, eds. (1993). *Madonnarama: Essays on Sex and Popular Culture.* Pittsburg, Pennsylvania and San Francisco, Calif.: Cleis Press.
Gottlieb, Joanne and Gayle Wald. "Smells Like Teen Spirit: Riot Grrrls, Revolution, and Women in Independent Rock." *Critical Matrix* 7.2: 11–43.
Handelman, David (1992). "Madonna's Head Trip." *Vogue* (October): 288–95, 393.
Harris, thomas allen (1993). "Phallic momma / sell my pussy / make a dollar." In Frank and Smith, *Madonnarama:* 35– 46.

hooks, bell. "Power to the Pussy: We Don't Wannabe Dicks in Drag." In Frank and Smith, *Madonnarama:* 65–80.

Irigaray, Luce (1985). *This Sex Which Is Not One* (1977). Trans. Catherine Porter. Ithaca, N.Y.: Cornell UP.

Labi, Nadya (1998). "The Next Generation: What Do Girls Want?" *Time* (June 29): 60–62.

Lentz, Kirsten Marthe. "Chameleon, Vampire, Rich Slut." In Frank and Smith, *Madonnarama:* 153–68.

Madonna (1992). *Sex.* Warner.

McConnell, Wendy (1993). "It's My Riot and I'll Whine If I Want To." *Fiz 7* (July/August): 3.

Roush, Matt (1998). "The Roush Review." *TV Guide* (October 10): 12.

Schwichtenberg, Cathy, ed. (1993). *The Madonna Connection: Representational Politics, Subcultural Identities, and Cultural Theory.* Boulder, Colo.: Westview.

Spivak, Gayatri Chakravorty (1988). "French Feminism in an International Frame." *In Other Worlds: Essays in Cultural Politics.* New York and London: Routledge: 134–53.

Trinh T. Minh-ha (1988). "Not You / Like You: Post-Colonial Women and the Interlocking Questions of Identity and Difference." *Inscriptions* 3/4: 71–77.

11

Migrant Landscapes

Iain Chambers

At the tip
  of the always dark
  of new beginnings.
  —A. H. Reynolds

Every philosophy also conceals a philosophy; every opinion is also
a hiding place, every word also a mask.
                                    —Friedrich Nietzsche[1]

To imagine is to begin the process that transforms reality.
                                    —bell hooks[2]

Migration is a one-way trip. There is no "home" to go back to.
                                    —Stuart Hall[3]

The imaginary landscape of an inquiry is not without value, even if it is
without rigor. It restores what was earlier called "popular culture," but it
does so in order to transform what was represented as the matrix-force of
history into a mobile infinity of tactics. It thus keeps before our eyes the
structure of a social imagination in which the problem constantly takes
different forms and begins anew. It also wards off the effects of an analysis
which necessarily grasps these practices only on the margins of a technical
apparatus, at the point where they alter or defeat its instruments. It is the
study itself which is marginal with respect to the phenomena studied. The
landscape that represents these phenomena in an imaginary mode thus has
an overall corrective and therapeutic value in resisting their reduction by a
lateral examination. It at least assures their presence as ghosts. This return
to another scene thus reminds us of the relation between the experience of
these practices and what remains of them in analysis. It is evidence,
evidence which can be fantastic and not scientific, of the disproportion
between everyday tactics and a strategic elucidation. Of all the things
everyone does, how much gets written down? Between the two, the image,
the phantom of the expert but mute body, preserves the difference.
                                    —Michel de Certeau[4]

1

To begin with these marks on the page, the movement of calligraphy: for to write is, of course, to travel. It is to enter a space, a zone, a territory, sometimes sign-posted by generic indicators (travel writing, biography, history . . .), but every-where characterized by movement: the passage of words, the caravan of thoughts, the flux of the imaginary, the slippage of the metaphor, "the drift across the page . . . the wandering eyes."[5] Here, to write (and read) does not necessarily involve a project intent on "penetrating" the real, in order to double it and re-cite it, but rather involves an attempt to add to it. To write, therefore, although an imperial-ist gesture, for it is engaged in an attempt to establish a path, a trajectory, a, how-ever limited and transitory, territory and dominion, is also the gesture of an offer, a gift that attempts to reveal an opening in the already given. This is the paradox in the belly of writing. It works with known materials—a language, a lexicon, a discourse, a series of archives—and yet seeks to release a supplement, an excess, an unforeseen and unknown possibility.

Writing depends on the support of the "I"—the presumed prop of the au-thorial voice—for its authority. Yet in the provisional character of writing this structure oscillates, is put in doubt, disrupted, and weakened. And so we begin to encounter a discourse that carries within itself the critique of its own language. For the travel of writing, unless it concludes in babble, or silence, also involves a return. Here something is lost, and something gained. What is lost is the security of the starting point, of the subject of departure; what is gained is an ethical rela-tionship to the language in which we are subjects, and in which we subject each other.

> For writing, like a game that defies its own rules, is an ongoing practice that may be said to be concerned, not with inserting a "me" into language, but with creating an opening where the "me" disappears while "I" endlessly come and go, as the nature of language requires. To confer an Author on a text is to close the writing. Eureka! It makes sense! *This is it!* I hold the key to the puzzle![6]

So, writing becomes a travelog, a constant journeying across the threshold between fact and fiction, taking up residence in that border country in which histories dis-solve into narrative. Here the actual authority of history is frequently queried and satirized, and the empirical claims of reality subject to irony.[7] The author becomes a collector, drawing together accounts in the hope that in their juxtaposition they may temporarily entwine and add up to something before continuing their sepa-rate ways. In this fashion the region of Patagonia, "the uttermost part of the earth," with its townships, railways, roads, hamlets, houses, and people of multiple de-scent, can be revealed and plotted not merely by geography or on a map, but through the narratives that traverse its mountains, lakes, rivers, and pampas. In Bruce Chatwin's writing, Patagonia is transformed into a landscape in which illusions and identities (Butch Cassidy, the Ancient Mariner, Charles Darwin, Caliban) become whispers, rumors, traces of tales. The land is redolent with speech, figures inscribed with (his)stories. This drifting nomadology of the imaginary directly recalls the Australian Aboriginal view of the land as a text, in which dreams, myths, and destinies are not so much constructed in words and language as "written" on the land itself.[8]

II

In all the charts of this country—both Spanish and English—a certain sound in Hoste Island bears the name Tekenika. The Indians had no such name for that or any other place, but the word in the Yahgan tongue means "difficult or awkward to see or understand." No doubt the bay was pointed out to the native, who, when asked the name of it, answered, "Teke uneka," implying, "I don't understand what you mean," and down went the name "Tekenika."

—E. Lucas Bridges[9]

L'étranger te permet d'être toi-même, en faisant, de toi, un étranger.
—Edmond Jabès[10]

The move into dialogue, into a sense of language that produces culture, history, and difference, involves a break with the romantic idea of the world as a separate entity attendant upon our attention, as though it were the diametrical "other" of our being and thought: the exotic elsewhere, the untouched difference, the world of the "natural" and the "native." To adopt this last stance is but to replay the nostalgia of difference, and to set up a presumed "authenticity" to be held against the corruption of modernity. It merely reproduces the power of existing positions: I, the nostalgic observer; you, the native, victim of my modernity. It establishes a blind circle that may comfort the observer, but that is powerless to address the conditions she or he nominates. We, in, and with, our differences are ultimately caught up in the same skein, the same net, the same topology. It is not to the "other," as separate entity and external interlocutor, that we should look, but rather to the conditions of dialogue in which different powers, histories, limits, and languages are inscribed. This, as Chandra Mohanty points out, draws us into an endless journey "between cultures, languages, and complex configurations of meaning and power."[11] It proposes, in James Clifford's words, "a new marking of 'the West' as a site of ongoing power *and* contestation, of centrality *and* dispersal."[12]

Beyond that recognition it also opens up for the children and offspring of a postcolonial world: "the possibilities of alter/native ficto-historical texts which can create a world in process while continually freeing themselves from their own biases."[13] There is a relentless transformation in postcolonial literature of time into space as the gap between worlds is negotiated and histories distilled into a sense of place and dwelling.[14] In the syncreticity of such cultural practices an imposed language—"English," Western "civilization," rock music—is frequently made into what the Palestinian author Anton Shammas calls a "homeland."

A_____, who brings us coffee, croissants, freshly squeezed orange juice and syrupy dates each morning, is Moroccan. He and his family have lived all their lives in Essaouira: a white-washed town, guarded by a pink Portuguese fort. With its back to the desert it faces the warm breezes of the Atlantic. There are few guests at the hotel. We strike up a friendship. No, that's too strong a word, too invasive, too romantic. We establish a "feeling," find each other "simpatico." That's better, more fitting for what we both know, despite the later exchange of addresses, is a transitory experience.

We don't talk much. I stumble through the remnants of schoolboy French. He nods, occasionally drenching me in a flood of sounds. Naturally, it is L_____ who frames these encounters. Her superior linguistic and social competence somehow giving a sense to the empty spaces between the men.

I sometimes wonder what is the nature of A_____'s interest in me, and mine in him.

I can't write A_____'s story, and yet his presence needs to be acknowledged. I can't present him as a unitary subject, complete his history, dreams, and passions. That would merely close the circle in a distorted mirror of my self. On the edges of that favorite postmodern metaphor—the desert—I meet a real man of the desert. Yet I can't represent him, I don't know how to make him figure in what I want to say.

Sure, I could provide him with a background by splicing together bits of the country's history, politics, and culture; even something of a foreground: the color of his "jellabahb," his sandalled walk, or his three children that we once glimpsed during an evening stroll. But even if I fragmented him and re-presented him in these splinters, that is still not quite the point. He has his own story. It is there in his clothes, his language, his house, in the gestures he makes when indicating the best places to go to eat "tajines," "bstilla," couscous, sardines.

A_____ has a voice, a presence. It is subaltern, still possibly colonized, certainly, by our standards, repressed, invariably hemmed in by the limits of locality, tradition and, why not, the tourism that likes him as he is. Our encounters are circumscribed, the exchange fixed by our respective locations, their sense starkly incomplete and not always comprehensible. Still, in the moments of our brief conversations, and in the connective gloss that L_____ seeks gently to construct around them, it is possible to recognize the ethics of a space. Here worlds meet. In the silence between the words we can hear the potential murmur of a dialogue barely begun.

The immediate surfaces of the world—language, clothes, faces, silence—can only appear mute to those who don't or haven't learned to listen.

III

Experience had taught him that reason could not be counted on in such situations. There was always an extra element, mysterious and not quite within reach, that one had not reckoned with.

Nothing in my experience had prepared me for the city.

—Angela Carter[16]

Cultures come to be represented by virtue of the process of repetition through which their "meanings" are vicariously addressed to— *through*—an Other.

—Homi K. Bhabha[17]

In the oblique gaze of the migrant that cuts across the territory of the western metropolis there exists the hint of a metaphor; a figure that might suggest how we all inhabit composite realities, diverse languages, fragmented memories and stories. In the extensive and multiple world of the modern city, with its languages of consumerism and images of difference, we become nomads, migrating across a system that is too vast to be our own, but in which we are fully involved—translating and transforming what we find and absorb into local instances of sense. As Michel de Certeau suggestively puts it, metropolitan space is made habitable as though it were borrowed for a moment by a transient, an immigrant, a nomad: "Since in short there is no *way* out, the fact remains that we are *foreigners* on the inside—*but there is no outside.*"[18]

It is above all here that we are inducted into a hybrid state and composite culture in which the simple dualism of first and third worlds snaps and there emerges what Homi Bhabha calls a "differential commonality," and what Felix Guattari refers to as the "process of *heterogenesis.*"[19] The boundaries of the liberal consensus and its centered sense of language, being, position, and politics, are breached and scattered as these other histories come to be rewritten in the contentious languages of the metropolis.

The stereotype—the "black," the "Indian," the "native," the "other"—collapses beneath the weight of such complexity, stretched between histories it tears, becomes piecemeal. Listening and moving to Soul II Soul, grooving to multiple histories configured in a hybrid sound mix, we recognize that we are all, with our often very different accounts, travelling through the networks of a world that is hooked to a shared destiny and increasingly participates in the same audiovisual circuits of communication. It is in this fractal culture of kaleidoscopic collision and collusion that we encounter a postcolonial genealogy of modernity in which color and a redeeming confusion is restored to the homogeneity of an officially bleached past.

In the migrant landscape of contemporary metropolitan cultures, deterritorialized and decolonized, drifting in the circuits between speech, image, and oblivion, the struggling into sense and history is pieced together. It is continually decomposed and recomposed in an open-ended dialog between what we have inherited and where we inhabit. It was surely to this continual and essential process of revealing that Heidegger was referring when he quoted Hölderlin's phrase: "poetically man dwells"? In the shifting insterstices of our world, whether moving to the acoustic patterns of our bodily beat or the technosurrealist design of computerized simulations, there lies the opening that redeems and reconstitutes our being.

It is perhaps something that we can hear when Youssou N'Dour, from Dakar, sings in Wolof, a Sengalese dialect, in a tent pitched in the suburbs of Naples. Only six months earlier I had heard his haunting voice in a New York club, this time singing in the context of the Japanese techno-pop/New Age sound of Ryuichi Sakamoto and No Wave New York guitarist Arto Lindsay.[20] It is surely in these terms, well before intellectual and institutional acknowledgment, that we come most immediately and effectively to recognize the growing territory in which the imaginary is being decolonized and the Eurocentric voice deconstructed.

This brings us to reconsider the histories we have inherited and inhabit: the histories of language, of politics, of culture, and experience. The politics of liberation, of freedom, have invariably appealed to the ultimate possibility of rational transparency: politics providing the communal insistence on the realization of this rational goal. But what if the world we live in proves to be more intractable? What if its opaque features are not susceptible to the mastery of a single, transparent gaze? What if that opaqueness, and the real differences it represents, is irreducible to a single explanation? What if in society, and between society and nature, there is no common rule? To accept this opaqueness, this intractability and incommensurability (Jean-François Lyotard's "différend"), means to extend and complicate our sense of "politics." It also means to critique not only the limits of the liberal ground of consensual management, but also the Marxist proposal of communal realization. For both persistently rule out difference and otherness. Referring to Hegel and Marx, William E. Connolly writes:

> The ontology each accepts is a precondition to the credibility of freedom and realization. But . . . each advances a theory of freedom which supports suppression and subjugation in the name of the realization for the self and the community. Because each ideal projects the possibility of drawing all otherness into the whole it endorses, any otherness which persists will be interpreted as irrationality, irresponsibility, incapacity or perversity. It can never be acknowledged as that which is produced by the order it unsettles.[21]

Yet, we have come to appreciate that the languages of resistance are inscribed on the inside of appearances. There, reversing the relationships of power, they hide and dwell in the rites of religion, in the particular inflection of a musical cadence;

they inhabit the space of everyday speech and provide the "surreptious creativities" (de Certeau) that lie in the use and abuse of consumerism. They produce "a skill ceaselessly recreating opacities and ambiguities—spaces of darkness and trickery—in the universe of technocratic transparency, a skill that disappears into them and reappears again, taking no responsibility for the administration of a totality."[22] It is where the familiar, the taken for granted, is turned around, acquires an unsuspected twist, and, in becoming temporarily unfamiliar, produces an unexpected, sometimes magical, space. It is where the languages we live in, precisely because we live in them, are spoken and rewritten. Drawing on an already existing lexicon of ready-mades to signify, to trope the trope, as Henry Louis Gates Jr. puts it, we can locate in such practices a script of traces, a particular way of picturing, signifying, and enframing the world we have inherited.[23] For it is our dwelling in this manysided space, inhabiting its languages, cultivating and building on them, that engenders our very sense of existence and discloses its possibilities.[24]

IV

It is, above all, the chronicles of diasporas—black, Jewish, rural migrations—that constitute the ground swell of modernity and which query and undermine any simple or uncomplicated sense of origins and traditions and lead us into mixed histories, mingled cultures and languages.

For example, the Jews who were expelled from Spain in 1492 and established themselves in the more tolerant world of the Ottoman Empire: in Salonica, Rhodes, Cairo, Istanbul. The subsequent histories of this expelled community, the "marranes" or "sefardita," involved poly-identities. Organized around the Mediterranean in a shifting combination of Occident and Orient, speaking a fifteenth-century Spanish dialect ("ladino"), such identities were shaped by migration and blended histories, full of linguistic and culinary traces: memories of Spain and Greece, that later included Italy and France in the case of Edgar Morin's father, Vidal; or Bulgaria, Russia, Turk, Armenian, and Romanian with Elias Canetti. Morin suggests that they represent an identity that is anterior to the subject/citizen of the modern nation state; we might add that they also suggest a possible posterior sense of identity with respect to the narrow confines of modem nationalism. One foot is here and the other always elsewhere, straddling both sides of the border.[25]

In varying degrees and comfort we all live in *and* between different histories, subject to their contiguous composition. It is under those conditions, inhabiting those shifting stories, conditions, and potential identities, that, as both Vico and Marx insisted, we make history. Beyond the abstract ideology of uniformity, stamped with the seals of tradition, nation, race, and religion, we are all destined to live in what the Chicano novelist Arturo Islas calls a "border condition."

I arrived in Naples in 1976. I came not as a tourist or in search of work, but for an appointment in love. From a certain point of view I didn't choose Naples, it was rather as though the city had chosen me. This pink, grey, and yellow-colored town on the sea offered a horizon in front of which a relationship, a life, could acquire form and develop. I, the son of a Scottish mother and English father, citizen of the North, found myself involved in a radically different world. It was one with which I had to struggle in order to render it comprehensible . . . livable. So, the city also came to represent the scene of an encounter and clash between diverse languages, reasons, and histories. My own cultural baggage, my particular story, was continually exposed in this play of difference. My logic and habits could no longer hide in the folds of common sense now that the sense of reality I inhabited differed so radically from the one in which they had been initially formed and recognised.

A sense of crisis can have many exits; a threat to one's sense of being can also lead to an unexpected opening, a further throw of the dice. I began to read the city, without always halting at the borders of its chaos, corruption, and decay. I began to experience it as the space of an alternative. It is perhaps in the dialogue that is installed between ourselves and this sense of "otherness" that our particular selves are most sharply revealed. In such encounters, in an ethics that respects that other voice, language invariably loses its previous anchorage, sense of center, and direction as it slips through the openings in dialogue towards a wider perspective.

To live "elsewhere" means to continually find yourself involved in a conversation in which different identities are recognized, exchanged, and mixed, but do not vanish. Here differences function not necessarily as barriers but rather as signals of complexity. To be a stranger in a strange land, to be lost (in Italian "spaesato"—"without a country"), is perhaps a condition typical of contemporary life. To the forcibly induced migrations of slaves, peasants, the poor, and the excolonial world, that make up so many of the hidden histories of modernity, we can also add the increasing nomadism of modern thought. Now that the old house of criticism, historiography, and intellectual certitude is in ruins, we all find ourselves on the road. Faced with a loss of roots, and the subsequent weakening in the grammar of "authenticity," we move into a wider landscape. Our sense of belonging, our language, and the myths we carry in us remain, but no longer as "origins" or signs of "authenticity" capable of guaranteeing the sense of our lives. They now linger on as traces, voices, and memories that are mixed in with other encounters, histories, episodes, experiences.

Naples, a city that is apparently deeply tied to its particular sense of roots, language, and history, is paradoxically also able to become an imaginary city, a place for nomads. This city, despite all its specific details and insular claims on experience, cannot avoid acquiring a part in other stories, other idioms, other possibilities. It is transformed from being a self-referring monument to becoming an intersection, a meeting place, a moment of rendezvous, in a wider network. Loosened from its moorings, and left to drift, the city reveals in its interior further spaces for a text that we are constantly rewriting.

5

Le nom autorise le je mais ne le justife pas.
—Edmond Jabès[26]

It is no more than a moral prejudice that truth is worth more than appearance; it is even the worst-proved assumption that exists. Let us concede at least this much: there would be no life at all if not on the basis of perspective evaluation and appearances; and if, with the virtuous enthusiasm and awkwardness exhibited by some philosophers, one wanted to abolish the "apparent world" altogether, well, assuming *you* could do that—at any rate nothing would remain of your "truth" either! Indeed, what compels us to assume there exists an essential antithesis between "true" and "false"? Is it not enough to suppose grades of apparentness and as it were lighter and darker shades and tones of appearances—different *valeurs,* to speak in the language of painters? Why could the world *which is of any concern to us*—not be a fiction? And he who then objects: "but to the fiction there belongs an author?" —could he not be met with the round retort: *why?* Are we not permitted to be a little ironical now about the subject as we are about the predicate and object.

—Friedrich Nietzsche[27]

To discuss the decentering of the white male voice, of the European cogito, and to bring into view the "other," a cultural and historical elsewhere, is this merely to draw that "otherness" back into the range of the voice and the discourse that nominates its own decentering? Perhaps it is. But it simultaneously forces a confrontation with the effects of instability that invariably follows the extension of the languages of recognition/misrecognition/nonrecognition. It means to live in oscillation between a displaced sense of center, of the "I," under the gaze of those other eyes/I's, and to subscribe to a subsequent weakening and uncertainty within the limits of *my* thoughts and actions.

This is not to endorse a retreat into self-reflection, but is rather about positioning, specifying, locating, and limiting a particular self. The insistence on limits, on a certain politics of reticence, even silence, does not necessarily involve recourse to the refuge of fixed or insurmountable barriers, but rather sees in that liminal, conjunctural and differentiated territory the space of questions, potential extensions, further dialogue and subsequent remakings. It is to suggest the modest gaze and curiosity of the stranger—the critic as a collector and wanderer: "un étranger avec, sous le bras, un livre de petit format" (Edmond Jabès). It is as though to propose a new type of intellectuality that, while trying to understand the "world from within" (Siegfried Kracauer), is profoundly marked by uncertainty and anxiety.

VI

"There are winners," said the imprisoned rabbi, the imprisoned saint. "Winners with their arrogance, their eloquence. And there are losers without words and without signs."
    "The race of the silent is tenacious."

—Edmond Jabès[28]

Representation: that which simultaneously speaks for and stands in for something else.

> These meanings are often run together because the notion of mediation underscores them both. As a consequence, the ethical and political motivation behind questions of representation in both its senses will similarly concern the possible conflict of interests between the mediator and the mediated. This expresses an obvious political asymmetry that is considerable because unavoidable.[29]

Language is not primarily a means of communication; it is, above all, a means of cultural construction in which our very selves and sense are constituted. There is no clear or obvious "message," just as there is no neutral means of representation.[30] This is further compounded by the shift in gaze from the local underworlds of Western culture, its hidden histories and subaltern cultures, to the even wider horizons and more extensive territories of contemporary metropolitan cultures in which the "typical" may no longer be London or New York, but Mexico City and Calcutta.

The breakup of universals decisively marks the body. By accepting historical and cultural differentiation, it is no longer possible to think of the body as the passive ground or constant of subsequent social activity. It too is a historicized and social site that can neither be considered fixed nor taken for granted. For, as Vicky Kirby argues, the assumed referent of the body becomes a flexible zone, interleaved, crossed, and composed by multiple discourses, constructed in different languages, tempos, and places, received and lived with different meanings that are diversely embodied.[31] To treat the world, its possibilities and its individuals, in a contingent manner brings us to the threshold of enabling differences to be, and "calls into question the project of perfecting mastery of the world on the grounds that, given resistances built into the order of things, the project would reduce everything to a straitjacket while pursuing an illusory goal."[32]

VII

Today, planned authenticity is rife; as a product of hegemony and a remarkable counterpart of universal standardization, it constitutes an

efficacious means of silencing the cry of racial oppression. We no longer
wish to erase your difference. We demand, on the contrary, that you
remember and assert it. At least, to a certain extent.

—Trinh T. Minh-ha[33]

It is when the western nation comes to be seen, in Conrad's famous
phrase, as one of the dark corners of the earth, that we can begin to
explore new places from which to write histories of peoples and
construct theories of narration.

—Homi K. Bhabha[34]

The Western intellectual through the language of nomination sanctifies his igno-
rance (the "Subject of Europe"), renders the rest of the world transparent ("Asia,"
"Africa," "Latin America"), and "erases" the real distance of location and difference and the subsequent "measure of silence."35 And yet there is a striking twist
in this story of unequal exchange. Jacques Derrida, unanimously condemned in
the 1980s by metropolitan left-wing critics for his supposedly depoliticized
language of deconstruction, has paradoxically elsewhere turned out to have
had the highest political impact, particularly in the zone of subaltern studies
and postcolonial criticism. Opening up the gaps in language, contesting its presumed unicity and metaphysical authority, Derrida's work has suggested the
spaces in which other worlds could appear and begin to collate the blankness surrounding the hegemonic European text.[36] Through suspending, interrogating,
and differentiating sense, deconstruction offered the chance to break a historical
silence and query the ethnocentric conclusion that invariably lead to "some domestic benefit."[37]

VIII

In *History: The Last Things before the Last,* Siegfried Kracauer argued that the mo-
tor of history lay in the nonidentity between reason and reality. He compared the
emergence of modern historiography to the rise of photography and their shared
proposal to, in Otto Ranke's words, show "how things actually were." The analogy that Kracauer draws between these two modern forms of representation—
photography and historiography—suggests a sense of time and memory enframed
by images.

Along with his Proustian research for "lost time," and an idea of historical
knowledge that comes to be most fully embodied in the figure of Ahasuerus, the
Wandering Jew, Kracauer insists on the epistemological value of the image. This
runs through his writings, from the early newspaper articles on mass entertainment, travel, dance, the detective story, and the hotel lobby, written during the
Weimar Republic, to his posthumously published book on the philosophy of his-

tory. For, as he puts it, images, however humble and marginal their origins, "help us to think *through* things, not above them."[38]

This immediately suggests that it is not simply the image, but knowledge itself, that has been secularized and has now lost its aura. And just as Walter Benjamin once argued that such a secularization led to the politicization of art, so we might extend that judgment to include what passes for knowledge. In the continual confrontation with contingency we are constantly having to breach the boundaries of that precarious concept.

Barcelona, December. Between Carrer del Carme and Carrer de Hospital there is the ancient Hospital de la Santa Creu. Here there is an installation by Francesc Abad: "La linia de Portbou. Homentage a Walter Benjamin." Closed for the holidays it provides a space for speculation. Walter Benjamin the collector, the pearl diver (Hannah Arendt), perpetually on the margins of European culture (German, French, Jewish), a migrant, in transit, a frontier spirit who in constantly travelling to the border speaks to our times.

Intellectually speaking the history of modernity has invariably been represented as a tragedy. We are encouraged to consider it as an epoch of decadence and decay; the moment when the promise of history is sullied and finally frustrated by the loss of authenticity. Yet, despite the immense horror revealed by modernity, there were scenes in its daily drama that although generally ignored were pregnant with promise. These were the concealed histories that accompanied the rhythms of modernity that were being written in the department stores and on the dance floors, as later in supermarkets and soap operas and a domestic, frequently female, space. Elsewhere such rhythms were also being scored and signified in the officially shunned "mumbo jumbo" (Ishmael Reed) of the poetry, literature, and music of exslaves and the subsequent formation of an urban black aesthetic—an aesthetic that has not only proved central to the modern metropolitan experience, but perhaps provides the secret, although invariably unacknowledged, heart of its vernacular avant garde. While denied a voice in the official account, these metropolitan stories have secretly undermined the presumptions of a single, monolithic culture and from their marginal and migrant formations helped forge the modern art of always "being in between" (Michel de Certeau).

IX

> The problem of the value of truth stepped before us—or was it we who stepped before this problem? Which of us is Oedipus here? Which of us sphinx? It is, it seems, a rendezvous of questions and question-marks.
>
> —Friedrich Nietzsche[39]

Today there is in act the break-up of ideological essentialism. Among its consequences is the fragmentation of a homogenous and transcendental sense of the "other."[40] It (for we are talking of a concept, not a specific, historical, body) is now plunged into time and circumstances; it comes alive. A fixed scheme of location and presumed identities shatters. A rationalizing totality in which everything was referred back to a center, presumably secured by the neutral voice of "knowledge," "science," "culture," and its associated Eurocentric accent, passes into vernacular confusion and slides toward a fragmentary complexity and "the bitter stubbornness of a wandering question."[41] The concept in becoming concrete is forced into movement. It travels, it finds itself involved in dialogue, exchange, interrogation. The abstract idea of difference dissolves to subsequently reappear in diverse, even incommensurable, histories that are heterogeneously incorporated in a differentiated culture.

There is a moment here in which we encounter the extreme extension of cognitive possibilities—war, death, our heart of darkness: "The horror, the horror." There is a city such as Beirut that can become the tangible zone of horror, the dark heart of the unsayable and the indecipherable. For when thought is organized by differences, rather than the levelling logic of contradictions, we are drawn out of the shelter of its presumed resolutions to travel under the wider skies of a troubling complexity. It is a mode of thinking

> that contemplates the present as a myriad of conflicts, none of which can be suppressed, in which frontiers are not barriers but thresholds, sites of transit, of movement. If one had to define the modern subject it would be as a frontier subject. The classical language of politics and philosophy is not able to describe this zone of shadows and horrors, nor dissolve them.[42]

It is a wet, grey afternoon in March, the drizzle slanting in the yellow headlights of the cars. I enter the Angelica cinema on Houston, near the corner of Broadway. Just a few minutes walk away there is the remarkable Mary Kelly exhibition Interim *at The New Museum . . . aah, the joys of New York. At the bar in the elegant foyer I order a cappuccino and a piece of cheesecake. I've decided to see* Black Rain, *not the Ridley Scott movie set in contemporary Osaka, but Shōhei Imamura's film based on the homonymous novel by Masuji Ibuse. It is on sale by the ticket booth.*

Downstairs, in the almost empty cinema that periodically rumbles with the passing subway trains, I follow the story of Yasuko. Yasuko is a young woman who experienced the black rain that fell on Hiroshima after the explosion of the atom bomb. Fleeing the destroyed city, she, her uncle, and aunt, go to live in the countryside. Despite her uncle's efforts to find a partner, she is unable to marry. All know that she was caught in the radioactive shower. She is forever marked, contaminated. Eventually, Yasuko succumbs to radiation sickness and death. The subtitled, black-and-white visuals underline the delicate bitterness of the story. In black and white it is not the aura of realism, retrospective, or documentary that is recalled, so much as the poetic starkness of a harrowing morality play. I, too, felt as though I had been marked.

Many months later my mother phoned me in Italy. She had just seen Black Rain *on British television. "It's terrible what people do to each other. They shouldn't do things like that." Taken off-balance, I could only mumble my assent.*

In *Le Monde* of 23 August 1990 there is an article on Poland, tourism, and postwar reconstruction. Warsaw was almost completely razed to the ground during World War II. Eighty-five percent of the buildings were destroyed. 800,000 died under the effects of Nazi bombs, mines, and flame throwers. 450,000 of the dead were Jews. Old Warsaw, the historical center, was subsequently rebuilt. Working from photographs, drawings, and memory, architects and engineers, employing the latest techniques and taking the opportunity to install modern plumbing, have reconstructed the ancient center and returned it to its prebellic appearance. In this simulacra of a previous Warsaw all traces of the ghetto have been removed. There remains only the giant Jewish cemetery and its "tombs without descendants."

In 1979 the concentration camps of Auschwitz and Birkenau became part of the UNESCO patrimony of protected historical monuments. In the guidebooks describing this "architecture of atrocity and its urbanization of genocide" the barracks reserved for the gypsies and homosexuals are still passed over in silence. The almost total destruction of a stable community and a recognized tradition still clings to memory. More marginal, less rooted, figures are expelled from remembrance, even from a collective participation in the shared oblivion of death.[43] But then the full impact of the Holocaust—not as an accidental aberration but as something intrinsic to the sense of modernity—has still, as Zygmunt Bauman has argued, to be fully inscribed into the body of contemporary experience.[44]

In all this evidence there lies an ethos. Like an open wound that calls for attention we are exposed to difference, interrogation, and ambiguity. It is this, as Hans-Georg Gadamer puts it, that constitutes the opening of experience. It is in this gap that we recognize our limits, learn to control our narcissism (personal, cultural, national), and finally come to recognize ourselves in the ethics of solidarity.[45]

X

Friends of the Good, know that we have met through the secrecy of the Word in a circular street, perhaps upon a ship plying a course unknown to me. This story has something of the night; it is obscure and yet rich in images; it should end with a feeble, gentle light. When we reach dawn, we shall be delivered. We shall have aged by a night, a long, heavy night, a half-century, and a few white pages scattered in the white marble courtyard of our house of memories. Some of you will be tempted to dwell in that residence, or at least occupy a small part of it suited to the dimensions of your bodies. I know that the temptation to forget will be great: oblivion is a spring of pure water that must on no account be approached, however thirsty you may feel.

For this story is also a desert. You will have to walk barefoot on the hot sand, walk and keep silent, believing in the oasis that shimmers on the horizon and never ceases to move toward the sky, walk and not turn around, lest you be taken with vertigo. Our steps invent the path as we proceed; behind us they leave no trace, only the void. So we shall always look ahead and trust our feet. They will take us as far as our minds will believe this story.[46]

Notes

1. Friedrich Nietzsche, *Beyond Good and Evil* (Harmondsworth: Penguin, 1973), p. 197.

2. bell hooks, at a talk in New York in April, 1990.

3. Stuart Hall, *The Real Me: Post-Modernism and the Question of Identity* (London: ICA Documents 6, London, 1987), p. 44.

4. Michel de Certeau, *The Practice of Everyday Life* (Berkeley, Los Angeles, and London: University of California Press, 1988), pp. 41–42.

5. Ibid., p. xxi.

6. Trinh T. Minh-ha, *Woman, Native, Other* (Bloomington and Indianapolis: Indiana University Press, 1989) p. 35.

7. This theme, that today can be theoretically summarized in the encounter between the new historicism and deconstructionism, is clearly central to many narratives in English in the 1980s: Jeanette Winterson, Graham Swift, Peter Ackroyd, Salman Rushdie, not to speak of Latin American "magic realism" and such North American writers as Vonnegut, Hawkes, Pynchon, and DeLillo. I was reminded of this by a paper given by Susana Onega Jaén—"British Fiction in the 1980s: Historiographic Metafiction, the Way Ahead"—at the XIV Congresso de asociacion española de estudios anglonorteamericanos at Vitoria-Gasteiz, Spain, in December 1990.

8. Which is what Bruce Chatwin, author of *In Patagonia,* directly takes up in the *Songlines.* Also see in particular, Krim Benterrak, Stephen Muecke, and Paddy Roe, *Reading the Country: Introduction to Nomadology* (Fremantle, W.A.: Fremantle Arts Press, 1984).

9. E. Lucas Bridges, *Uttermost Part of the Earth* (London: Hodder and Stoughton, 1951), p. 36.

10. Edmond Jabès, *Un Etranger avec, sous le bras, un livre de petit format* (Paris: Gallimard, 1989), p. 9.

11. Chandra Mohanty, quoted in Lata Mani, "Multiple Mediations: Feminist Scholarship in the Age of Multinational Reception," *Inscriptions* 5 (1989): 5.

12. James Clifford, "Notes on Travel and Theory," in *Inscriptions* 5 (1989): 179.

13. Bill Ashcroft, Gareth Griffiths, and Helen Tiffin, *The Empire Writes Back* (London, and New York: Routledge, 1989), p. 154.

14. Ibid., p. 36.

15. Paul Bowles, *The Sheltering Sky* (New York: Vintage, 1990), p. 134.

16. Angela Carter, *The Passion of New Eve* (London: Virago, 1982), p. 10.

17. Homi K. Bhabha, "Interrogating Identity," *The Real Me: Post-Modernism and the Question of Identity* (London, ICA Documents 6, London 1987), p. 9.

18. Michel de Certeau, *The Practice of Everyday Life* (Berkeley, Los Angeles, and London: University of California Press, 1988), p. 14.

19. Felix Guattari, "The Three Ecologies," in *New Formation* (Summer 1989): 139.

20. For this shifting mix of different cultures and diverse contexts, in which identities are crossed and contaminated but not for that necessarily debilitated or lost, listen to Youssou N'Dour's *The Lion* (1989) and *Set* (1990), and Ryuichi Sakamoto's *Beauty* (1989).

21. William E. Connolly, *Political Theory and Modernity* (Oxford and New York: Blackwell, 1989), p. 132.

22. Michel de Certeau, *The Practice of Everyday Life* (Berkeley, Los Angeles, and London: University of California Press, 1988), p. 18.

23. On overturning the trope and resignification in black literature, see Henry Louis Gates Jr., *Figures in Black* (New York: Oxford University Press, 1988).

24. Martin Heidegger, "Building Dwelling Thinking," in *Basic Writings* (New York: Harper and Row, 1977).

25. Edgar Morin, *Vidal et les siens* (Paris: Seuil, 1989).

26. Edmond Jabès, *Un Etranger avec, sous le bras, un livre de petit format* (Paris: Gallimard, 1989), p. 11.

27. Friedrich Nietzsche, *Beyond Good and Evil* (Harmondsworth: Penguin, 1973), pp. 47–48.

28. Edmond Jabès, *The Book of Questions,* vol. 1 (Middletown: Wesleyan University Press, 1976), p. 50.

29. Vicki Kirby, "Corporeographies" in *Inscriptions* 5 (1989): p. 112.

30. Ibid., pp. 112–13.

31. Ibid.

32. William E. Connolly, *Political Theory and Modernity* (Oxford and New York: Blackwell, 1989), p. 161.

33. Trinh T. Minh-ha, *Woman, Native, Other* (Bloomington and Indianapolis: Indiana University Press, 1989), p. 89.

34. Homi K. Bhabha, *Nation and Narration* (London and New York: Routledge, 1990), p. 6.

35. Gayatri Chakravorty Spivak, "Can the Subaltern Speak?" in C. Nelson and L. Grossberg, eds., *Marxism and the Interpretation of Culture* (Urbana: University of Illinois Press, 1988), pp. 272–80.

36. Ibid., pp. 292–94.

37. Jacques Derrida, quoted in ibid., p. 293.

38. Siegfried Kracauer, *History: The Last Things before the Last* (New York: Oxford University Press, 1969), p. 192.

39. Friedrich Nietzsche, *Beyond Good and Evil* (Harmondsworth: Penguin, 1973), p. 15.

40. See Angie C. Chabram and Rosa Linda Fregoso, "Chicana/o cultural representations: reframing alternative critical discourses," *Cultural Studies* vol. 4, no. 3 (October 1990).

41. Edmond Jabès, *The Book of Questions,* vol. 1 (Middletown: Wesleyan University Press, 1976), p. 26.

42. Franco Rella, "Nella zona dell'orrore," *il Manifesto,* 9/9/90: 34

43. Quotes from Frédéric Edelman, "Les simulacres de la nuit," *Le Monde,* 23/8/90.

44. Zygmunt Bauman, *Modernity and the Holocaust* (Cambridge: Polity, 1989).

45. Hans-Georg Gadamer, 12 November 1990, Istituto Italiano di Studi Filosofici, Naples.

46. Tahar ben Jelloun, *The Sand Child* (New York: Ballantine Books, 1989), pp. 7–8.

12

Leave It to Beaver
The Object of Pornography

Kelly Dennis

For to assume that the woman herself takes on the role of fetish, only raises the question of the difference of her position in relation to desire and to the object.

—Jacques Lacan

I don't know what it is but I know it when I see it.
—Justice Potter Stewart

Contrary to conventional wisdom on the subject, the primary—even obsessive—focus of mainstream, heterosexual pornography is, in fact, female orgasm. One might even say that the history of visual technology is a prolonged quest for establishing proof of female sexual pleasure—an attempt to realize that which does not conform to perceptual conventions. What cannot be seen in pornography is displaced onto what can be seen: onto both the "hydraulics of male ejaculation"[1] and the *expression* of ecstasy on the woman's face—often coupled in the film cum shot onto the woman's face. Within the order of the visible, women can only *look like* they are coming.

In her book-length study of the pornographic film genre, *Hard Core: Power, Pleasure, and the "Frenzy of the Visible,"* Linda Williams notes that the early motion-stop photography of Eadweard Muybridge established Leland Stanford's "hunch"—in opposition to conventional and even scientific belief in 1878—that "at a certain moment in the fast trot all four feet [of the horse] do leave the ground" (37). Muybridge's photographs rendered motion visible, in accordance with "the phenomenon of the persistence of vision"[2]—and provided undeniable visible evidence of Stanford's horse sense. Williams also notes, as a poem by Albert Goldbarth reasons: "Studying the horse, we understand / how hard-core followed the invention / of photography."[3] Photography's "greater accuracy of vision" made visible what had been only imagined and fed the desire to establish other "unseeable 'truths'." Unlike the ecstatic moment of the fast trot made visible by photography, however, female pleasure does not accommodate itself to the "accuracy of vision" and as such threatens the conventions of the primacy of vision. If truth is based in visibility and visual technology is based in establishing truth, then the "truth in sex" is always potentially faked by women.

The primary difference between hard-core film and hard-core photography is the difference between the cum shot and the beaver shot. The hard core film's climactic cum shot, or "money shot," is a relatively recent innovation in porn history, one particular to the emergence of the full-length, narrative porn film in the sixties and seventies.[4] Prior to the cinematic epiphany of the cum shot onto the woman's face, pornography's primary concern was the display of female genitalia in both photography and film. Photography not only privileges but "can be credited with the invention of the beaver shot, an image so constructed that its sole purpose is the exposure of the female genitalia."[5] Early stag films are in fact little more than moving versions of the photographic "beaver shot," progressing from still, "split beavers" (legs apart, genitals visible); to "action beavers" (which added motion—masturbation or cunnilingus—to the essentially still beaver shot); to the "meat shot" (genital or anal penetration by the penis), which although it included slightly more elaborate narrative justification—boy meets girl, boy fucks girl—quickly abandoned what little narrative had been evoked in the display of the event.[6]

In the absence of the cum shot—due partly to censorship laws that regulate print and film by different standards—contemporary porn photography, such as that in *Hustler* magazine, continues the photographic tradition of the beaver shot, explicitly attempting to represent that which in psychoanalytic parlance is *lacking*. Indeed, psychoanalyst Jacques Lacan's rethinking of the lack will have much to tell us about the perceptual conventions that underlay pornography's representation of feminine sexuality. Hard-core photography attempts to represent female sexuality by the splayed labia of the beaver shot and open mouth of the model, who *looks like* she is coming.

The distinction between pornographic film and pornographic photography resides in their respective relation to the fetish and to fetishism. Christian Metz writes that "film is more capable of playing on fetishism, photography more capable of itself becoming a fetish."[7] According to Metz, the movement and duration of film implies temporality and, coupled with its auditory component, utilizes a number of sense perceptions synchronously, conforming to the illusion of the spectator's subjective unity. The "authority" of the photograph, on the other hand, is its stillness and silence. Unlike film, which begins, and then ends, and in which "nothing can be *kept*" (83), photography fixes its objects and freezes them within a temporality that is *retro-spective;* as such, "its significance is not limited to the immediacy of sight."[8] Unlike film, in which nothing remains fixed, the photograph is itself a fetish:

> The photographic *take* is immediate and definitive, like death and like the constitution of the unconscious, fixed by a glance in childhood, unchanged

and always active later. . . . The fetish, too, means both loss (symbolic castration) and protection against loss. . . . Not by chance, the photographic act (or acting, who knows?) has been frequently compared with shooting, and the camera with a gun.[9]

If the synchronous deployment of visual and aural perceptions in film affirms the viewer's subjective unity, then the photograph's stillness and temporal fixity can be said to challenge subjective unity.[10] What, then, is the relation of the photograph, as fetish, to the fetishization of the female sex? What prey is hunted by the photographic beaver shot?

Although porn photography depends on the medium's presumed indexical status—its titillation dependent primarily on the fiction that the women are not modelling but are truly aroused and caught on camera—photography's relation to the fetish of the beaver shot is itself fetishistic. Pornography does not fetishize woman: woman is herself a fetish and a symbol of fetishism. Objections to pornography as sexual exploitation invariably grant photography's claim to realism; that is, pornography's referent, the woman, is presupposed. But in fact "woman" is an ambiguous object insofar as the desire for the signification of the lack in subjectivity has been displaced onto her: *standing in* for the missing phallus, she signifies its *absence*. Pornography's referent is not the woman but the fiction of lack she must come, visibly, to signify.

A rereading of the relation of the fetish to pornography is crucial to understanding photography's realism, since photography's realism is pornography's fetish.[11] The realism of the porn photo permits the viewing subject the fantasy of seeing, yet the subject gets a *symbolic* thrill, too. In pornography, the viewing subject is represented in relation to the scopic drive: The viewing subject is determined and instituted by the gaze, becoming "that punctiform object, that point of vanishing being with which the subject confuses his own failure."[12] The beaver shot represents both *the origins and the goal* of representation, identifying the lack which is the condition of representation, as well as constituting that lack as *other* to representation. Perhaps more than any other image, the beaver shot constitutes that "failure" by which the subject is, as Lacan states, "photo-graphed."[13]

As fetish and presenter of fetishes, photography duplicates the function of Lacan's notion of the gaze; it presents the viewer with the image of lack, thereby reproducing that relation by which the image is constructed as a mediation of the other. As will be shown here, the failure of this mediation, whose force back upon the subject could only be called "perverse," is equally duplicated in the medium of photography, which as Metz states, "endlessly mimes the primal displacement of the look between the seen absence and the presence nearby" (87). The implications of the Lacanian gaze for pornography and photography will be developed throughout this chapter, particularly as regards the commonly held belief that voyeurism is the basis of pornography. The classic definition of the voyeur as one who sees but is not seen, a position generally understood to be one of (male) power, is only as secure as the autonomy of the subject it supposedly affirms. Through images and texts from both art history and *Hustler* magazine I propose to examine how pornography works—and how it does not work—and how the subject is, to take a liberty with Lacan, *porno-graphed.*

The Split (Beaver) in Subjectivity

The intervention of the specular relation in the imaginary plane demonstrates that the structure of subjectivity, *grounded on a decisive* coupure, is in itself fetishistic.

—Jacqueline Rose

Throughout his career, Freud placed increasing emphasis on female genitalia as site of the split in subjectivity; that is, on the perception of the mother's genitals and on the castration complex as crucial to the constitution of the subject as split in the process of the defense and disavowal of difference. In the castration complex, castration is significant only as castration of the female.[14] This perception and discovery of lack in the mother is a crucial point for a number of psychoanalytic concepts. The castration complex not only institutes oedipal triangulation and a turning toward the Law of the Father; it also constitutes the site of fetishism. Ultimately, it is realized in the splitting of the ego [*Ichspaltung*] that signals the subject's entry into the symbolic and the realm of desire. The latter, the splitting of the ego in the process of defense, is initially formulated in Freud's essay "Fetishism."[15]

Although Freud identifies the little boy's belief that his mother has a penis in his 1910 foray into art criticism,[16] it is in the later essay "Fetishism" that he argues not only that the fetish is specifically a substitute for the mother's penis, but that the structure of fetishism is that of a "divided attitude" (157) in which the child's belief that the mother has a phallus is simultaneously retained and given up (154). The fetish, Freud states, is some object or part-object onto which the disavowal of the perception of the mother's lack is displaced:

> When the fetish is instituted some process occurs which reminds one of the stopping of memory in traumatic amnesia. As in this latter case, the subject's interest comes to a halt half-way, as it were; it is as though the last impression before the uncanny and traumatic one is retained as a fetish. Thus the foot or shoe . . . fur or velvet . . . crystallize the moment of undressing, the last moment in which the woman could still be regarded as phallic. (155)

Invested in the fetish is the denial of *having seen:* the child does not *deny* that his mother does not have a penis, he denies that he *saw* that she does not have a penis. Through this disavowal, the penis that the mother lacks becomes the phallus that she possesses.

The disavowal of *having seen* in the process of fetishism is Freud's first observation of the split in the ego, wherein "[t]he attitude which fitted in with the wish and the attitude which fitted in with reality exist side by side" (156). This "side by side" relationship of imaginary and real constitute the subject's entry into the symbolic within an ambiguous relation to perception; it is here that the problem of subjectivity converges with that of sexuality.[17]

The primacy of seeing is established in the perceptual discovery of the mother's lack and thus in the acknowledgment and hierarchization of sexual difference. As such, "[a]natomical difference," as Jacqueline Rose states, "comes to *figure* sexual difference, that is, it becomes the sole representative of what difference is allowed to be."[18] The primacy of looking, of visual verification, is indissociable from the dominance given to the phallus as the *figure* of sexual difference: "[t]he phallus thus indicates the reduction of difference to an instance of visible perception" (66). It is no wonder, then, that feminists have criticized the role of vision in the history of art and cinema. However, as Rose further notes, "what counts is not the perception but its already assigned meaning"—not the *perception* but, as in fetishism, *the ontological reasons for its disavowal.* The hierarchization of sexual difference preexists the "discovery" of sexual difference in the mother. Perception is the institution of sexual difference in as much as the penis is its anatomical sign. In other words, the primacy of vision is accorded *its* significance based on the principle of sexual difference, the latter according the phallus *its* significance based on the visibility of the penis as the signifier of that difference.

Given the phallic import invested in vision, it is not surprising to find that Freud comments on the "substitutive relation" between the eye and the penis and on the coincidence of the fear of blindness with the fear of castration in his essay "The Uncanny."[19] The fear of blindness is a double for the fear of castration, the eye a double for the penis. Doubling is a common motif in dreams, Freud notes, which represent castration by the multiplication of genital symbols (235). What is uncanny about the double is that although it functions ostensibly as preservation against castration, it "reverses its aspect" and doubles as "harbinger" of castration or death (235). Not unlike the fetish, "both the disavowal and the affirmation of the castration have found their way" into the construction of the double.

Thus, the primacy of perception doubles for the primacy of the phallus. The reduction of sexual difference to an *instance* of perception (note that the primacy of perception is itself *temporal*) both insures the place of the phallus within sexual hierarchy and exposes its dependency on the visibility of its supposed referent, anatomical difference. The primacy of perception within sexual difference guards against *difference being other than visible.* In guarding against lack, against castration, the phallus therefore signifies lack, signifies castration: In guaranteeing that the phallus will stand for presence, the perception of difference becomes the perception of lack. Thus, the primacy of perception upholds sexual difference as a law signified by the phallus. This is why, for Lacan, "the subject's entry into the symbolic order is equally an exposure of the value of the phallus itself. . . . The status of the phallus is a fraud (this is, for Lacan, the meaning of castration)."[20] This is why, for us, the status of the phallus equally exposes the primacy of vision as a fraud.

The subjective import of castration and perception thus bears upon representation [*Vorstellung*] as "repress-entation," by which Freud specifies that something is repressed.[21] Freud notes that the definition of uncanny [*unheimlich*] is un-homely, or that which was once homely or familiar become un-familiar. The female genitals are a primary example of what is most often perceived as "uncanny,"[22] and thus the "the prefix 'un' is the token of repression" (245). "This reference to the factor of repression," Freud states, "enables us, furthermore, to understand Schelling's definition of the uncanny as something which ought to have remained hidden but has come to light" (241). The function of the phallus is precisely this: To disavow and keep hidden that which has "come to light," the lack that has been perceived in the mother's genitals and thus the lack for which the phallus itself stands. The phallus is also a "token" of repression, and therefore, as Lacan notes, it plays its role "veiled."[23] For Freud, what is at stake in castration is the "subjective import of the perception of the female genital organ. . . . This moment of castration is the mode of representation of a lack from which the subject finds himself suspended in his relation to desire. . . ."[24] Representation, the confrontation with a lack that can only be figured as what cannot be seen by what *can* be seen, itself places into question both the primacy of the phallus and the primacy of perception within sexual difference and the structure of subjectivity.

As symbolized by female genitalia, the uncanny's relation to castration, death, and representation relates to Freud's notion of *das Ding*—the Thing as "sublime object: a positive, material object elevated to the status of the impossible Thing."[25] Freud's Thing is not an object as such but the uncanny, material doubling of the fear of castration, a harbinger of death. Within representational paradigms of the primacy of perception, the displacement of woman's *jouissance* onto the sight of her genitals as "impossible Thing" marks representation itself, as Lacan notes, as an issue of how feminine sexuality comes into play.

Prehistory of the Beaver Shot

A cunt is he who sees.
—Jean-François Lyotard

Sexuality is the vanishing-point of meaning.
—Jacqueline Rose

Although photography is credited with having invented the beaver shot, there is no lack of historical precedent in Western painting.[26] The beaver shot, in fact, constitutes in no small way the originary vanishing point of Western perspectival realism. The earliest "beaver shot" in Art History is simultaneous with the discovery and invention of perspective in Albrecht Dürer's "how to" treatise, *A Course in the Art of Measurement with Compass and Ruler,* 1525 [fig. 12.1]. An illustration in the treatise performs a telling act: The artist presents the beholder with the traditional reclining nude while at the same time showing the artist himself rendering this view with the aid of the perspectival grid. At the moment when perspective and anatomy are codified as modes of visual experience in the Renaissance,[27] the artist's desire to establish a scientific means of perception is at odds with his conformity to artistic conventions of the nude. The view the artist has of his model is not the spectator's; rather, the artist's view is a "beaver shot" perceived through the grid. The artist's view is metaphorically framed by the window behind him: The artist's eye peers, with the aid of a phallic vertical axis, along a direct horizontal axis straight into and through a bush; the woman, on the other hand, is framed by a window that likewise encloses an equally curvaceous mountain landscape whose receding distance demonstrates one-point perspective. The coincidence of the construction of visual knowledge with the point of the invisible, what is unknown in woman, is marked by the vanishing point of perspective that renders Renaissance art a "window on the world."

As a means of adding knowledge to visual experience—depicting visually the "depth" we "know" the body to have[28]—perspective is analogous with the desire to know the woman's body and *its* vanishing point. The vanishing point of perspective, that which secures geometrical distance in visual representation by attempting to account for the third dimension of an object in the two-dimensional medium of pencil or paint, is illustrated here by the "confrontation with a lack" in the object perception of the female genitals. The constructed origin of perspective is doubly figured by the fetish: Dürer's "beaver shot" here both signifies and substitutes for the lack remanded to vision through perspectival construction as the representational project of both art and science.

The beaver shot implied in an eighteenth-century painting by Jean-Honoré Fragonard, *The Swing* [fig. 12.2], also figures a point "vanished from" the beholder's gaze and rendered the exclusive property of a lover's privileged view of his mistress. Additionally, however, the beholder's point of view completes a joke at the expense of her cuckolded husband. The painting, commissioned by a wealthy nobleman, depicts the aristocrat's mistress in a pastoral garden seated in a swing and pushed by her husband. The aristocrat requested the artist to depict him in the foreground of the scene—not insignificantly behind a bush—where he could "see the legs of this charming girl, and more, if you want to enliven your picture still further."[29] Although the viewer of the painting does not have the lover's privileged view, we are nonetheless positioned to enjoy the cuckold's ignominy. The husband is excluded from the visual exchange between the lover, his exposed mistress, and the witnessing viewer.

Despite the mistress's position at the center of the painting, a feminist interpretation might object that the authority of her look is eclipsed by our knowl-

Figure 12.1

Albrecht Dürer, *Man Drawing a Nude in Perspective*, circa 1525, Foto Marburg/Art Resource, NY

Figure 12.2
Jean-Honoré Fragonard, *The Swing (Les hasards heureux de l'escarpolette)*, 1768–1769, by kind permission of the Trustees of the Wallace Collection

edge of the true spectacle of the painting—the lover's view of his mistress's genitals. Indeed, as Mary Ann Doane has interpreted a similarly structured image, woman's status as a "spectator" is sacrificed for the sake of a dirty joke. Despite woman's centrality within a tableau, as Doane notes, "[t]he real site of scopophiliac power is on the margins of the frame."[30] The would-be spectacle of the beaver shot is displaced onto the lover's hat, held aloft and gaping by his phallic, extended arm which directs our look to that which he views. However, woman as spectacle rather than spectator, her regard elided by her genitals, is not inconsistent with her centrality to the tableau: she is, in fact, its very condition. Our inability to see her vanishing point reproduces the conditions of the possibility of representation.

The multiple substitution of the woman's regard onto her genitals and her genitals onto the hat demonstrates not merely her erasure as an autonomous viewing female subject, but the threat of castration represented by the doubling of genital symbols. Their metonymic confusion as "the object" of the painting signifies, more succinctly, the configuration of another "eye" in the painting. Differentiating between the structure of the gaze and that of perception, Lacan tells his audience, "You no doubt eat oysters, innocently enough, without knowing that at this level in the animal kingdom the eye has already appeared," playing upon the word *l'huître*, oyster, the French slang for vagina.[31] As Lacan implies in his reference to the female genitals, the gaze is an "eye" that does not "see" but places into question the supposed primacy of seeing on which not only sexual hierarchy but subjectivity itself is founded. The supposed object of the painting is neither singular nor unseeing. Rather, the impact that the unseen but seeing *l'huître* has on the "marginal, real site" of scopophilic power displayed in the painting is *uncanny*. Within the primacy of seeing in representation, the repressed fear of castration "comes to light" in the gaze represented by the female genitals.

The erotic image privately commissioned from Gustave Courbet, *L'origine du monde* (1866) [fig. 12.3], foregrounds the sublimity of representation as "confrontation with a lack." Possibly taking its cue from early pornographic photography, *L'origine* brings to light the signifying process by which the female nude is a primary subject of Western realism—as fetish, as possessing the fetish, as fragmented by her fetishization. *The Origin* is remarkable not simply for its startling subject matter and the exquisitely modeled detail with which it is rendered, but even more so for the photographic cropping of its subject. Courbet's display of the female genitals reproduces the detailed acuity of painterly realism, but clearly owes its framing to photography. In historical proximity to photography's invention of the beaver shot, Courbet presents the "eye" of the female genitals, explicitly asserting that which is the primary function of painting: To satisfy what is demanded by the gaze in the dialectic of desire; namely, to provide an image of the lack "with which the subject confuses his own failure"[32] in order to disavow it.

Like pornography, *L'origine* is neither gratuitous nor without narrative context. Its title, *The Origin*, explicates the relation of the fetish to representation as the originary lack on which representation is constructed and constructed to ob-

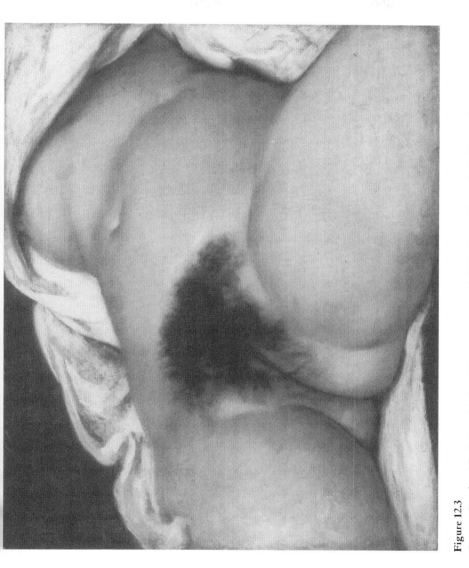

Figure 12.3

Gustave Courbet, *The Origin of the World* (*L'orgine du monde*), 1866, Musée d'Orsay, Paris, France, Réunion des Musées Nationaux/Art Resource, NY

viate. Michael Fried has argued that the image is one of a series of attempts by Courbet to *em-body* the project of representation.[33] Perspectival realism, if followed to its formal extreme, would culminate in the assimilation of the beholder to the painting's surface. Perspective's "realism" is one of space rather than vision. As such, the photographic cropping of the model by the edges of the painting reveals painting's artificially constructed perspective by refusing background or context, and thus confirms woman's fragmentary condition as a condition of representation itself. Following Fried, Stephen Melville argues that Courbet "displays the extent to which the Western realist project moves toward a radical assimilation of body to paint and painting."[34] Perspectival realism would culminate in the assimilation of the beholder to the painting's surface, its "realism" the order of space rather than vision. Thus, the proximity of Courbet's "beaver shot" alludes to the conditions of the possibility of dissolution into the origin—the fictive lack— of subjectivity.

"The classic dialectic around perception," Lacan states, "derives from the fact that it deals with geometral vision, that is to say, with vision in so far as it is situated in a space that is not in its essence the visual."[35] Perspectival realism conquers space, explicating the depth we "merely know" the body to have, rather than vision, the surfaces we "really see." As such, perspectival representation is not in its essence visual but is primarily concerned with locating the body in space and, subsequently, the viewer's body before the painting. Visual representation, then, concerns itself with the *place or position* of subjectivity, compensating for the *site,* rather than the *sight,* of the subject as "split."

Perspectival realism, by which the geometrical penetration of space masquerades as the visual knowledge of objects, lends itself, as Fried argues Courbet demonstrates, increasingly to an incorporation of the beholder to the surface of the canvas. Fried argues that the consequent emphasis on "flatness" in modern painting is the result of that frustrated penetration. The implication of Courbet's painting is that the presumed masculinity of painting, the perspectival penetration of space, is one that would be confounded by the assimilation of the beholder to the painting's surface, understood to be feminine. In other words, if perspectival representation is supposedly a "masculine" endeavor that objectifies the bodies of women, so that femininity is associated with the surface rather than the depth of representation,[36] then this masculine project is itself confounded by "femininity." The intervention of the painting's surface points to *the failure of realism to objectify;* that is, the failure of painting to create an *object* other than itself. [37] Like Dürer's perspectively rendered nude, the tradition of Western realism and the tradition of representing the nude are born of the same impulse—or origin.

What this means, finally, is that representation is not simply a process by which the viewer's gaze is one of (constructed) mastery and the object depicted is itself mastered. According to Lacan, the gaze is not the possession of any (gendered) subject but figures the encounter with the division of subjectivity and implicates the eye as inadequate within the castration complex. As such, the gaze is "a threat to the autonomy of the subject rather than an exercise of that autonomy."[38] As *l'huître,* the subject of *The Origin* has special implications for the (male) subject who seeks in it the representation of his (phallic) identity.

Ironically, the origins of Courbet's *L'origine du monde* were, for a long time, unknown. Linda Nochlin has elaborately documented that *L'origine* had been frequently reproduced within art historical texts despite the fact that no one could identify the painting's provenance. Without the painting, the "patriarchal origin," the material, incontrovertible evidence of Courbet's name and patrimony, Nochlin writes, "*The Origin* is literally indistinguishable from standard, mass-produced pornography—indeed, it is identical with it."[39] This, however, is simply not true. Although her point about the author-function is well taken, it obviates the fact that *L'origine* is neither a photograph, nor does it mime period pornography. Conventional pornographic display in fact included the model's body, her face, unless obscured or turned away, and some contextual background—a boudoir, brothel, or outdoor setting. Albeit technologically feasible, the kind of cropped display of the female genitals in Courbet's *The Origin* was not conceptually likely.[40] There are no extant photographs of cropped genitalia prior to *The Origin*. Nor does *The Origin* display the minor labia and clitoris: Like pornography conventions of the period, the genitals are signaled by the spreading of the model's legs, visible pubic hair, and cleft of the major labia. Although extant, the kinds of display of labia, vagina, and anus that typify *Hustler* magazine today were not prominent in nineteenth-century pornography until the Belle Époque.

Although I am sympathetic to Nochlin's critique of the patriarchy of authorship, the painting's subsequent discovery (in the Lacan estate!), sale, and exhibition in the permanent collection of the Musée d'Orsay does not assure us in the least of the masculinity of its origins. It is neither the masculine subjectivity of the artist/beholder, nor the art historical patrilineage of Courbet's name that is reaffirmed by *The Origin*'s recovery. Rather, *The Origin* implicates artist *and* spectator in a process of viewing—of representation—that is not about looking but is about the *gaze.* If photography invented the beaver shot, what are the conditions for the representational capture of its elusive prey? How *is* photographic pornography different from *The Origin*?

The Technology of the "Small Apparatus"[41]

> How does the cameraman compare with the painter? . . . Magician and
> surgeon compare to painter and cameraman. . . . For contemporary man
> the representation of reality by the film is incomparably more significant
> than that of the painter, since it offers, precisely because of the
> thoroughgoing permeation of reality with mechanical equipment, an
> aspect of reality which is free of all equipment.
>
> —Walter Benjamin[42]

Early photographic technology was instrumentalized in theories of criminal physiognomy and phrenology to establish archives of the "criminal type" in the latter half of the nineteenth century.[43] Police archives instituted universal norms and classified deviant particulars of anatomy and physiognomy by another universal—undesirability. As Allan Sekula has argued, photographs of known criminals were shot and archived in order to substantiate theories that criminals shared physiognomic traits such as cranial and ear shapes, which were invested with "characterological significance,"[44] enabling police to better identify and apprehend recidivists who "looked like" criminals. Based on a "conventional notion of space and objectivity whose development preceded [its] invention,"[45] photography seemed to promise more than mere optical detail, "reduc[ing] nature to its geometrical essence,"[46] in order to realize the perspectival dream of "knowing" and articulating the body in space.[47] In the interest of identifying social others—both racial and criminal types—physiognomy and phrenology invested in "the belief that the surface of the body, and especially the face and head, bore the outward signs of inner character."[48] Influenced by physiognomy and phrenology, early criminology instrumentalized photographic technology to exteriorize invisible, inner character onto visible, facial and "anatomical stigmata."[49]

In concurrent studies, Italian craniologist Cesare Lombroso posited a "quasi-Darwinist" theory that criminals suffered from a limited cranial capacity, attempting to prove their inferior brain size through extensive, standardized criminal portraits.[50] Ironically, female criminals—primarily prostitutes—did not fit his hypothesis since they possessed above-average cranial capacity.[51] Lombroso accordingly changed his paradigm, focusing instead on the prostitute's genitals. There he sought aberrations and irregularities that he equated with the abnormal and primitive genitals of Hottentot women[52] in order to explain the female criminal's behavior through anatomical stigmata particular to her sex.

It is a small leap from establishing the truth in physiognomy to the truth in sex as instrumentalized by photography in the nineteenth century. The body was constituted as a series of fragments in archives of criminal photographs, where part-objects of anatomy came to signify the *visibility* of human character as a series of "*contingent instances* of deviance and social pathology."[53] In "The Body and the Archive," Allan Sekula notes, photography simultaneously poses a "threat and promise," not merely to the criminal but also to the bourgeois identity against which "deviancy" is defined. Despite criminology's "almost exclusive emphasis on the head and face" (12), which subverted the tradition of portraiture as a "ceremonial presentation of the bourgeois *self* inherited from the seventeenth century" (6), it is the "criminal body" that is defined as a new "object" in the latter half of the nineteenth century. "Photographs and technical illustrations were deployed," Sekula notes, "not only against the body of the representative criminal, but also against the body as a bearer and producer of its own, inferior representations" in the form of tattoos, for example (40). However, the photographic threat to the subjective autonomy invested in the body goes much further than this, and can be seen in the status of the subject positioned both before and behind the camera lens.

The camera not only fragments perception but fragments the subjects of perception, *fixing* them into "shots." Walter Benjamin compares Eugène Atget's turn-of-the-century photographs of deserted Paris streets to "scenes of a crime" due to the "withdrawal" of man from the photographic image.[54] Benjamin states that the deserted scene of a crime is "photographed for the purpose of establishing evidence"—of what?—of a murder *having taken place*, of subjects *having been there*. Although photography becomes the means of establishing proof of the *former presence* of the subject, it is also the means by which that absence is ominously emphasized as a condition of photographic representation: A condition in which, as Lacan states, "the dependence of the visible [is] on that which places us under the eye of the seer . . . something that I would prefer to call the seer's 'shoot' (*pousse*)—something prior to his eye."[55] "Shot" by photography, the subject is arrested as an effect of the gaze, both victim and perpetrator of the ontological investment in seeing.

The camera, then, is not merely an apparatus of power: Subjectivity is itself an "apparatus" of the gaze as Lacan differentiates it from Sartrean (and by extension, Foucauldian) paradigms of vision and power. The camera "takes" but does not return the look, frustrating the subjective myth of autonomy invested in our ability to exercise vision. The camera permits virtually any point of view, situating itself anywhere vis à vis its subject, as well as dislocating the "eye" from the subject who would author it. The camera displaces and dislocates the proper place of the subject in spatial paradigms of representation as a *function of the gaze,* rather than merely victimizing the (autonomous) subject within paradigms of visual epistemology.[56] Criticism of the predominance of vision in representational and epistemological paradigms is inevitably based on—and therefore reinscribes—the autonomous subject in possession of the gaze as *"look."* Seeing as an activity in and of itself is neither denied nor negated here; but the subjective import of the gaze is lost when construed simply as a type of looking or as a theory of the "spectator."[57] The power of surveillance is not simply a function of visual control but a condition of modern subjectivity. The fragmenting and dividing of the subject's fictive unity is not merely a result of being seen and not himself seeing, but of encountering an unrepresentable other. As such, the power of visual technology in surveillance is not only that of observational control but of displacing the subject as the source of his own autonomy. The authority of the police is not only *panoptic,* a function of visual monitoring which itself is not visible, but *unrepresentable,* that by which the criminal subject is nonetheless himself represented—here, by a universalized archive of criminals.[58]

As an eye able to see, identify, and facilitate the *arrest*—both photographic and penal senses of the word—of undesirables, the photograph's authority in criminal identification resides in its archival expansion and repetition, thus serving a "panoptic principle" in everyday life as Sekula suggests.[59] The criminal photograph not only excises the subject from his/her social context but severs his/her organs and members from the gestalt of the individual body. Photography figures the perception of the body as fragmented, problematizing the unity of the modern subject as either corporeally or perceptually whole.

Further, perception itself is fragmented, dismantled into a series of photographic *gestures*[60] including choosing the shot or frame, focusing the lens, the newly unconscious "snapping" of the button which "clicks" the shutter and fixes the image—deferred to be developed later. One of the primary distinctions between painting and photography, Benjamin notes, is the instrumentalized modes of perception in photography. Photography concentrates artistic functions solely on the eye[61] and the convergence of a series of processes which "fix" a moment of vision; that is, fixing vision as *moment* by a single, abrupt gesture of the hand—the "snapping" of the photographer's finger.[62] The photograph, we noted earlier, has the status of a fetish due to its fragmentary nature which refers back to an instance of perception. The sequence of photographic processes fragments perception, as Metz suggests, lending to photography's status as fetish and "resulting from a singular and definitive cutting off which figures castration and is figured by the 'click' of the shutter."[63]

We are now in a position to understand Benjamin's claim that photography gives the moment a "posthumous shock."[64] The photograph, as Metz states, "marks the place of an irreversible absence, a place from which the look has been averted forever." But like the fetish the photograph is also a keepsake of the averted glance and marks the presence of that absence. The photograph both fixes the sight of the object as well as dislocates the site of the subject, *dis*illusioning the immediacy of vision and instituting *retro*spection, the significance of which is not primarily visual but signifies *temporal* distance. The photograph is a fetish insofar as it compensates for the absence of a "unified," autonomous subject as well as figures this absence as a condition of representation.

The camera, like the surgeon, as Benjamin observes, does not "face" the subject but "penetrates" its gestalt and radically undermines its unity by fragmenting perception as well as the body. Unlike painting, then, photography does not participate in the perpetuation of the dialectic of desire, does not present the viewer with the lack which he may disavow in order to feel "whole."[65] According to Benjamin,

> the painting we look at reflects back at us that of which our eyes will never have their fill. *What it contains that fulfills the original desire would be the very same stuff on which the desire continuously feeds.* What distinguishes photography from painting is therefore clear . . . to the eyes that will never have their fill of a painting, photography is rather like food for the hungry or drink for the thirsty.[66]

Contrary to the physiognomist's dream of executing Dürer's study of human bodily proportions on an "extended scale"—an ideal based in the perspectival situation both of the eye of the subject and the body of the object in space—the photographic study of anatomy fragments and fetishizes the unity and autonomy of the subject. The photograph's capacity for detail gives the illusion of resolving desire, of "feeding the hungry" and fulfilling "that of which our eyes will never have their fill." However, the subordination of anatomical particulars to universal paradigms of normal and abnormal is a manifestation of the perception of the body as fragment rather than gestalt. The fragmented body is a manifestation of what Benjamin calls a "crisis in perception" which is constitutive of the modern subject.

Thus, it must be asked whether pornography exists prior to the invention of photography, or prior to what we understand as *modernity*. By the 1860s the photographic documentation of criminals originating in the 1840s had become quite common,[67] coinciding not only with early pornographic photographs but also the very definition of pornography: it has been noted that our contemporary use of the word "pornography" originates in the nineteenth century.[68] Pornography's modern etymology is concurrent, therefore, not only with the first pornographic photographs but also with the "crisis" in perception and representation of the bourgeois subject. This is not to deny that erotica appeared in classical Greek vase painting nor that the etymology of the word *pornographos* predates photography, but to bring to bear a series of historical associations on what it is *we* think we mean by "pornography." What is it that distinguishes Lombroso's genital "portraits" of female criminals from early photographic pornography? How do we "know" and how does such knowledge become erotic?

Any Narrative Will Do

> For the first time, captions have become obligatory. And it is clear that they have an altogether different character than the title of a painting.
>
> —Walter Benjamin

> This is the look . . . of the object of a love which only a city dweller experiences, which Baudelaire captured for poetry, and of which one might not infrequently say that it was spared, rather than denied, fulfillment.
>
> —Walter Benjamin

It is for their realism that the first photographs of nudes are banned from the *Société Français de la Photographie* in the 1850s.[69] The indexical, unmediated relation presupposed between the model and the photograph disrupted conventions of the idealized painted nude. Unlike the photographic nude, the painted nude possessed no pubic hair, and, more importantly, did possess a coy, inviting, and complicitous look that, as Walter Benjamin characterized painting, fed "that which will never be fulfilled." As Abigail Solomon-Godeau has observed, the photographic nude included "not just pubic hair, but dirty feet, and, perhaps most disturbingly, the face of the real woman, often including her direct and charmless gaze. The look of these women is rarely the inviting, compliant expression that signals complicity between the desiring subject and the object of desire."[70] The photograph rendered the undeniable reality of the woman depicted as something other than ideal, even as other than a model; she was often assumed to be a prostitute.

Representing that which she lacks, the female nude is constructed by a set of conventions that secure her—as well as the viewer—from the implications of the female body and its functions. Photography's realism subverts the idealization of the woman's body by reproducing aspects heretofore absented from the painted reproduction. Photographic nudes, familiar rather than ideal, disrupt the aura of the painted nude.[71] The aura, as Benjamin observes, disappears from the work of art in the age of its technological reproducibility. Defined in Benjamin's later essays as meeting the "expectation that our look will be returned by the object of our gaze," the aura is entrenched in the art object by its embeddedness in history and tradition, and invests art with "the ability to look at us in return."[72] Photography, on the other hand, does not fulfill the expectation aroused by the look. Rather, as Benjamin notes, the look of the figures in the photograph or earlier daguerreotype was "inevitably felt to be inhuman, one might even say deadly. . . ."[73] The intervention of the real person in the photograph, rather than the ideal represented in the painting, was discomfiting if for no other reason than s/he seemed dead. Photography fulfilled our desire for the real only to discover that it was already dead. The photograph *shoots* this death while compensatory captions and narratives serve to reanimate the dead life documented by the photograph, giving its deathful reality an aura of its own.[74]

Dependent on and compensated by captions, pornography is, if nothing else, *not* gratuitous: It is compelled to define itself by degrees of realism, and, more importantly, to justify itself through a contextualizing narrative. Opponents of pornographic film often complain about its minimal attention to plot; however, the plot that is missing is the one that sanctifies sexual relations—bourgeois romance. Hard-core pornographic films for the most part dispense with romance and provide instead a dizzying display of seemingly arbitrary scenes of sexual intercourse. Often it is not clear how an identifiable character arrives from one scene to the next, nor when and where that character "met" his/her new partner. Hard-core pornography depends on a careful balance of realism and spectacle. The viewer wants to believe that these are real people copulating, which, of course, they are, but their "real" pleasure is subordinated to the temporality imposed on them by the movie camera—the number of takes each scene requires and the accompanying necessity for restimulation between scenes and takes.[75]

Without the seamless construction of film, porn photography relies on being sutured into a generic magazine format for its justification. Unlike the softcore *Playboy,* whose realism depends on the interview format of its centerfold pictorials and the reproduction of the model's handwritten biographical fact sheet,

Chic's and *Hustler*'s "honeys" come equipped with alliterative, extended-metaphor narratives.[76] A centerfold layout on the beach or poolside, for example, is accompanied by a text that describes "Tricia" as waiting for the fleet, or headlined, "Michele: Born to Sun." The narratives describe this exhibitionist nudity as a normal event, as one the reader could potentially encounter. More specifically, the narrative stages the images *as encounters*. The perspectival distance foreclosed by photographic realism is additionally performed by the intervening text. The texts in *Hustler* magazine address the viewer, conducting the exchange between the image of the model and the viewer as an omniscient author who addresses the reader's complicity:

> MICHELE: "You'd be surprised how many guys I've caught spying on me while I'm sunning!"
> TEXT: *"Wanna bet?!"*[77]

Unlike soft-core porn magazines, which permit the illusion that "I only read it for the articles," and assure the reader that it is assumed that s/he is, of course "getting it" at home (and therefore merely enjoys but does not *need* dirty pictures), hard-core porn magazines acknowledge that they serve a generally isolated audience member and explicitly encourage masturbatory interaction with the magazine. Like the "wanna bet?" addressed to the reader in response to "Michele's" ingenuous comment, the magazine repeatedly refers to its readers' presumed physical response and activities, warning its reader not to "burn your bone"[78] by enjoying a particular model "too much"—not to get, as it were, "too close."[79]

I would therefore argue that hard-core pornography is not based on voyeurism, traditionally defined.[80] This is not to say that the model's look is not complicitous like the painted, ideal nude, or that pubic hair and grains of sand haven't achieved some sort of acceptable fetish status as well. However, the magazine problematizes voyeurism *by acknowledging the viewer's look*. The viewer is acknowledged, however, as a reader, and, as such, the textual accompaniment to the photo spreads both supplements and supplants the photographic nude.

That the textual narrative supplants the images may seem surprising, but becomes less so on further examination. There are a number of discrepancies between the image and the text: The text describes what cannot *take place* in the photograph. Since, unlike hard-core film, hard-core pornographic magazines cannot show oral-genital or anal/genital-genital contact between two people, the most explicit *proximity* is attempted. The narrative textual accompaniment, however, blithely describes the union as if it were, in fact, taking place in the photographs, referring to penetration, and licking, and sucking, as if they were, at least imminent rather than indefinitely suspended, never to be consummated in the photograph.[81] But the impossibility of consummation, both within the photograph and between spectator and image, is exactly the point of pornography: The confrontation with lack is always suspended and deferred, allowing the illusion of symbolic mastery constitutive of the fictive unity of the viewing subject. Despite the emphasis of the hard-core magazine on the display of the female sex organs, her excitement is displaced, as in both pornographic and mainstream cinema, onto her facial expression, arched back, and textual narrative. The idealizing tradition remains in the rather hygienic display of the female genitals: No perceptible signs of arousal are visible—rather, they are present in the narrative text, which describes the sight as "throbbing," "sopping," "succulent," "dripping," and "lubricious," which, clearly, the site is not.[82] Despite her exposure, woman's desire and her sexuality are displaced because they cannot be *placed;* she represents the originary lack and dislocation of the subject and thus she must ultimately remain unseen.[83]

The primacy of the text in hard-core pornography is also evidenced in the phenomenal success of *Hustler*'s "Letters" and *Chic*'s "Confessions" sections. Both magazines have a general letters to the editor page (usually praising a particular model or layout from a past issue) as well as a confessions page: letters sent to the magazine describing erotic encounters experienced by readers. The confessions section of the magazines proved to be popular enough (and profitable enough) to warrant a separate magazine composed entirely of letters. Like *Penthouse Forum, Hustler Letters* is supplemented by small photo layouts and brief, authored fiction, the latter acting as fictive counterpoint to authenticate the letters. The format of the letters within the magazine in particular is the point at which Foucault's assertion of the Western *scientia sexualis*[84] is most evident in contemporary hard core. The letters are assembled in sections according to a classification of sexual activity: anality, voyeurism, sapphic/lesbian sex, bondage and domination, kink, and oral sex. The letters function both as the confession of pleasure and as the pleasure of *knowing* pleasure by their compilation in magazine form.

Similarly, *Hustler* functions as a forum for amateur erotic modeling and amateur photography. "Beaver Hunt," a monthly feature of *Hustler,* is an amateur photo contest: eight photographs are displayed each month, and subscribers cast votes for their favorite once a year.[85] Photos published each month receive $100, while the annual contest winner receives an extended, professional "photo-feature worth $1,000." "Beaver Hunt" photos stand in marked contrast to the professional, airbrushed pictorials of the centerfold and are themselves an interesting reading of the pornography of *Hustler* since they are significantly less aestheticized than their professional counterparts. But this difference is itself of interest: The amateur status of the photographs is coyly signaled by their haphazard, skewed layout against the background of a refrigerator door in the magazine's layout. Each photo is held to the refrigerator by a small toy magnet—cars and trucks, guns, monsters—much as one would display a child's finger paintings, signaling their status both as amateur and as domestic. The contest's only stipulations are that the "models" be "totally nude, and faces must be visible." The former rule is generally ignored, as the models appear in assorted jewelry, stockings, lingerie and disarrayed clothing. The latter rule, that faces be visible, is scrupulously honored: so much so that, in conjunction with the distance of the nonprofessional photograph and the mundane, homey details of the model's surroundings, "Beaver Hunt" photographs appear to be portraits rather than spectacularized porn.

As such, "Beaver Hunt" serves as a significant rereading of the pornographic image, both undermining as well as reinforcing the structure and function of pornographic representation. The limitations of the amateur photographer and the insistence on the visibility of the woman's face force a distance not present in the professional photographs. This distance permits the intervention of the model's surroundings: the flowered bedspread or couch upholstery, the mismatched pillowcase, the vase of plastic flowers, doilies, and the teddybear on the headboard, the poster, radiator, or electrical outlet on the wall—all giving clues to the "model's" status as a white, heterosexual, working-class woman.[86]

Although the narrative details of "Beaver Hunt" serve to authenticate the amateur originality of the photos, they also push the limits of the genre conventions of pornographic representation to the point of absurdity. The homey details function both as the reminder of the domestic arena that pornography subverts as well as signal the domestication of pornography. Despite their marginality within *Hustler* magazine, the amateur photographs reiterate sex and sexuality's implication within an "implantation of perversions," that Foucault argues "transforms sex into discourse" in order to "constitute a sexuality that is economically useful and politically conservative."[87] Whereas both pornography *and* its critics would have us believe that it transgresses the "normative" sexuality of marriage-sanctioned, monogamous sex, clearly pornography is reappropriated by this traditional monolith. Indeed, the two may be tied to one another far more than they are opposed.[88]

It would be tempting to read the amateur photographs of "Beaver Hunt" as a kind of pure eroticism since they do not have recourse to the painterly means of fetishizing the nude—the trick lighting, camera lenses, airbrushing, and professional makeup that help create the spectacular beauty of the professional model. The models for "Beaver Hunt" range in age from twenty to forty-five and few have the perfect—or surgically enhanced—bodies of the professional models. Additionally, despite consciously adopting poses and lingerie from *Hustler,* the amateur photographs are also uniform in their nonconformity to other standards of the magazine. Few adopt the facial expression of the woman-in-ecstasy, opting instead to look directly into the camera lens much as the nineteenth-century pornographic models did. The distance imposed by the requirement that the "Beaver Hunt" model's face be visible is one which itself supplants the "beaver shot." The few women who touch or display themselves do so self-consciously, appearing neither aroused, nor caught in the act, and thus fail to invoke a merely voyeuristic narrative. As such, "Beaver Hunt" calls into question the immediacy upon which pornography's realism relies. Attempting to mime the pornographic beaver shot, the "Beaver Hunt" photographs foreground instead photography's function as an index of the bourgeois fetish of identity rather than as the indeterminate fetish of female sexuality. "Beaver Hunt" models are, in fact, posing for the camera rather than acting for it.

It is not that these self-porn-portraits in any way escape the patriarchal ordering of woman as fetish, but that something in the awkward pleasure of these
photographs both subverts and reinforces professional porn. More pose than act,
more intimate than polished, more distance than encounter, the amateur photographs of "Beaver Hunt" expose pornography's dependence on realist paradigms
of immediacy that are dependent on both spatial and symbolic distance.

Like the professional layouts, biographies accompany each "Beaver Hunt"
photograph giving the name, age, hobbies, and occupation of each model. Additionally, there is a space on the entry form for "Sexual Fantasies" that stand as
the narrative text for each photograph. Unlike the outrageous, sex-toy fantasies
written to accompany the professional centerfold layouts, most of the fantasies
of the women who pose for "Beaver Hunt" are conservative, romantic fantasies
in which the model asserts she wants to "make love to my hubby in the mountains while it rains." Indeed, the photo credits by and large are "Photo by Husband" or "Photo by Boyfriend" (with the occasional, daring "Photo by Self"), au-
thenticating the model's desirability and justifying her exhibitionism: they are
implicitly some other guy's woman. "Beaver Hunt" photographs thereby undermine the realism of the professional models in the confession and enactment of
their own exhibitionist fantasies. Though the unattainable beauty and desirability of the professional models serves to enhance pornography's marginal stance,
the reappropriation of this form within the traditional boundaries occupied by
the amateur models denies that pornographic desire is abnormal or marginal at
all.[89] Letters to the editor of *Hustler* exclaim over the amateur models, many of
whom cannot even remotely be construed as resembling the ideal physiognomic
and anatomical beauty of the professional models. It seems reasonable to conclude, therefore, that pornography's fascination is not limited to the sight of
beauty, breasts, or beavers, but is located at some other site. What is suggested by
the "Beaver Hunt" photos in their assertion of real woman over fetishized ideal,
and their reappropriation of the erotic within traditional boundaries of home
and monogamy, is that the fantasy is not sex so much as it is the possibility of fantasy itself.

The Family Values of Porn

Join the *Hustler* family:
    Hustler
    Hustler Letters
    Hustler Humor
    Hustler Busty
    Hustler Most Sensuous Pictorials
    . . . On Sale at Newsstands Everywhere.
    —*Hustler* advertisement, emphasis added

Ward, I'm worried about the Beaver.
—June Cleaver

Even before the proliferation of newspaper commentary on pornography in the wake of the censorship of the 1989 Robert Mapplethorpe retrospective in Washington, D.C.,[90] there had already been a considerable increase in the amount of academic scholarship and feminist inquiry into pornography. Particularly compelling is the point of view that pornography has a subversive and transgressive value since "it challenges sacred cows like the nuclear family, monogamy, heterosexuality and the tie between sex and reproduction. Pornography, *like sexuality itself,* has a deeply subversive side."[91] In displaying sexual diversity—the number of positions as well as the number of partners and gender combinations—pornography depicts sexual activity and enjoyment outside the boundaries of monogamy and class and social hierarchy. Sex, not money, appears as the great leveler. In this light, liberal feminists and right-wing religious fundamentalists make strange bedfellows in their antipornography stances.[92]

Both religious and feminist antipornography positions rest on attitudes of sexual "norms."[93] The Religious Right asserts that sex belongs within the boundaries of marriage for the purpose of procreation, while antiporn feminists hold that the display of women in a sexual manner or in positions of sexual submission are inherently exploitative. Whereas the Religious Right's position that sex belongs only in marriage would seem to be one that feminists would rally against as repressive of sexual equality and reproductive freedom, the view that pornographic representations of women, particularly the "feminist norm regarding the inherently submissive nature of fellatio,"[94] are equally repressive since they condemn any pleasure derived from these acts as well as imply a normative, politically correct sexuality for women. The feminist slogan, "Pornography is the theory, and rape the practice," condemns pornography for inciting violence against women, citing sexual practices—such as fellatio—depicted in pornography.[95] Condemning the representation of a particular sexual practice in pornography, however, stems from an evaluation of those practices as exploitative in "real life."

This is not to say that pornography is without sexism, or that pornography simply influences or reflects sexual attitudes.[96] Yet, the feminist promotion of sexual norms in the name of a true female sexuality that pornography suppresses is dangerous; not only for its desire to establish a precultural origin of female sexuality but for its prudish condemnation of alternatives of pleasure in favor of political correctness. "Are feminists," Linda Williams asks in her book *Hard Core,* "to declare themselves against representations of fellatio, against being on their knees during sex, against anything other than absolutely egalitarian forms of mutual love and affection? Indeed, what forms of sex *are* egalitarian?"[97] Would "original" female sexuality preclude, for example, lesbian sexuality? And given that a portion of the lesbian population engages in sado-masochistic sex, would that originary sexuality necessarily—or desirably—exist in the absence of power?[98] Is politically correct sex exclusive of power in its pleasure?[99]

Claims for the so-called transgressive power of pornography against patriarchal culture and values deserves further examination as well, however. Not surprisingly, soft-core magazines such as *Playgirl* and *Playboy* subordinate sexuality—their "dirty pictures"—to dominant narratives of heterosexual, monogamous, romantic love or to a discourse on relationships. The two magazines share an overall format, including celebrity interviews and gossip columns, lifestyle marketing, erotic fiction and letters, fashion and nude pictorials, and sex-advice columns. Both have "Men's" and "Women's" columns representing the mysterious opinions and alternative attitudes of the "other" sex, which ultimately emphasize the similarity of their vulnerabilities and desires. With the exception of the nude pictorials, either magazine could be mistaken for *GQ, Esquire, Vogue,* or *Cosmopolitan* with their advice on how to meet/date/mate the opposite sex. Even the bios accompanying the single-nude pictorials (as opposed to the seminude couples pictorials) profess the girl/guy-next-door attitude, claiming either current participation in a steady, "normal" relationship (as opposed to the promiscuous relations a reader might wish or assume of a person who poses nude) or their desire to meet Mr/Ms Right.

Hard-core pornography, such as *Hustler, Chic,* and the gay *Advocate Men* and *Mandate,* on the other hand, also follows the standard formats of letters, advice, gossip, celebrity interviews, and pictorials not only with significantly more emphasis on sex, rather than on "relationships" or "lifestyle," but with significantly more emphasis on politics. Larry Flynt, publisher of *Hustler* and *Chic* magazines as well as distributor of the bulk of periodical gay pornography,[100] has long proclaimed himself an advocate of the First Amendment, free speech, anticensorship, and sexual freedom; moreover, Flynt has a history of association with leftist publishing.[101] The freedom-of-speech-anticensorship rhetoric of hard-core pornographers such as Al Goldstein (of *Screw* magazine) and Flynt have frequently been dismissed as smokescreens, or as a masturbatory ruse and means of perpetuating the "conflict" on which both mainstream morality and pornography depend.[102] However, Flynt's *Hustler* and *Chic* magazines consistently report on legislation attempting to govern sexual practices, feature conservative political figures as "Asshole of the Month," and publish freelance advocate and investigative journalism on AIDS research, prostitution, religious fundamentalism, circumcision, corporate dominance, and government spending—reporting that can be found elsewhere only in alternative presses such as *The Village Voice,* the *LA Weekly,* and gay and lesbian-feminist presses such as *Outweek, The Advocate,* and *Off Our Backs.*[103]

The intersection between pornography and political leftism[104] may seem less anomalous when considered from the point of view of gay and lesbian publications, which have an explicitly vested interest in political advocacy. Within the long history of mainstream repression of homosexuality, gay and lesbian porn publications provided a much-needed forum for political and health information and a sense of community for a long-excluded population. With the proliferation of AIDS and prejudice, gay presses provided increasingly important health information, promoted safe sex and safe-sex alternatives, including nude photography (as in *The Advocate*'s porn offshoot, *Advocate Men*) and phone-sex advertisements, the latter which additionally provided the necessary alternative funding for these publications. In other words, the politics of these politically alternative and pornographic publications has undertaken the guiding principle of the early feminist movement: the personal is political.

Despite the legitimate criticism that can be directed at pornography, there is an underlying realism implied in the dogma, "Pornography is the theory, and rape the practice." Even most anticensorship criticism confesses either an uneasiness with regard to the status of pornography and the societal inequality and oppression of women, or falls back onto the distinction between pornography and erotica and, of course, the exclusion of child pornography from the realm of acceptability. The criticism of pornographic representation rests, for the most part, on a criticism of pornographic realism, assuming an unmediated status of representation. Such criticism has two very significant results: one, the presumption of complicity on the part of any woman who enjoys pornography—thereby masochistically assuming the male subject position to whom porn is presumably directed—and two, a concomitant blaming of the "object" of pornography, namely the woman who complies, by posing, with her own oppression by this representational system. Yet, how desirable a feminist tactic is inscribing the complicity of the female subject, as either masochist or unconscious object? The presumptive third term in the statement, "Pornography is the theory, and rape the practice," is "woman is the object."

Conclusion: The Stakes of Voyeurism

> Even if the ultimate enemy is the patriarchal gaze, the phenomenal site
> of critical assault . . . is the object. Objects are bad. They sit there, naively
> ignorant of the extent to which their mere objecthood constitutes a tacit
> assent to the dominant male gaze. Objects are wicked because they give
> themselves to be looked at.
>
> —Stephen Melville, Bill Readings

Thus far I have suggested that pornography is both traditional and subversive in its politics and morality, and that porn both subverts and maintains visual paradigms of representation. I have also suggested that pornography is not necessarily based on voyeurism, although it is clear that *both consumers and critics of pornography have a vested interest in maintaining voyeurism as an exercise of power over the object of the look.* If, to reiterate Mary Ann Doane's assertion, the real power of the scopic drive is exercised from the margins, then what implications does this have for the center? That is, if perversion and its powers are marginal rather than normal, and pornography is considered a marginal practice, then it takes place not, as Doane suggests, at the *expense* of the center but *because of it*. As a "perversion" of normal sexuality, pornography is indissociable from sexual "norms."

An article on pornographic film quotes an anonymous man's frank response to pornography, in which he notes with puzzlement his relation to different pornographic media:

> When I look at a porn magazine, I don't care about the way the scene is visualized, even if the men and women are ugly or something else isn't quite right. In my fantasy they exist in a way that excites me. Besides, it's up to me which picture I choose to look at, and I can always turn the page or go back to a certain picture . . . . The viewer of a porn film always remains alienated from the situation he's observing, because he has to keep his clothes on and can't touch, even though the pictures arouse him. He becomes confused.[105]

The viewer here articulates the difference in his response to porn film as one that obviates his *control* of the viewing situation. He cannot author the sequence of images or the amount of time he is exposed to them; he cannot touch himself or disrobe "like when" he looks at the magazine. This would *seem* to be the classic complaint of the voyeur: that s/he cannot author her/his glimpses in the movie theater because s/he can her/himself be *seen* by others in the act of seeing. The purported impulse of the voyeur to see and not be seen is frustrated in the cinema. The above response is cited, however, in order to ask why porn films are nevertheless so popular, and the author suggests that the porn cinema experience may in fact be the logical extension of voyeurism. As author Gertrud Koch argues, "inside the porn theater desire actually becomes transformed into the fetishism of the aficionado, who only needs to know what is available, then sits back down to watch—the ultimate triumph of the eye over the body" (17).

Though I've no doubt as to the acuity of Koch's observation that in porn film, voyeurism is "transformed" into the "fetishism of the aficionado," this is less a *result* of voyeurism than its originary impulse. The viewer's frustrated complaint that he cannot touch himself problematizes the classic definition of voyeurism, particularly since he does not specify what it is he cannot touch but that it has to do with not being able to disrobe. Unlike the photograph, cinema is more capable of playing on fetishization than itself being fetishized, and unlike photography it cannot "be kept, mastered, held, like the photograph in the pocket."[106] The viewer's relation to cinema is imaginary, while his/her relation to photography is symbolic: It is worth remarking the shift in the viewer's prose above from the "I" (the subject) encountering the photographs to the more objectified reference to himself as "he" (the object) who experiences film. These differing responses indicate the subject's relation to the fetish (photography) and to fetishism (film). If the function of the fetish is to disavow the lack by disavowing the look, what, then, does the so-called voyeur attempt to "see" in the fetish of the beaver shot? Or, more precisely, what is it that the voyeur attempts *not* to see?

Walter Benjamin, uncannily taking his cue from Freud, analogizes the desire to look (the scopic drive) with the desire to eat (the oral drive) when he states that painting "reflects back at us that of which our eyes will never have their fill," while photography is "rather like food for the hungry or drink for the thirsty."[107] The assumption that photography, unlike painting, can fulfill the scopic drive is based on the idea that it can realize a meticulously detailed realism. The desire for "realism," however, is nothing less than the desire for the object. Freud, as Lacan notes, equates the scopic drive (*Schaulust*)—voyeurism-exhibitionism and sado-masochism—with the oral and the anal drives, neither of which can be satisfied like hunger and thirst. The scopic drive has as much to do with seeing as the oral and anal drives have to do with eating and shitting, which is to say, nothing. It is in these "unsatisfiable" and therefore "partial" drives, Lacan states, that sexuality is (im)possible or comes into play. The completion or satisfaction of the scopic, oral, and anal drives is not in the attainment of the object of desire, nor in copulation, but in the circuitous return of the drives to their "origin" in the self. This circuit however, must pass through the other and depends on the "introduction of the other"[108] insofar as it is through the other that the drive is *returned rather than completed.*

So what is it that the subject seeks from *Hustler?* The subject seeks "the object as absence."[109] But the subject perversely and unsatisfyingly seeks this absence from the presence of the phallus, the woman as fetish. The subject seeks evidence and reassurance of his state of wholeness and he seeks it from the phallus itself—the fetishized body of the exhibited woman—just as the voyeur seeks in the exhibitionist the absence of the phallus in order to realize it in himself. The subject seeks the absence of the phallus in the presence of THE phallus, since "what one looks at is what cannot be seen."[110] What Lacan calls the "perverse" sense of the scopic drive may be understood if we note that he discusses it in conjunction with the sadomasochistic drive, reiterating Freud's assertion that "pain has nothing to do with it." According to Lacan, the sadist without knowing it occupies the place of the object to the benefit of another—the masochist, whose pleasure depends upon *making* him/herself seen (*se faire voir*) by the sadist. The sadomasochistic drive is but one drive, Lacan states, the masochist's. Sadism is merely the disavowal of masochism (186), the disavowal of the object position assumed by the masochist. We can likewise state that voyeurism and exhibitionism are but one scopic drive, exhibitionism. The voyeur disavows his position as the object for the exhibitionist, and it should be remembered that the object, ultimately, is of the utmost indifference as far as *the drive* is concerned. It makes no difference whether the "exhibitionist" is conscious (in the strip show) or unconscious (the innocent "victim" spied upon by the voyeur) since, Lacan reiterates, "[i]t is not only the victim who is concerned in exhibitionism, it is the victim as referred to some other who is looking at him" (183). Within the structure of the scopic drive *there is only exhibition-*

ism and its disavowal. When the voyeur stares he makes himself the object of another *and simultaneously denies doing so* in order to constitute himself as subject. He is looking for the lack in order to reassure himself whole.

By its insistence on sexual norms that pornography perverts by instigating or perpetuating scopophiliac power "from the margins of the frame," criticism of pornography plays sadist to pornography's masochist. That is, pornography is positioned as the object identification that "sexual norms" disavow and with which, perversely, it is one and the same. Lacan merely humors us in his use of the word "perverse" to distinguish voyeurism from the gaze. *Perverse* is a term Lacan uses to distinguish voyeurism, a partial drive, from the gaze insofar as the gaze itself figures as voyeurism's *objet petit à* in the structure of sexuality. Voyeurism has as much to do with "seeing" as does the gaze, which is nothing. Voyeurism and the gaze are themselves less dissimilar than similar, both functions of the self-referential, immanent legitimation of subjectivity. The voyeur who makes him/herself the object of another and simultaneously denies doing so in the constitution of subjectivity illustrates the gaze in the subject's encounter with the division of subjectivity. That is, the subject always attempts not to *be* but to *make* him/herself the object of another ("You never look at me from the place from which I see you")[111] and simultaneously disavows doing so. The subject always assumes the position of an object ("I see myself seeing myself")[112] in his/her constitution as subject and thus always fails to make him/herself a subject.

In criticizing a transhistorical "male gaze," feminist criticism of pornography often forgets the ontological critique it learned from psychoanalysis. As a result, criticism of pornography reasserts the phenomenality of its objects and grants pornographic realism its mimetic authority, its art historical, perspectival claim for having realized the body. Many of the resultant criticisms of pornography, or theories of an alternative or women's pornography, culminate in a kind of criticism of the object's referent: woman is complicit in her pornographic representation. This criticism is documented, for example, by the initial feminist response to Linda Lovelace's autobiography, *Ordeal,* in which she claims to have been a victim of abuse and forced to perform in the now-classic hard-core film, *Deep Throat.*[113] Feminists such as Gloria Steinem initially rejected Lovelace's account because she "looked like" she was enjoying herself in the movie and was thereby an affront to antiporn feminists. Once convinced of her story—or its usefulness to the antiporn movement—Steinem revised her position, taking Lovelace under her wing as a pornography "victim."[114] Conversely, theories of alternative or women's pornography inevitably legitimate pornography by reinscribing it within the boundaries of monogamous, heterosexual relationships, and emphasize touch over sight in an implied theory of originary female sexuality.[115]

If, as Lacan states, perversion—the subject's determining itself as object— is the inverted effect of fantasy—the subject's determining itself as subject (in the encounter with the division of subjectivity)—then "normal" sexuality is that which maintains the fiction of the unified subject while perverse or marginal sexuality problematizes the homeostasis of the unified subject *in its willful identification as object rather than the object disavowal of the subject.* As such, pornography is not merely a (empty) threat to the myth of the normalcy of heterosexual, monogamous, reproductive sex, but to the authority of the subject on which this narrative is based.[116] Thus, we might say of antipornography rhetoric that it would prefer to maintain the fiction that woman is an immutable object than to face being a mutable subject.[117]

My claim that representation is not simply a voyeuristic act—or that voyeurism is not what we think it is—seems to be one of the art historical lessons of Michael Fried's work on absorption and theatricality in the history of painting.[118] Emphasizing visual representation as the arena where questions of ontology are indissociable from those of sexuality is *not* to claim that representation is simply the visual exploitation of an object (woman) by a subject (man) who "possesses" the gaze and therefore possesses the "power" to represent. The classic understanding of voyeurism is that the voyeur sees but remains unseen. What Fried seems to claim for Courbet and what I would claim for *Hustler* is that these images "see" the subject seeing them, which is to say that, like Lacan's sardine can,[119] they do not "see" at all; instead, they problematize the subject's ability to claim to "see" them. It is not vision that is at stake in the gaze but the fiction of the subject's autonomy. I would therefore be remiss were I not to include Marcel Duchamp's *Étant donnés* (1946–66) in the history of the beaver shot, particularly since Nochlin couples it with Courbet's *L'origine du monde* in her critical catalog note for the latter.[120] Contrary to Nochlin's claim that *Étant donnés* "foregrounds the role of voyeurism in artistic experience," I would argue instead that the gallery goer cannot be implicated in voyeurism as s/he is positioned to peer through a peephole at a splayed, pornographic nude and, in the gallery context, is positioned to be seen or "caught" doing so. The subject is not implicated in voyeurism but in the *impossibility* of voyeurism as the possession of the gaze by one autonomous subject over another. It is not that representation is inherently voyeuristic and that the viewing subject is complicitous in this structure: It is not that the viewing subject is "caught looking," but that the subject is inevitably *caught trying.*

Notes

This chapter was originally published in *Strategies: A Journal of Theory, Culture and Politics* vol. 6 (1991): 122–67. Since the article's drafting in 1988, the field of pornography studies has greatly expanded, influenced by developments in gender studies and queer theory. An updated and expanded version of the argument will appear in my book-length study on the art historical conditions of pornography.

    1. Linda Williams, *Hard Core: Power, Pleasure and the "Frenzy of the Visible"* (Berkeley and Los Angeles: University of California Press, 1989); 2d. ed. (1999), p. 94.

2. Marshall Deutelbaum, "'Rounds of Amusement': The Thaumat-rope," in *"Image" on the Art and Evolution of the Film* (New York: Dover, and the International Museum of Photography, 1979), p. 1.

3. Quoted in Williams, p. 34.

4. The feature-length porn film emerged from the "golden years" of the stag film in the early half of the century. The "golden years" of the stag film or "smoker" are recounted by Al DiLauro and G. Rabkin in *Dirty Movies: An Illustrated History of the Stag Film* (New York, London: Chelsea House, 1976). The "nostalgia" of their account is contested by Williams, p. 92. The cum shot's primacy has been challenged by the widening of the porn video market to include lesbian and heterosexual women. Susan Faludi documents the effects of this transformation on ideas of American manhood in a portion of the porn community in "The Money Shot," *The New Yorker,* vol. 71 no. 34 (October 1995).

5. Abigail Solomon-Godeau, "The Legs of the Countess," *October* 39 (Winter 1986): p. 97.

6. See Williams, chapter 2.

7. Christian Metz, "Photography and Fetish," *October* 34 (Fall 1985): p. 90.

8. Mary Ann Doane, "Film and the Masquerade: Theorising the Female Spectator," *Screen* vol. 23 nos. 3–4 (Sept–Oct. 1982): 85.

9. Metz, p. 84.

10. Part of photography's challenge to the unity of the subject resides in its identity as a document of subjective memory. See especially Eduardo Cadava, *Words of Light: Theses on the Photography of History* (Princeton: Princeton University Press, 1997).

11. Pornography is not alone in fetishizing photography's presumed realism; documentary photography and photo-journalism are but two additional examples.

12. Jacques Lacan, *The Four Fundamental Concepts of Psycho-Analysis* (New York: Norton, 1981), p. 83.

13. Ibid., p. 106.

14. Freud notes in "The Dissolution of the Oedipus Complex" that the threat of castration brings about "the destruction of the child's phallic genital organization" (175) but that prior to observing the female genitals, the child has experienced numerous losses or threats that he does not believe. "The observation which finally breaks down his unbelief," Freud asserts, "is the sight of the female genitals. . . . With this, the loss of his own penis becomes imaginable, and the threat of castration takes its *deferred* effect" (176, emphasis added). In the *Standard Edition* (hereafter referred to as *SE*) vol. 19 (London: Hogarth, 1953), pp. 173–79.

15. Freud, "Fetishism," *SE* vol. 9, pp. 149–57.

16. "Leonardo and a Memory of His Childhood," *SE* vol. 11, pp. 56–137.

17. For a fine explication of the link between sexuality and the unconscious in Freud and Lacan, see Jacqueline Rose, *Sexuality in the Field of Vision* (London: Verso, 1986), pp. 51–52.

18. Ibid., p. 66.

19. Freud, "The Uncanny," *SE* vol. 17, p. 231: "anxiety about one's eyes, the fear of going blind, is often enough a substitute for the dread of being castrated. The self-blinding of the mythical criminal Oedipus, was simply a mitigated form of the punishment of castration."

20. Rose, p. 64.

21. Jacques Lacan, "Guiding Remarks for a Congress on Female Sexuality," in *Feminine Sexuality: Jacques Lacan and the école freudienne,* eds. Juliet Mitchell and Jacqueline Rose (New York: Norton, 1985), p. 90.

22. Cf. Freud's essay on Leonardo, p. 45, as well as "The Interpretation of Dreams," *SE* vol. 5, p. 399, and "Fetishism," p. 155.

23. The phallus, like the gaze, is "lacking in the real" and yet is constitutive of the real. The phallus plays its role "veiled" in as much as its signifying function, like Parrhasios's painted veil which fools Xeuxis into believing that the real painting lay behind it, is to fool us into believing that the penis, and not the fiction of lack in subjectivity, is its referent (Lacan, *The Four Fundamental Concepts,* pp. 101–103). The eye is fooled insofar as it believes Xeuxis's painted veil to be a real veil covering another image; i.e., that the eye participates in the desire for a real behind the veil. The eye is thus revealed in the *trompe l'oeil* as inadequate, as itself implicated in the castration complex.

24. "The Phallic Phase and the Subjective Import of the Castration Complex," collective publication from *Scicilet* (1968), in Lacan, *Feminine Sexuality,* p. 113.

25. Slavoj Zizek, *The Sublime Object of Ideology* (London: Verso, 1989), p. 71.

26. I have yet to discover the full etymology of "beaver shot." During the period of the earliest porn photographs (ca 1840–50), the word "beaver" became common slang for a man's beard. The word "beard" has a longer history as a reference to the female genitals, dating at least to 1400, the publication date of Chaucer's *Canterbury Tales.* Absolon of the infamous "Miller's Tale" knows he has been falsely played when he discovers that he kissed his lover's "beard" instead of her mouth:

> But with his mouth he kiste hir naked ers,
> Ful savourly, er he was war of this.
> Abak he sterte, and thoughte it was amis,
> For wel he wiste a womman hath no berd:
> He felte a thing al rought and long y-herd
> And seyde, "Fy! allas! what have I do?"

Additionally, the beaver (*castor, castores, castrando*) is known as a castrated— or rather self-castrating—creature: Fables have the beaver castrating himself in order to avoid being hunted for the valuable oil secreted by his testes. I owe this latter observation to Guy Wheatley's invaluable research assistance.

27. Kenneth Clark, *The Nude* (New York: Doubleday, 1956), p. 258.

28. For an elaborate discussion of theories of seeing and perspective and the necessity to visually compensate in representation for what is otherwise "known" but not immediately presented to vision, see E. H. Gombrich, *Art and Illusion* (Princeton: Princeton University Press, 1960), especially his discussion of the infamous *trompe l'oeil* story of Xeuxis and Parrhasios. Lacan's use of the story in his discussion of mimesis is not unrelated: *trompe l'oeil* reproduces "perceptual depth" only insofar as it "fools the eye" by letting it "perceive" in a "triumph of the eye over the gaze" (*The Four Fundamental Concepts,* p. 103).

29. Saint-Julien, as quoted in Albert Boime, *Art in an Age of Revolution* (Chicago: University of Chicago Press, 1987), p. 47.

30. Doane, "Film and the Masquerade," p. 85. The similarly structured image that Doane analyzes is Robert Doisneau's photograph, *Une regard oblique,* in which a couple looks into a display window. The wife, positioned at the center of the tableau, points out something in the window to her husband, who is instead glancing furtively at a painting of a female nude on the wall. Doane argues that the wife's gaze is eclipsed by the nude and she thus becomes the butt of a "dirty joke."

31. Lacan's pun is observed by Jonathan Elmer in "The Exciting Conflict: The Rhetoric of Pornography and Anti-Pornography," *Cultural Critique* no. 8 (Winter 1987): 67. The pun occurs in the introduction of Lacan's seminar "The Line and the Light," p. 91. Chaucer's Absolon, it should be noted, is also referred to as having kissed his lover's "nether ye" or "lower eye" in having kissed her bearded "naked ers."

32. Lacan, *The Four Fundamental Concepts,* p. 83.

33. Michael Fried, "Courbet's 'Femininity'," *Courbet Reconsidered,* ex. cat., ed. Sarah Faunce and Linda Nochlin (New York: Brooklyn Museum, 1988), pp. 43–53.

34. Stephen Melville and Bill Readings, "Feminism and the Exquisite Corpse of Realism," *Strategies* nos. 4–5 (1991): 242–88.

35. Lacan, *The Four Fundamental Concepts,* p. 94.

36. See, for example, Laura Mulvey's distinction in cinema between the masculine as penetration and the feminine as surface in "Visual Pleasure in Narrative Cinema," *Screen* vol. 16, no. 3 (Autumn 1975): 12–13; and Doane, pp. 76–77. Cf. Kelly Dennis, "Playing with Herself: Feminine Sexuality and Aesthetic Indifference," *Solitary Pleasures: The Historical, Literary, and Artistic Discourses of Autoeroticism,* ed. Paula Bennett and Vernon A. Rosario II (New York: Routledge, 1995), 49–74.

37. Fried, "Courbet's Femininity," pp. 50–52.

38. Lacan as paraphrased by Melville and Readings, p. 286, note 11.

39. Linda Nochlin, "Courbet's Real Allegory: Rereading "The Painter's Studio," *Courbet Reconsidered,* ex. cat., ed. Sarah Faunce and Linda Nochlin (New York: Brooklyn Museum 1988), p. 84.

40. This point is debatable. In terms of photographic technology this kind of shot was feasible but conceptually and culturally unlikely at this point in time. My thanks to Therese Mulligan, Curator of Photography at George Eastman House, for engaging these issues with me.

41. The reference here is to the end of chapter 12 in Lacan's *The Four Fundamental Concepts,* in which he refers to a photograph of a little girl with her skirt pulled up and displacing the "eye" of the camera which "exposes her" with her own "small apparatus," p. 160.

42. Walter Benjamin, "The Work of Art in the Age of Mechanical Reproduction," *Illuminations* (New York: Schocken Books, 1969), pp. 233–34.

43. Allan Sekula, "The Body and the Archive," *October* 39 (1986): 11.

44. Ibid.

45. Hubert Damisch, "Notes for a Phenomenology of the Photographic Image," *Classic Essays on Photography,* ed. Alan Trachtenberg (New Haven: Leete's Island Books, 1980), p. 289.

46. Sekula, p. 17.

47. Belgian astronomer and statistician Adolphe Quetelet, whose work Bertillon drew upon, professed his theory of *l'homme moyen* in his *Treatise on Man* as explicitly based on Dürer's anatomical and perspectival studies. Quetelet stated that his "aim had been, not only to go once more through the task of Albert [sic] Dürer, but to execute it also on an extended scale." Quoted in Sekula, p. 23.

48. Sekula, p., 11. See also Sander Gilman, *Difference and Pathology: Stereotypes of Sexuality, Race, and Madness* (Ithaca: Cornell University Press 1985); and Sander L. Gilman, "Black Bodies, White Bodies: Toward an Iconography of Female Sexuality in Late Nineteenth-Century Art, Medicine, and Literature," in *"Race," Writing, and Difference,* ed. Henry Louis Gates Jr. (Chicago: University of Chicago Press, 1986). pp. 223–26.

49. The phrase is Stephen Jay Gould's in *The Mismeasure of Man* (New York: Norton, 1981), p. 127.

50. See Gould, chapter 3.

51. Cesare Lombroso and William Ferrero, *The Female Offender* (New York: Philosophical Books, 1958).

52. Gilman, *Difference and Pathology,* pp. 245 and 248.

53. Sekula, p. 7, emphasis in the original.

54. Benjamin, "The Work of Art," p. 226.

55. Lacan, *The Four Fundamental Concepts,* p. 72.

56. See also Melville and Readings for a discussion of the distinction of Lacan's notion of the gaze from Sartre's and Foucault's. This distinction seems to me to be absolutely crucial not only for my argument here, but for understanding Lacan's work generally.

57. This seems to me the fundamental error in Martin Jay's criticism of what he characterizes as the "antiocularcentrism" of contemporary French thought.

See his *Douncast Eyes: The Denigration of Vision in Twentieth-Century French Thought* (Berkeley and Los Angeles: University of California Press, 1993).

58. The reference to panopticism is of course to Michel Foucault, *Discipline and Punish: The Birth of the Prison* (New York: Vintage, 1979), pp. 195–308. I am indebted to Samuel Weber for my discussion of subjectivity in relation to structures of authority.

59. Sekula, p. 7. Sekula also notes that "arrest" within the ranks of bourgeois portrait photography acts as an insurance of social status, freezing one's place within the social hierarchy from which one peered either up or down.

60. Lacan, following Merleau-Ponty, distinguishes between "gesture" and "act"—the former he specifies as a movement that is terminated, "a blow that is interrupted. It is certainly something that is done in order to be arrested and suspended." Lacan, *The Four Fundamental Concepts,* p. 116. That his example of "gesture" is the painter's brushstroke by no means contradicts my argument; rather, photography is that which figures the temporal-ontological significance of representation itself, which is not to say that these implications are not present in painting, but that photography more explicitly "pictures" the gesture of picturing.

61. Benjamin, "On Some Motifs in Baudelaire," p. 219.

62. Ibid., p. 175.

63. Metz, "Photography and Fetish," p. 87.

64. Benjamin, "On Some Motifs in Baudelaire," p. 175.

65. Hubert Damisch has made a useful distinction between the perspectival construction of painting and the "framing" of photography. Unlike painting, whose "world" is constructed within the frame of the canvas, beyond which "perspective" would necessarily become distorted and disfigured, photography "frames" its "world picture" as one excised from the illusory continuity of its surroundings. For the implications of Heidegger's notion of the "world as picture" see Stephen Melville, "The Temptation of New Perspectives," *October* 52 (1990): 3–15.

66. Benjamin, "On Some Motifs in Baudelaire," p. 187, emphasis added.

67. Sekula, p. 5.

68. Walter Kendrick, *The Secret Museum: Pornography in Modern Culture* (New York: Viking, 1987), pp. 1–12.

69. Solomon-Godeau, "The Legs of the Countess," p. 98.

70. Ibid.

71. Ibid.

72. Benjamin, "On Some Motifs in Baudelaire," p. 188.

73. Ibid.

74. See also Angelika Rauch on the function of the woman's body as "corpse" in order to be the repository for meaning in modernity: "The *Trauerspiel* of the Prostituted Body, or Woman as Allegory of Modernity," *Cultural Critique* vol. 1 (1988): 77–88.

75. See, for example, Spaulding Gray's "The Farmer's Daughter," in *Wild History* (New York: Tanham, 1985), a fictionalized account of the trials and tribulations of a porn actor and the attending "fluffers"—women whose job it is to restimulate and sustain the actors' erections off-camera for their on-camera performances. Also commenting on this disjunction between pleasure and production is David James, "Hardcore: Cultural Resistance in the Postmodern," *Film Quarterly,* vol. 42, no. 2 (Winter 1988–89): 31–39. Fluffers are a porn industry perk lamented by the actors interviewed by Faludi, "The Money Shot."

76. Hard-core porn magazines are also distinguished from soft-core pornography such as *Playboy, Playgirl,* and *Penthouse,* by a slightly different, if literal, set of visual codes. The primary difference between hard- and soft-core magazines is literally the "hardness" of the male sexual organ. Hard-core magazines like *Hustler, Chic* and gay hard-core magazines *Advocate Men* and *Mandate* show the erect penis, while soft-core magazines like *Playgirl* show only the unerect penis. Soft-core *Playboy* and *Penthouse* rarely show the male organ at all, although blow jobs are alluded to in couples photography. Unlike hard-core film, mainstream hard-core photography cannot show sexual intercourse: Censorship laws prevent it from showing genital-genital or oral-genital contact, although any other oral-body or digital-body contact may be shown. This is clearly not the case for underground hard core that evades censorship laws.

77. *Chic,* November 1988 (Los Angeles: Larry Flynt Publications), p. 21. Full disclosure: In 1988 I worked as a freelance typographer for Larry Flynt Publications, Inc.

78. *Hustler,* September 1988 (Los Angeles: Larry Flynt Publications).

79. On the implications of being "too close" to the image, see Kelly Dennis, "Playing with Herself," in *Solitary Pleasures: The Historical, Literary, and Artistic Discourses of Autoeroticism,* ed. Paula Bennett and Vernon A. Rosario II (New York and London: Routledge, 1995), pp. 49–72.

80. For examples of the argument that pornography is based on voyeurism, see David James, p. 34 and the discussion in the final chapter of Linda Williams's *Hard Core.*

81. Times have changed. *Hustler* now shows oral-genital contact, digital penetration, and dildo-genital contact between women.

82. In contrast, however, the cartoons (for example, "Chester the Molester") have a decidedly scatalogical bent, showing in exaggerated detail the genitals and sexual organs as anything but hygienic. Rather, genitals are represented in *Hustler* cartoons as hirsute, as dripping juices, and as manifesting malodorous vapors and around which flies hover.

83. Since the origination of this article in 1988, the visual displacement of female sexuality has become increasingly represented by photographing the labia with a drop of whitish fluid—suggesting either semen or female ejaculate. Chris Straayer has written on the fetishization and politics of female ejaculate in "The

Seduction of Boundaries: Feminist Fluidity in Annie Sprinkle's Art/Education/ Sex," in *Dirty Looks: Women, Pornography, Power,* eds. Pamela Church Gibson and Roma Gibson (London: BFI, 1993), pp. 156–75.

84. Michel Foucault, *History of Sexuality* (New York: Random House, 1980), pp. 51–75.

85. This feature has since been expanded to include "Beaver Hunt Video Contest."

86. In "Hardcore: Cultural Resistance in the Postmodern," David James argues that amateur mail-order porn video "shamelessly proclaims erotic representation as its *raison d'etre,* [and] is not obliged to disguise itself as either narrative or documentary" (33). By contrast, such domestic details in amateur porn photos provide a narrative context that is both similar and dissimilar to the narratives of professional photographic pornography. For a class-based analysis of pornography and feminist objections to pornography see Laura Kipnis, "(Male) Desire and (Female) Disgust: Reading *Hustler*" in *Cultural Studies,* ed. Lawrence Grossberg et al. (New York: Routledge, 1992), pp. 373–78; reprinted in Kipnis, *Ecstasy Unlimited: On Sex, Capital, Gender, and Aesthetics* (Minneapolis: University of Minnesota Press, 1993).

87. Foucault, p. 36.

88. Porn publisher Larry Flynt claims transgression with his antirepression tirades and his claims *not* that porn is normal for a majority of the public but that the majority of people are perverse in their desire for pornography.

89. A condition verified by pornography's status as a multibillion-dollar business: "Contemporary pornography is a hugely profitable industry which thrives on being thought illicit." Rosalind Coward, "What Is Pornography? Two Opposing Feminist Viewpoints," *Looking On,* ed. Rosemary Betterton (London: Pandora, 1987), p. 175.

90. For a thorough discussion and documentation of opinions and events surrounding censorship of the exhibition, see Richard Bolton, *Culture Wars* (New York: New Press, 1992) and Steven C. Dubin, *Arresting Images* (New York: Routledge, 1992).

91. Eleanor Heartney, "A necessary transgression," *New Art Examiner* vol. 16, no. 3 (1988): 21, emphasis added.

92. Since this article was written in 1988, the "pro-sex" feminist position has made itself more prominently known through numerous articles and anthologies. See especially Carla Freccero, "Notes of a Post-Sex Wars Theorizer," *Conflicts in Feminism,* ed. M. Hirsch and E. Fox Keller (New York: Routledge, 1991), pp. 305–25. However, the antiporn feminist position maintains a stronghold.

93. Williams, *Hard Core,* p. 25.

94. Ibid.

95. See Williams for an excellent summary of this argument in her final chapter of *Hard Core.*

96. It seems that we "know" pornography is sexist and exploitative, but that this should not, as Heartney states, "surprise us."

97. Williams, p. 25.

98. It should be noted here that most commercial *heterosexual* S&M is male submissive, female dominant. See, for example, Dolores French, *Working* (New York: Pinnacle, 1988), Mistress Lilith Lash, "Pain, Pleasure and Poetry," in Priscilla Alexander and Frederique Delacoste, *Sex Work: Writings by Women in the Sex Industry* (Pittsburgh: Cleis, 1987), pp. 50–52; a special issue of *Social Text* 37 (1993) on the bondage sex trade, edited by Anne McClintock; "The Kat Box," bondage and domination advice column in *Chic* magazine, Larry Flynt Publications; and the phone-sex advertisements in the back pages of any alternative newspaper (*Village Voice, LA Weekly*) or any sex-oriented magazine.

99. The answer to this is a resounding "no" by radical lesbians who accept both S&M and pederasty as forms of sexuality. SAMOIS refutes the idea of S&M as a "mirror" of the power structure of patriarchal society into "butch" and "femme" relations, in contrast to feminist and "vanilla lesbian" politics. Documented and discussed by Pat Califia in "A Personal View of the History of the Lesbian S/M Community and Movement in San Francisco" in SAMOIS, *Coming to Power: Writings and Graphics on Lesbian S/M* (Boston: Alyson, 1981) pp. 245–84. A number of essays in *Sex Work* and *Social Text* explicitly state that sex workers, lesbian and straight, feel that they are marginalized and misrepresented by academic feminists.

100. Gay pornographic publications distributed by LFP, Inc., in 1988 included *Advocate Men, Inches, Mandate, Torso, Rods, Heat, MI (Male Insider), Jock,* and *Honcho.*

101. See Denise Hamilton, "Evolution from Underground: The *LA Weekly* and Alternative Journalism," *Enclitic* vol. 10, no. 2 (1988): 20.

102. Elmer, "The Exciting Conflict."

103. Alas, corporate ownership has long since dulled the alterity of these alternative presses.

104. Kipnis refers to *Hustler*'s place in a long tradition of Rabelesian tactics of deprivileging those in power by depicting them nude or in an otherwise obscene fashion. Some of this tradition is likewise covered in Lynn Hunt, ed., *The Invention of Pornography: Obscenity and the Origins of Modernity, 1500–1800* (New York: Zone, 1993).

105. Cited in Gertrud Koch, "In the Body's Shadow Realm," *October* 50 (Fall 1989): 16. It is interesting to note the coincidence of this description of indifference to beauty with that of letters to the editor praising *Hustler*'s "Beaver Hunt" amateur models.

106. Metz, "Photography and Fetish," p. 87.

107. Benjamin, "On Some Motifs in Baudelaire," p. 187.

108. Lacan, *The Four Fundamental Concepts,* p. 183.

109. Ibid., p. 182.

110. Ibid.

111. Ibid., p. 81.

112. Ibid., p. 80.

113. Linda Lovelace, *Ordeal* (New York: Berkeley Books, 1980). I do not, in fact, doubt Lovelace's tale, but it is a tale *not* of pornography but of abuse. Linda Lovelace, née Boreman now Marchiano (1949–2002), and antiporn feminists point to her abuse by former husband Chuck Traynor as exemplifying the violence of pornography; however, it would make as much sense—perhaps more—to equate marriage itself with the sexual, verbal, and emotional abuse of women.

114. This response is documented in Linda Lovelace's sequel, *Out of Bondage* (New York: Berkeley, 1987). Lovelace describes initial femininst resistence to her claims of abuse and then her credibility due to her consciousness raising by and friendship with Gloria Steinem. According to Marchiano/Lovelace, Steinem abandoned their "friendship" once Lovelace had served her purpose.

115. See Williams, *Hard Core*, pp. 261–64. Williams has since revised this stance. See her preface to the second edition of *Hard Core*.

116. C. Carr points out that every artist under attack by Jesse Helms and others opposed to the NEA has challenged the hierarchy of the "sexual order." Artists Robert Mapplethorpe, Annie Sprinkle, and Karen Finley, among others, assert "other" sexualities; other definitions of what it means to be male and female—that is, being gay or demystifying the female body. See "War on Art: The Sexual Politics of Censorship," *Village Voice* (June 5, 1990), p. 27; reprinted in C. Carr, *On Edge: Performance at the End of the Twentieth Century* (Hanover and London: Wesleyan University Press and University Press of New England, 1994), pp. 249–59.

117. Lacan criticizes the so-called feminist inscription of women as objects in their criticism of the phallocentric order: "It is quite striking to see that the representatives of this sex in the analytic circle are particularly disposed to maintain the fundamental belief in feminine masochism. It may be that there is a veil here, concerning the interests of the sex, that should not be lifted too quickly." Lacan, *The Four Fundamental Concepts*, pp. 192–93.

118. Cf. Michael Fried, *Absorption and Theatricality* (Chicago: University of Chicago Press, 1980); see also Stephen Melville, *Philosophy beside Itself: On Deconstruction and Modernism* (Minneapolis: University of Minnesota Press, 1986).

119. Lacan, pp. 95–96.

120. *Courbet Reconsidered*, pp. 176–78.

13

Heretical Marxism
Pasolini's Cinema Inpopolare

Kriss Ravetto

His [Dionysos] cult is the cult of awakening . . . a power that still shows its ambiguity. Phallic Dionysos gives drunkenness and ecstasy. Calls beyond. Sets absence within and between bodies. He heralds a rupture with life . . . he returns again and again to nature pouring forth. His love and his hate have yet been polarized. He still mixes everything up together.

—Luce Irigaray

The divine enters the world surreptitiously. No break-ins, no bloodshed. At least in general, at least not visibly or even tangibly. Apollo establishes the Olympian Regime which will rule over men by means of a voice that speaks to them from within. The empire of the Father of gods is founded by a mutation in the nature of signs. The mediator par excellence between heaven and earth, earth and heaven, will henceforth be the word. The God's sovereignty is installed through the privilege given to the word over any other system of exchange.

—Luce Irigaray

I am not a Hegelian: there is indeed a thesis, the sacred, and an antithesis, the profane, but there is no synthesis, only juxtaposition.

—Pier Paolo Pasolini

Pier Paolo Pasolini's affiliation with the Communist Party has always been tenuous. After his death the party has reclaimed him as one of their own, but his expulsion or, as Naomi Greene calls it, his "excommunication" on the basis of his homosexuality left Pasolini to live out "lo scandalo del contraddirsi, dell'essere con sè e contro sè; con sè nel cuore, in luce, controsè nelle buie viscere" (the scandal of contradicting himself of being with it/him [the party/Gramsci] with it/him in his heart, in the light [publically], but against it/him in the dark viscera [sexually]).[1] Like many postwar Italian intellectuals who turned to Communist ideology as the only legitimate opposition to fascism, Pasolini followed the teachings of Antonio Gramsci. In his poem *"Le Ceneri di Gramsci"*/The ashes of Gramsci, Pasolini articulates that his relationship to Communist ideology is more than a moral attitude. Instead it is a visceral fascination with the subproletariat that extends beyond both class consciousness and historical materialism: "è per me religione la sua allegria, non la millenaria sua lotta; la sua natura, non la sua coscienza" (for me it is a religion, its joy; not its millennial struggle, its nature, not its consciousness) (*"Le Ceneri di Gramsci,"* 72). This is not to say that Pasolini's interest can be depoliticized or reduced to pure sexual desire, which some reactionary writers have claimed. By introducing sexuality as a component in the ritual of human interaction instead of what has been perceived as merely sexual preference translated into political discourse, Pasolini not only challenges the political left in terms of its moral connection to the bourgeoisie, but questions its ideological goals of reconstituting its historical subject, the working class.

Oswald Stack's argument that "Pasolini has an uncritical attachment to the peasantry [revealing] a contradiction between marxism and communist analysis and backward looking romanticism." This overlooks Pasolini's critique of both Marxism—and Communism—as providing the protagonist's own romantic narrative of history as the history of class struggle in which the proletariat will assume its position as protagonist. In fact Pasolini clearly indicates his understanding of the proletariat as well as Partito Communista Italiano as inevitably entrenched in the process of becoming its own historical subject, within an ultimately unnegatable bourgeois narrative.[2] It is the failure of both the ideology of dialectic materialism and that of staid millenarian progression (peasant to proletariat to bourgeois to socialist to Communist) to produce any valid revolutionary praxis in the postwar period. Pasolini marks his point of departure from Marx's and Gramsci's critiques of capitalism as a movement toward what he defines as the prehistoric (the prebourgeois). I will discuss Pasolini's view of an impossible future and of an irrecoverable past in which he expands the notion of the subproletariat to include the third world, homosexuals, woman. I also discuss his notion of the sacred disempowered mythic past. Pasolini's privileging of the sacred over the profane reveals not only a desire to awaken the mythic/Dionysian explosion of the passions—"a power that still shows its ambiguity," that "still mixes everything up together"—but also to (re)call beyond patriarchal history to a timeless mythic place of origins, a place of sexual ambivalence and "innocent" erotic violence.

Pasolini sets this prehistoric radical otherness apart from the Western political economy that he perceives as historically determined by a system of symbolic exchange that promises technological modernization at the expense of conforming to a model of perpetual consumption and acquisition of status and wealth within the confines of the patriarchal structure.[3] For Pasolini it is this patriarchal "system of exchange" that demands submission to the laws of the repressive sexual apparatus of the bourgeois family and the punishing Word of the Father. In his contempt for conformity to the "fascism" of the bourgeoisie, Pasolini creates the "other" as a construct that symbolizes the celebration of the body and the blood, the ambivalence of the Dionysian erotic experience, the ironic delegitimation of hegemonic order in the masquerade of the carnival.

In his earlier films—such as *Accattone* (1961), *Mamma Roma* (1962), *Il Vangelo Secondo Matteo* (1964), *Uccellacci e Uccellini* (1965–66), and even as late as *Teorema* (1968)—he inscribes the sacred within a revolutionary political discourse. He draws the subproletariat, the peasantry, and the third world from the periphery to the center to coagulate them as the locus of a revolutionary force. The subproletariat, the peasantry, and the third-world peoples embody subversive values and virtues of a prehistoric past. Since the future represents only a light that *"non cessa un solo instante di ferirci,"* ("that does not stop, for an instant, to hurt us."),[4] Pasolini "calls beyond": *"accerto un bisogno struggente di minoranze alleate. Tornate, Ebrei, agli albori di questa Preistoria"* because *"per chi é crocifisso alla sua razionalitá straziante, macerato dal puritanesimo, non ha piu senso che un'aristocratica, e ahi, impopolare opposizione."*[5] "I find a pressing need for a minority alliance. Turn back Jews, to the dawn of this prehistory" because "for those who are crucified by their torturing rationality, marked with Puritanism, do not have anymore sense than an aristocratic and unpopular opposition." This *"impopolare opposizione"* translates into an idealistic if not consciously privileged turn toward the periphery: a process of regression to a prehistoric, prelinguistic, and preoedipal "space"—a "return to nature pouring forth." Yet this turning toward the periphery, reveals not only Pasolini's self-positioning as the (albeit entrapped) center, but also his collapsing of time into space. The economic and geographic others (the subproletariat and the third-world peoples) become a construct that he calls the prehistorical. Although the series of films that Pasolini labeled *"cinema inpopolare"*—*Edipo Re* (1967), *Porcile* (1968), *Teorema* (1968–69), and *Medea* (1970)—symbolize a further regression into the mythic past, this extended reach beyond reflects not only a desperate search for a place of spiritual purity and natural origin, but also the inability of the *"minoranze alleate"* to provide a space outside of the bourgeois regime and its capitalist language of exchange. Pasolini documents the disappearance of the other (or at least his imaginary construction of the other) and the growing migration of the periphery toward modernization/conformism (sameness) in films such as *Sopraluoghi in Palestina, Il Vangelo Secondo Matteo* (both 1964), *Appunti per un'Orestiade Africana* (1969–70), and *Le Mura di Sana'a* (1970–71), all shot where he always seems to have arrived too late to find a precapitalist culture. For Pasolini this disappearance or detachment of humankind from its place of origin—albeit a problematic projection of Pasolini's cosmic values on the third world and, in the case of Medea, women—represents a closure of the past and simultaneously the impossibility of a future transcendence that would reunite modern man with a sense of natural wholeness.

The movement from a nostalgic idealization of the subproletariat to their narrativization in what Bakhtin calls the "absolute" or "epic past" corresponds to Pasolini's profound disillusionment with the political promises of the Left that lead him to present the subproletariat as a politically disruptive force. The advent of the *"cinema inpopolare"* heralds Pasolini's dismissal of *"il rosso straccio di speranza"* ("the red rag of hope") and leads him to the conclusion that *"La rivoluzione non e più che un sentimento"* ("the revolution is not more than a sentiment") (*Se-*

lected Poems, 202). Therefore, the use of a mythic distance itself reflects Pasolini's inability to locate the Dionysian cosmic sense of wholeness in the periphery, which he saw moving toward if not being appropriated by the omnipresent and ever expanding culture of global capitalism.

The regression to a mythical prehistory reduces Western history to a tragedy of loss (prehistoric wholeness) and betrayal (the promise of the future which turns out to be only a wound). History is reduced to an irreconcilable split of the sacred and the profane. In the above-mentioned series of films Pasolini posits the irrevocable autonomy of bourgeois capitalism. Even in his call for a return to prehistoric origins Pasolini reflects that the sacred is no longer a viable path, since it has already been seduced by the patriarchal colonialist father, and has already been corrupted by the desire to become one and the same with the capitalist system (as Medea is seduced by Jason). *Edipo Re* (the first of the series of mythic films) serves as an analogy to Pasolini's abandoning all hope of returning to a prior form of innocence—a meaningful (cosmic) wholeness. It is Edipo's very search for the place of origin (womb) that brings about the knowledge that reveals that he is guilty of killing his father and that he has defiled his place of origin (his mother's womb). He realizes that unbeknownst to himself, he is guilty of being the very destroyer of that place of origin. Oedipus rests on what Luce Irigaray calls the "edge of a precipice." In the vertigo of the abyss he "seeks the secret of his birth and his death [. . . ; however,] to repeat his own birth is simply impossible and by wishing for it, he chooses to die."[6] Thus, knowledge as a search beyond can only be the conduit to understanding that he can never return to his original innocence (to the preoedipal, prelinguistic, and prehistoric womb), and must live in the guilty knowledge that once uprooted from his origins he must live forever in exile—aimlessly destined to wander/wonder in the modern city.

Although as Adorno postulates, "the myths as the tragedians came upon them are already characterized by discipline and power,"[7] Pasolini interprets these myths as allegories of the clash of the sacred (prehistorical/Dionysian) and the profane (Bourgeois capitalism/Apollonian) and attempts to delegitimize the messages of discipline (bourgeois moralism) and decenter the power structures (patriarchal regimes). The very juxtaposition of these two forces undermines the empire of the Father's claim to a historical and political dominance. Since man can never return to the sacred as a return to "nature pouring forth," the sacred reserves only the power to "herald a rupture with bourgeois life," where desire can only be "an exodus towards death." Therefore, the mythical series of films replaces a "synthetical" transcendence with a negative dialectic—a vengeance that sacrifices its own existence for the disappearance of its "antithesis." According to Adorno this process of "determinate negation" is set into motion in order to "reject [the] defective ideas of the absolute," or in the case of Pasolini, it is a return of the oppressed (repressed) passions that wreck (counternarrate) the infinite autonomy (narration) of the bourgeoisie (*Dialectic of Enlightenment,* 24). According to Pasolini: *"Solo un mare di sangue può salvare il mondo dai suoi borghesi sogni destinati a farne un luogo sempre più irreale! Solo una rivoluzione che fa strage di questi morti, può sconsacrarne il male!*" ("Only a sea of blood can save this world from its bourgeois dreams / certain to make it more and more unreal / Only a revolution that slaughters these dead men can deconsecrate their evil") ("*La Realtà*" *Selected Poems,* 134).

Medea distinguishes itself from the rest of the "*cinema inpopolare*" series in that it presents a closure; not only by negating the patriarchy's self-regeneration—ending the Oedipal dialectic of sons replacing (killing) fathers—but by making the culmination of an affirmative negation. The only escape from the (prison) marriage of exiled sacredness (Medea) with nomadic or more likely cosmopolitan "profanity" (Jason) rests in the consumption of their offspring—a negation of any possible past or future, regressive or progressive. In addition, *Medea* proves to be an anomaly in respect to the canon of Pasolini's works, by the mere fact that it locates the "voice" and symbolic presence of the sacred and its radical potential for rupture in woman, who in previous films served as a silent background figure associated with the sacred only by her disassociation with the profane.

Although it is constructed as a series of juxtapositions similar to *Edipo Re, Porcile,* and *Teorema, Medea* emphasizes a chronological development: the movement from the sacred (prehistoric) to the profane (Western bourgeois society as well as its ideological and economic structures). First, *Medea* delineates the sacred in the various forms Pasolini had attributed to it—the prehistorical, the prelinguistic, the third world, and woman as mother. Second, it signifies the alienation from nature created by a forced assimilation to the economy of exchange and submission to the laws of the patriarchy. Last, it represents the revenge of the sacred that is reduced to an object of appropriation and exchange, a mere vessel through which the profane narcissistically reproduces itself. This revenge articulates itself by devouring the offspring (Medea's sons/future patriarchs), decapitating the power structure (Aeetes and Kreon) and its possibility of mimetic procreation (Glauke), devaluing the system of exchange and reducing the linguistic mediation (the Word) to silence. Medea, as an emblematic figure of radical otherness (prehistorical, prelinguistic, erotic-violence, the third world and the mother), becomes "*un vaso pieno di sapere non mio,*" (a glass full of knowledge that is not [hers]); in fact she embodies Pasolini's construction of the other, and its potential of violent negation, leaving the only creative opening for Pasolini in the imagination—the sexual fantasies portrayed in "*La trilogia di vita.*"[8]

Although Medea is constructed as a multiplicity of polarized forces, these forces intersect in respect to their association or division along the axis of the sacred and the profane. These various dimensions within Pasolini's thesis (sacred) and antithesis (profane) are primarily framed in a philosophical discourse that divides the sacred and the mythic cosmos from the profane logos. Yet the placement of the two forces reveals not a regression but a migration toward the profane in its various facets. The philosophical prologue serves not only as a structural but also an ideological model for the film, which continues to move from the larger categorical oppositions to more and more specific (confining) ones—from the opposition of the cosmos to the logos (the division of man as an individual from nature), to the juxtaposition of two cultures (one prehistorical, the other posthistorical), to the irreligiosity of the bourgeois state that divides the *isonomia* (same) from the *barbaroi* (non-Greek speakers, slaves, women, and animals), and finally to the division of the *polis* from the *oikia* (house) that divides and devises the respective gender placement within the patriarchy.

Even though Medea, like Jason, symbolizes the intersection of various marginal others in respect to the Western-centered gaze, these levels of otherness are not reducible to a general sacredness or profanity, nor are they exchangeable. Although modeled after Euripides' classical tragedy, Pasolini's *Medea* reaches beyond the realm of tragedy—already "characterized by discipline and power"—to the world of myth—a depoliticized world/word, of beginnings, and participation with (or a repetition of) the past. While the retelling of the myth and the retelling of Euripides' tragedy provide the film with narrative continuity, the juxtaposition of the two genres depicts a rupture of ideological processes. In fact it is through the two centaurs that Pasolini symbolizes the departure from the sacred and its unexplainable movement toward the profane: initially the centaurs serve to narrate the mythical origins of Jason and Medea, connecting the two together in a common story, while simultaneously functioning as representatives of the opposing forces of the sacred and the profane. Yet the centaurs' reappearance in the second half of the film reinforces the movement from the mythic world (*"fatto di cose"*/made of things) to the internalization or psychologization of myth itself in the realm of the profane (*"fatti di pensieri"* /made of ideas).

Medea might begin at sunrise—the (son)rise of civilization—but even though it begins within a discourse of the cosmos, it already establishes itself within the Western male tradition (both mythic and philosophical), anticipating the rise of patriarchal hegemony. By foregrounding the educational process and the corresponding maturing of Jason—the resituating of the Western male from the mythic hero to the modern political and philosophical man—Pasolini identifies Jason not only as the figure of transition who embodies both attributes of the sacred and the profane, but also symbolizes the central reference (subject) in relation to which all otherness is defined.

The first form of Cheiron as a centaur represents the *"uomo antico"* (the ancient man) with the understanding that *"tutto é santo"* (everything is sacred) and *"non c'é niente naturale nella natura, tutto é possenduto di un dio, . . . ma la santitá é insieme un maledizione, gli dei che amano nel tempo stesso odiano,"* (There is nothing in nature that is natural, everything is possessed by a god . . . but sacredness is also a curse, the gods that love at the same time hate) (*Medea,* 548). In addition this figure also presents, as much as he represents, the aspect of myth that identifies Jason within the legacy of Greek heroes, not only by establishing a direct lineage of Jason to a series of heroic forefathers, but by association to Cheiron's previous pupils—Asclepius, Achilles, Aeneas, and Herakles. Thus, the symbolic past becomes a means of reference, a legitimation of Jason's noble lineage (*"un discendente di Eolo"*/descendant of Aeolo who is associated with the wind), yet at the same time it subjects him to the chaotic power of nature (the wind itself), which "still shows its ambiguity." The very form of Cheiron incarnates this ambiguity, "where everything is still mixed up together": his sexual ambivalence, which would allow him to claim that he was both mother and father of Jason, and the fusion of his human frame with that of an animal. Cheiron recalls the excess of the cosmic wholeness, the "yet to be polarized love and hate," as the excess of erotic violence, aggressive sexuality, drunkenness, and ecstasy which are usually attributed to male virility. But the centaur is a symbolic manifestation of the act of sexual intercourse itself, both heterosexual and homosexual. The Centaur's asymmetrical formation is mirrored in his hybrid qualities: on the one hand he represents the old lyrical world (poetic language), and on the other, the alternative to the culture of the polis, the uncivilized, bestial, drunken wildness. The allusion to the Centaur is reminiscent of the timelessness that Euripides' Jason (and maybe Pasolini) advocates—a masculine *autakeia,* self-sufficiency, a society with no need of women.[9] For Pasolini, the centaur not only signifies the hidden meanings and the omnipresence of the sacred, but also the antithesis to the bourgeois family, that which is not only nonreproductive but sexually aggressive (as Medea), while still being sexually ambiguous.

According to Bakhtin "in ancient literature it is memory [as participation in the past] and not knowledge [as the Socratic message of 'know thy self'] that serves as the source and power for the creative impulse."[10] It is this very mythic language (as memory) that is delegitimized (as only a "creative impulse") at the onset of the film with Cheiron's annunciation to Jason: "*Tu non sei mio figlio e non ti ho trovato nel mare, . . . tu non sei bugiardo, Io si, mi diverto a dire le bugie . . . Io non sono tua madre e tuo padre*" (You are not my son and I did not find you in the sea . . . you're not a liar, I am, I like to tell lies . . . I am not your mother and your father) (*Medea,* 548). Here Cheiron divides the world/word of myth from that of the truth—that which he does not speak since he has defined himself as a liar. And hence, his excessive use of language, recounting of the world as "*fatto di cose,*" is regarded as noncomprehensible babbling, especially by Jason (as the child) who falls asleep. However, Cheiron's expression of nature as having hidden meaning (as being "*fatto di cose*") reveals the inability of language as a mimetic form to express the world of experiences that is always in flux and undergoing metamorphosis. As Luce Irigaray explains, "How is one to mimic something that has no identity, cannot be encompassed, something eluding capture and catalog, except for the mask [language]—death" (*Marine Lover of Friedrich Nietzsche,* 58). The process of life (as the sacred) is inexplicable, since it has no form and no language—no formal construct. The form or meaning given to life (roles, symbols, language) can only be given to a closed/dead or historical form. In fact for Pasolini, it is the incarnation of the word, the process of naming, as the internalization of meaning (the replacement of myth and ritual for the inner experience of the modern man) in a fixed platonic form that causes the loss of spiritual meaning. Pasolini's philosophical centaur armed with the weapons of the discursive (roles, symbols, language, and the idea)

negates or kills the sacred understanding of the world as an indistinguishable external cosmic wholeness, by dispossessing the cosmos of its "holiness" and its
meaning, as *"un lontano ricordo che non ti riguarda più, infatti non c'é nessun dio"* (A
distant memory that you don't recall anymore, in fact there is no god). According
to Pasolini, *"La morte non é nel non poter comunicare ma nel non poter più essere com-
presi"* (Death is not in not being able to communicate, but in no longer being able
to understand) (*"Una Disperata Vitalità," Selected Poems*, 150).

For Adorno "the separation of sign and image is irreversible, language itself gave what was asserted, the conditions of domination, the universality that
they had assumed as the means of intercourse of bourgeois society" (*Dialectic of
Enlightenment*, 22). The replacement of the sacred centaur with the secular one
reflects the social power of language that not only "robes" the centaur with the language of the logos but reflects the death of "the real" as having meaning outside
of language: *"solo ció che é mistico é realistico, solo ció che è realistico è mistico"* (Only
that which is mystical is real, only that which is real is mystical) (*Medea*, 551). This
mysticism does not refer to the modern world where the supremacy of thought
(consciousness) pronounces the impotence of thought in the empirical world (human existence), but to the prelinguistic world of Medea where the "sign and the
image" are one and the same. With the advent of Platonic thought, the logos itself
(dis)places the real in the abstraction of forms, reducing the cosmos to mere appearances and the passions to a sense of lack (of knowledge of the forms).[11] The
cosmos merely becomes a mimetic copy of an original form outside of the cosmic
or natural world itself.

The "philosophical or modern" centaur symbolizes the triumph of the word
as the "mediator par excellence, the mediator between heaven and earth" (the
mind and the body) by positing the replacement of the sacredness of the real, as
"esperienza concreta" (concrete experience), for the *"profonda esperienza personale"*
(professional personal experience). The transformation of discourse from the
"uomo antico," who was *"troppo poetico"* (too poetic) to *"uomo moderno"* reveals not
only the internalization and the psychologicalization of experience, as well as the
subsequent loss of spiritual meaning, but also the reorientation of the myth to a
materialistic discourse on the acquisition of social status—a discourse that reveals
its source of meaning in sociopolitical and economic structures. Whereas the old
centaur embeds the story of the golden fleece within a mystical realm, *"il vello por-
tava fortuna ai re"* (the fleece brought fortune to kings), the new centaur uses the
fleece as an example of a conquest (where appropriation equals proof of ability to
master or colonize) but also as a means to gain status within the social structure
(exchange value). Therefore, for Jason as a modern man (a prototypical bourgeoisie), the fleece only has symbolic value in the sense of exchange value. The
fleece no longer contains power in and of itself, but is made meaningless as an object of exchange (as Medea herself will be objectified, once removed from Colchis).

Pasolini depicts the process of civilization as the clothing of the natural or
the sacred with the profanity of engendered language, and the introduction of un-

equal exchange that solidifies meanings only in relation to social institutions (patriarchal) and economic conditions that ultimately reduce all meaning to an abstraction of exchange and accumulation of possessions/power. According to Irigaray the domination of the philosophical logos

> stems from its power to reduce all others to the economy [capitalist] of the Same [patriarchal], the teleologically constructed project it takes on is always also a project of diversion, deflection, . . . creating the other of the Same—which could be interpreted as submitting the real to the imaginary of the speaking subject.[12]

The positing of the logos rests on an economy of binary oppositions (the sacred and the profane)—a process of othering already attributed to hegemonic power structures as an artifice that separates and legitimizes its own dominance. The identity of the Same/*isonomia,* as the Greek male, depends on a negation, the other—*barbaroi,* non-Greek, slaves, women, and animals. Therefore, the exotic foreign culture contributes to the socratic dictate, "know yourself." Language no longer corresponds to reality, since identity itself (as self-knowledge) is constructed on not only a negation (the not-self), but on the construction of the other as "an imagination of the (Greek) speaking subject"—a constructed identity in relation to the gaze of the speaking subject. Pasolini himself appears as a prisoner of a certain economy of the logos, defining difference (sexual and cultural) by giving an a priori value to sameness (precluding the domination of Western patriarchal capitalism). Even though he divests from the established power structure he reinvests in its binary opposite, creating an imaginary other—*"una forma del sentimento, fossile, immutabile che lascia in ogni altro sentimento diretta o indiretta, la sua orma"* (A form of feeling, immutable fossil which impresses on every other feeling direct or indirect traces of itself) (from "*La religione del mio tempo,*" Selected Poems, 90). As Herbert Marcuse explains, "Even where the critical abstraction arrives at the negation of the established universe of discourse, the basis [in this case binarism] survives in the negation and limits the possibilities of the new position."[13]

Pasolini's process of othering proves to be only a submission to a system against which he protests—a system that disenfranchises the other via a series of separations, differences, and divisions (prelinguistic, precapitalist, preoedipal, etc.). The very choice of myth already signifies an inevitable outcome that validates the emergence and domination of the Same. In addition, by placing the other into a mythic past, Pasolini not only presumes the disappearance of the other in the present but constructs the other in what Edward Said calls the "synchronic" panopticon, a vision of domination. This western-oriented gaze toward the periphery views the Orient (Colchis as the third world) as static or stable—projecting an image of the Orient as a fixed (mythic) identity. The other that emerges from such a gaze is an other not governed simply by empirical reality, but by an attempt at saming (assimulating) via a "battery of desires, repressions, investments and projections."[14] The act of othering manifests itself as a certain violence, not only in respect to the implicit control of the process of representation itself (as knowledge/power), but also as a confinement of the subject and object to the prison house of the binary ("territorialized knowledge").

Pasolini presents the cultural juxtaposition of the first world (Greece) and the third world (Colchis, the land across the sea) as a movement from one meta-narrative to another: one of homogenization (as archaic, purer, and more sacred), the other of emergence (the history of the culture of the invader, the colonist, the capitalist), one of loss, the other of invention (monumental history). This transition from the homogeneous world to the world of emergence is reflected in the historicity of the opposing centaurs: for the first centaur (who represents homogeneity), "tutto è santo," the world is an undifferentiated play of forces that cannot establish a hierarchy, and myth as history links Medea and Jason in a common history of mythic order and disorder. The logocentric centaur already perceives his predecessor as the *"uomo antico,"* thus establishing a difference (hierarchy of the progressive and the regressive) by the transcendence or the emergence of individual consciousness. He distances himself both historically (in relation to modernity) and geographically from Colchis (part of the mystical world of the *"uomo antico,"* as well as a land across the sea). Cultural otherness is defined both progressively, in relation to the modernity of the Western center, and geographically, in relation to that very site of Western historical emergence.

According to Adorno the emergence of the motif of adventure shows the hero "to be a prototype of the bourgeois individual, a notion originating in the consistent self-affirmation which has its ancient pattern in the figure of the protagonist compelled to wander" (*The Dialectic of Enlightenment,* 43). More importantly for Pasolini this model of adventure not only reveals the Western bourgeois hero as a wild nomad but as an invader (of other cultures) and a plunderer, robbing their symbolic and sacred wealth while seducing them with the (mythic) image of historical greatness (modernization). Pasolini demonstrates the Western response to the other through Jason and his Argonauts, a nomadic horde of men who encounter the geographic otherness as exotic or beautiful. Yet their reaction is only one of appropriation/self-gratification—Jason's first comment is, *"che bei cavalli, prendiamoli"* (What beautiful horses, let's take them). Their adventure is not only one of acquisition but also one of denial and erasure of all meaning (otherness) that is not related to the self or does not directly enrich the self. Jason displays a complete lack of recognition of the sacredness of the other by not only robbing it/them of its/their riches, but also by tossing back a single coin (as the capitalist might do to a colonized other) to a priest and commenting *"prega per noi"* (Pray for us). While the Greek world is ordered under the law of exchange—the fleece is established by Pelias as the object of exchange for Jason's acquiring status within the patriarchy—this order does not apply to the (inferior) prehistoric or non-Western world. Thus, Pasolini establishes the economy of the Western (Greek) world as an appropriation from the non-Western world. It legitimizes this appropriation by the fact that (as Jason legitimizes his treatment of Medea) it brings "civilization" and the process of modernization to what it considers socially and morally inferior. Although Pasolini engages in a certain violation of the other through a representation that homogenizes (as static and regressive) his construct of otherness, he purposefully delegitimizes the violent processes of modernization, revealing the West's tendency to erase the marks of otherness, and attributes interpretation of this other to the Western imaginary. Although to some degree mimicking the process of modernization or Westernization, Pasolini mimics (reveals) the process of othering and the dynamics of forced assimilation.

While Jason and his Argonauts represent "*i figli fascisti [che] veleggeranno verso i mondi della Nuova Preisotria*" (the fascist sons [who] will sail toward the world of a new prehistory) (from "*La Realtà,*" 174), both as the original and the allegorical repetition of the return to prehistory, Medea and Colchis "embody" the prehistoric: "[. . .]*la semplice sacralità di dueo tre sillabe, piene, appunto, del biancore del sole trionfante— diviano una realtá, maturata nel profondo e ora giá matura, come il sole, a essere goduta, o a fare paura*" (The simple sacredness of two or three syllables, as though full of the triumphant sun's whiteness—divining a reality, matured in unseen depths and now ripe, like the sun to be enjoyed or feared) (from "*le Belle Bandiere,*" 138). Instead of validating a teleological understanding of the Western Master Narrative (as progressive), Pasolini posits history as the unfolding of the death drive—a "fictive" continuity that inevitably consumes/appropriates its (m)others. In juxtaposition to the enculturation of Jason, the society of Colchis appears as a regression to a prelinguistic, pre-Western (cosmic) womb of otherness that is organized on a model of the sacred. Colchis appears as reduced to silence (other than pre-linguistic chanting, "*dueo tre sillabe*"), but also as a community headed by men (as the givers of the sperma/seed/ "sole trionfante") and managed by women (as workers of the fertile land). This juxtaposition of patriarchal and matriarchal societies not only reveals the "*mondo antico*" as inaccessible—it cannot be understood or represented via symbolic language—but also unrecognizable, since Pasolini sets *Medea* in a timeless (ideological) past void of any reference that would allow for a historical contextualization of the sacred.

Even though Pasolini locates Colchis in northern Africa, the iconography, dress, and ritual practice present an otherworldliness that distinguishes itself from the West through its inaccessibility rather than its incomprehensibility. He reverses the Hegelian dialectic: rather than "rationally" progressing toward a new synthesis (Fascist/conformity), he calls beyond to a reality that does not rely on a model of binary oppositions, a reality before masters and slaves, yet a reality that is already unreachable. Therefore, Medea (as a symbol of the sacred alogos) is located beyond the dialectic of polarization, beyond the logos where she is not an opposite of Jason but a force that does not need teleology in order to exist. However, the logos and the telos need her for their own, to determine their origin and separate themselves from that very site of (in)difference.

Pasolini's Colchis reflects a world (the womb) of ambiguity, a wholeness/holiness that has not been polarized, where violence and sensuality are inextricable, where birth (the fertility of the earth or harvest) is paid with death (the blood sacrifice of a young man), where a sacrificial victim celebrates his own death (the ritual itself mixes sensuality with *spargamos*) "*gli dei che amano nel tempo stesso odiano.*" His first introduction to Colchis is one of visceral religiosity (prior to the ordering of phallic language), the celebration of blood in a ritual that connects and orients the body (society) to the mother (earth), where the blood itself serves as the sperma/seed, a source of value and power. Here, as Irigaray explains, the body is not yet separated from the cosmic womb:

> They tear him apart, and he carries and receives life and death at the same time. And as he returns to the cycle of his nurses, his mother, his sister, in order to be reborn, [. . .] the blood and milk he drinks carry him into an otherworldly state of intoxication. (*Marine Lover of Friedrich Nietzsche*, 131)

The representation of the prehistorical other as an "intoxicating otherworldliness," a headless (voiceless) body that talks in (excessive) traces of its own return to the cosmos, presents Pasolini's notion of the real as fluid bodies and sensations that resist interpretation. This "intoxicating" ritual of obsessive dismemberment, inextricably linked to fertility, emphasizes the connection of body and blood to that of earth/rebirth. Yet it simultaneously represents a cleansing of social violence via a carnivalesque series of reversals. Even though Pasolini constructs Colchis as diametrically opposed to the cosmopolitan consumption (of Jason and his Argonauts), the mere introduction of the carnival draws attention to the already existing hierarchical structure, dividing women from men and rulers from subjects. The ritual not only displays women partaking in one of the most violent masculine activities (although they do not partake in the actual *spargamos*), but also the violation of order by the disempowered—where the subjects metaphorically decapitate the social structure, by spitting in the face of their king and queen and flogging the ruling family's children (a ritual that will be mimicked by Medea). While the event of the ritual symbolizes an in-seme-nation of the earth by the dis-member-ment of the male body, it also strives to eliminate violence as a form of resentment for those in power, and a violent return to order—an order where men protect women, the body or earth, while women work, cultivate the land in order to prepare the table where the men will be seated.

By foregrounding the ritualistic excessive dis-order, Pasolini makes an effort to disrupt any conveyance that could be interpreted as legitimizing a rigid social structure. He envisions the social structure of Colchis as a quasi-balanced distribution of power, divided between mothers, daughters (Medea), fathers (Aeetes), and sons (Apsytus). This society functions on the model of ritual reciprocity—that entails the fierce laceration of a birth paid by death and an order reestablished via disorder. In addition to the symbolic inversion of the power structure, the ritual foregrounds the interchangeability of gender roles not in relation to the division of labor, but in relation to the positions of power within the cosmos. According to Renè Girard, the Dionysian ritual involves "the feminization [victimization?] of men and the masculinization of women; [it reflects a] lost reciprocity."[15] More important, for Pasolini, than a simple reversal of gender roles is the creation of sexual/sensual otherness. He naturalizes the objectification (feminization?) of the male body (which is mirrored in Medea's assessment of Jason's body), destabilizing the Western gaze by decentralizing the masculine subject, but also creating a sense of sexual ambivalence (already tied to victimization) by centering the gaze (identification or feminization) of Apsytus and Aeetes on the chosen victim in a series of shot reverse shots, linking the three characters in a a circle of looks. Thus, Pasolini places man as the object of his own gaze—a disturbing reflection of self-victimization. As Pasolini constitutes the "gaze" as an excessive exploration of the senses (violence, sensuality, eroticism, etc.), he also reveals the inherent violence of the gaze that exposes the viscera of the other (turns the other inside out) to the interpretation of modern man/woman. And here we as spectators must identify with Jason in our attempts to interpret and translate the ritual into symbolic discourse.

Although the sensual immediacy and the sexual ambivalence created by the fertility ritual confuse the boundaries of the self, the combination of sexual attraction (albeit ambiguous) with identification implies a narcissistic sensuality (homosexual identification). Yet, Pasolini complicates (castrates) this process of identification or homoeroticism by (re)introducing the elements of violence and sacrifice. Both Apystus and Aeetes mirror the facial expressions of the victim in a series of full-faced reverse shots, identifying with their symbolic placement as the seed/sperma as well as with their placement (as the victim) within the process of the ritual. Their own gaze reveals themselves as the viscera exposed to the Western gaze. However, the expectation of, as well as the actual event of, *spargamos,* suggests an already existing sense of "absence within and between bodies" (a conscious distancing), the impossibility (if not threatening violence) of embracing that (homo)sexual desire. Although close, as Irigaray explains, "they no longer join up—the indefinite unfolding of their caresses has become an immensity of space that they cannot cross. Stock still, they look at each other, and no longer touch except with lightning" (*Marine Lover of Friedrich Nietzsche,* 134). As Irigaray suggests, the eroticism of the Dionysian ritual already reflects a lack, a nostalgia, where ritual contact can only come to fruition in its expressions of violence. The female counterparts, Medea and Aeetes' wife disrupt (pene-trate) the continuity of the gaze; their gaze reveals only half of their face—an intrusion in the process of identification. In this series of glances toward the victim, Medea as gaze replaces (cuts off) those of Apystus and Aeetes: while she remains the farthest from the victim (in the background or on the periphery), the camera pans across the blurred faces of the king and his son focusing only on Medea. She presents the other faces of the life force: "the shadow [that] imposes its lofty form outlines itself as a unit and cuts itself off from the harmony of the whole" (*Marine Lover of Friedrich Nietz-*

sche, 136). Not only does the emergence of Medea's desire manifest itself as a "cutting off from the harmony of the whole," but also, ironically, as the individuation of the self—a self-possession through a self-dispossession based on the desire to be possessed by Jason.

Pasolini does not represent the other (Medea as the symbol of the sacred, the non-Western, and woman) as a passive victim in this process of Westernization, but implicates the other in this process of Westernization. By ignoring the process of colonization, Pasolini reduces the movement of prehistory (the periphery) into the historical (the Western center) to the singularity of desire based on the eroticization of the Western male hero—a vision that leads to the annihilation of the sacred and ultimately, of the object of desire itself. Although Medea embodies all facets of Pasolini's sacred, it is the very force of her "natural" desire that causes her to nullify the regenerative powers of the sacred (excluding its destructive qualities, which Medea will utilize against Glauke and Kreon). By stealing the fleece, she defrauds her father of his symbolic source of power, but also that of his son—killing the seed (as she will kill her own children) she kills the potential perpetuation of the *"mondo antico."* As opposed to the sacrificial victim who *"rinasce con i semi"* (is reborn with the seeds), the dismembering of Aysptus symbolizes the severing of the umbilical cord of the cosmic family (father). This establishes Medea as an individual (a figure of rupture), not only of the prehistorical harmony, but also of the archaic or mythic order (procession) of kings. Ironically, this mutilation of the family and the effacement of order (of the pre-oedipal father) symbolizes the advent of the sexual economy of the couple, the binding of Jason ("la mia destra"/my right) to Medea—a marriage Pasolini condemns not only as the cause for the depravity of the sacred, but also as one of the expressions of consumerism under the guise of bourgeois moralism. Irigaray describes this "sterilizing" economy as "woman's maternal destiny banishing the autoerotic homosexual, or fetishistic character of the relationship of a man to a woman [and] emphasizes the production of a child" (*This Sex Which Is Not One,* 32). Medea also becomes engendered (as the other of the man) by her desire/seduction that leads her not to a return to nature (as the earth mother), but forever fixes (objectifies) her in the sexual economy (exchange of women) of the production of the patriarchy—the narrative of monumental or patriarchal history. Thus, the process of engenderment or the singularity of desire appears as not only a loss of wholeness, but a mutilation of the natural passions—a mutilation of the self and the reduction of that very self to the opposite of the desired object that has power over the self, since it possesses what the self lacks. In desiring what Irigaray calls the "Same or the One" (Man), the self identification that Medea has created is submitted to the position of a negation, the other of the Same.

Like Jason's, Medea's acts are motivated by self-interest or self-gratification. However, her acts of blood or cruelty, which are represented in detail, exhibit her constant attachment to more "primitive," "natural" expressions of desire. On the other hand Jason prefers muted, hidden violence, the violence of *"il mondo che ig-*

nora cioè che in lei è sempre creduto" (the world that ignores everything that she always believed in) (from *Medea,* 556). For Pasolini, the violence of modernization/capitalism masks itself with images of seduction (Jason blowing kisses to those women who have influential power over his destiny), which draws its other resources into its (concealed) mode of appropriation on account of its own brilliance. Within this economy the masculine subject (hers) enriches itself by raping/robbing the other. According to Irigaray the sacredness of the blood "becomes covered with other forms of wealth; gold [the system of exchange], the penis [the domination of power by the patriarchy], and the child [the infinite mimesis or reification of the system itself], blood rights are neglected [since] sperm has capitalized authority in the name of the father."[16] In fact, Jason announces that (Medealike) the *"pelle d'oro, non ha nessun significato fuori del suo posto,"* (the golden fleece no longer has any significance away from its place of origin), indicating the epistemological shift from a culture where blood is the measure of value to a culture based on exchange and use value. For Pasolini, it is the "cover-up" (the process of seducing the other) of these forms of wealth that violates the sacred: a masked violence that consumes for personal gain, that "domesticates" and uses its others, and requires the reform (repression) of the "primitive passions," concealing the rape/robbery of Medea as the sacred (both physically and metaphysically) under the guise of seduction (an embellished image) and the Law/Word (the embellished sign).

Jason's own destiny (like Apollo's) "isolates him from women—for them, there begins a period of abandon[ment], a period in which the god-man embraces himself indefinitely through them, by the mediation of their flesh which is transformed into airs and out of which he creates his dream or works of beauty" (*Marine Lover of Friedrich Nietzsche,* 155). Thus, by inscribing (desiring) herself in Jason's narrative of appropriation, Medea (unbeknownst to herself) marks the passage of the ecstasy of delirium or desire as an "exodus toward death," submitting herself to a radical reordering—this is an adhesion to a civilization of uniformity with a well-defined cultural model, a culture that Pasolini (as Euripides) depicts as a desperate wasteland of exclusion (of difference). Although this new order initially veils itself in the seductive charm of Jason, it becomes manifest when, returned to Greece, Jason and his Argonauts reposition themselves in relation to Medea and her culture, primarily by interpreting the language of the sacred as a discourse of hysteria. As a spokesperson for the sacred media, Medea is reduced to silence (a sign Freud considers the mark of hysteria), like all others who have no access to the Western Logos. She desperately searches for some type of grounding, a voice from the past or a return to (her own) nature on the dried-out, cracked earth of supposed Greece. Medea's (hysterical?) cries (*"parlami terra, parlami sole, tocca la terra con i miei piedi, ma non lo conosco, vedo il sole, ma non lo conosco,"*/speak to me earth, speak to me sun, I touch the earth with my feet, but I do not know it, I see the sun, but I do not know it) reflect the realization of her exile from the prehistorical sacred world (the death of her previous self as well as the negation of her cultural identity) and simultaneous exclusion (as a women and a foreigner) from the phallocentric (Apollonian) scene of the modern world. Although Medea awakens the desire to return to the cosmic order, she is like Pasolini himself: "*con il cuore cosciente di chi soltanto nella storia ha vita, potrò mai più con pura passione operare, se so che la nostra storia è finita*" (with the conscious heart of one who can live only in history, will I ever again be able to act with pure passion if I know that our history is over) ("*Le Cenere Di Gramsci,*" 22). Here, as in the case of Oedipus, knowledge itself becomes the knowledge of loss, the impossibility of return/regression and the guilt of separation. In order for Medea (the emblem of the periphery in its various facets) to gain access to the circle of men she must become a prostitute to the interests of the dominant ideology. Her only access to logocentric and phallocentric discourses is through mimicking already subordinate (reformed/conformed) positions, woman (sexual other), foreigner (cultural other), and sacreligious other. Therefore "the joy of departure fails in the pain [of loss]. [The sacred subject] arrives in port dead. The rebirth out of the great depths is frozen in the mask [the other of the Same]. In the still, spell-binding [Apollonian] beauty of an arrested movement. A suspended desire" (*Speculum of the Other Woman*, 125).

Although Pasolini laments the loss of the sacred, he emphasizes that the very construction of the profane (of the logos, the phallus, and telos) is created out of that very same sense of loss (a rape) of a center (the cosmic womb) and of meaning (the sacred process of becoming). The center, womb, or earth, which Pasolini locates as the cosmic place of birth and death, sinks into an unreachable prehistoric past, leaving the modern man/woman to wander in exile on a groundless social and economic order. This order of total exchangeability dissolves into absolute meaninglessness, except for the inexchangeable repressed violence that awaits appeasement. Medea draws attention to the meaninglessness of a sociopolitical order that "*non ha un centro*"/does not have a center (as she exposes the meaninglessness of the Word), but she also threatens as much as she prophesies that the "land will sink."

Although Medea exits "il mondo antico" in a violent manner, she enters the patriarchal world "surreptitiously": Medea becomes a Greek wife not only through her association to Jason, but also through a change of clothes (masks). It is Pelias's daughters who robe/disguise the sacred/otherness of Medea only to present her as the same (a simulacrum or semblance). They try to submit her to the "same" incestuous social ideology or at least to the patriarchal Father, while simultaneously stripping her of her "vecchio costume" (source of power). For Pasolini, Pelias and his (multi)phallic crown symbolize a specific stage in the historical movement from the prehistoric order of the sacred to the advent of the hierarchical/patriarchal order. Ironically, Pelias's exaggerated phallic symbolism is undermined by the fact that he has no male progeny. Pelias presents the predominance of the penis, establishing greed and appropriation as the driving forces of action—divesting meaning from the fleece as well as the oath (the Word) which leads to its historical end in Corinth. In addition, Pelias, who initially sent Jason out on a quest for the fleece promising that Jason would inherit all that he had, turns the Word into an act of deception. Pelias teaches Jason the lesson that *"il re non sempre mantiene le promese"*/the king does not always maintain his promises, a precedent which Jason follows in regard to the vows he makes with Medea.

With the movement into (Corinth) the prototypical world of bourgeois moralism and capitalism, Pasolini shifts his focus from the juxtaposition of two cultures to the juxtaposition of the outside (*extramuros*) to the inside (*intramuros*)— the juxtaposition of the powerless and the Law. Within the Greek city-state, Medea is not only viewed as the xenon/foreigner (outside), but also the other/woman. She is ghettoized as the non-Greek, living outside the walls of the city, and imprisoned as a woman, living inside the oikia/house. Not only is Medea's desire to leave the house met with resistance by her *"nutrice,"* but when Medea finally convinces the *nutrice* to accompany her, she must pass through a labyrinth of walls—a walling off of different symbolic domains that correspond to different political zones. As Medea moves from inside the walls of the house, she is met with the walls of the city that prohibit her entrance (as a cultural other and as a woman). Finally, as she steals into the city, she must walk along the inner walls (the very sign of exclusion) of the city, emphasizing both her confinement and transgression of these legal boundaries. Pasolini changes the film's location in accordance with the division of the extramuros from the intramuros. As a metaphor for her perspective, Medea's dwelling remains in the third world (extramuros), while the view of the city-state from the outside is actually located by Pasolini in Northern Africa. Instead the world of Jason (intramuros) is represented by the marble walls of Pisa, the domain of the polis, representing the perspective from inside the Western cultural center. Although Pasolini juxtaposes the natural realm (in which both Medea and Jason were initially framed) to the (confinement of the) modern city— the site where bourgeois moralism, capitalist economy, and the Western patriarchy converge—it is in the world of Corinth that Pasolini's conception of sociopolitical divisions along the hierarchical axis becomes definitive. Pasolini uses the city-state of Corinth as an allegorical model of the structure of the modern world, a world that distinguishes its different domains and their relations of power in terms of gender, race, and class. "Political life (*politikos*) stands in opposition to home life (*oikia*), [while the *polis* represents the realm of freedom] the house is ruled by despotic powers."[17] What follows is the legitimation for this division of gender-rule-and-class-related domains. Since the *oikia* functions in the realm of necessity (*ananke*, the remnants and reminiscent of the archaic powers), chaotic "nature pouring forth," and represents a regressive order in comparison to the polis, it must be governed accordingly (not as a rational equal, but a degenerate wilderness). All women (and here I include the feminized non-Western other) are exiled from the polis to the realm of nothingness—"Being [a waste product] as [they] are, [they] do not achieve the enunciatory process of the discourse of History, but remain its servants, deprived of self (as same), alienated in this system of discourse as in [their] master and finding some hint of [their] own self, . . . a You, or a He, who speaks" (*Marine Lover of Friedrich Nietzsche,* 139). The construction of the subject who is confined to language (or History) maintains the phallus as its symbolic reference (the location of power and meaning); therefore, the walls encircle Western culture and its patriarchal structure, preserve only the presence of the Western male, while His others are forced (economically, politically, and ideologically) into the position of the negative—becoming a pretense of a non-self.

The placement of women in the realm of *ananke* reveals the dual significance of woman within the patriarchal order: first women function as a means to patriarchal power (Glauke); and second they function as that which Irigaray calls "death's detour" (the mother/Medea). Woman's ability to reproduce affords her the status of "death's detour":

> The new detour along the road to death, through the construction of narcissistic monuments [children], involves pulling the libido back from the object onto the self and desexualizing it, so it can carry out more sublimate activities, woman [as a vessel of duplication] gives man back his image and repeats it as the same—she facilitates the same. (*Speculum of the Other Woman*, 54)

Although Medea provides Jason with two duplicates of himself (sons) assuring his own "detour of death"—at least ensuring mimetic linking of the chain of fathers and sons—Jason privileges his own monumental placement within the "regime of Fathers," as the direct heir to the throne over the love for his narcissistic reproductions. By abandoning Medea, Jason not only (metaphorically) kills or exiles his family, but he humiliates Medea by exiling her from his bed ("desexualizing her"), and by killing or ignoring the sacred passions within himself (the fact that "he indeed loves Medea"). Jason's replacement of Medea with Glauke does not reflect his lack of desire for her but reveals his stronger desire for power, even at the expense of his family's death. Jason's love lasts only as long as he can absorb Medea's manifest powers. Pasolini "illuminates" the tenacity of woman's position as the desired (love) object of man, a tenacity Irigaray describes as a series of riddles:

> Where has "I love" gone? What has become of me? "I love" lies in wait for the other. Has he swallowed me up? Spat me out? Taken me? Left me? Locked me up? Thrown me out? What is he like now? When you say I love you, . . . you're saying I love myself . . . You "give" me nothing when you touch yourself, touch me, you [only] touch yourself again through me. (*This Sex Which Is Not One*, 206)

Jason "gives Medea nothing" but a lie, an oath consisting of empty words, merely for the purposes of "touching himself." In addition Jason does not acknowledge Medea's role in his own material destiny—his profit from Medea's acts of violence—but he only recognizes Medea's ("illogical"/threatening) anger. Jason denies her "historical" significance (*"tutto quello che ho fatto, lo ho fatto io stesso"*/all that I have done, I have done it myself), and he reinterprets her acts of violence as savage (denying that he was the impetus or "reason" for such actions) and claims that he has done her a greater favor by "bringing" her to civilization. He adopts the justification of the colonist who "rapes/robs" the other, and erases the marks of (her)story. Her own history and origins are represented as a story, not a story of loss, but of lack—of Reason, culture, and civilization. Ironically, it is Jason who relies on acts of violence, but the violence of seduction, a language that he reinterprets at his own volition in order to gain what he lacks—property and, therefore, symbolic status.

Although the repudiation of a wife might have been common in ancient Greece—a process that involved sending the wife back with her dowry to her father or another male—Pasolini exaggerates the impossibility of a return to a previous order, by representing Medea as radically "cut off" from the past (geography, family, and religion), thus leaving her in complete exile (inside and outside of the modern world). Jason's abandonment of Medea causes her to not only identify with but also to symbolize the Other/woman, who like Glauke, is not only framed by the camera as a separate entity from (outside of) male society but imprisoned within the *oikia*—a realm of immobility, or stasis, reminiscent of the archaic orders of nature. Medea, like Glauke, has no choice (voice) in the selection of a husband (the One who will become her new master), she is subject to the needs and the will of the patriarchal system and its systematic exchange (consumption and disposal) of women. However, Medea's desire for vengeance does not simply stem from her passions (a regressive quality attributed to women), but from a conscious reaction to the failures of the patriarchal system. As Julia Kristeva explains: "The pitiful power of the femme [within the patriarchy], be it drive or murder, is in fact unleashed only with the help of masculine degradation or bankruptcy, the bankruptcy of the father, and [his] manly authority."[18] Medea uncovers the bankruptcy of the Word by bringing to the foreground the lies on which its formal reality rests. Jason becomes a counterfeit hero by having his own oath or Words exposed as lies (for personal gain) which reflects the system of the patriarchy and its Law as an apparatus of deceit. The patriarchal system, as Pasolini portrays it, is a system of seduction, physical and material appropriation of otherness, and ultimately of laws that only serve to exclude (the other from the Self and their own sacred otherness) or decree the exile of the now disempowered other. Just as Jason exiles Medea from the family and its symbolic order, Kreon exiles Medea from the city-state and its political order.

The juxtaposition of Medea the domesticated *"maga"* (witch) and Jason the breaker of oaths and teller of lies, (re)calls attention to the fact that *"questo posto [mondo] sprofonderà è infondato,"* also recalling the repressed passions that facilitate Medea's regression. According to Irigaray, the other (woman) must obediently form the periphery in order for the patriarchal center to constitute itself as central: "For if woman does not religiously blindly support the attributes of power of the king, judge, or warrior, the power may well decline or prove useless, since the real issue is always men's competition for power" (*This Sex Which Is Not One,* 117). Hence, Medea's evocation of a self-proclaimed power (albeit borrowed from her past) in an attempt to erase the totalizing boundaries of the hegemonic system constitutes her as an element of corrosion, as a counternarrative that deconstructs the foundations of the discursive (authority of the Word), philosophical (*logos*), political (patriarchy), and economic (capitalist) models from within their own boundaries, laws, or language games. By refusing to adhere to her assigned position within that hegemonic order, as the disempowered other, Medea causes a crisis of authority.

Although Medea directs her anger at the modern institutions of the family and the state, her will for revenge forces her to regress—a return to her sacred archetypes, to her forefathers and the womb of history—recalling another knowledge beyond the logos, an alien wisdom, a borrowed wisdom ("*un sapere non mio*") that she articulates with borrowed authority (*il giudizio di dio/*the justice of god). Medea not only signifies the spurned woman, but also the return of the oppressed, whose "permanent dream," according to Frantz Fanon, "is to become the persecutor" (*Wretched of the Earth,* 51). In this case revenge becomes polyvalent, directed on both the psychological and political level at the repressive Father (the symbolic Fathers) at his enforcing counterpart the patriarchal oppressor, and from multiple points on the margin (historical, cultural, economic, gender specific, political, etc.). By fooling Jason and Kreon with alien wisdom, using guile (playing the part they want her to play as a woman), Medea not only manipulates Kreon and Jason but also becomes an emblem of ambivalence, the pharmakon which deconstructs all *sophia.* Unlike her sophistic husband and king, Medea puts on different masks: the one of the "maga" who conjures up an alien logic (a mimicked discourse), the one of the rejected wife (a mask she presents to Jason), and finally that of the desperate mother—she coneals her ambitions and her private grief with a discourse of self-pity, a language of emotions that reveals the impotence of reason. It is through a dream or an hallucination that Medea regresses to her sacred past, recalling the power of the *pharmakon.* Medea's knowledge of the *pharmakon,* a remedy that is always at once a cure and a poison, transforms her into both the mediator of that ambivalent source of knowledge and a metaphor of the pharmakon itself. She is both the medicine and the poison, the cure and the destruction, the killer and the liberator, the murderer and the victim. This dream sequence, which appears as a repetition of events (the murder of Glauke and Kreon), actually ties Medea to Glauke through the play of mirrors (a series of reflections and identifications). Glauke not only receives the "gift" of Medea's "vecchio costume," which Medea enchants with the *pharmakon,* but when she puts on this costume she no longer sees herself as Glauke, but as the other, an outsider in her own house. Although Medea dreams of killing Glauke with the pharmakon (which may be read as an act of rivalry among women for the love of the Same), the actual death of Glauke is not induced by the *pharmakon* (or Medea's anger), but her own conscious suicidal jump into the abyss (following her own realization that "*si ama Medea, e é anche donna*" you love Medea, and she is also a woman). In addition the repetition of the dream reveals that Glauke escapes the house, not in flames but in fear of the image in the mirror (her own likeness to Medea) and her desire to escape from her father the king and his rule. Hence, while the first presentation of the death of Glauke reflects both Medea's desire for revenge against her husband for abandoning her and her regression into a "more primitive" order (the mimicry of the classical tragedy), the actual event of Glauke's death reveals Glauke as Medea's double whose only act of individuality within the modern world is suicide. Death becomes, metaphorically, the only means of individuality, but it also performs the rite of purification. It cleanses, first, rivalry as the subjection of women to competition for the Man/king (corresponding to a greater competition, the competition among men for power) that makes her only an appendage to that power structure; and, second, it signifies the cleansing of the "already dead or fixed" community (society) and the false laws that confine One and all to its own rigidity. Similar to the death of Glauke (the vessel of the future patriarchy), the death of Kreon (the patriarchal king) appears as a realization that the death of his daughter symbolizes his own castration, barring from the future. Thus when he commits suicide he is already dead (symbolically and historically impotent, with no products to exchange). For Pasolini, as for Medea, the pharmakon is no longer both a means to self-preservation and an act of self-destruction. Within the modern world the pharmakon can only perform as a negation.

Medea destroys all that binds her to the other (Jason), the state, its laws, her children, the future of her family (as well as the future propagation of the patriarchy), logocentric language (reason), and phallocentric narrative, providing only an apocalyptic ending. However, the most subversive breakdown of language and signs is the act of filicide, a death of the future, which Pasolini treats as an almost motherly act. This killing of the maternal instinct reflects the absolute emptiness of desire (passion/*thymos*), and the self-negation or self-mutilation necessary to return to a lost self. Yet that desired return is also impossible. Medea warns Jason he cannot cross the fire to appropriate his sons' bodies for burial. Nor can she cross into a past she has destroyed. The killing of her sons is conducted as a sacrifice, not a ritual of visceral religiosity (as the fertility sacrifice). It is, as Girard explains, a sacrifice of "violence seeking appeasement—the replacement of revenge with a victim because that victim is vulnerable and close at hand" (*Violence and the Sacred*, 2). Unlike Euripides' Medea, Pasolini's character does not simply choose "a victim close at hand" as a result of some violent frenzy. Pasolini portrays Medea's acts of violence as (although provocative) motherly—as a cradling and caressing of the children who are viewed as a part of the self. It is the ultimate possession, by Medea, of her sons who belong to Jason. At the same time, the filicide merely continues the cleansing process: ridding the world of the possible reification of not only the patriarchal or capitalist system but of the repetition and proliferation of the rule and lineage of Jason (the Same). Although Pasolini presents Medea's acts of "violence" as calculated, he confuses the reading of the filicide as a purely violent act, by combining murder with a bedtime lullaby. Julia Kristeva expresses this confusion of symbols (mother/murderer) as the most powerful subversive threat to symbolic power:

Any crime, because it draws attention to the fragility of the law, is abject, but premeditated crime, cunning murder, hypocritical revenge are even more so because they heighten the display of such fragility. He who denies morality is not abject; there can be grandeur in amorality and even in crime that flaunts its disrespect for the law, rebellious, liberating, and suicidal crime. Abjection is a terror that dissembles, a hatred that smiles, a passion that uses the body for barter instead of inflaming it, a debtor who sells you up, a friend who stabs you. (*The Powers of Horror,* 27)

For Kristeva, abjection is in fact the recognition of the very want which hinges any being or desire. Medea becomes abject only in relation to her position within the modern world; whereas her actions in the '*mondo antico*' are not presented as abject. It is her recalling of her former powers within the "*mondo moderno*" that reconstitutes her symbolic positioning within the realm of abjection. Pasolini confounds (if not reverses) the boundaries that classify Medea as the abject. Medea serves as an allegorical figure heralding a rupture with modern life (or rather death). Her resistance to the patriarchal system amounts to the sacrificial death of sacred Nature in exchange for the death of its binary opposite, profane logic, or Reason. For Pasolini such a person is the root of abjection. It follows that—in order to decapitate this "abject" power structure—the soul or the passions must consume themselves to eradicate the power of the profane mind that oppresses them. According to Pasolini, Medea's act of revenge is motivated by her own death (symbolic placement or fixture within the hierarchical structure that denies her access to her natural powers and passions) and by her exile from the bourgeois institutions of the family and state (to a nonexistent outside). This "bourgeois death" is repaid with death (a negation of the bourgeois "resemblance" of life). Pasolini leaves no room for a playful carnivalesque reversal (an ironic mimicry of the ideological apparatus). Such a laughter that would reverse or at least confuse hegemonic positions of power, and would also mock the "great many regimes that mold the body—the rhythms of work rest, and holidays, poisoning by food, values, eating habits, moral laws."[19] Instead, for Pasolini the only resistance is a severe rupture with all that is considered human: "*Non c'e piú niente oltre la natura—in cui del resto è effuso solo il fascino della morte*" ("mio tempo," 94). "There is no longer anything beyond nature, which in any case, is only permeated by the fascination of death."

Notes

1. Pier Paolo Pasolini, "Le Cenere di Gramsci," from *Operere di Pier Paolo Pasolini,* Garzanti, Milano, 1957, p. 71. Gramsci, who Pasolini posits is a "humble brother," not as a castrating, fascist father like his own bourgeois father, represents for Pasolini one side of a political enigma that Pasolini internalized: that of the

"enlightenment" of Gramsci's antifascist thought and his tragic death; however, Gramsci is also implicated in the oppressive moral agenda of the Communist Party. The poem constructed in the form of a eulogy, takes on other functions— that of a confession of Pasolini's attraction to the peasantry and, at the same time, his denunciation of the Communist Party's conservative moralism, yet a similar interest in the plight of the victims of capitalist exploitation, namely the subproletariat and the third world (Naomi Greene, *Pasolini: Cinema as Heresy,* Princeton: Princeton University Press, 1990). Greene points out that the consequences of the public denunciation of Pasolini in the Communist newspaper *L'Unità* describing him as a "decadent poet" along with Gide and Sartre, who "seem to be progressive, but in reality present the most harmful aspects of bourgeois degeneration," caused him to lose his livelihood as a teacher (p. 13). Hence this moral judgment on the part of the Communists not only forced him out of his native Friuli, but left him penniless. Although as Greene suggests, this caused Pasolini to rethink his relationship to Communism, I would like to stress that the "denunciation" of Pasolini on the grounds of his homosexuality does not amount to a simple reaction against Communist ideology on the part of Pasolini.

2. Oswald Stack, *Pier Paolo Pasolini,* ed. Paul Willemen, London: BFI, 1977, p. 2. Stack argues that by "increasing stress on the need to restore an epic and mythological dimension to life" Pasolini "emphasizes the spirituality of the peasantry, their semipagan consciousness of supernatural meanings and forces, which is hard to reconcile with Marxist political analysis, and in fact it is sex which Pasolini now seems to see as the main threat to the bourgeoisie." Although I agree that Pasolini unrealistically romanticizes both the mythic world and the subproletariant as its historical agent, I find the effect of such a search for a historical subject a crucial problem for not only Pasolini, but more importantly for Communist ideology in the postwar period.

3. Geoffrey Nowell-Smith defines the prehistoric of Pasolini as not "ancient times . . . but a world about which all we can say for sure is that it is not the world of our own world, by clearly preceding it." It is a world of primitive drives, primitive aggression, and primitive eroticism. "Pasolini's Originality," from *Pier Paolo Pasolini,* ed. Paul Willemen, London: BFI, 1977.

4. Pier Paolo Pasolini, "*Il pianto della scavatrice,*" from *Pasolini: Selected Poems,* ed. Norman Macafee and Luciano Martinengo, London: John Calder, 1984, p. 50. Here Pasolini presents the future as a hope that "*non cessa un solo instante di ferirci.*"

5. Pier Paolo Pasolini, "*Progetto di opere future*" (1963), from *Pasolini: Selected Poems,* pp. 200, 202. "*accerto un bisogno struggente di minoranze alleate. Tornate, Ebrei, agli albori di questa Preistoria*" because "*per chi é crocifisso alla sua razionalitá straziante, macerato dal puritanesimo, non ha piu senso che un'aristocratica, e ahi, impopolare opposizione.*"

6. Luce Irigaray, *Marine Lover of Friedrich Nietzsche,* trans. Gillian C. Gill, New York: Columbia University Press, 1991, pp. 55, 57.

7. Max Horkheimer and Theodor W. Adorno, *Dialectic of Enlightenment*, trans. John Cummings, New York: Continuum, 1989, p. 7.

8. Pier Paolo Pasolini, *Medea,* Rome: Garzanti, 1991, p. 552.

9. Euripides, *Medea,* trans. Robert W. Carrigan, New York: Dell, 1965, p. 41. Although Jason realizes that children are not the reason he leaves Medea, but the acquisition of higher status, he exclaims: "How good it would have been if mortal men begot their children in some other way; men would not be subject to this curse."

10. M. M. Bakhtin, *The Dialogic Imagination,* trans. Caryl Emerson and Michael Holquist, ed. Michael Holquist, Austin: University of Texas Press, 1981, p. 32.

11. Plato, *The Symposium and The Phaedo,* trans. Raymond Larson, Collegeville, Minn.: Saint John's University Press, 1980.

12. Luce Irigaray, *This Sex Which is Not One,* trans. Catherine Porter, Ithaca: Cornell University Press, 1985, pp. 79, 98.

13. Herbert Marcuse, *One-Dimensional Man,* Boston: Beacon, 1964, p. 134.

14. Edward W. Said, *Orientalism,* New York, Vintage, 1978, p. 252.

15. Rene Girard, *Violence and the Sacred,* trans. Patrick Gregory, Baltimore: Johns Hopkins University Press, 1979, p. 132.

16. Luce Irigaray, *Speculum of the Other Woman,* trans. Gillian C. Gill, Ithaca: Cornell University Press, 1985, p. 225.

17. Hannah Arendt, *The Human Condition,* Chicago: University of Chicago Press, 1958, p. 32.

18. Julia Kristeva, *The Powers of Horror,* trans. Leon S. Roudiez, New York: Columbia University Press, 1982, p. 169.

19. Michel Foucault, *Language, Counter-Memory, Practice,* trans. Donald F. Bouchard, Ithaca: Cornell University Press, 1977, p. 153.

14

Missing Marx
Or, How to Take Better Aim

Laurence A. Rickels

The MTA claims subway ridership is down because of the homeless sleeping all over the place—on benches, in cars—making the subway stations look like Calcutta. Panhandlers walk up and down the subway trains with cups in their hands or stand at the token booths, antagonizing riders, and people just don't want to ride, says the transit authority. So, the MTA has taken well-publicized steps to remove the homeless from its facilities, chasing them out of subway stations, off trains and out of terminals.

But the MTA may be going after the wrong guys. Actual ridership has not fallen off nearly as dramatically as MTA statistics indicate. Rather, the MTA is being robbed blind by subway "vampires"—people who make a living by stealing tokens. . . .

Police sources say that most of the subway token thieves and vampires are former chain and purse snatchers. This, they say, is because it is a lesser criminal charge to steal from a machine than from a person, regardless of the amount of the theft. "I used to do robberies in my old days," says Curtis, a subway vampire. "But it's easier to do tokens. Most of the people I know that do it just do it to get drug money." . . .

When the transit police arrive, the thieves are nowhere to be found. Instead, the transit police find homeless people sleeping on benches or sitting down with a cup or sign. The police chase the panhandlers and wake up those sleeping on benches, because they are visible.

—Joe Homeless and Eric Berman,
"Ripping Off the MTA: Subway Vampires
Bleed the Transit Authority Dry"

CC Writer

Down to their available component parts, the technical media were in the ready position for assembly centuries before their first emergence.[1] The delay built into their realization on the outside was synchronized, on the parallel internal fast lane, with their alternating or preceding analogical hookup with (and within) master discursivities. Hegel's embargo on noise, for example, delayed the invention of the gramophone, while Freud's discovery of transference pushed back the "live," non-transferential transmissions of TV or teen culture—all the way to the (psychotic) outside of the psychic apparatus (while nevertheless tuning in, in Freud's second system, as the tech-no-future of modern mass psychology). The Marxian challenge to stress placed on a discursive reception of this constitutive delay in the invention and broadcast of every technical medium would instead establish a timetable for the emergence of media via shifts of capital, modes of production, and social or class relations. Only certain socioeconomic conditions, which were available only at a certain time, could afford to capitalize on and produce media-technological invention (which, however, turns on, on its own, same time, same station). Owing to a presupposed lineup of effects, the Marxian argument and proof would remain endlessly in sync with a tautological outcome. But the analogical inside-out relations between (for example) psychic apparatus and mass-media culture are temporalized and delineated via their endless out-of-phasednesses. Was Freud right or has mass-media culture consumed Freudian theory? The Freudian corpus thus contains the ideology (the consumer protection and projection) of mass culture and, at the same time, consumerism's only internal critique. Thus Marxian insistence on a one-way dialectic of material relations and their socioeconomic effects amounts to a third instance of discursive postponement of invention and reception of our ongoing media technologization. The consumerist incorporation and acting out that receive and complete the TV picture remain tuned out.

Group psychology emerged within Freud's second system to contain and counter the *TV Guide* or Führer of perpetual adolescence, conversion, and the television set of responses (depersonalization and imposture) which teen self-esteem shares with borderline psychosis. Group psychology's reconstruction and excavation as (perpetual) adolescent psychology can be beamed back across certain marginal anticipations and connections already in place inside Freud's two systems. The emergence of group psychology (and thus of media technologization—and thus of the intersection between technology and the unconscious) can be followed inside the Marxian discursivity through the retreat it beats behind a series of exclusions, implications, and exceptions (in *The Holy Family* and *The Eighteenth Brumaire of Louis Bonaparte*).

The fun Marx and Engels make of Bruno Bauer and Co.'s Critical Critique has its blast via the endopsychic perceptions contained in the butt of the joke.[2] Can post-Freudians join in the laughter that the notion of the internality of all censorship is expected (by Marx and Engels) to provoke (87)? Is not censorship in fact a mass projection that alternates on the internal side with public opinion or "the phrase"? According to Critical Critique, philosophy has supported and supplied this side with simple concepts or "shibboleths" that get their meanings over with once and for all (97). But, Marx and Engels point out, Critical Critique (hereafter CC), which claims to reproduce its opponent, must also hold a share in phrase making (104). That's dialectics. But CC laid hold of opposition itself, which it called—resistance [*Widerstand*]: "The 'mass opposition' to it is therefore 'dangerous' only to 'the masses' themselves" (104). As "spirit," CC openly internalizes the masses, thereby creating a "critical mass." But CC thus also invites or prepares for its own contamination by the real masses (82, 153). The projective residue of this internalization or identification must be reclaimed and worked out through an exchange of letters, in which corresponding exponents of CC confess that they seek release from their ineluctable status as mass members.

CC becomes the masses in order to establish interrelations with the Christian mass (9, 105). The correspondence of confessions kicks in once CC replaces its absolute object and opposite—the masses—with itself. The attempted sublation/sublimation of CC's share in the masses (of that share or bond at the same time distributed via postal exchange) models itself after Christian askesis. The epistolary correspondence, as placeholder of media technologization, gets synchronized with the ongoing, remote-controlled release of (unconscious) Christianity.

Although Marx and Engels deride CC on account of its tendency to "sublimate" (150), the history of philosophical materialism, through which they at one point situate themselves and their target within the delegations of the Cartesian machine model, in turn sublimates (that is, casts the subliminal veil over) the technological cabling systems that got them to this juncture. Thus Marx and Engels disown as one-sided caricature the machine-model Descartes first established in the place of our pets (that is, totemically speaking, in the place of father) and its followup syndication by La Mettrie in which man's own body (in other words, the mother's body) gets mechanized (133, 137).

According to CC, systems conceived for the organization of the masses have been the result of fantasizing about the usability of the masses (142). Instead CC focuses on a rapport of telepathy or wish fulfillment between writing and history. Marx and Engels object that the "quill" (which in German [*Feder*] is a metonym not only of writing but also of technology) would thereby be placed ahead of the writing subject who thus gets divorced from the historical person who wrote (106). But via the telepathic cable it lays down, CC comes closer to anticipating group psychology than it does to challenging Marx's critique of capital. A near miss links Bruno Bauer's mass psychology to psychoanalytic rereading via a kind of reverse projection: Ida Bauer was Freud's Dora, the star of the psychoanalytic discovery (via another near miss) of transference: that is, nontransference. Dora was thus Freud's first encounter with adolescent psychology (which, in the second system, is conveyed via and recombined with the matricentricity of group psychology and female sexuality). But twenty years prior to the advent of group psychology's socialization and teenagerization of breakdowns of mourning and couplification around a bisexual constitution—which sponsors the release and retraction (within a sadomasochistic distribution of pleasure or couplification of drives) of the impulse that goes outside as happy face and inside as suicide—Freud was measuring the father function as it lit up the symptoms and orifices of regression on Dora's person and slid out of her adolescent cult of friendship (her bond with Frau K.). To this end, Freud recycles an analogue from *The Interpretation of Dreams* that remains his sole articulation of the unconscious with capitalism. This mark of exception comes full circuit within the Bauer legacy of teen psychology. (In *The Eighteenth Brumaire of Louis Bonaparte* Marx plugs into this discovery of remote control via the exception he uncovers within the history of class interest [as *the* interest that accrues to capital]. At this end Benjamin shows us the way—back to Freud.)

> The wish to replace Herr K. by her father provided the necessary motive power for the dream. Let me recall the interpretation I was led to adopt of Dora's intensified train of thought about her father's relations with Frau K. My interpretation was that she had at that point summoned up an infantile affection for her father so as to be able to keep her repressed love for Herr K. in its state of repression. . . . But the concern by itself would not have produced a dream; the *motive power* required for a dream had to be contributed by a wish; and it lay with the concern to provide itself with a wish which would act as the motive power for the dream. To use a simile: it is quite possible for a thought from waking life to play the part of an *entrepreneur* for a dream. But the *entrepreneur,* who, as they say, has an idea and thirsts to put it into effect, can nevertheless do nothing without capital. He needs a capitalist to meet the expenses; and this capitalist, who can supply the psychological outlay for the dream, is invariably and inevitably, whatever the thought from waking life may be, *a wish from the unconscious.*[3]

Parcel Post

Benjamin's group-psychological outlet (first mounted in "Über einige Motive bei Baudelaire") was recircuited through the *Passagenwerk* at the time of group psychology's greatest test drive: National Socialism's at once phantasmatic and practical realization of crowd theory's worst projections or ideologizations. Benjamin's original tribute to Freud (the Baudelaire essay), which cast the group bond as the residue of identificatory inoculations in the service of shock absorption or catastrophe preparedness, was superseded by focus on Marx's *The Eighteenth Brumaire of Louis Bonaparte* at the time total war or suicide entered the rapport of self to other, of the ego to its introjects. Benjamin's shift covers the conditions and coordinates of the experiment that has been on ever since the Frankfurt School first gave it a go: Freudian psychoanalysis and Marxism could be conceived as convertible or compatible only on the ground of group psychology—the ground that dropped out of the classes of Marxism's theorizing.

Freud's group psychology bills post-Marxian precursors who recast the crowd's occult rapport with delusions and superstitions (the underlying bond of crowd behavior according to studies current at the time Marx left implicit and excluded a psychology of the group) along hypnotic (and thus media-technologized) lines. Marxism emerges during a first funereal phase of technologization (or industrialization) that gives way, around 1870, to the illuminated, plugged-in, consumerist context—of group psychology. The crowd psyche, which Gustave Le Bon was the first to penetrate and plug into, at the same time grows (under the cover of secularization or journalism) increasingly (that is, unconsciously) Christian. The Christian mass and the modern masses form a direct hit via or as mass identification (or *mass*-ochism) which renders the "individual" a transistorized, hypnotized group of one, while blasting the couple (the only other of group formation). Le Bon's crowd psychology, which downs Christianity to come up with auto-hypno-technologization, receives its ultimate synchronization, syndication, or demonstration in Stoker's *Dracula:* the vampire hunters form a band of gadget lovers whose techno-group bond outblasts and outmodes Dracula's telepathic blood bonds—just as telegraphy, gramophone, and typewriter surpass the ancient postal order of life's journey into death (the uncanny trip on which Count Dracula was destined to continue booking passage). But in the course of busting the vampiric ghost, the group that grows out of the blood bath of vanquished vampirism (and out of the media devices it plugged and turned into in the course of the hunt) is, in fact, a new improved vampirism. One identifies (always) with that which you cannot (otherwise) lick. The autotechnologization of the vampire hunters represents that inoculative, identificatory exchange of catastrophe's direct hit for the group's state of preparedness and anticipation (some call this state California).

As Benjamin confirms: no group psychology without catastrophe preparedness. The first disasters to be contained by the group they at the same time built were techno-accidents and crashes that always recalled, all agreed, earthquakes. So-called natural disasters were thus simulcast (via antidotal group identification or shock absorption) alongside the accidents brought to us by technology. In other words: no group psychology without media technology (which transmits, on station identification, our participation in or anticipation of catastrophes preprogrammed to tune in, thus, as techno-accidents).

The inoculative logic Benjamin ascribed to group formation in the face of shock is set on Freud's group psychologization of Darwin's evolutionary take on change. Darwin's primal-horde model of human history, which tuned in same time, same station as Marx's model (in *The Eighteenth Brumaire*) of dictatorship without class representation or conflict, owed its admission into the Freudian system to the primal father who, in the second system, would be prime candidate for leadership of the group—if, however, the group did not in the meantime consist of mutual identifications that no longer follow the leader. In place of leadership there is a phantom that takes pleasure in the prospect of the group members or identificatory friends not getting no satisfaction. These egoic-atomic units of sadomasochistic release build the evolving technobody—of the group. The primal paternal apparatus, the superego, does not suit the egoic attention span, which is as short as it is internal, that is, eternal. The generational plan that promotes the continuation of larger units of "life" (the one the superego advertises) is not an egoic turn-on. Instead the ego turns on and turns into the "prosthesis god": the ego (or, same difference, its double) doesn't want to go. In 1870 (in Samuel Butler's *Erewhon*) Darwinian theory was rewired for machine development: mankind embodies the selective synchronic context for an evolutionary movement that aims over man to complete itself in machines (the members of the horde are at once the horde's genitals and the reproductive organs of machines). These machine-fed psychologies of change mark the withdrawal of the superego, which Marx registers on his side as a haunted state.

The *Eighteenth Brumaire* contains repeated mention of ghosts uncontained by the smaller number of references to burial.[4] At the center of the haunted group formation, which through repetition of repetition (i.e., identification) allows its classless, homeless members to be all they can be—namely, anything at all (namely zombies in uniform)—is the *Parzelle* ("small holding") peasant or unit. The *Parzelle* is an egoic-atomic unit of property, the proper, or, in other words, of the kind of narcissistic self-relation that does not admit having already admitted a dead other.

The *Parzelle* is the identificatory core—and half-life—of a wealth of sublimations which, first encoded in Napoleon's name, had, by 1852, reversed itself and turned around into simulation or repression. It was, as Adorno said of both the Californian Culture industry and National Socialism, "psychoanalysis in reverse." The state—which Napoleon peeled off society as the maxi-shield of protection or projection supplied at bottom by each *Parzelle*—has in the meantime turned into a "state machine" that runs on automatic (129). The Napoleonic surplus of armed forces originally grew out of the phantasmic need to protect the *Parzelle*. The fatherland was the fantastically "extended and rounded-off *Parzelle*" and "patriotism the ideal form of the sense of property" (136–37). The parceling out of property and identity also served as the foundation for an all-powerful and immense bureaucracy, which has (by 1852) turned into a "terrible parasitic body" (128). An *idée fixe* shared by the peasant class and its dictator (131) produces the second coming of Napolean; but by 1852 the *Parzelle* economy has turned the peasant farmers into "troglodytes" enslaved to capital. (Their cavelike dwellings bear windows the way a body leaves open its sense organs and orifices.)

Marx lists the ingredients of the *Parzelle* economy, which can be read off the back of Benjamin's brand of crowd theory:

> The *Parzelle,* the peasant farmer and the family; next to it another *Parzelle,* another peasant farmer and another family. A shock of these (*Ein Schock davon*) makes a village, and a shock of villages makes a department. In this way the masses of the French nation are formed through simple addition of units bearing the same name. (130)

The wealth of sublimations or *idées napoleoniennes* that emerged from the *Parzelle* can refer only to the "undeveloped, youthfully fresh *Parzelle.*" "They are a contradiction for the outlived *Parzelle.* They are but the hallucinations of its death struggle, words changed into phrases, spirits into ghosts" (135).

Shifting back and forth between the edge and the abyss, the *Parzelle* peasants thus end up supplying the mobile forces of uncanniness or homelessness (135). One of the distractions the second Napoleon must introduce to keep the *Parzelle* units feeling good about themselves—while alleviating the pressure of their uncanniness and homelessness—is a lottery that bestows on the winners (or losers) one-way trips to California (89–90, 138). The bourgeois order that provided the state as protection for the *Parzelle* had thus collapsed onto the identificatory core of the *Parzelle* economy (from which it then rebounded). "The bourgeois order . . . has become a vampire" (134). Whatever remains after vampirization is complete is cast into the "alchemist's kettle of capital" (134). The bourgeois order—the vampire—is mass culture and group or adolescent psychology. Every other so-called class also gets absorbed within the vampire's circulatory system, within a mass structure that, according to *The Eighteenth Brumaire,* is not grounded in social class. Even the psychotic or psychoticized uncanny or homeless form a peer group that, teenage at heart, aims to achieve self-esteem.

Quotation Marx of Vampirism

Money, according to Marx, compares neither to language nor to blood because the transformative circulation of and into a certain alien character [*Fremdheit*] which we find in currency exchange is not conveyed by the other two systems:

> Ideas do not exist separately from language. Ideas which have first to be translated out of their mother tongue into a foreign language in order to circulate, in order to become exchangeable, offer a somewhat better analogy; but the analogy then lies not in language, but in the foreign quality of language.[5]

But the transformation or translation brought to us by the vampiric blood bond dissolves the uniqueness of an individual life by releasing its social character or caricature, which runs alongside the transformed life, like price alongside the commodity. But that's the Christian mass—which is why Marx brings the transformation inherent in capital into focus as transubstantiation. Capital, which lies at the vampiric heart of the bourgeois order, is at the same time, via Marx's own analogy, the mass or communion in which father and son become one.[6] In vampirism (in the bourgeois order—in mass-media culture) the parallel tracks of price and commodity also release and keep separate Marxian and Freudian ideologies. At the heart of their common disconnection we find the massification of the father function. Thus the *Parzelle* economy or group-protection plan betrays a suicidal metabolism, which every form of bourgeois organization—of mass-media culture—symptomatically shares (112).

Just as identification at once organizes the group via projection and remains in some other place as nonintegrated and noncontextualized unit, so the *Parzelle* of vampirism releases "a serial mass of people almost wholly ignorant of their common social being."[7] This serial group bond nourishes *Varney, the Vampyre; or, The Feast of Blood,* which was first simulcast in 1847 with the detonation of events and then, in 1853, was granted another origin when it got controlled/released as "penny-dreadful" serial novel. The mass of readers invited to feast on the dreadful flow (of ink) encountered representations of the masses as inflammable or inflatable (through belief in and rumor of vampiric existence) into a body more destructive and autodestructive than any realization of the vampire's own threat and hunger.[8]

> "Fire—fire—fire the house! Burn down the house! Bum out the vampyre!"
> Amidst all this tumult there came a sudden blaze upon all around, for the
> pile had been fired. "Hurra!" shouted the mob—"hurra!" and they danced
> like maniacs round the fire; looking in fact, like . . . demons at an infernal
> feast. (230–31)

The infernal feast has already dropped and downed the internal funereal repast (or primal past). Consumer relations with a father's death otherwise parceled out as personalized works of mourning seek protection—projection—in masses that aggress, "go forward," or go for it. From Goethe's *Faust* to Jonestown: the internal—eternal—rapport with the imaginary father or big brother has grown at once immortal and suicidal, that is, perpetually adolescent, group bound, matricentric, and friendly.

According to Freud, mania and melancholia are the two extremes of out-of-control response (unchecked by the father's death) to a loved one's passing. Melancholia's loss retention is reflected back in group format as the mutual admiration society and its likeability principle: the group member likes to be different—like everyone he likes—to be like. On the manic side, group violence devours and expels the objects in its path; whatever is rapidly lost was also never in fact possessed. The metabolisms of retention and fast-food annihilation of objects prove and perform the malfunction of the paternal order. The body of the group keeps in projective disconnection from its founding relation; instead identification is spread around or shared among friends whose personal space remains interchangeable, uninvaded, untouchable.

The primal props and conditions that with each repetition of Varney's invasion of yet another household must be recycled and met fall into place (each time around) around the rescue of the vampire from one of his suicide attempts. In return for the family's rescue mission, which admits the vampire into the household, Varney vampirizes the young and beautiful daughter, whom he subsequently tries to marry. This, then, is Varney's scene: suicide attempt, rescue via the hotline of the family, vampirization of the daughter, marriage attempt (which almost succeeds on account of parental thirst for the vampire's capital). The series cannot, however, come full circle and complete itself but is always and again interrupted by a messenger from an earlier scene. The clownish (and phallic) Admiral Bell returns three times from the opening story to recognize and uncover the groom-to-be in the series finale as "Varney the Vampyre." The Bell name, which is made to ring and resound in its literalness, is handed down (together with the price or promise of the Admiral Bell inheritance) to the couple (to the future)—even though it is the groom's (the Admiral's nephew's) mother's name that runs alongside the price and must therefore first be made over as transmittable, in other words, transubstantial (father and son are one on the lap—Pieta style—of mother). The couple that thus rests on the assumption of the maternal Bell name has survived a paternal household that was shaped and shattered from all sides by suicide.

The opening shot of vampirization (the first release, in other words, of the suicidal impulse) does not belong to the series of the vampire's repetition compulsion. In fact what gets dropped down the opening takes effect or comes into focus (as already in place right from the start) only via controlled time-release action. The countdown begins with Varney's first forced entry locked onto the beam of his uncanny resemblance to the portrait of an ancestor he in fact shares with those he persecutes—"an ancestor of ours, who first, by his vices, gave the great blow to the family prosperity" (10). But the ancestor who comes back as his portrait, was buried as his portrait, namely, in his clothes: "this one of my ancestors . . . committed suicide, and was buried in his clothes" (21). The ancestral suicide, however, is the diachronically displaced double of the more immediate or synchronic axis of the family's dissolution, which first deserves mention as the recent calamity of the father's death: "He was found lying dead in the garden. . . . He had endeavoured to write something previous to his decease. . . . The probability was that he had felt himself getting ill" (26). Indeed, the tomb, which the band of sons and brothers must penetrate to check out the portrayed and doubled ancestor's remains, had not been opened, they are compelled to recall, since the father's death ten months ago (35). Over one hundred pages later the father's fatal illness is granted a more precise diagnosis. At first it is the vampire who makes reference, over the father's dead body, to "a crime only second to murder itself" (151). Only a heartbeat later the vampire draws out the father's daughter's confirmation of the family "catastrophe":

"You know that this spot has been the scene of a catastrophe fearful to look back upon, in the annals of your family."
"I know to what you allude; 'tis a matter of common knowledge to all."
"Your father, here, on this very spot, committed that desperate act which brought him uncalled for to the judgment seat of God." (158)

Another delay must be dropped before the catastrophe surrounding father can move out beyond his suicide to the external charge of murder (indeed, the father as murderer was all along in league with the vampire, a bond his suicide sealed). Before taking himself out (after taking in "spirits" that maddened him with remorse), the father concealed the murdered man's loot (including the vampire's share) in the ancestor's portrait (387).

Vampirism first penetrates the family plot under the theatrical (Oedipal) cover of a burial plot. The vampire puts on vampirism to conceal his designs on another system of circulation. A disorder at the level of capital (possession and dispossession of a secret) plugs into a Freudian, consumer projection—as though without symptomatic connection. But the capital (indeed, the secret) is supplied by the unconscious.

The origin of Varney's vampirism tunes in (Cromwell's time and place) in the era of regicide, that is, patricide. In his human phase, Varney was a revolution-opportunist who smuggled royalists to the continent. An audience with Cromwell later, Varney becomes a double agent who must henceforward turn the clients he agrees to take secretly out of danger in to the authorities. On his way back from the audience that puts him on two sides at once, he encounters his twelve-year-old son who already (or in flashback) shares with his father the one identity required to form their corporation of espionage. To constitute a(n) (in)corporation (only) one identity is required. But thus doubled via a patricide's dictation, the father already carries his son's corpse:

> "When we reached the doorway of my house, the first thing I saw was my son wiping his brow, as if he had undergone some fatigue; he ran up to me, and catching me by the arm, whispered to me. I was so angry at the moment, that heedless of what I did, and passion getting the mastery over me, I with my clenched fist struck him to the earth. His head fell upon one of the hard round stones with which the street was paved, and he never spoke again. I had murdered him." (856)

The murder of the son—the transubstantial murder of the internal father—sets off the vampire charge: Varney goes off in a techno-flash of transformation and remains down during a two-year trance. When he comes to (in the restoration period) he does not know that he is consumed with blood lust until he has exhumed in the ruins of his former home (at the murder site) the hidden remnants of his capital. The murder (or suicide) that doubled father onto son (and created the vampire) turned over in a household where mother could only be found—missing. Hence Varney discovers that he requires a certain blood type ("blood of the young and the beautiful" [861]), which he draws from the child's blood bond with mother. This typecasting of the victim saturates the repetition compulsion but not the primal condition or motive force that drives a split between desire for capital and blood lust, between Oedipalization and mass identification (or group psychology). And yet the missingness of mother, which comes prior to the murder and corporation of father and son, is covered by Varney's first confession of his primal origin. It was at the instant an original love object fell victim to his human murderousness that Varney got turned on by the serialization of his vampiric existence.

> "I it was who listened to the councils of a fiend, and destroyed her who had given up home, kindred, associations, all for me." (771)
> "Oh when will the crime of murder be cleansed from my soul. I killed her. Yes, I killed her who loved me." (771)
> "I killed her—I killed her, and she was innocent. Then I became what I am. There was a period of madness, I think, but I became a vampyre." (772)

> *"The blood seemed to curdle at his very heart—*
> *a film spread itself before his eyes." (781)*

The abusive father struck the masturbatory strokes of the child. Gambling—which Freud situates within the repression of infantile autoeroticism—guides the spirit-fueled degeneration of fathers who fall ("without any previous intention") not for the desire to win but for the "desire to retrieve . . . loss" (304). A case book of crowd delusions contemporary with *Varney the Vampyre* stakes its claims on the consequences of gambling: "Money, again, has often been a cause of the delusion of multitudes. Sober nations have all at once become desperate gamblers, and risked almost their existence upon the turn of a piece of paper. . . . Men, it has been well said, think in herds; it will be seen that they go mad in herds, while they only recover their senses slowly, and one by one."[9]

In *Varney the Vampyre* the alternation between live transmission of shock and recovery of one's senses isolates members from or within the group which emerges to take the charge.[10] The "dreadful and maddening fraternity" (199) of vampirism is therefore the projective aspect of a crowd parceled out internally section by section. Once the pack prepares to exhume a corpse suspected of vampiric comeback, we are confronted with a "melancholy fact":

> Those who have never seen a mob placed in such a situation as to have cast off all moral restraint whatever, at the same time that it feels there is no physical power to cope with it, can form no notion of the mass of terrible passions which lie slumbering under what, in ordinary cases, have appeared harmless bosoms, but which now run riot. (203–204)

The vampire, who "was there" when the mob (which belief in him created) turned violent, recalls his insider's response and inside view: "'I shall never forget the crowd of frightful sensations that came across my mind'" (389).

The crowd—of sensations—is distributed via shocks that electro-charge both the body of the group and the vampire's person. The exhumation efforts of the crowd of vampire hunters proceed "with a rapidity that seemed almost the quick result of the working of some machine" (206). At the other end: "The vampyre sprang to his feet, as he had been suddenly impelled up by some power-ful machinery" (348). The vampire's existence which fades in and out of super-natural reality whenever blood lust or identification alternates with desire for cap-ital in its motivation is given another double origin through the galvanic experiment performed postexecution on his corpse. The doctor in attendance as-cribes the vampire's continued existence to electroshock alone. While the vampire claims that "it was but accident which produced a similar effect upon the latent springs of my existence" (354), and that moonbeams alone did the trick, he at one point dates his own realization that his existence was vampiric in its duration or unbeatability to the first reanimation he underwent after the galvanically moti-vated return from death (391). As his corpse keeps on coming back to life (thus proving the supernatural schedule of his ghost appearances) the reanimated corpse each time looks "as if a galvanic battery had been applied to it" (536).

> *"A poor boy, a brother's only child, 'twas left an orphan.*
> *He slew the boy, and he is one of us." (753)*

The rumor or belief—that the vampire exists—builds the group via the openness of the secret, the *Parzelle*-like serialization of that which everyone comes into con-tact with without conscious connection: "tell everybody to keep it secret" (371)— each rumor spreader tells another. A rumor center must be established for the ab-sorption of the techno-crowd effect of belief in the vampire by the priest who becomes Varney's "best friend" in order to contain the vampiric phantasm. "He knew that nothing could be more dangerous than allowing any such story to pass current as a wonderful fact" (819). Indeed, the "wonderful" or "melancholy fact" (which releases a "mass of sensations") soon shoots up the crowd:

> The excitement too in the village was immense; for the story of the vampyre's attack upon the young girl was fresh in everybody's mouth, and it lost nothing of its real horrors by the frequency with which it was re-peated, and the terror-stricken manner in which it was dilated upon. (831)

The melancholic fact pits the vampire's ability to "die late" against the crowd's re-peated manner of die-lating upon it. The shock that thus hits hardest—right into the very foundation of the group's absorption capacity or attention span—is the "greatest evil of all—a false friend" (128):

> "This is the greatest shock I have yet received" (124).

Shock value begins in the one-on-one, which gets dissolved, in the after shocks, within the group (of friends):

The effect of my wife's death was a very great shock to me, and such a one I could not forget. (309)

The vampire's attack (which represents the group's invasion of the couple) administers doses of the shock that otherwise comes naturally. The attack victim has each time "received a severe shock":

Most important in the affair, is the impression it has produced upon her mind; that, you see, may last her all her life, and produce very unfortunate consequences. (638)

The shock, the mind and nervous system have sustained, will only be eradicated by time and change. (642)

When the "'shock to the nervous system'" (798) administered by the vampire is too great, the victim can nevertheless share the returns on vampirism's life-insurance investment with her own vampiric double. (When the father witnesses his dead daughter file her claim—with the vampire—he "started as if a shock of electricity had been applied to him" [802].)

The light show of mourning must simulate and push back via fond memories and images the return vampirism advertises. As the family of survivors or vampire hunters enters the crypt to confirm the rumor of little sister's vampiric lifestyle, they first touch base with the protective image of and idealized identification with the mourned dead, the antibody, and the absorbed shock:

The sons having by accident cast their eyes upon the coffin that contained the remains of their mother, regarded it in silence, while memory was busy, too, within them in conjuring up her image. (837)

But the daughter's return is thus sprung from a crypt in which the mother's image is on the rise.

The work of mourning that does not kick in is described by the fraternal band (prior to the return to the mother's crypt) in the negotiable terms or bonds of ambivalence:

They had hopes that time would soon produce its usual effects upon that feeling which of all others is, while it lasts, the most poignant, at the same time that it is the most evanescent—grief for the dead. And well it is that it should be so, otherwise we should be a world of weepers and mourners.

But the image still summons the corpse from the crypt and the "desire to retrieve loss" (as in gambling) is not "at the same time . . . evanescent" because the *Parzelle* economy of the vampire-hunting and vampire fraternities alike remains based on a double denial—that of "the poor privilege of all." Sympathy with the vampire's condition produces a reflection—and then shortcircuits:

> It was sad—very sad, indeed, that such a being could not die when he chose, the poor privilege of all. (806)

Suicide would appear to be, then, the most basic privilege of human existence. As the vampire "'beset by a parcel of people who do not mind cutting a throat if they can get an opportunity of doing so'" knows best, the act that conjures and grounds the mob is self-destructive:

> When there is a popular excitement against any man, he had better leave this part at once and altogether. It is dangerous to tamper with popular prejudices. . . . It is a sheer act of suicide. (232)

The vampire's return to his continued existence models itself after the survival of catastrophe, an experience of rescue that safeguards the suicidal impulse. The survivor of disaster knows, like the vampire, that there are far worse states to be in than death's dominion:

> To have passed the barrier of life, and to become insensible to all, and then to be recalled to life, is an agony not to be described. I have seen men who have been restored to life, and who have solemnly declared that the pangs of death they could encounter, and not those of a return to life. (703)

The catastrophe of shipwreck, which has prompted this innocent bystander to share the fantasy of undeath, counted among its casualties the vampire—who was then moon-beamed back. Upon his return Varney shares the fantasy with his "rescuers":

> Yet I feel as if the whole mass of my blood was changed, and that I should never again be what I was; that, in fact, I shall always carry about me the appearance, and certainly the feeling, of a man torn from the arms of death, and made to live. (707)

The mass death Varney alone survives (by once again surviving himself) rides the surf of the *Parzelle* economy:

> The vessel was no more; a mere mass of boards; . . . nothing but a confused mass of planks was to be seen, with here and there a human being clinging to them for life; . . . they were dashed to mummies. (700)

Varney is the immortalization of the untenable—"dashed"—mummy-bond that each egoic-atomic unit shares in group-formational phantasm. To be released (if

only for a season) from the series in which he must obtain a victim and (thus) renewal always with "'the pangs of death,'" Varney seeks "'the voluntary consent of
one that is young, beautiful, and a virgin'" (686). The vampiric projections and
group formations of the *Parzelle* economy observe, then, an alternation and serialization of origins (of, that is, identifications):

> "Those who know about vampires say that there are two sorts, one sort al-
> ways attacks its own relations as was, and nobody else, and the other always
> selects the most charming young girls, and nobody else, and if they can't get
> either, they starve to death." (745)

The two sets of vampiric existence or identification are interchangeable yet
nonsuperimposable. The attack upon family relations is paternal in scope (it recycles death wishes that originally targeted father); the thirst for virgin blood draws
from the mother's blood. But although the voluntary gift of virgin blood would
fulfill the vampire's ultimate desire, it is offered only in the series of its withdrawal.
At the close of the series (at which point the opening secret is released), Varney
kills himself without remainder but with a witness (a third party or pater) in attendance. The one identification has always contained the other in the mode of
shock absorption: The one-on-one (of the maternal relation), which shares its un-
witnessed immediacy with mass murder, is contained via the shock administration of vampiric attack as the kind of catastrophe or techno-accident which, unlike the selective randomness of mass murder, contains itself. At one point—of
injection—Varney experiences in a dream an inside or endopsychic view of the
dose of group formation or preparedness he shoots up into technologizing (and
maternalizing) accident identification:

> "But it was a dream of such absolute horror, that I shall dread to close my
> eyes in rest again, lest once more so fearful a vision should greet me. It was
> a dream of such frightful significance, that it will live in my remembrance
> like a reality, and be dreamed of again as such." (453)

> "A proposition yelled out . . . to place me in the tomb even as I was, a living
> man. . . . Endow him with the rare gift of immortality, and then let him lie
> buried for thousands of years yet to come." (454)

The tension between immortality and the suicidal impulse is the vampire's own
legacy, which gets control-released, in the face of shock, within the group the vampire forms with his victim.

The consumerist hunger that craves mother while sinking teeth always only
into the paternal antibody (which thus, in the intake of identification, is rendered
"maternal," that is, friendly) alternates with a paternal, that is, patricidal impulse.
On this side the vampire seeks possession of capital only always to fall for (or into)

the encrypted secret dimension the vampire himself put on to cover up designs on the secret of another circulation and disposal system.

Within the *Parzelle* economy, then, Freudian and Marxian takes alternate as each of the other's concealment (of their common but double origin or identification). In the adolescent psychology body built out of egoic-atomic units, the underlying (maternal) mutual identification at the same time remains border-line or interchangeably disconnected (in accordance with the paternal order). The organizing interchange—between immortality and suicidal impulse—is shared with the vampire. Because the other is always the first to go: we are immortal. But because the other is always the first to go—we are suicidal. The vampire (who is us) has not learned to survive immortality.

"I am some nameless, homeless thing." (770)

That's why television was not the "liberator" of the Eastern European countries (which we last visited, while they were still veiled by the iron curtain, in *Shoah*). TV comes full circuit in 1991 in the mideast media war, which pits allies and en-emies who are fighting World War II against antiwar activists who are resisting the Vietnam war. In the meantime the war's TV coverage is more real (if only be-cause friend and foe alike are tied, gadget-lover style, to the same "live" broadcast) than the war itself. TV was first conceived as a surveillance device not only for use in espionage and thought control but also (and more fundamentally) to monitor weapons experiments and, by extension, to exercise remote control over the bombs themselves. The war's live transmission is coextensive with the video control that (right down to detonation) gives us the inside view, second by second, from the point of view at the end of the missiles. A media war features, unlike wars said to be in history, the eternal return of the same phantasms. The phantasm of portable gas chambers (made in Germany) conveyed by the buzz bombs of the Battle of Britain is one of the secret (that is, openly admitted) weapons. In the midst of this eternal return of phantasms, the patriot system gets repress-released to challenge, ultimately, Nazi control of the airwaves. (The German response to the opening shot of the war followed the leader: World War II was back online.) In a battle zone of repetition (of repetition) class representation withdraws into both wings of the inner/outer arena of dictation. In other words, the left wing is the right wing.

This war appears to be the projective release from (that is, of) a dead end of internalization (of the loss of the Vietnam War). But when it comes to live trans-mission (as opposed to the psychic mechanisms of pre-TV technology) the alter-nation of origins (that is, of identifications and projections) no longer takes on (or in) the full-scale format of the superego (the agency that safeguards sexual love and the couple). Instead, the machine-fed body-ego alternates its absorption in mass murder (which is the p-unitive realization of its most fervent wish) with its own absorption within the fraternal group bond of catastrophe preparedness.

What gets synchronized is death, in other words, suicide: the death of all at the same time.

As the first twelve American casualties threatened to preempt U.S. war readiness by switching on the pre-TV newsreel technology of Vietnam's funereal commemoration, the media war flipped to the sitcom: Most of the war dead had been shot by their own side. The Californian concept of "friendly fire" instantly unblocked the metabolism that threatened to shut down (already and again) as grief-stuck. The war effort was so efficient (that is, friendly) that not only were enemies killed, but even some of one's own had to go. It's a different way (it works!) to plug into the "live" transmissions of total war.

In Jeffrey Mehlman's Freudian words, which alternate with Marx's words (cited from *The Eighteenth Brumaire*):

> Emptied of its dialectical content, history seems "without events," that is, barely history, "wearying with constant repetition of the same tensions, the same relaxations." For it is as though the movement of dialectic had been frozen. Whereas the *higher* was inevitably to be overthrown by the *lower*— the *bourgeoisie* by the proletariat—those two poles remain constant and are mutually impoverished by a strange irruption of something lower than the low . . . at the top.[11]

The leftovers or over-men who take over mass culture follow out (leader-and-the-pack style) the beam of a dictation that the dictator takes down. The homeless generation of *Parzelle*-units puts on uniforms to be all it can be. To be anything you can be, namely, all that's left, is to serve as dispossessed or uniformed medium of the dictation that withdraws within a sensurround of repetition of repetition (in other words, of mutual identification).

But the classless, homeless "troglodytes" of the bourgeois or mass society that has turned vampiric have already been body counted along the fronts of another media war expanding and disbanding within the "live" transmissions of AIDS.[12] With AIDS everything is the same difference. The disease spreads neither according to recognizable spatial coordinates nor in accord with temporal laws: it's ubiquitous and omnipresent and yet at the same time seems to delimit and target certain groups on the margin they share with vampirism. AIDS (comes and) goes with the flow: it's the maternal blood bond and Christian mass all over (and out) again. The melancholic fact alone that even and especially the recipients of blood transfusions have counted among the casualties of AIDS shows us the way the disease transgresses all margins and boundaries. AIDS is the ultimate guarantor, sign, and symptom of global transmissions. The myths of its origin advertise the most fantastic connections. Its first diseased transmitter was a Canadian airplane steward; its first "case" was that of a Norwegian sailor and his family. Transmission in every sense. Steamship travel belongs to the first significant applications of classical mechanics: transmission of energy. Following the 1912 Titanic conference, transmission, in the sense of "wireless" broadcasting of information or the news, became the pioneer undertaking of radio technology; in mechanical flight these techniques of transmission reached a highpoint. Transmission of power or energy and transmission of information have come to occupy the interchangeable places from which diseases (and drugs) can also be transmitted.

AIDS, drugs, homelessness, and TV confront us with an uncanny truth; namely, that in an era of universal and global transmissions all of us (humans and machines alike) form one body—the tech-no-body of the group. Tuned in within an at once short and uninterruptible, untreatable attention span, we, together with our machines or gadgets, belong to one body which can thus be afflicted by one disease, the disease of the One (in other words, the narcissistic object). This is the other (or under) side of the group formation that is under way (if it hasn't already come and gone): we will have aspired to be, that is, to pretend to be (rather than become) the One—one nation, one god, and (Michael Jackson style) one race and one gender—in other words, the exquisite corpse that comes in the one size that fits all.

Notes

Epigraph: *Crossroads Magazine* vol. 1, no. 2 (September 1990): 8–9.

1. See Rickels, "Psychoanalysis on TV," *SubStance* 61 (1990): 39–52, The problems of this vampirological reading of the two ideologies or identifications that go (without saying) with the names Freud and Marx are given rigorous explication by Samuel Weber in "Capitalizing History: *The Political Unconscious,*" in *Institution and Interpretation* (Minneapolis: University of Minnesota Press, 1987), 40–58.

2. *Die heilige Familie oder Kritik der Kritischen Kritik. Gegen Bruno Bauer und Konsorten* in Karl Marx and Friedrich Engels, *Werke,* ed. Institut für Marxismus-Leninismus beim ZK der SED (Berlin: Dietz Verlag, 1957), 2: 7–223. Page references are given in the text.

3. *Fragment of an Analysis of a Case of Hysteria* in Sigmund Freud, *Collected Papers,* ed. Ernest Jones, trans. Alix and James Strachey (New York: Basic, 1959), 3: 104–105.

4. Karl Marx, *Der achtzehnte Brumaire des Louis Bonaparte* (Berlin: Dietz Verlag, 1988). Page references are given in the text.

5. Cited in Marc Shell, *Money, Language, and Thought* (Berkeley: University of California Press, 1982), 106.

6. Karl Marx, *Das Kapital,* ed. Institut für Marxismus-Leninismus beim ZK der SED (Berlin: Dietz Verlag, 1969), 1: 169–70.

7. *Varney, the Vampyre; or, The Feast of Blood* (New York: Arno, 1971), 459. This edition gives Thomas Preskett Prest as author. It is now believed that James Malcolm Rymer was the serial novel's author. Further page references are given in the text.

8. In *The Living and the Undead: From Stoker's "Dracula" to Romero's "Dawn of the Dead"* (Urbana and Chicago: University of Illinois Press, 1986), 278–80, Gregory A. Waller reads the mob in *Varney the Vampyre* as the side-effect of violence control that has gone out of control.

9. Charles Mackay, *Memoirs of Extraordinary Popular Delusions and the Madness of Crowds* (New York: L. C. Page, 1932), xx. The cited passage is from the preface to the 1852 edition (the book was first published in 1841).

10. "It is astonishing, as well as amusing, to find how the mind assimilates itself to the circumstances in which it is placed, and how society, being cut up into small sections, imagines different things merely as a consequence of their peculiar application. We shall find that even people living at different ends of a city will look with a sort of pity and contempt upon each other" (433).

11. Jeffrey Mehlman, *Revolution and Repetition: Marx/Hugo/Balzac* (Berkeley: University of California Press, 1977), 12–13.

12. In the following rundown of the AIDS phantasm I am indebted to a joint proposal I worked on with my colleague, Wolf Kittler. My choice of title for the project and proposal, "'Live' Transmissions: Media Technology, Drugs, AIDS," was inspired by the interview with Derrida on drugs, "Rhetorique de la drogue," published in *autrement* 106 (April 1989): 197–214.

CONTRIBUTORS

TERESA BRENNAN is Schmidt Distinguished Professor of Humanities at Florida Atlantic University and is the author of *The Interpretation of the Flesh: Freud and Femininity* (1992), *History after Lacan* (1993), *Exhausting Modernity: Grounds for a New Economy* (2000).

WILLIAM CHALOUPKA is Professor of Political Science at the Colorado State University. His books include *In the Nature of Things: Nature, Language, and Politics* (co-edited with Jane Bennett) and, most recently, *Everybody Knows: Cynicism in America*. Both volumes were published by the University of Minnesota Press. Chaloupka currently serves as co-editor of *Theory and Event,* a journal of politics and culture.

IAIN CHAMBERS is Professor of Cultural and Postcolonial Studies at the Istituto Universitario Orientale, Naples, Italy. He is author of *Culture after Humanism* (2001), *Migrancy, Culture, Identity* (1993), *Popular Culture: The Metropolitan Experience* (1996), and co-editor of *The Postcolonial Question: Common Skies, Divided Horizons* (1996).

KELLY DENNIS teaches art history at the University of Connecticut and is currently completing a book on the art historical conditions of pornography.

ERNESTO LACLAU teaches in the Centre for Theoretical Studies in Humanities and Social Sciences at the University of Essex and is the author of *Politics and Ideology in Marxist Theory* and *New Reflections on the Revolution of Our Time,* and co-author of *Hegemony and Socialist Strategy* (with Chantal Mouffe) and *Contingency, Hegemony, Universality* (with Judith Butler and Slavoj Zizek).

JOHN P. LEAVEY JR. is Professor of English at the University of Florida. He is a noted translator of Jacques Derrida's work, including *The Archeology of the Frivolous: Reading Condillac* (1980), *Edmund Husserl's Origin of Geometry* (1989), and *Glas* (with Richard Rand) (1986), and is the author of *Glassary* (1986).

BRADLEY J. MACDONALD teaches political theory at Colorado State University and is author of *William Morris and the Aesthetic Constitution of Politics* (Lexington Books, 1999).

MARILYN MANNERS teaches Comparative Literature at UCLA and is the author of numerous articles on literary theory, popular culture, and popular music.

DONALD PREZIOSI is Professor of Art History at UCLA and author of *Rethinking Art History: Meditations on a Coy Science* (1991), editor of *The Art of Art History : A Critical Anthology* (1998), and co-author of *Aegean Art and Architecture* (2000).

269

KRISS RAVETTO is currently a visiting scholar at Emerson College and is the author of *The Unmaking of Fascist Aesthetics* (University of Minnesota Press, 2001) and of numerous articles on film and cultural theory.

LAURENCE A. RICKELS is Professor of Germanic, Slavic, and Semitic Studies at the University of California, Santa Barbara. He is a regular contributor to *Artforum, Art + Text,* and *Flash Art,* as well as the author of *Aberrations of Mourning* (1988), *The Case of California* (1991), and *The Vampire Lectures* (1999). In Spring 2002, his three-volume study *Nazi Psychoanalysis* was published.

R. L. RUTSKY is the author of *High Techne: Art and Technology from the Machine Aesthetic to the Posthuman* (University of Minnesota Press, 1999), as well as numerous articles on film, media, and cultural studies.

MICHAEL RYAN teaches English at Northeastern University. His books include *Marxism and Deconstruction, Politics and Culture, Camera Politica,* and *Literary Theory: An Anthology.*

KEITH TOPPER teaches political theory in the Department of Political Science at Northwestern University. He is the author of *Sciences of Uncertainty: Perspectives on Naturalism, Politics and Power* (Harvard University Press, forthcoming 2003), as well as articles on American pragmatism, democratic theory, contemporary social and political theory, continental philosophy and political thought, theories of international politics, and the philosophy of the social sciences.

GREGORY L. ULMER, Professor of English and Media Studies at the University of Florida, is the author of *Applied Grammatology* (Johns Hopkins, 1985), *Teletheory* (Routledge, 1989), and *Heuretics: The Logic of Invention* (Johns Hopkins, 1994). His current projects include *Miami Miautre; Mapping the Virtual City* (with the Florida Research Ensemble), and *Internet Invention: From Literacy to Electracy.*

SAMUEL WEBER, Avalon Professor of Humanities at Northwestern University, was a founding editor of *Glyph: A Journal of Textual Studies* and is the author of such books as *The Legend of Freud* (1982), *Institution and Interpretation* (1987), *Return to Freud: Jacques Lacan's Dislocation of Psychoanalysis* (1991), and *Mass Mediauras: Form, Technics, Media* (1996).

INDEX

174; industry, ix; mass, ix, viii, 67, 250; metropolitan, xiv, 169–183; overintegrated conceptions of, 136; political, 83; polyphonic, 142; postmetaphysical, xiii, 115–116; postmodern, ix, xiii, 68; taking for granted, x; teen, 250

Culture, popular, ix, viii, 169; as form of capitalist contagion, ix; in opposition to leftist political theory, ix; women's sexuality in, xiii

Custer, George Armstrong, 147–155

D

Dafoe, Willem, 161

D'Amico, Robert, 51

Damisch, Hubert, 220*n65*

Darwin, Charles, 253, 254

Davis, Mike, 143

Debord, Guy, ix

de Certeau, Michel, 169, 173, 175, 180

Deconstruction, xiii, 4–5; critics of, xii; demonstration of present and, 14–15; Derrida and, 3; discursive machinery of, 52; elements of, 5; of Eurocentric voice, 174; as extension of spirit of Marx, 23; familiarity with, 3; language of, 179; of Marxism, 58; new historicism and, 183*n7;* political usefulness for, 52; politics and, xi, 8–9, 12, 41; post-Marxism and, xii; reinterpretation of identity and, 4–5; relation to person, 55; representation in popular press, 146; staging in, 11; tactics of, 52

Deep Throat, 214

Deleuze, Gilles, 25, 152

De Man, Paul, xii, 39, 52

Della Volpe, Galvano, 57

Democracy, 127; indeterminate character of, 69; liberal, 127, 128; North American, 130*n13;* participatory, 126; radical, xii, 65, 69, 72; role of intellectual in, 72; struggles for, 65; "superhard" and, 71

Dennis, Kelly, xiii, xv, 187–215

Derrida, Jacques, vii, xii, xii, 8, 42; on apartheid, 54; on aphorism, 43; on dancing table, 12; deconstruction and, 3, 146, 179; deconstruction of identity and, 4; feminism and, 52; focus on ghost in *Hamlet,* 15–21; on Husserl, 4; ideality and, 4; iterability and, xi, 11; notion of the subject, 53–54; on philosopher's signature, 46; redescription of instrumentalization, 151; rereading of Marx, 6–21, 9, 23; signature and, 46; *Specters of*

Marx, 4–21, 23; on tempo, 44; time out of joint and, xii; *Truth in Painting,* 90*n20;* use of "invaginated text," 52; validity of linguistics of, 154; writing theory, 147

Description, thick, 121

Desperately Seeking Susan, 161

Determinism: voluntarism and, 120

Dickless, 159

Difference: allowable, 191; anatomical, 191; discourse as, 58; images of, 173; incorporation of, 7; nostalgia of, 171; racial, 136; sexual, 191; visible perception and, 191

DiLauro, Al, 216*n4*

Direction: political, xii; temporal, xii

Discourse: academic, 145, 146; characteristics of, 63; classical, 103; commonality and, 128; constructing one's as difference, 58; contact across, 153; of daily life, 146; eliciting, 101; of entertainment, 154, 155; epistemological, 93*n50;* of equality, 65; ethical, 93*n50;* evidentiary value of, 100; exchange across, 147; of family, 146; of female sexualities, 163; feminist, 162; as horizon of constitution of objects, 63; of hysteria, 239; ideological, 104; of imperialism, 95; of knowledge, xiii, 96, 152; legitimate, 65; of liberalism, 125; male literary, 100; Marxist, 59; materialistic, 232; metaphysical, 93*n50;* of moderation, 110; phallocentric, 240; political, 226, 227; of power, xiii, 95, 96, 98, 101; propositional, 12; public, 125, 126, 127; racial, 136; of racial difference, 136; revolutionary, 227; scientific, 96–112; social, 120; symbolic, 65; of television, 155; theory of, 100; unconscious in, 151

Doane, Mary Ann, 196, 211, 218*n30*

Dominance: phallic, 191; scientific, 96–112

Domination: conditions of, 232; of others, 104; ritualized, 108, 109; of self, 104; shifting relations of, 137; of women, 104

Dostoyevsky, Fyodor, 42

Dreams, 171; doubling in, 191

Du Bois, W. E. B., 136

Duchamp, Marcel, 215

Dürer, Albrecht, 202; *Course in the Art of Measurement with Compass and Ruler, A,* 193; *Man Drawing a Nude in Perspective,* 194*fig*

E

Eaton Centre (Toronto), 79

Ecology, 59

Gilroy, Paul, xiv, 135, 136, 137, 142, 143
Girard, Renè, 237
Goldbarth, Albert, 187
Goldstein, Al, 210
Gorz, Andre, 36n1
Gramsci, Antonio, xv, 58, 68, 225, 226, 246n1;
  concept of the intellectual, 72; hegemony in,
  70; new political logic of hegemony and, 59;
  organic ideology and, 72; on organic
  intellectualism, 71
Graves, Michael, 77
Greene, Naomi, 225
Grimes, Milton, 138, 139, 140
Groening, Matt, 162
Guattari, Felix, 25, 152–153, 173

H
Habermas, Jürgen, 41; on Derrida, 146
Hall, Stuart, 169
Hammerbox, 159
Handelman, David, 160
Hanhardt, John, 156
Hanna, Kathleen, 163
Harris, thomas allen, 160
Haunting: logic of, 23
Hegel, G. W. F., 7, 44, 48, 115, 150, 174; cunning of
  reason in, 63; edginess of, 45; *Of Grammatology*
  and, 45; noise and, 250; signature of, 45
Hegemony: construction of new culture and, 67;
  defining, 63; as field of articulatory practice,
  67; genealogy of concept of, 59–60, 61;
  Gramsci and, 59; logic of, 63; new political
  logic of, 59–60; planned authenticity and, 178;
  politics as, 57; as start of post-Marxist
  discourse, 62; theoretical, xiii
Heidegger, Martin, 28, 49, 90n20, 128, 174; on
  irony, 123; on metaphysics, 115;
  phenomenological project, 69
Heine, Heinrich, 42
Helms, Jesse, 224n116
Hermeneutics, 148
Heterogenesis, 173
Heterosexuality: construction of masculine ideal
  and, 106; expulsion of feminine traits and,
  106; mandatory, 106, 107; S&M and, 223n98
Heuretics, 148, 151
Heuristics, 155
High Scholasticism era, 86–87
Hip hop, 137, 165
Hirsch, E. D., 147, 152

Historicity: contingency and, 119; recognition
  of, 115–116, 119; reduction to teleology, 58
History: being of, 62; "Capitalized" 92n45;
  contingency and, 61; cultural, 99; doctrine of,
  75; as experience of necessity, 84; negativity
  and, 60, 61; objective, 61; as objective process,
  60; philosophy of, 63; poststructuralist view,
  68; rational, 61; revised agendas for, 76; as
  single unfinished plot, 85; as space including
  all things, 84; subject in, 84–88; of term
  modern, 41; as text, 84; as totalization, 92n43;
  universalization of, 66
Hobbes, Thomas, 51
Hobsbawm, Eric, 36n4
Hole, 159, 162
Holocaust, 182
Homelessness, 8
Homophobia, 166n2
Homosexuality, 210; absence of discursive
  evidence on, 106; as catamitic practice, 102;
  coerced submission of boys to older men, 101,
  108; detecting existence of, 101; discursive
  violence and, 102; emergence into discourse,
  97, 98; exclusive, 99, 105; Greek, 101–112; as
  initiation into power elite, 101, 108, 109, 110;
  invention of, 96, 98, 102, 110; as invisible
  object, 96; *kinaidos,* 101, 103, 105; nonexistence
  of, 106; as point of resistance, 96; as positive
  object of knowledge, 96; preexistence of
  science that discovered it, 103; prostitution
  and, 108; during Renaissance, 102; repression
  of, 210; as systemic form of child abuse, 97,
  102, 110; as threat to constructed heterosexuality, xiii; threat to heterosexuality, 111
hooks, bell, 160, 169
Horkheimer, Max, ix
Horton, William, 138
Horton Plaza (San Diego), 88
Huggy Bear, 159
Humiliation, 123, 124
Husserl, Edmund, 4; idealization and, 4
Hustler, xv, 188, 189, 205, 206, 208, 210, 213, 215,
  221n81
Huyssen, Andreas, 39, 49
Hybridity: language of, 136; legitimating value
  of, 143; theorization of, 136

I
Idealism: German, 117
Ideality, 4; nonpresence and, 5; repetition and, 4,
  5

Warhol, Andy, 145–146
Weber, Samuel, vii, xi, xii, 3–21, 84, 85, *92n43,
93n50, 93n51*
West, Cornel, *92n39, 93n50*
Wexner Center for the Visual Arts (Columbus),
88
White, Hayden, 75
Wilde, Oscar, 98
Williams, Linda, 187
Wittgenstein, Ludwig, 117, 118
Work: archaeo-teleological model of, 14
Wright, Richard, 136

Writing: academic, 147; the body, 161;
gendering in, 149–150; mystory, 147–157; as
ongoing practice, 170; popcycle in, 147, 154,
155; separation from literature, 146; support
of "I" in, 170; travel of, 170

Y
Yeastie Girlz, 159

Z
Zahn, Paula, 138, 139, 140